Computer Programming and Architecture: The VAX

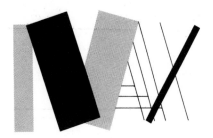

Digital Press digital™

Computer Programming
and Architecture: *The VAX*

Second Edition

Henry M. Levy / Richard H. Eckhouse, Jr.

9 8 7 6 5 4 3 2 1

Order number EY-6740E-DP

Printed in the United States of America.

Interior design: Richard Bartlett
Cover design: David Ford
Art coordination: Carol Keller
Illustrations: Network Graphics
Production coordination: Nancy Benjamin

Trademarks

AT&T Bell Laboratories: UNIX

Bolt Beranek and Newman, Inc.: Butterfly

Control Data Corporation: Cyber

Cray Research, Inc.: Cray-1, Cray-2, Cray X-MP

Digital Equipment Corporation: DEC, VAX, MicroVAX, VMS, Ultrix, VAXclusters, PDP, UNIBUS, BI, MASSBUS

Intel Corporation: 8086, 80286, 80386, 80387, iPSC

International Business Machines Corporation: System 360/370, System 4300

Motorola, Inc.: 68000, 68010, 68020

Sequent Computer Systems, Inc.: Balance, Symmetry, Dynix

Thinking Machines Corporation: Connection Machine

Library of Congress Cataloging-in-Publication Data

Levy, Henry M.
  Computer programming and architecture.

  Bibliography: p.
  Includes index.
    1. VAX computers. 2. VAX computers—Programming. 3. Computer architecture.
I. Eckhouse, Richard H.   II. Title.
QA76.8.V32L48   1988   005.2'45   88-22887
ISBN 1-55558-015-7

In memory of Samuel J. Levy

Contents

Preface

Like the first edition of our book, the intention of this second edition is twofold: to teach the architecture and organization of computer systems, and to provide a single reference on the details of one specific computer system, the VAX. Since the first edition, there have been many changes in the field and we wanted to reflect those changes in this edition. Also, we have used this book for several years to teach an undergraduate course in computer architecture and assembly language at the University of Washington. Based on this experience, we wanted to revise and expand the book to further develop our conceptual and pedagogical approach, particularly with respect to assembly language programming.

The book is divided into two parts. The first part, Chapters 1 through 10, is concerned with the architecture of a computer as seen by the assembly language or systems programmer. Chapters 1 through 8 cover the essentials normally taught in an assembly language or systems programming course. We have expanded the material from the first edition, added more examples, updated our coverage of the VAX and the VAX family, and provided a complete chapter on the assembler and debugger. Our examples use the VAX/VMS assembler syntax and I/O routines, but for those who wish to use Ultrix or Berkeley VAX/Unix, Appendix A describes the Ultrix assembler and how it differs from the VAX/VMS assembler. Chapter 9 is a short but unique new chapter on systems performance evaluation. It describes methods used to evaluate architectures and presents measurements that show how the VAX is used by real programs.

We believe that the best way to understand computer architecture is first to gain detailed experience with one specific architecture, and then to examine general principles. Thus, after examining the specifics of one machine, the VAX, Chapter 10 turns to architectural concepts that apply to all computers. The reader is introduced to instruction set design and the instruction-level architectures of four diverse computers for comparison with the VAX. The four systems chosen are the IBM 370, the CDC 6400, the Intel 80386, and the Berkeley RISC. The final section of that chapter examines the move toward reduced instruction set computers and the reasons for that trend, as well as describing the Berkeley RISC architecture.

The second part of the book, Chapters 11 through 16, considers system-level issues in computer architecture, including high-level operating system support and low-level implementation alternatives. We believe that these chapters contribute to the unique aspect of our book, and have therefore developed them in several directions. Chapter 11 considers physical level I/O and related issues, such as network interconnection alternatives. Chapters 12 and 13 are a study of the relationship between architecture and operating systems. Chapter 12 provides a substantial discussion of architectural support for operating systems, and how the VAX architecture supports virtual memory, protection, processes, and so on. Chapter 13 describes the structure of the VAX/VMS operating system, concentrating on how it uses the architectural features described in Chapter 12.

Caches are now essential for increasing system performance, even on low-end computer systems, and Chapter 14 concentrates on the design of caches and translation buffers. The chapter describes issues and alternatives in cache design. Additionally, the chapter includes a discussion of the difficulties encountered with today's high-performance machines, such as cache coherency in multiprocessors and the need for multilevel caches.

To understand how a complex instruction set such as the VAX is implemented, and to appreciate alternatives such as the reduced instruction set (RISC) and very-long instruction word (VLIW) machine designs, one must examine the use of microprogramming. Chapter 15 is a new addition to the book; it presents the concepts and develops the multiple facets of microprogramming. Once the general concepts are presented, this chapter describes the microarchitecture of a real VAX implementation, examines the format and operation of its microinstructions, and shows how those microinstructions are used to execute the VAX instruction set.

Our final chapter, also new to the second edition, is concerned with parallel processing techniques that are becoming commonplace in the computer marketplace. Chapter 16 examines the internal use of parallelism within a processor (for example, pipelining), as well as the external use of parallelism through different interconnection structures to build multiprocessor systems. Examples of important multiprocessor systems are presented.

The reader of this book will most likely have programming experience in a high-level language and a knowledge of basic data structures. With that background and a thorough reading of our text, the reader will gain a sound understanding of computer organization and the important issues in contemporary computer architecture. The reader will also come to appreciate the relationship between the complex demands of today's operating systems and applications and the underlying support that is provided by the hardware.

Although the story is told with the VAX as the main character, we believe the book is generally applicable to the understanding of any computer system. The techniques developed should enable the reader to quickly master any new machine encountered. It should also aid the reader in assessing the strengths and weaknesses of a particular architecture. Therefore, we believe that this book can be used successfully both as a teaching text for the college student and as a guide for the practicing professional.

Acknowledgments

We would like to thank the many people who helped in the production of both the first and second editions of this book. The many readers of our first edition and the reviewers of this second edition gave us valuable feedback on content and style. In particular, the students and teaching assistants of CS378 at University of Washington provided us with a wealth of experience in the use of the book for teaching, which we have used to produce this second edition. Robert Short helped us in understanding the operation of the MicroVAX microarchitecture. Finally, we would like to thank Digital Equipment Corporation and Digital Press for their technical and production support.

Henry M. Levy
Richard H. Eckhouse, Jr.

1

Architecture and Implementation

There are two major levels at which we usually examine any computer system: architecture and implementation. Because we often refer to these terms, it is important to understand the distinction between them.

The architecture of a computer system is the user-visible interface: the structure and the operation of the system as seen by the programmer. Implementation is the construction of that interface and structure from specific hardware (and possibly software) components. There can be several different implementations of an architecture, each using different components, but each providing exactly the same interface to the user.

For example, let's examine the architecture of a piano. The definition of a piano's architecture is the specification of the keyboard, as shown in Figure 1.1a. The keyboard is the user (player) interface to the instrument. It consists of eighty-eight keys, thirty-six black keys and fifty-two white keys. Striking a key causes a note of specified frequency to be played. The size and the arrangement of the keys are identical for all piano keyboards. Therefore, anyone who can play the piano can play any piano.

There are many implementations of the piano, as shown in Figure 1.1b. The implementation is concerned with the materials used to build the instrument. The kinds of wood used, the selection of ivory or plastic keys, the shape of the instrument, and so forth, are all implementation decisions made by the piano builder. Regardless of the implementation decisions made, however, the final product can be played by any piano player.

In a computer system, the architecture consists of the programming interface: the instruction set, the structure and addressing of memory, the control of input/output (I/O) devices, and so on. There can be several implementations of an architecture, for example, one with vacuum tubes, one with transistors, and one with very large scale integrated (VLSI) circuits. Clearly, each of these implementations would have different size, cost, and performance characteristics. However, a program that runs on one machine would run on all of the machines following the architecture.

Organization of This Book

This book deals primarily with the architecture of one computer system: the VAX. VAX computers are manufactured by Digital Equipment Corporation. The best way to learn about the VAX architecture is by using

1

Figure 1.1   Architecture and implementation of the piano

a. Piano keyboard architecture

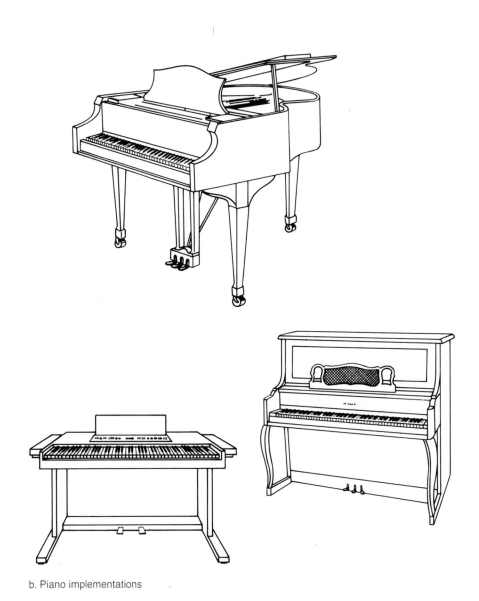

b. Piano implementations

it, and to use it you must become an assembly language programmer. As an assembly language programmer, you will learn how to control the operation of the hardware system directly. You will also gain a better understanding of how a compiler translates a high-level language program, and how the processor executes that program.

The first half of this book develops the basics of assembly language programming on the VAX. First, the elementary concepts of processors, memories, and instruction execution are introduced. More sophisticated addressing techniques are presented, and we build an instruction repertoire suitable for problem solving. From there, you will see how the VAX instruction set is used to manipulate more complex data structures.

Later, we use the concepts developed through the VAX to examine the instruction set architectures of several other machines: the IBM 360/370, the Control Data Corporation Cyber, the Intel 80386, and the Berkeley RISC II. This material provides an interesting basis for comparison and helps solidify the material already learned.

The second half of the book deals with the VAX architectural features used by the operating system. We show how the VAX supports the resource management activities of the operating system and how the VAX/VMS operating system uses these facilities. We also examine caches, which are memory buffers used to increase performance; microprogramming, a technique used for implementing complex systems such as the VAX; and multiprocessing, which is becoming a common technique for building cost-effective computer systems.

Review of Number Systems

Before beginning our examination of computer structures, it is worthwhile to review the basics of number systems. Throughout the book we use decimal, binary, and hexadecimal number systems. Therefore, the reader should be comfortable with these representations and with converting one to the other. Some readers may want to skip this section.

Number Systems

All data stored and manipulated in the computer is stored in binary form. Integers, floating-point numbers, characters, and instructions are all represented as a sequence of binary zeros and ones. When the value of a data item is output to a terminal or printer, or when we specify a value for input, we usually *display* the contents using base 8 (octal), base 10 (decimal), or base 16 (hexadecimal). These bases are easier for humans to deal with than long strings of binary digits. However, the *value* of a unit is the *same* regardless of the base used to represent it. Different bases are suitable for different applications. Bases 8 and 16 are particularly useful for looking for patterns of bits within a word, while base 10 is useful for understanding the decimal value of a word.

In the weighted numbering system, the value of a numeral depends on its position in a number. For example, in base 10

$$347 = \begin{array}{rl} 3 \times 100 = & 300 \\ +4 \times 10 = & 40 \\ +7 \times 1 = & \underline{7} \\ & 347 \end{array}$$

The value of each position in a number is its *positional coefficient*. The second factor or power of the base is called the digit-position weighting value, weighting value, or simply *weight*.

Using the positional coefficients and weights, we can express any weighted number system in the following generalized form:

$$X = x_n w_n + x_{n-1} w_{n-1} + \cdots + x_{-1} w_{-1} + \cdots + x_{-m} w_{-m}$$

where

$$w_i = r^i \quad (r^i = \text{weighting values and r} = \text{radix or base})$$

and

$$0 \le x_i \le r-1 \quad (x_i = \text{positional coefficients})$$

This formalism makes it clear that the largest value of a positional coefficient is always one less than base value. Thus, for base 2 (binary), the largest coefficient is one; for base 10 (decimal), it is nine. Although this may seem intuitively obvious, it is not uncommon for the novice programmer or even some old-timers to write illegal numbers while coding programs, for instance, 10853 in base 8 or 102 in base 2. Equally confusing are bases greater than 10, in which positional coefficients are denoted by letters rather than numbers. In hexadecimal, for example, the letters A through F represent the numerical values 10 through 15, respectively.

Examples of writing the full expressions for weighted number systems follow:

$$\begin{aligned} 140 &= 1 \times 10^2 + 4 \times 10^1 + 0 \times 10^0 \text{ (base 10)} \\ &= 1 \times 2^7 + 0 \times 2^6 + 0 \times 2^5 + 0 \times 2^4 + 1 \times 2^3 \\ &\quad + 1 \times 2^2 + 0 \times 2^1 + 0 \times 2^0 \text{ (base 2)} \\ &= 2 \times 8^2 + 1 \times 8^1 + 4 \times 8^0 \text{ (base 8)} \\ &= 8 \times 16^1 + C \times 16^0 \text{ (base 16)} \end{aligned}$$

In other words,

$$140_{10} = 10001100_2 = 214_8 = 8C_{16}$$

Although these examples assume a positive radix, negative radices are also possible. For example, assuming a radix of -3, the value 140 can be expressed as

$$140_{10} = 2 \times (-3)^4 + 1 \times (-3)^3 + 1 \times (-3)^2 + 2 \times (-3)^0 = 2122_{-3}$$

It is even possible to conceive of nonweighted number systems—and such systems do exist—such as "Excess -3" and "2 out of 5," but discussion of these systems is beyond the scope of this book.

Binary and Hexadecimal Representations

Because of the inherent binary nature of all computer components, modern digital computers are based on the binary number system. However, no matter how convenient the binary system may be for computers, it is exceedingly cumbersome for human beings. Consequently, most computer programmers use base 8 or base 16 representations instead, leaving it to the various system components—assemblers, compilers, loaders, and so on—to convert such numbers to their binary equivalents. Modern assemblers also permit decimal numbers, both integer and real (floating-point), to be input directly, a useful convenience for most applications programs. Table 1.1 shows the binary, octal, and hexadecimal equivalents of the decimal values zero through sixteen.

Table 1.1 Conversion Table

Decimal	Binary	Octal	Hexadecimal
0	0000	0	0
1	0001	1	1
2	0010	2	2
3	0011	3	3
4	0100	4	4
5	0101	5	5
6	0110	6	6
7	0111	7	7
8	1000	10	8
9	1001	11	9
10	1010	12	A
11	1011	13	B
12	1100	14	C
13	1101	15	D
14	1110	16	E
15	1111	17	F
16	1 0000	20	10

Base 8 and base 16 representations of binary numbers are not only convenient but also easily derived. Conversion simply requires the programmer to separate the binary number into 3-bit (for octal) or 4-bit (for hexadecimal) groups, starting with the least significant digit and replacing each binary group with its equivalent. Thus, for the binary number 010011100001,

$$010\ 011\ 100\ 001_2 = 2341_8$$

and

$$0100\ 1110\ 0001_2 = 4E1_{16}$$

This process is performed so naturally that most programmers can mentally convert visual representations of binary numbers (computer displays) to their octal or hexadecimal representation without conscious effort. Special pocket calculators that operate in both octal and hexadecimal are available as an aid in debugging programs. Fortunately, the tools of the assembly language programmer—the program listings, linker maps (showing locations of variables and modules), and dumps (displays of the contents of memory)—are expressed in at least octal or hexadecimal. Programmers need not be concerned with bits and binary numbers unless they choose to. However, when examining the bit patterns that make up the different data elements within the computer, the programmer has no alternative but to use bits and binary numbers. The next section examines these patterns.

Negative Numbers

For any base, there are three common ways to represent negative numbers. Negative binary numbers, for example, can be represented in sign-magnitude form, one's-complement form, or two's-complement form. One might ask, therefore, which form a computer would use in performing arithmetic calculations.

Sign-magnitude numbers are represented by treating the most significant bit as the sign bit and the remaining bits as the magnitude. Therefore, the 6-bit representation of ± 18 would be:

$$+18_{10} \quad 010010_2$$
$$-18_{10} \quad 110010_2$$

Addition and subtraction require a consideration of both the signs of the numbers to be added as well as the relative magnitudes in order to carry out the required operation.

Complement form for negative numbers takes advantage of the

continuum of representation. While the most significant bit remains the sign bit, the representation of the magnitude is different for negative numbers and positive numbers. The one's-complement representation is formed by taking the positive number and inverting all the bits. The two's-complement representation is formed by adding one to the one's-complement representation. For example, the 8-bit representations of ± 18 are:

$$+18_{10} \quad 00010010_2$$
$$-18_{10} \quad 11101101_2 \quad \text{One's-complement form}$$
$$-18_{10} \quad 11101110_2 \quad \text{Two's-complement form}$$

Sign-magnitude form is rejected in favor of complement form because it is more complex to add or subtract numbers using sign-magnitude arithmetic. Thus, the choice of form for negative binary numbers is really between one's-complement and two's-complement representations. In reality, the choice is frequently one of the designer's preference. Generating one's-complement numbers is easier than generating two's-complement form. Moreover, from the computer hardware point of view, it is more "uniform" to build a one's-complement adder than a two's-complement adder. On the other hand, one's-complement notation has two representations of zero, both a positive and a negative zero:

$$0000 \quad 0000_2 \quad \text{Zero}$$
$$1111 \quad 1111_2 \quad \text{Minus zero in one's complement}$$

whereas only one zero exists in two's-complement form:

	0000	0000$_2$	Zero
	1111	1111$_2$	One's complement
		+1$_2$	Plus one
discarded → 1)	0000	0000$_2$	Two's complement of zero

Mathematically speaking, it is inconvenient to have two representations for zero. It is also more difficult to test for zero, an operation performed frequently on computers. As a result, most machines today use two's-complement notation to represent negative numbers. Remember that one's-complement and two's-complement are simply methods for *representing* signed integers in binary. Positive integers have the same representation in both one's complement and two's complement, but negative integers have different representations.

Forming the complement of a hexadecimal number may seem strange at first. Compared with binary, where one simply "inverts" the bits, hexadecimal complementation requires a subtraction of each digit from hexadecimal "F" (and an addition of one for the two's-complement result). For example,

3C8E	Original number
C371	One's complement
+1	
C372	Two's complement

Fortunately, as with all such techniques, familiarity comes with use.

After this brief digression, we can now turn our attention to the general structure of computer systems and the architecture of the VAX. You will find that an understanding of hexadecimal and binary number systems is helpful to your understanding of computer concepts.

Exercises

1. Describe the architecture of a typewriter. What parts of the typewriter are not part of the architecture? What are some implementation differences among different typewriters?

2. Why do you think it is important to define precisely a computer's architecture?

3. Why do you think different computer manufacturers build computers with different architectures? What does this imply about the importance of high-level languages? Why is there a need for standardizing high-level languages?

4. What effect do you think the standardization of operating systems will have on computer architectures?

5. What range of integers can be represented in a 12-digit unsigned binary number? In a 12-digit two's-complement signed number?

6. Why are octal and hexadecimal useful for recognizing patterns of binary digits but decimal is not?

7. Is 10234 a legal value in base 8? base 16? base 5? base 4? Express the value 10234_5 in base -3.

8. Convert 101010101 into hexadecimal and octal. Convert $10A34_{16}$ into octal and decimal. Negate both values using 32-bit binary two's-complement form.

9. Add +18 and −18 using each of the three representations for negative numbers. Use 8-bit arithmetic and either binary or hexadecimal representations.

10. Perform the following hexadecimal arithmetic:

a. 205 − 6
b. AF9 + 9
c. 10 * 10
d. 1CFF + F2FF

11. Write a high-level language program that inputs a decimal number and a radix and outputs the value of that decimal number in the specified radix. For example, if the inputs are 10 and 16, the output should be A (that is, the value of 10 decimal is A in base 16). Limit yourself to bases less than or equal to 16.

12. Subtraction can be implemented by complementation followed by addition. Suppose you are to subtract -56_{10} ($C8_{16}$) from 27_{10} ($1B_{16}$). Show how this could be done.

2 Computer Structures and the VAX

Depending on the nature of the application and the language chosen, programming a computer requires different levels of understanding. For most programmers writing in Pascal, for example, the computer appears to be a machine that executes Pascal statements and manipulates high-level data structures. The structure of the underlying hardware is invisible.

This chapter introduces the fundamentals needed by the assembly language programmer. To program at the assembly level, you need a thorough understanding of the structure of a computer system, the process of program execution, and the nature of memory addressing. Once you have this foundation, you can begin to focus on the basics of instructions and elementary programming for a particular machine.

Computer Structures

Most general-purpose computers have the same basic structure, consisting of the high-speed primary memory, the arithmetic control unit (typically called the *central processing unit*, or CPU), and the peripheral *input* and *output* devices (the I/O system). One or more *buses* (described in more detail later) move data between these components. Although there are other components of interest, these units are directly visible to the machine-level programmer and are part of the user architecture. Figure 2.1 shows an organizational representation of this basic structure.

The Memory

The memory of a computer is a repository for both instructions and data. Memory can be implemented by any device that can retain two or more distinguishable states that can be set and sensed. All common memories are composed of two-state devices that can represent the values zero and one. Hence, each device—such as a magnetic core, a semiconductor flip-flop, or a two-sided coin—can represent one binary digit, or *bit*.

Bits in memory are arranged as an array of information units, with each information unit composed of a fixed number of bits. Each information unit resides in a distinct location in memory, and each location is capable of holding one such unit, as shown in Figure 2.2.

Figure 2.1   Basic computer structure

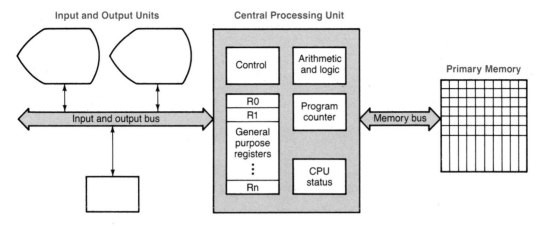

All memories share two organizational features:

1. Each information unit is the same size.

2. An information unit has a numbered address associated with it by which it can be uniquely referenced.

Thus, we say that a memory unit is characterized by two things:

1. An *address*, which is its relative position in memory.

2. The *contents*, which is a number that is physically stored at the particular location in memory.

As Figure 2.3 shows, memory can be viewed as a large one-dimensional array, *M(i)*, where each element of the array contains one unit

Figure 2.2   Memory organization

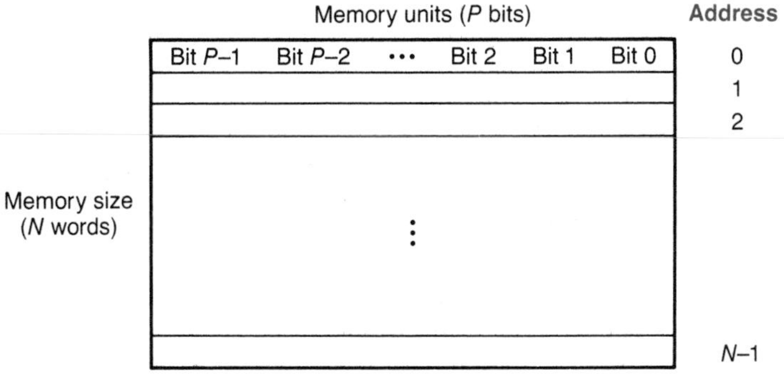

	Memory units (*P* bits)						Address
	Bit *P*–1	Bit *P*–2	•••	Bit 2	Bit 1	Bit 0	0
							1
							2
Memory size (*N* words)			⋮				
							N–1

Figure 2.3   Memory as an array

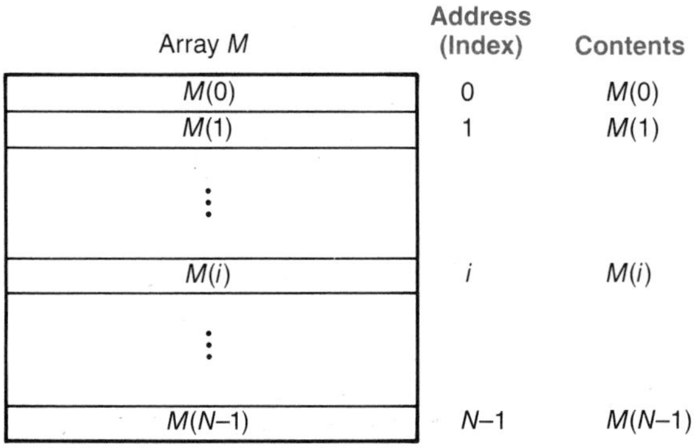

(word) of information. The index, i, is the address of the unit. Using its address, we can determine the contents of any unit. It is important to remember, however, the difference between the address of a unit, i, and the contents of the unit, $M(i)$.

When a computer is designed, the size of its information units is chosen according to the applications for which the computer is intended. On many machines, each information unit is known as a *word*. Word sizes typically range from 8 bits on early microprocessors to 64 bits on large scientific computers. A word is usually divided into a number of *bytes*, with each byte representing one character. Machines designed for administrative data processing, in which information to be processed includes names and letters as well as numbers, are often *byte addressable*. In these machines, the byte is the basic information unit, and each byte has a unique address by which it can be accessed. On the other hand, word-addressable machines are generally used for scientific calculations in which large numbers are manipulated and precise numerical results are required.

The key difference between byte and word machines is the size of the smallest addressable information unit. For a byte machine, this unit is one byte, that is, a unit of information capable of holding a small number or representing a letter of the alphabet or a digit. For a word machine, the smallest addressable unit is one word, a unit of information capable of holding several characters or a large number. Words can often be subdivided into a fixed number of characters or digits. In a true word machine, however, we can reference only the collection, not the individual characters. Thus, the value of the subdivision is its storage efficiency.

The *address space* is the set of all addresses, or the collection of distinct information units that a program can reference. The size of the address space is determined by the number of bits used to represent an address. An address is usually less than or equal to the word size for a given machine. Early minicomputers and microprocessors typically used 16-bit addresses, yielding 2^{16}, or 65,536, unique memory locations. Programmers quickly discovered, however, that 16 bits of address were insufficient for representing large data structures or solving complex problems. Typical modern computers, including the VAX, use 32-bit addresses that provide a memory address space of 2^{32}, or 4,294,967,296, unique addresses and therefore can support much larger programs and data structures. While it may be hard to imagine using up 4 *gigabytes* of address space, programmers are ingenious in their ability to consume all available computer resources. Some applications do require this much data, and we can already see machines with address spaces even larger than 2^{32}.

The Central Processing Unit

The central processing unit (CPU) is the brain of the computer. The CPU is capable of fetching data from and storing data into memory. It requests instructions from memory and executes them, performing arithmetic and logic operations specified by the instructions. The CPU can manipulate addresses as well as data. In addition, the processor can examine a memory location and follow different program paths, depending on its value. Finally, the CPU can execute instructions that initiate input and output operations on peripheral devices.

Internal to the CPU are a number of *registers* that provide local, high-speed storage for the processor. These registers can hold program data and memory addresses. Some computers have different sets of registers to perform different functions, for example, to address arrays or to represent floating-point numbers; others have general-purpose registers that can be used for any function.

Also internal to the CPU are one or more status words that describe the state of the processor, the instruction being processed, any special conditions that have occurred, and the actions to take for special conditions.

Instruction Execution

A computer is controlled by a *program*, which is composed of a sequence of *instructions*. Each instruction specifies a single operation to be performed by the CPU. Instructions can be classified into five basic categories:

1. *Data movement* instructions move data from one location in memory to another or between memory and I/O devices.

2. *Arithmetic* instructions perform arithmetic operations on the contents of one or more memory locations, for example, they add the contents of two locations together or increment the contents of a location.,

3. *Logical* instructions perform logic operations such as AND, OR, and EXCLUSIVE OR.

4. *Comparative* instructions examine the contents of a location or compare the contents of two memory locations.

5. *Control* instructions change the dynamic execution of a sequence of instructions by causing program execution to be transferred to a specified instruction, either unconditionally or based on the result of a comparative, arithmetic, or logical instruction.

Instructions are stored in memory along with the data on which they operate. The processor fetches an instruction from memory, interprets what function is to be performed, and executes the function on its operands. Each computer has its own representation of instructions, but all instructions are composed of two basic components:

1. An *operation code* (opcode), which specifies the function to be performed, for example, Add, Subtract, Compare.

2. One or more *operand specifiers*, which describe the *locations* of the information units on which the operation is performed. These information units are the *operands* of the instruction.

An instruction in memory can occupy several consecutive words (or bytes): one for the operation code and, optionally, several more for the operand addresses. For instance, an instruction to add the contents of memory location 100 to memory location 200, shown symbolically as

ADD   100,200

can be represented in computer memory as follows:

ADD operation code	Instruction word 0 (opcode)
100	Instruction word 1 (first operand address)
200	Instruction word 2 (second operand address)

⋮

\<next instruction\>

⋮

The processor executes a program by fetching and interpreting instructions. The location (memory address) of the next instruction to be executed is held in a special internal CPU register called the *program counter* (PC). When the program is loaded into memory, the PC is loaded with the address of the first instruction. Using the PC, the CPU fetches this instruction, along with any operand specifiers. The operands themselves are then fetched, the operation is performed, and any results generated are

Figure 2.4   Instruction execution

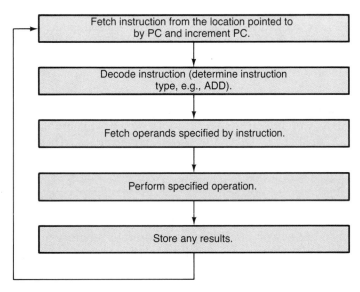

stored back in memory. Figure 2.4 shows the complete cycle of fetching, interpreting, and executing an instruction.

Note that each time an instruction is fetched, the PC is modified to point to the next instruction. Thus, the processor executes instructions one after another. Some instructions, like "branch" (the machine-level GO TO), affect the flow of control by explicitly changing the contents of the PC so that a new location, not the next one in sequence, is taken to be the one containing the next instruction to be executed. Otherwise, instructions are fetched and executed sequentially from memory.

A computer program, then, consists of two parts: instructions and data. When loaded into memory, each instruction and data element is located at a unique address. Looking at the program as a string of words or bytes, we are unable to differentiate data from instructions because both are merely strings of numbers coded in binary. We are also unable to differentiate data types because integers, floating-point numbers, character strings, and so on, are represented as strings of binary numbers, too. Only in context does the program have meaning.

The key to making sense of the string of numbers representing a program is the starting address of that program, since that tells the CPU where to find the first instruction to execute. The first instruction in the program can be located anywhere in the memory of the computer. The programmer specifies the starting address of the program by means of a directive to the language translator or to the program loader. (In a high-level language, this is the main program or procedure.) When the operating system loads the program into memory, it transfers control to that initial instruction by making sure that the initial contents of the PC "point to" the address of the starting instruction. As each instruction and operand is fetched in sequence, the PC is incremented so that it points to the next byte or word to be fetched.

Classes of Instruction Architectures

Computer instruction sets vary greatly from machine to machine. A later chapter looks at some different architectures to contrast them with the VAX, which is presented in more detail. In general, however, we can classify instruction sets into several categories. These categories are chosen based on the operand-addressing techniques available in the machine.

Simplest of the categories are *zero-address* instruction sets, also known as stack-based instruction sets. Part of the processor state for such a machine includes a stack pointer to the top of a stack. The stack, which is simply a last-in first-out list, can be stored in memory or in the processor. The stack pointer is an implicit operand for most instructions and does not need to be specified explicitly. For example, on such a machine, the instructions

```
PUSH    A
POP     B
```

cause the contents of memory location A to be placed on the top of the stack (as a result of the PUSH); the contents of the top of the stack are then removed and copied into memory location B (as a result of the POP). Arithmetic instructions always operate on the top one or two elements of the stack, depending on whether they are unary or binary operations. For example, the instruction

```
ADD
```

would add the two top elements of the stack together, popping those elements from the stack and pushing the sum onto the top of the stack. Such machines are called zero-address machines, because arithmetic operations such as ADD have no operands; the operands are implicitly known to be the top two stack elements. Not only do some computers operate in this fashion, but some calculators use stacks also.

A *one-address* instruction set has, as its name implies, instructions with one address. Typically, such machines have a single register, called the *accumulator*. Just as the stack is an implied operand for instructions on the stack machine, the single accumulator is the implied operand for instructions on the one-address machine. Suppose we want to add the contents of memory locations A and B, putting the result in location C. On a one-address machine we would probably write

```
LOAD    A
ADD     B
STORE   C
```

The LOAD instruction loads the contents of memory location A into the accumulator, while the ADD adds the contents of location B to the accumulator. Finally, the STORE instruction copies the contents of the accumulator into memory location C. Architectures such as this, in which arithmetic can be done only in registers, are known as *load and store* machines. In such machines, it is not possible to add a number directly to a memory location. Instead, one operand must first be loaded into a register and the summation formed there.

A *two-address* instruction set allows two operands to be specified in the instruction, for example,

```
ADD    A,B
```

adds the contents of location A to the contents of location B. When the addition is completed, the contents of location A are unchanged, and location B contains the sum. Finally, *three-address* instructions such as

```
ADD    A,B,C
```

allow the result of the summation to be written to a third location.

These are just some of the options available to the designer of an instruction set, and many tradeoffs can be made. Some instruction sets have characteristics of several of these options. In general, the more operands an instruction set allows, the more powerful instructions tend to become. But as the instruction set becomes more powerful, the hardware required to implement that instruction set becomes more complex.

The Input/Output System

Connected to the processor and memory are several input and output (I/O) devices. The I/O devices allow the processor to communicate with humans, with other processors, and with secondary storage devices that are slower than main memory but larger in capacity.

The most common devices are magnetic disks, magnetic tapes, terminals, and printers. Magnetic disks and tapes provide large online or backup storage for programs and data. These devices are usually capable of transferring large blocks of data directly to primary memory. In contrast, the processor must feed or retrieve one character at a time to or from most terminal devices.

Because all these devices are slow compared to the execution speed of a modern CPU, systems are designed to overlap processing with I/O. That is, the processor begins an I/O operation on a device and then continues executing program instructions. The processor can check later to see if the operation is complete, or the device can signal when it is done.

One or more data buses can be used to interconnect the CPU, memory, and I/O devices. Some computers have two (or more) buses, one to connect the memory to the CPU, another to connect I/O devices to the CPU. Other computers use one bus for all transfers among I/O devices, memory, and the CPU. Figure 2.5 shows some alternatives in the interconnection of the CPU, memory, and I/O devices.

Whether there is one bus or several, the purpose remains the same: to carry address, data, and control signals among the devices connected to the bus. The address and control signals specify the device and the function to be performed on the data. The bus is like a common highway for computer information flow. Any device connected to it can place information onto the highway; conversely, any device can take information from the bus. The bus thus provides an efficient means for passing information among the functional units connected to it.

Describing Computer Structures

From a structural level, computers consist of the basic components we have described: processors, memories, buses, I/O devices, and so on. One way to describe the structure of a computer is to use a notation called PMS, for processor, memory, and switch. PMS notation is described in detail in *Computer Structures: Principles and Examples* by Siewiorek, Bell, and Newall. The objective of PMS is to provide a pictorial means of showing the high-level organization of a system.

A PMS diagram consists of a stick-figure drawing of a system's components connected with lines showing the physical interconnection. Some of the component types shown are

- P (processors). The central processor, shown as P_c, controls the overall operation of a computer. However, a computer can have other processors, for example, an I/O processor, $P_{i\ o}$, or a slave processor, P_{slave}.

- M (memories). Computers have several levels of memories, such as the primary memory, M_p, or secondary memories, M_s.

- S (switches). A switch is a bus or any device that interconnects several components of the system, transferring information to one or more components at a time.

- L (links). A link is a point-to-point interconnect between two specific components of a system.

- T (transducers). A transducer changes information from one form to another, for example, from electrical impulses to mechanical actions.

Figure 2.5   Alternative bus structures

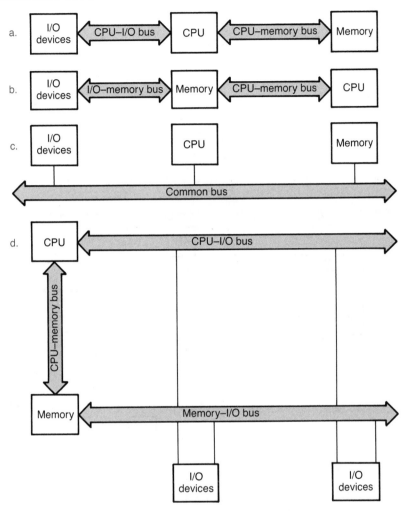

Terminals, line printers, tape readers, and card readers are all transducers.

- *K* (controllers). A controller is a unit that manages the actions of another device, typically an I/O device.

Figure 2.6 shows a PMS diagram of a VAX 8800 configuration. A component description can be augmented with details about specific characteristics of the component, or the details can be listed as a footnote, for example,

P_c['CVAX; 80ns cycle time; technology: CMOS VLSI microprocessor]

Figure 2.6   VAX 8800 PMS diagram

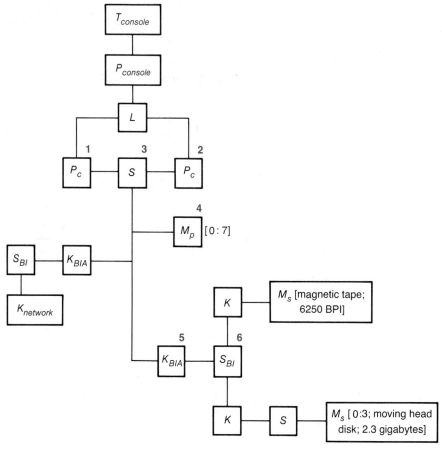

Notes

1. P_c['VAX 8810; 45ns cycle; 64 KB cache; variable-length instructions; 8-, 16-, 32-, 64- and 128-bit data types; technology: 1200-gate ECL gate array]
2. P_c['Second processor on dual processor VAX 8820]
3. S['Memory interconnect bus; 32-bit; synchronous; 4/16/32 byte transfer; 45ns cycle; 60 megabytes/second]
4. M_p[16 megabytes/module; MOS dynamic RAM]
5. K['Memory bus to BI adapter]
6. S['BI bus; 32 bit; synchronous; 200ns cycle]

Introduction to the VAX

The VAX is a general-purpose digital computer manufactured by Digital Equipment Corporation. The VAX architecture was designed to extend the addressing capabilities of its predecessor, the PDP−11 minicomputer; hence, the name VAX, for Virtual Address eXtension. Over a dozen VAX implementations have been produced.

The VAX has a high-level architecture that contains many features to support operating systems and compiler code generation. The VAX instruction set currently includes over 300 instructions and over 20 formats for operand specifiers, called addressing modes. This flexibility enables the programmer and the compiler to select instruction and addressing combinations that are both space- and time-efficient. Thus, algorithms implemented with the VAX instruction set architecture are generally compact (compared to the same algorithm implemented on other architectures, including the PDP−11) and fast (compared to programs running on other machines using the same hardware technology).[1]

Figure 2.7 shows the logical organization of a VAX 8810 computer system. In fact, each VAX implementation has a different internal structure that was chosen for the particular price and performance range of the machine. Figure 2.7 resembles the structure of the general computer shown in Figure 2.1. The VAX CPU shown in the center of Figure 2.7 is the

Figure 2.7   VAX organizational structure

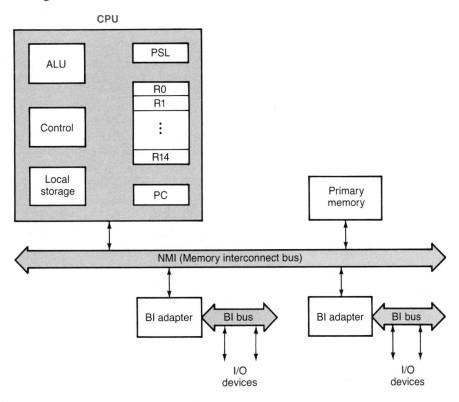

---

[1]In fact, there is controversy as to whether high-level architectures like the VAX or much simpler "reduced instruction set computers" (RISCs) will achieve better performance. We discuss this further in Chapter 10.

master controller of the VAX system. The processor contains sixteen 32-bit general-purpose registers that provide high-speed local storage for programs. Several of these registers have special uses; in particular, one is the program counter and one is used as a stack pointer. Also internal to the CPU is the 32-bit processor status longword (PSL) that contains information about the processor and the current state of the program being executed. The PSL is composed of two 16-bit words. The lower 16 bits, called the program status word (PSW), contain information about the user program and are user accessible. The upper 16 bits contain privileged processor information and can be modified only by the operating system. Thus, the user program can examine and change program state information, but processor state is protected from user modification.

A common system bus connects the CPU, memory, and I/O buses. Through this bus, all input and output devices are connected so that they can communicate with each other, as well as with the CPU and memory. Indeed, it may be possible for I/O devices to send and receive data among themselves and memory without processor intervention.

A memory controller connects the CPU to the memory subsystem. The controller can perform functions such as reading large amounts of data at a time in anticipation of future requests, buffering read and write requests, and so on. Current large VAX systems allow for several hundred megabytes of primary memory; smaller single-user VAXes are typically configured with 10 to 20 megabytes.

New VAXes are typically designed with their own internal system bus through which memory and components of the CPU communicate. To allow existing I/O devices to be attached to the new bus, special *bus adapters* are designed. These adapters allow existing devices to be connected to the VAX system without change, thereby offering benefits in development cost and time. Devices can thus be made immediately available for a new machine by providing an interface between the new computer bus and existing I/O buses.

For example, many VAX implementations use an I/O bus called the backplane interconnect (BI), to which numerous device controllers connect. If a user has peripherals that use an older bus called the Unibus, a special BI-to-Unibus adapter can be used; the older Unibus devices connect to a Unibus, which attaches to the BI-to-Unibus adapter, which attaches to the BI bus.

VAX Information Units and Data Types

We have already described byte-addressable and word-addressable machines. In the context of that discussion, it is appropriate to say that the VAX is a byte-oriented computer. The basic information unit on the VAX is the 8-bit byte. However, the instruction set is also capable of operating on a

Figure 2.8   VAX information units

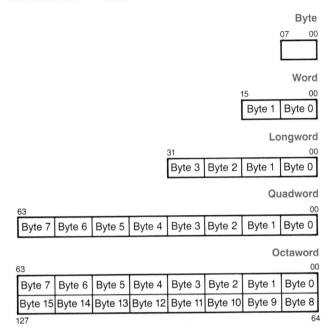

number of other information units formed by groups of bytes and bits. The multiple-byte units are the 16-bit *word* (two bytes), the 32-bit *longword* (four bytes), the 64-bit *quadword* (eight bytes), and the 128-bit *octaword* (16 bytes), shown in Figure 2.8. Each of these information units is formed by a sequence of contiguous bytes. The unit is always addressed by the low-order byte of the group. Note that the bits within any information unit are numbered from the least significant bit, bit 0, on the right. The most significant bit (bit 7, 15, 31, 63, or 127 for byte, word, longword, quadword, or octaword, respectively) is on the left.

For example, suppose the bytes beginning at location 400 in memory have the values shown below:

08	07	06	05	04	03	02	01	:400

Location 400 is the address of a byte whose value is 01_{16}. It is also the address of the word whose value is 0201_{16}, the longword whose value is 04030201_{16}, and the quadword whose value is 0807060504030201_{16}. Similarly, location 401 is the address of the byte whose value is 02_{16}, the word whose value is 0302_{16}, and so on. Every information unit is addressed by its low-order byte; it is up to the compiler or the assembly language programmer to determine what information units are stored at which addresses and to use the proper instructions to manipulate them.

Figure 2.9   Variable-length bit field

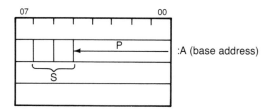

VAX registers can store any of the VAX information units. Since each register is 32 bits, a register typically holds a single longword. However, two adjacent registers can hold a quadword and four adjacent registers can hold an octaword. In this case, the entire information unit is named by the lower numbered of the adjacent registers. That is, if a quadword is stored in register 2 (R2) and register 3 (R3), we specify the unit by R2.

Another information unit found in the VAX is the variable-length *bit field*. The bit field is different in that the basic addressable unit is based on a length measured not in bytes but in bits. A bit field can be from 0 to 32 contiguous bits in length and can be located arbitrarily with respect to the beginning of a byte. To describe a bit field, three attributes are required: (1) a *base address* of a particular byte in memory chosen as a reference point for locating the bit field; (2) a *bit position* that is the starting location of the field with respect to bit 0 of the base address byte; and (3) a *size* giving the length of the bit field in bits. For example, Figure 2.9 shows a bit field with base address A, bit position P, and size S.

Bit fields are commonly used to pack multiple information fields tightly together. For example, Boolean values (sometimes called "flags") can be packed eight per byte. In this context, bit field instructions allow the programmer to manipulate fields smaller than a byte.

The byte, word, longword, quadword, and octaword are the fundamental information units of the VAX. Built on these information units are *data types*, which are *interpretations* of the bits contained in the units. All information units contain a string of binary digits, but a unit can represent an integer, a letter of the alphabet, a real number, and so forth. The VAX processor is capable of manipulating a great variety of data types. The choice of data type allows the programmer (or the compiler) to produce compact programs using those data types most closely tailored to his or her needs. There is also a full set of instructions for converting easily from one data type to another, which reduces the complexity of many programs.

Integers

Integers are represented as both unsigned binary numbers and two's-complement signed numbers, and can be stored in byte, word, longword, quadword, or octaword elements. The choice of storage representation for an integer determines both the maximum value of the number to be stored and the efficiency of the representation (that is, the number of bits used effectively). Table 2.1 shows the numeric range for the various integer sizes. The VAX has a complete set of instructions for adding, subtracting, dividing, multiplying, complementing, and shifting integers. (In fact, quadword and octaword arithmetic is not fully supported by VAX instructions, for example, there is no single instruction to add quadwords or octawords, so programmers should be careful when designing algorithms using those information units. However, the VAX does have instructions for implementing multiprecision arithmetic on large unsigned numbers using multiple longword add with carry instructions.)

A complete set of conditional branch instructions allows the programmer to alter the flow of control based on the result of previous arithmetic operations. Because the most significant bit of a two's-complement number always indicates the sign, the hardware can easily test for positive or negative.

Table 2.1   Integer Data Types

| | | Range (decimal) | |
Integer Type	Size	Signed	Unsigned
Byte	8 bits	-128 to $+127$	0 to 255
Word	16 bits	-32768 to $+32767$	0 to 65535
Longword	32 bits	-2^{31} to $2^{31}-1$	0 to $2^{32}-1$
Quadword	64 bits	-2^{63} to $2^{63}-1$	0 to $2^{64}-1$
Octaword	128 bits	-2^{127} to $2^{127}-1$	0 to $2^{128}-1$

Floating-Point Numbers

Integers are useful for data representation and problem solution in many areas, but they often lack the dynamic range necessary for a variety of scientific applications. Although integers represent the data with sufficient precision, the magnitude of the data or the intermediate results may exceed the range defined by the width of the data word. A *floating-point* number, like an integer, is a sequence of contiguous bits in memory. However, the bits are interpreted as having two distinct parts, the *fraction* (or mantissa) and the *exponent*. That is, a floating-point number might be stored in a computer word as

S	m	S	n

Exponent   Fraction

and interpreted as $\pm 0.n \times 2^{\pm m}$, where n represents the bits in the fraction field and m represents the bits in the exponent field. Note that we have arbitrarily allocated two sign bits to allow positive and negative fractions and exponents. It is more common to assign only one sign bit to a word. Thus, a different representation is used in which the most significant bit of the word is the sign of the fraction and the exponent is represented as a positive (*biased*) value. In other words, although the exponent is a positive number in the range 0 through $m-1$, half of the exponent range (0 to $m/2-1$) is used to represent negative numbers while the other half ($m/2$ to $m-1$) represents positive numbers.

The VAX has four floating-point formats: F_floating, D_floating, G_floating, and H_floating. The formats of these floating-point data types are shown in Figure 2.10, and their range is described in Table 2.2. Originally the VAX had only F and D, which were designed to be somewhat compatible with the PDP−11 (hence, their somewhat unusual format, with the sign on a 16-bit boundary instead of a 32-bit boundary). While D has more fraction bits than F, it has the same size exponent and therefore no more range (just greater precision). G and H (sometimes called "grand" and "huge") were added later to provide a larger exponent range in 64 bits and a larger exponent and fraction range in 128 bits, respectively. A floating-point data type can start on any byte boundary and is addressed by the byte containing bit 0. Bit 15 of the first longword contains the sign of the number.

Figure 2.10 *VAX floating-point data type formats*

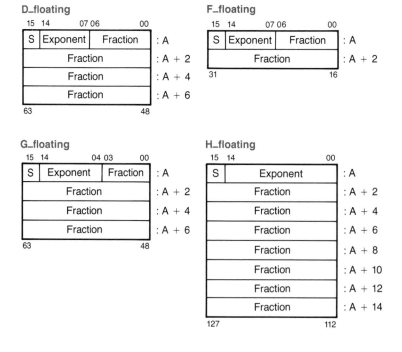

Table 2.2   VAX Floating-Point Data Types

Data Type	Total Size	Exponent Size	Fraction Size	Range	Precision
F	32	8	23	$.29 \times 10^{-38}$ to 1.7×10^{38}	7 digits
D	64	8	55	$.29 \times 10^{-38}$ to 1.7×10^{38}	16 digits
G	64	11	52	$.56 \times 10^{-308}$ to $.9 \times 10^{308}$	15 digits
H	128	15	112	$.84 \times 10^{-4932}$ to $.59 \times 10^{4932}$	33 digits

Let's take a close look at G_floating, which is now the standard double-precision floating-point representation for VAX high-level languages.

- The fraction is expressed as a 53-bit positive fraction, where $0.5 \leq$ *fraction* <1, with the binary point positioned to the left of the most significant bit. (This is similar to scientific notation, although in scientific notation we typically show a number with the decimal point to the right of the most significant digit.) Since the most significant bit must be 1 if the number is nonzero, it is redundant and not stored. This effectively enables the fraction to be stored in 52 bits. This form is called a *normalized* fraction.

- The exponent is stored as a biased 11-bit positive integer, providing what is called an *excess 1024* binary exponent. That is, when 1024 (2^{10}) is subtracted from the exponent, the result represents the power of 2 by which the fraction is multiplied to obtain the true value of the floating-point number. Thus, exponent values of 1 through 2047 indicate binary exponents of -1023 through $+1023$. An exponent of zero together with a sign bit of of zero indicates that the value of the number is zero, regardless of the value of the fraction.

- The sign of the number is positive when S, the sign bit, is 0, and negative when S = 1.

A floating-point number represented by the 64-bit G_floating datum is described by the equation

$$X = (1 - 2 \times S) \times fraction \times 2^{(exponent - 1024)}$$

where

$$2^{-1024} = .56 \times 10^{-308} \leq X < 2^{1023} = .9 \times 10^{308}$$

As an example, suppose we have a G_floating number whose hexa-decimal representation is

```
00000000 18004080
```

and we want to convert this to decimal. If we rearrange the digits to correspond to the G_floating format shown in Figure 2.10, we have

15	14	04 03	00
0		408	0
		1800	
		0000	
		0000	

The sign bit is 0, so we know this is a positive number. Next, the exponent field contains 408_{16}, or 1032_{10}. Because this is a biased, excess 1024 exponent, we know that the value of the exponent is $1032 - 1024$, or 8. The fraction field is formed by concatenating the high-order part in bits <0:3> with the low-order bits below, giving us a fraction of 0180000000000_{16}. In binary this is

```
0000 0001 1000 0000 ... 0000
```

However, the fraction is actually stored as a normalized fraction with the decimal point to the left of the most significant one bit, and that one bit is not stored. The value of the fraction (in binary) is thus

```
.1 0000 0001 1000 0000 ... 0000
```

We had an exponent of 2^8, so we simply shift the decimal point eight digits to the right, and the value of our G_floating number in binary is

```
10000000.11
```

To convert to decimal, $10000000 = 80_{16} = 128_{10}$ and $.11 = 1/2+1/4 = .5 +.25 = .75$, so the number stored is 128.75 decimal.

As with integers, floating-point data types can be stored in registers. For D, G, and H floating-point formats, the data types are stored in adjacent registers. Once again, a data type stored in multiple adjacent registers is addressed by the lowest numbered register. For example, if we move a G_floating number to R5 (register 5), the low-order 32 bits of the number will be placed in R5 and the high-order bits of the number will be placed in R6.

Alphanumeric Characters

Although all information units contain binary numbers, alphanumeric characters can be represented by a numeric code for each character. In the VAX, the American Standard Code for Information Interchange (ASCII) is used. The ASCII character set includes both uppercase and lowercase alphanumeric characters, the numerics (0 through 9), punctuation marks, and special control characters. The ASCII code, shown in Table 2.3, was developed by the American National Standards Institute (ANSI) to allow the connection of computers and peripherals by different manufacturers. Therefore, all ASCII character-oriented peripherals, such

Table 2-3   ASCII Character Encoding

Hex Code	ASCII Char	Hex Code	ASCII Char	Hex Code	ASCII Char	Hex Code	ASCII Char
00	NUL	20	SP	40	@	60	`
01	SOH	21	!	41	A	61	a
02	STX	22	"	42	B	62	b
03	ETX	23	#	43	C	63	c
04	EOT	24	$	44	D	64	d
05	ENQ	25	%	45	E	65	e
06	ACK	26	&	46	F	66	f
07	BEL	27	'	47	G	67	g
08	BS	28	(	48	H	68	h
09	HT	29	)	49	I	69	i
0A	LF	2A	*	4A	J	6A	j
0B	VT	2B	+	4B	K	6B	k
0C	FF	2C	'	4C	L	6C	l
0D	CR	2D	–	4D	M	6D	m
0E	SO	2E	.	4E	N	6E	n
0F	SI	2F	/	4F	O	6F	o
10	DLE	30	0	50	P	70	p
11	DC1	31	1	51	Q	71	q
12	DC2	32	2	52	R	72	r
13	DC3	33	3	53	S	73	s
14	DC4	34	4	54	T	74	t
15	NAK	35	5	55	U	75	u
16	SYN	36	6	56	V	76	v
17	ETB	37	7	57	W	77	w
18	CAN	38	8	58	X	78	x
19	EM	39	9	59	Y	79	y
1A	SUB	3A	:	5A	Z	7A	z
1B	ESC	3B	;	5B	[	7B	{
1C	FS	3C	<	5C	\	7C		
1D	GS	3D	=	5D	]	7D	}
1E	RS	3E	>	5E	^	7E	~
1F	US	3F	?	5F	—	7F	DEL

Figure 2.11   ASCII representation of the string My VAX

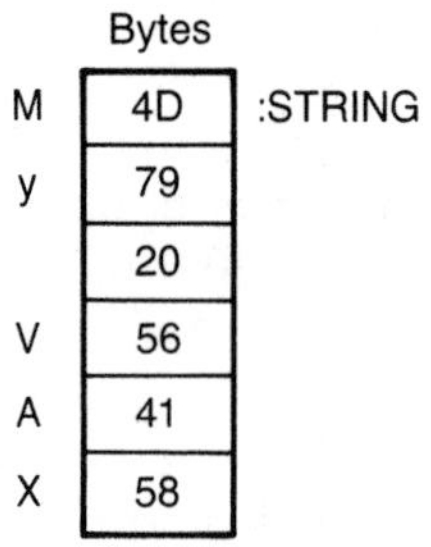

Bytes

M	4D	:STRING
y	79	
	20	
V	56	
A	41	
X	58	

as line printers and terminals, will output an A when the ASCII code for A (41 hexadecimal) is presented. The ASCII table also includes values for special control characters. When you press a line feed key on a keyboard, the terminal transmits the eight-bit value 0A (00001010). Another useful feature of the ASCII encoding is that the uppercase and lowercase characters differ by only a single bit. Uppercase *A* is 41 hex (01000001), and lowercase *a* is 61 hex (01100001). This simplifies case conversions.

Figure 2.11 shows the ASCII representation for the alphanumeric string *My VAX*. Note that each character uses one byte of storage, or two hex digits. The string is referenced by the address of the first byte, the one containing the character *M*, at symbolic address STRING. The space is an ASCII character whose value is 20 hexadecimal.

The VAX has instructions to manipulate strings of contiguous bytes, called character string instructions. A character string has two attributes: an address and a length in bytes (or characters). On the VAX, character strings can be from 0 to 65,535 bytes in length.

Decimal Strings

In addition to binary representations, numbers can be represented within the computer as a string of decimal digits. Numbers are usually entered in ASCII format and converted to binary for arithmetic operations. For some applications, however, it may be more convenient to operate in a decimal format. This is often true in a business (COBOL) environment, where programs require only simple computations.

The VAX supports two forms of decimal strings. In the form known as numeric string, each digit occupies one byte. Numeric strings can be in leading separate or trailing numeric format depending on whether the sign appears before the first digit or is superimposed on the last digit. The second decimal form, known as packed decimal, packs two decimal digits per byte.

Table 2.4 shows the format for a packed decimal string. A packed decimal string is composed of a sequence of bytes in memory, with each byte divided into two 4-bit nibbles. Each nibble contains a representation for one of the decimal digits. The last nibble contains a representation of

Table 2.4 Decimal String Representation

Digit or Sign	Decimal Value	Hex Value
0	0	0
1	1	1
2	2	2
3	3	3
4	4	4
5	5	5
6	6	6
7	7	7
8	8	8
9	9	9
+	12	C
−	13	D

the sign of the number. Figure 2.12 shows the packed decimal string representation for the number −12345. If we were just writing the hexadecimal contents of these three bytes, we would write them as 5D3412.

A decimal string is specified by two attributes: the address of the first byte of the string (shown as DECIMAL in Figure 2.12) and the length specified as the number of digits (not bytes) in the string. The VAX has instructions to perform arithmetic operations on decimal strings and to convert decimal strings to other formats. For some simple operations on numbers entered in ASCII, it is easy to convert from ASCII to a decimal string, perform the operation, and convert back to ASCII for output.

Summary of Data Types

Although only binary values are contained in memory, we can place almost any interpretation on the contents, because the computer instruction set recognizes and operates on a number of interpretations. Selecting the correct representation depends on the intended application and its requirements. Figure 2.13 shows the data types supported by the VAX.

Figure 2.12 Decimal string representation of −12345

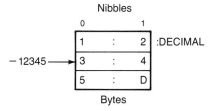

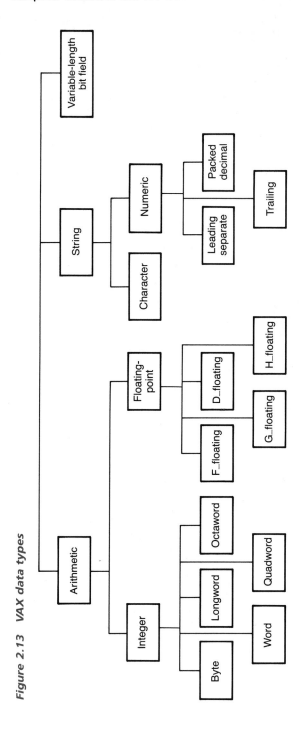

Figure 2.13   VAX data types

Interestingly, we can take the same information and represent it in many different ways. Figure 2.14 shows how the number 8800 can be represented by four different data types: packed decimal string, longword integer, G_floating, and ASCII string. Each representation is shown as a string of hexadecimal bytes.

In the same way that we represent alphabetic letters by encoding them, we can also encode machine instructions. However, we would still refer to the machine instructions by their binary codes if it were not for the symbolic assembler that lets us use memory assisting names, or mnemonics, in place of the codes. A later chapter looks at the actual VAX encodings. For now, however, it is necessary only to understand the basic instructions in their symbolic form.

Summary

This chapter introduced the basic elements of the computer as seen by the assembly language programmer. The most important concepts to understand at this point are the instruction–execution process, the addressing of memory, and the encoding of various data types. To be able to write assembly language programs, we must be comfortable with the fundamentals of computer operations.

Before you can write assembly programs, you must become familiar with the assembler that translates programs into binary machine code. Chapter 3 describes the assembler, the assembly process, and the debugger, which can help you to understand and debug your programs dynamically during execution.

Figure 2.14 **Representations of the number 8800**

Packed Decimal String

C0	00	88

Longword Integer

00	00	22	60

G_floating

30	00	40	E1
00	00	00	00

ASCII String

30	30	38	38

Exercises

1. Name the three major components of the computer system. Describe the function of each.

2. What is an address? In Figure 2.2, the last address is given as N−1. Why? If a memory unit has address 37, how many memory units precede it?

3. Compare and contrast the computer memory system to the human memory.

4. What is the address space? How is the size of the address space determined? If a machine has a 4-bit address, how many addressable memory units are there? How are they numbered?

5. What are the parts of an instruction? Describe in detail the steps in the execution of an instruction. Why are instructions stored (and executed) sequentially in memory? Can you think of an alternative?

6. You have seen the CPU execution cycle: instructions are fetched from sequential memory locations and executed, one after another, until a branch or change of control occurs. Can you imagine a machine in which instructions are not fetched sequentially? How would such a machine function? What would its instructions look like?

7. Give a PMS diagram for a computer you have used in the past or for one whose structure you can determine.

8. What are some of the characteristics of I/O devices? What are some of the differences between the bus organizations shown in Figure 2.5?

9. If we wish to run a program with 69,326 bytes of instructions and data, what does this imply about the size of addresses (in bits) needed on the computer?

10. Suppose we have two machines with 16-bit addresses, but one has byte addressing and one has word addressing. What does this imply about the size of the programs that the two machines can execute?

11. What are the information units on the VAX? What distinguishes an information unit from a data type? What are the VAX data types and what is each data type used for?

12. In Figure 2.11, if the M is stored in a byte with address 1248(hex), what is the address of the byte containing the X?

13. Show the ASCII representation for this sentence.

14. We say that the VAX is an ASCII machine. What does this mean? Suppose we used another encoding besides ASCII. Would this have any impact on the instruction set?

15. What is a normalized fraction? Why are normalized fractions used in floating-point number representations?

16. Show the hexadecimal VAX G_floating representation for the decimal number 512.5. Show the hexadecimal VAX G_floating representation for the decimal number 512.6. Which was harder to compute and why?

17. Can all decimal numbers be represented in floating-point format? Why or why not?

18. Why can decimal string digits be stored in 4-bit nibbles, when ASCII characters use a byte of storage?

3 *The Program Assembler and Debugger*

You are probably familiar with one or more high-level languages such as Pascal, Modula, FORTRAN, or PL/I. For these languages, programs are encoded in an algebraic English-like style. A language translation program called a *compiler* reads the high-level language program (called the *source* program) and translates it into a machine language program (called the *object* program). Because the source language can express concepts not directly executable by the computer hardware, the compiler often generates many machine instructions for a single source-language statement.

One major advantage of high-level languages, besides the ease with which they can express algorithms, is their machine independence. They hide the specifics of the hardware machine and the instruction set. Programs written in high-level languages are therefore said to be portable, that is, they can be easily moved from machine to machine with few if any modifications.

Nonetheless, there are still a number of reasons why understanding machine language programming is valuable. First, it gives us a better appreciation for computer architecture and the way a computer functions. Second, it makes us appreciate how a compiler must generate instructions from our high-level language programs, thus allowing us to write better high-level programs. Third, there are still a few applications, usually involving careful manipulation of specific hardware features of a particular computer, for which programming at the machine level is required. For example, the parts of an operating system that manage memory and I/O devices may be written in machine language. If one's goal is to develop a basic understanding of the machine, then a knowledge of machine language is worthwhile.

Of course, we would not want to code instructions for a computer in their binary machine language form for several reasons. The chance of making errors would be extremely high. In addition, because instructions specify operand addresses, inserting an extra instruction or data item would change the ordering of all succeeding addresses, requiring massive changes to those instructions that reference them within the modified program.

Assembly language programming solves those problems by allowing us to specify machine operations using symbolic names for memory locations and instructions. A program called the *assembler* translates the assembly language program into binary machine code, just as the compiler translates the high-level source program into binary machine code. The assembler does all the work of remembering the values of symbols and the addresses of data elements. However, unlike the high-level language, each assembly language instruction corresponds to exactly one machine instruction.

There are two major operating systems that run on the VAX: DEC's VAX/VMS operating system, and AT&T's Unix system. Unix is supported by different sources, including AT&T, University of California, Berkeley, and DEC. VMS and Unix have different VAX assemblers, and the syntax supported by each assembler is slightly different. In this book, we use the VMS assembler and associated programs. For historical reasons, the VMS assembler is probably better suited to assembly language programming and has better debugging support. The Unix assembler is intended primarily for use as an intermediate language by Unix compilers. We believe that it is fairly simple to move between the two assemblers. The Unix assembler is described in Appendix A.

Assembler Statement Types

The process of programming in assembly language involves using imperative, declarative, and control statements to specify what is to be produced and how it is to be produced.

- *Imperative* statements are the actual machine instructions in symbolic form (for example, ADD for the add instruction, CMP for the compare instruction, MOV for the move instruction).

- *Declarative* statements control assignment of storage for various names, I/O, and working areas. These are not really instructions but rather reservations of space, definitions of symbols, and assignments of contents to locations (for example, .LONG to initialize a longword, .BLKW to reserve a block of words).

- *Control* statements allow the programmer to have some control over portions of the assembly process.

Declarative and control statements are directives to the assembler. They do not generate machine instructions to be executed at run time.

We use these statement types casually in the following discussion without giving careful definitions or precise meanings. Basically, we are concerned with understanding computer architecture and organization and will therefore leave the actual details of assembly language programming to the *VAX Macro and Instruction Set Reference Manual.*

VAX Instruction Format

A VAX instruction is specified by an operation code and from zero to six operand specifiers. The assembly language format of the instruction is

```
LABEL: OPCODE SPECIFIER1,SPECIFIER2,... ; COMMENT
```

where

- LABEL is an alphanumeric symbol that can be used to refer to the address of an instruction.

- OPCODE is a mnemonic (symbolic name) for one of the VAX instructions.

Table 3-1   Simple VAX Instructions

Name	*Symbolic*	*Form*	*Operation*
Move Longword	MOVL	A,B	Copy the contents of the longword at address A into the longword at address B.
Move Address of Longword	MOVAL	A,B	Move the address of longword A into the longword at address B.
Clear Longword	CLRL	A	Zero the longword at address A.
Add Longwords	ADDL	A,B	Sum the longwords at locations A and B and store the result in B.
Add Longwords (3 operands)	ADDL3	A,B,C	Sum the longwords at locations A and B and store the result in the longword at address C.
Subtract	SUBL	A,B	Subtract the longword at address A from the longword at address B, storing the result in location B.
Increment	INCL	A	Add one to the longword at address A.
Decrement	DECL	A	Subtract one from the longword at address A.

- SPECIFIER is the symbolic name or specification for the address of an operand.

- COMMENT is an English-language description of the function of the instruction.

The label and comment fields are optional; the number of required specifiers is determined by the opcode.

To help you understand the form of VAX instructions and to prepare you for the addressing fundamentals of Chapter 4, a simple subset of the VAX instruction set is given in Table 3.1. These instructions, the ones most commonly used by beginning programmers, include one-, two-, and three-operand instructions.

Table 3.1, continued

Name	*Symbolic*	*Form*	*Operation*
Compare	CMPL	B,A	Compare the longwords at locations A and B. This evaluates the quantity A−B.
Test	TSTL	A	Evaluate the longword at location A. This compares the contents of A to zero.
Branch Equal	BEQL	X	Branch to X if the result of an arithmetic operation, compare, or test was equal to zero.
Branch Not Equal	BNEQ	X	Branch if the result was not equal to zero.
Branch Less Than	BLSS	X	Branch if the result was less than zero.
Branch Less Than or Equal	BLEQ	X	Branch if the result was less than or equal to zero.
Branch Greater Than	BGTR	X	Branch if the result was greater than zero.
Branch Greater Than or Equal	BGEQ	X	Branch if the result was greater than or equal to zero.
Jump	JMP	X	Branch unconditionally to location X.

To understand how instructions operate, examine a simple longword Add instruction that sums two 32-bit longword integers in memory. We can specify the locations of the operands to be added by their addresses. For instance, the instruction

```
ADDL 200,204
```

causes the longword stored at location 200 to be added to the longword stored at location 204. The result for the two-operand arithmetic instructions is always stored at the second operand address. That is, the contents of location 204 are modified by this instruction.

Suppose memory locations 200 and 204 contain the following values before the execution of the ADDL instruction:

```
Address        Contents
200            1765
204              23
208             152
```

Following the execution of ADDL 200,204 instruction, the contents of the memory will appear as follows:

```
Address        Contents
200            1765
204            1788
208             152
```

The VAX also allows three-operand forms of most arithmetic operations. To preserve the contents of locations 200 and 204 and store the result in location 208, we would instead code

```
ADDL3   200,204,208
```

Following the execution of that instruction, the contents of memory would appear as follows:

```
Address        Contents
200            1765
204              23
208            1788
```

It is important to remember the order in which operands are evaluated for operations that are not symmetric. For example

```
SUBL   200,204
```

subtracts the contents of the longword at location 200 from the contents of the longword at location 204, leaving the result in location 204.

We usually do not specify addresses numerically. Instead, we assign symbolic names to the data locations and let the assembler keep track of the numeric values. A symbolic name is created by labelling a particular line of code or data. The resulting symbolic address, or label, provides a means of referencing the location.

In VAX assembly language (called VAX Macro in VAX/VMS), the notation LABEL: at the beginning of a line creates a symbol and equates it to the address of that statement. VAX Macro also has declarative statements (called pseudo-operations, or *pseudo-ops*, because they do not generate instructions) that allocate and initialize data locations. For example, the statement

```
A:    .LONG   5
```

causes the assembler to allocate a 32-bit longword of memory and initialize it with the value 5. The symbol A is given the value of the *address* of the longword.

Using symbolic labels, the previous Add example could be coded as shown below:

```
Address         Assembly Statement
200             A:    .LONG   1765
204             B:    .LONG   23
208             C:    .LONG   152
  .                   .
  .                   .
  .                   .
400                   ADDL3   A,B,C
```

The addresses shown to the left appear only for the sake of this example and are not part of the instructions coded by the programmer. The assembler does all the work of remembering addresses, thus providing the programmer with a symbolic way to reference them.

It is important to remember that the symbols A, B, and C represent the *addresses* of three longwords, not the values stored there. The value of the symbol A in the preceding example is 200, while the value of the longword stored at location 200 is 1765. This is quite different from the concept of a symbol A in most high-level languages, where the symbol and its value are synonymous. When programming in assembly language, always keep in mind the distinction between an address and the data stored at that address.

The Functions of a Symbolic Assembler

As we have said, the VAX assembler performs the clerical task of translating the symbolic assembly language program into the binary machine language program. To translate a symbolic assembly program, the assembler performs the following functions:

1. It generates a *symbol table* that contains the values of all user-defined labels and symbols.

2. It maintains a *location counter* that tells where the next instruction or data item will be placed in memory.

3. It translates the symbolic instruction names and operand specifiers into binary machine code (called the *object program*).

4. It produces a listing for the programmer, showing the instructions and data and how they are translated and assigned to unique memory locations.

To understand how an assembler works, we next look at the mechanisms it utilizes in performing the translation process. These mechanisms include the location counter, the definition and use of symbols, storage allocation, expression evaluation, and control statements.

The Location Counter

Programs are generally written on the assumption that successive instructions are stored in successive memory locations. While it is common to have decision statements or instructions that alter the flow of control from one statement to the next, programmers normally write blocks of statements in which the implicit flow of control is sequential. Consequently, most instructions do not include an address field in which the address of the next instruction to be executed is given.

Because it is implied that instructions are to be executed in sequence, they must be stored that way in memory. Then, when the program counter is automatically incremented between instructions, it necessarily points to the next instruction in memory to be executed after the previous one is completed. Analogous to the CPU's program counter, the assembler maintains a location counter to keep track of where the next byte of instruction or data will be placed.

The assembler usually assumes that the first byte of a program will be placed in the first location of memory, that is, at address zero. As the assembler reads the instruction and data specifications from the source program, it translates and outputs each byte to the object program. The location counter is incremented as each byte is output; thus, it always points to the address at which the next byte will be placed.

In VAX Macro, the period (.) is the symbol for the location counter. When used in the operand field of an assembler directive, a period represents the address of the current byte. For example,

```
MANGO: .LONG .    ; refers to location MANGO
```

causes the assembler to place the address of the location MANGO in the longword at MANGO. In general, it is preferable to use labels rather than to reference bytes through the location counter, because the resulting program is easier to read and also because the use of the period can lead to errors. For example, the statements

```
MANGO:  .LONG   MANGO
        .LONG   MANGO
```

and

```
MANGO:  .LONG   .
        .LONG   .
```

are not equivalent. In the first set, both longwords are initialized to the address of MANGO. In the second set, the second longword refers to its own address, which is MANGO+4.

Symbols

A symbol is a string of alphanumeric characters. It can contain any of the characters of the alphabet (both uppercase and lowercase), the digits 0 through 9, and the special symbols period (.), underline (_), and dollar sign ($). A symbol can be up to thirty-one characters long, for example, A_LONG_SYMBOL, but its first character cannot be a digit.

A symbol can be defined in two ways. First, a symbol is defined when it is used as a label. For example, the source line

```
OAK:   SUBL  LEAF,TREE    ; defoliate
```

defines the symbol OAK. The assembler equates OAK with the address at which the instruction will be assembled, that is, the value of the location counter.

The second way a symbol is defined is by direct assignment using the equal sign (=). For example, the statements

```
SIX = 6
COUNT = 50
ARRAYSIZE = 100
```

equate the symbols with the specified values. Such assignments are provided for programming convenience and documentation only. They are *not* assignments in the programming language sense; they are constant declarations. They do not generate machine instructions and they are not executed by the machine; constant assignments simply equate symbolic names to assembly-time constant values.

Symbols that are defined as labels (by following them with a :) or by direct assignment (by equating them with a value through the = sign) are local to the program in which they are defined. To specify a symbol that can be referenced globally (that is, outside of the current program), the notations :: and == are used.

Constants

The assembler interprets all constants as decimal integers. However, a unary operator can be used to specify a constant in another radix or representation, as shown in Table 3.2. For example, the statement

```
BYTE_OF_ONES = ^XFF
```

equates the symbol BYTE_OF_ONES to hexadecimal value FF. To define an ASCII constant, a delimiter character must be placed before and after the string. All of the statements

```
ABC = ^A/ABC/
ABC = ^A.ABC.
ABC = ^ADABCD
```

equate the symbol ABC to the ASCII equivalent of the three characters ABC.

Storage Allocation

The allocation of storage for data is provided by declarative statements or assembler directives, some of which are listed in Table 3.3. These directives exist for initializing bytes, words, longwords, etc., and for allocating large blocks of storage. For instance, the statement

```
NUMBERS: .BYTE 1,2,3
```

stores three bytes of data containing the integers 1, 2, and 3 into consecutive bytes and defines the label NUMBERS as the address of the byte containing the 1. The statement

```
LIST:   .LONG  156,718,0
```

stores the integers 156, 718, and 0 into consecutive 32-bit longwords. Here the symbol LIST can be used to address the first longword, whose initial value will be 156. The longword at address LIST+4 will have the value 718, and so on, as shown below:

156	:LIST
718	:LIST+4
0	:LIST+8

Table 3.2   Assembler Unary Operators

Operator	Representation
^B	Binary
^D	Decimal
^O	Octal
^X	Hexadecimal
^A	ASCII
^F	Floating-Point

Table 3.3   Assembler Storage Allocation Directives

Directive	Meaning
label: .BYTE value_list	Store specified values in successive bytes in memory at symbolic address "label."
label: .WORD value_list	Store specified values in successive words in memory
label: .LONG value_list	Store specified values in successive longwords in memory.
label: .QUAD value_list	Store specified values in successive quadwords in memory.
label: .OCTA value_list	Store specified values in successive octawords in memory.
label: .ASCII /string/	Store ASCII representation of the delimited character string in successive bytes in memory.
label: .ASCIC /string/	Store the one-byte string length, followed by the ASCII representation of the string.
label: .ASCID /string/	Store a 64-bit string descriptor that contains the string's length, type, and address.
label: .ASCIZ /string/	Store the ASCII representation of the string, followed by a zero byte.
label: .ADDRESS address_list	Store the 32-bit address of the specified locations in memory.
label: .BLKB count	Reserve a contiguous block of "count" bytes of memory. The bytes are initialized to zero.
label: .BLKW count	Reserve a contiguous block of words.
label: .BLKL count	Reserve a contiguous block of longwords.
label: .BLKQ count	Reserve a contiguous block of quadwords.
label: .BLKO count	Reserve a contiguous block of octawords.

To allocate large blocks of storage without specifying the contents of each element, the .BLKx directive is used, where x specifies the size of each element in the block (B, W, L, Q, O). The statements

```
        ARRAYSIZE = 50
ARRAY:  .BLKW   ARRAYSIZE
```

allocate fifty words of contiguous storage. As a convenient feature of the assembler, the storage space is automatically initialized to zero. The value of the symbol ARRAY will be the address of the first byte of the data space.

The assembler also has directives (not listed in Table 3.3) to allocate floating-point data or storage blocks with the directives .F_FLOATING, .D_FLOATING, .G_FLOATING, .H_FLOATING, .BLKF, .BLKD,.BLKG, and .BLKH. Floating-point constants can be specified with or without (if the fraction is zero) decimal points, and with or without exponents, for example:

```
FLOATS:   .G_FLOATING  25, 63.556, 40.997E10
BIGNUM:   .H_FLOATING 12345678987654321.123456789
```

Finally, you should remember that the assembler is not a typed language. The directives defined in this section simply allocate storage; that is, they simply place binary data in memory. The assembler does not check the data types you declare against the data types you use to access data in instructions. At execution time, all data and instructions are just indistinguishable bytes in memory; it is impossible for hardware to tell where one variable starts and another stops. For example, if we declare

```
STUFF::
    .BYTE   1,2,3
    .LONG   4
    .BYTE   5,6,7
    .WORD   8
```

and at execution time, the linker places STUFF at address 200, then memory at address 200 will appear as follows:

```
00080706 05000000 04030201
```

There is no run-time information to tell the hardware how this information was defined or how it should be treated. It is up to you to use instructions that produce a correct result.

Storing Strings

The VAX Macro Assembler has several ways to represent strings. Because strings are typically variable in length, the programmer using a string must know or be able to compute its length. The simplest declaration for strings, .ASCII, simply stores the ASCII representation of the characters in consecutive bytes in memory. If the declaration

```
MYSTR:    .ASCII  \hello\
```

was assembled at location 300, ASCII *h* would be placed in byte 300, ASCII *e* in byte 301, and so on. In this case, the program would probably need to know explicitly how long the string is. Note that the string is surrounded by a delimiter that is not part of the string (in this case, \). Any character can be used to delimit the start and the end of a string, as long as it is not part of the string itself.

There are three other storage methods and corresponding directives for strings. A *counted* ASCII string is a string in which the first byte contains the length of the string. Since the count is limited to a byte, the string can be no longer than 255 characters. The directive .ASCIC allocates a counted ASCII string, automatically storing the length. If the declaration

```
MYSTR:    .ASCIC  \hello\
```

was assembled at location 300, byte 300 would contain the integer 5, byte 301 would contain ASCII *h*, etc. A similar directive, .ASCIZ, allocates a *zero terminated* string. In this case, there is no count, but a byte whose value is zero is placed following the string. A program processing the string will test for zero to know when the string is terminated. Strings are typically stored this way in the Unix operating systems.

Finally, a string can be represented using a *string descriptor*. String descriptors are typically used when passing strings to VMS operating system procedures. A string descriptor is 64 bits long and has the format shown below:

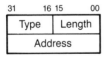

The descriptor contains the length of the string in the first 16 bits, a type indicator in the second 16 bits, and the address of the string in its second longword. The string itself can be stored anywhere in memory and can be up to 65,535 bytes in length. The declaration

```
MYSTR:    .ASCID  \hello\
```

would have a similar effect to the declaration

```
MYSTR:  .WORD    5        ; string length
        .WORD    0        ; string type
        .ADDRESS HERE      ; location of the string
        .
        .
        .
HERE:   .ASCII   \hello\
```

Always handle the string length field as a 16-bit word, since the following 16 bits will not necessarily be zero. In the preceding .ASCID declaration, the type field might contain an indication that the descriptor points to a simple ASCII string (as opposed to a decimal string, for example).

Expressions

Expressions are combinations of terms joined by binary operations. A term can be either a numeric value or a defined symbol. The binary operators are shown in Table 3.4.

The expression and all terms are evaluated as 32-bit values. The expression is processed left to right, with no operator precedence. However, angle brackets (<>) can be used to change the order of evaluation. For example,

A + B * C   and   A + <B * C>

have different values. Angle brackets can be nested, as in the expression

<<A ! B> @ - C>

Expressions can be used anywhere within the program that values are

Table 3.4 Assembler Binary Operators

Operator	Example	Meaning
+	A + B	Sum of A and B.
−	A − B	Difference of A and B.
*	A * B	Product of A and B.
/	A / B	Integer quotient of A and B.
@	A @ B	Arithmetic shift of A by B bits. If B is positive, A is shifted left, and zeros are shifted into the low order bits. If B is negative, A is shifted right and the high order bit of A is duplicated in the high order bits.
&	A & B	Logical AND of A and B.
!	A!B	Logical OR of A and B.
\	A \ B	Logical EXCLUSIVE OR of A and B.

used. As a result, all of the following expressions are legal:

```
.LONG   35*<7 + 6>
.BLKB   ARRAYSIZE*4
LENGTH = 4*8*ARRAYSIZE
```

All terms within an expression must be assembly-time constants or symbols.

Control Statements

Four assembler control statements are used frequently in this text. The title directive

```
.TITLE module_name    comment
```

defines the name of the program module and contains a comment string that is printed on the top line of each page of the listing. The subtitle directive

```
.SBTTL comment
```

contains a comment string to be printed on the second line of each listing page. The .TITLE directive is always the first line of the module, while the .SBTTL directive is used before each routine within a module. The assembler also uses the subtitle declarations to produce a table of contents on the first page of the listing.

The entry directive is used to declare procedures in VAX assembly language. The .ENTRY directive

```
.ENTRY procedure_name, register_mask
```

defines the *entry point* to a procedure whose name is specified as the first parameter. As we will see later, an assembly language procedure is responsible for saving any registers it modifies. The second parameter to .ENTRY is a 16-bit mask that specifies which registers should be saved when that procedure is called.

Finally, the end statement

```
.END   label
```

informs the assembler that this is the last source line to be processed. The label operand of the .END statement tells the assembler the starting address for the translated program. When the program is executed, it will begin at the specified location. This is typically a procedure name defined by a .ENTRY statement. If the module contains only subroutines and no starting point, the label is omitted.

Labels

As previously described, an instruction or storage declaration can begin with an optional label that refers symbolically to the address at which that storage or instruction will be placed. In the VMS assembler, there are actually three ways of declaring labels. First are normal alphanumeric labels, delimited by a colon (:) from the rest of the line. These symbols can be referred to anywhere within the module being assembled. However, if the label is to declare a symbol that will be referred to *outside* the current module, for example, a global variable or a globally referenced procedure entry point, then the label should be followed by a double colon (::). As a general programming style, global variables should be kept to a minimum.

Finally, the VMS assembler has a local label facility. In high-level languages, labels are rarely used. This is because the purpose of a label in a high-level language is to declare the target of a GOTO, and GOTOs are rarely used. In assembly language, however, the assembly equivalent of the GOTO is used frequently, since it is the basic control structure. A local label is a number followed by a dollar sign. The scope of a local label is limited to the instructions between the previous nonlocal label and the following nonlocal label. As an example, consider the following code skeleton:

```
GLOBAL_1::  .LONG 0  ; visible outside of this module
MYVAR:      .LONG 0  ; visible within this module
              .
              .
              .

START::                ; global procedure entry point
            <instruction>
10$:        <instruction>
            <instruction>
20$:        <instruction>
            <instruction>
LOOP:       <instruction>
            <instruction>
10$:        <instruction>
              .
              .
```

Two local labels, 10$ and 20$, are used in the code section begun by START and terminated by LOOP. The scope of these labels is limited to that code section. A Branch instruction whose target is 10$, which appears after START and before LOOP, will branch to the 10$ following START. No instruction either before START or following LOOP can refer to these labeled instructions. Following the label LOOP, a new local label block begins, and the local labels 10$ and 20$ can be reused. Now, however, they refer to different instructions.

There are two reasons for providing local labels in the VMS assembler. First, because labels are used so frequently in assembly language, local labels avoid the need for inventing senseless names that might be hard to locate when scanning a listing. Second, the use of local labels guarantees that a label cannot be referenced outside its local label block.

The Listing

Figure 3.1 shows a typical listing produced by the VAX macro assembler. For each line on the listing, the assembler prints the following information:

1. A decimal line number for reference.

2. The source line from the source input program.

3. The hexadecimal address at which the first byte generated from the source line will be placed (printed as an offset from the start of the program section).

4. The hexadecimal representation for the binary values to be placed in memory for data or the generated machine code for an instruction.

The assembler also prints a symbol table at the end of the listing, giving the numeric value for each symbol used in the assembly language program.

The Assembly Process

Now that we have examined the syntax and the semantics of assembly language, we will briefly describe the process of assembling a program. The assembly process is easily illustrated by examining a simple, two-pass assembler. The two-pass assembler is so named because it reads the source program twice. Two passes are required because all symbol values must be known before the translation can begin.

The objective of the assembler is to read the user's symbolic source program and to produce the binary object program and the listing. To do this, the assembler must be able to perform three functions:

1. Remember the addresses and values of the symbols used in declarations and instructions.

2. Translate the symbolic operation names into binary opcodes.

3. Convert the symbolic operand specifiers into their binary forms.

The purpose of the first pass, then, is to build a symbol table that contains the values of all labels and symbols defined in the program. For

Figure 3.1 Typical VAX macro listing

```
                                       0000    1          .TITLE  CIRCULAR BUFFER ROUTINES
                                       0000    2 ;
                                       0000    3 ; Storage for the buffer and pointer variables
                                       0000    4 ;
                                       0000    5
                             00000064  0000    6          BUFSIZE = 100                   ; define size of buffer
                             00000064  0000    7 BUFFER: .BLKB   BUFSIZE                 ; define character ring buffer
                             00000000  0064    8 COUNT:  .LONG   0                       ; initial count is zero
                             00000000  0068    9 BOTTOM: .LONG   0                       ; start bottom at 0
                             00000000  006C   10 TOP:    .LONG   0                       ; start top at 0
                                       0070   11
                                       0070   12         .SBTTL  INSBUF - Routine to insert in Circular Buffer
                                       0070   13 ;++
                                       0070   14 ;
                                       0070   15 ; ROUTINE DESCRIPTION:
                                       0070   16 ;
                                       0070   17 ;       This routine inserts a one byte character into the
                                       0070   18 ;       circular buffer.
                                       0070   19 ;
                                       0070   20 ; CALLING SEQUENCE:
                                       0070   21 ;
                                       0070   22 ;       CALLS OR CALLG
                                       0070   23 ;
                                       0070   24 ; INPUT PARAMETERS:
                                       0070   25 ;
                                       0070   26 ;       CHAR(AP) - the low byte of the first argument contains
                                       0070   27 ;                  the character to be inserted
                                       0070   28 ;
                                       0070   29 ; OUTPUT PARAMETERS:
                                       0070   30 ;
                                       0070   31 ;       None
                                       0070   32 ;
                                       0070   33 ; RETURN VALUES:
                                       0070   34 ;
                                       0070   35 ;       R0 =
                                       0070   36 ;               0 →  buffer is full
                                       0070   37 ;               1 →  character successfully inserted
                                       0070   38 ;--
                                       0070   39
                             00000004  0070   40         CHAR = 4                        ; offset to first argument
                                       0070   41
                                 0000  0070   42         .ENTRY INSBUF,^M<>
                 4            50   7C  0072 3 43 1       CLRQ    R0           2          ; assume full buffer error and zero
                                       0074   44                                         ; ... R1 for EDIV instruction
 E8 AF   00000064 8F               D1  0074   45         CMPL    #BUFSIZE,COUNT          ; is buffer full
                  1B               13  007C   46         BEQL    10$                     ; exit with error if so
          50   E7 AF               D0  007E   47         MOVL    BOTTOM,R0               ; get last entry index
    FF77 CF40  04 AC               90  0082   48         MOVB    CHAR(AP),BUFFER[R0]     ; insert char. in buffer
               D8 AF               D6  0089   49         INCL    COUNT                   ; note one more in buffer
D2 AF   51   50   00000064 8F      7B  008C   50         EDIV    #BUFSIZE,R0,R1,BOTTOM   ; wrap pointer by using
                                       0096   51                                         ; ...MOD(pointer,bufsize)
                     50   01       9A  0096   52         MOVZBL  #1,R0                   ; insert success code
                                   04  0099   53 10$:    RET                             ; return to caller
                                       009A   54
                                       009A   55         .END
```

example, a symbol table for the program listed in Figure 3.1 might contain the following information:

Symbol Name	Value (hex)	Symbol Type
BOTTOM	68	Label (address)
BUFFER	0	Label
BUFSIZE	64	Symbol
CHAR	4	Symbol
COUNT	64	Label
INSBUF	70	Label
TOP	6C	Label

Figure 3.2 shows the simplified flow of control for the assembler's first pass. As the figure shows, the first pass begins by setting the location counter to zero. As each line is read, it is syntactically analyzed and interpreted to determine what type of statement it contains. If the line contains a label, the label is assigned the current value of the location counter and is stored in the symbol table. Equated symbols are placed in the symbol table with their specified values. If an instruction or storage space declaration is found, the assembler increments the location counter by the size of the instruction or allocated data.

The second pass is shown in Figure 3.3. During this pass, the assembler uses the symbol table to translate the program. Once again, the location counter is initialized to zero and the source program is read. The assembler composes a listing line for each source line consisting of the source text, the line number, the location counter, and hexadecimal representation for any instruction or data. As each line is read, it is again analyzed for syntax and any errors are noted in the listing line. Label and symbol definitions are usually checked against the symbol table for consistency. If an instruction is found, the assembler uses the symbol table to find the values of any symbolic operand specifiers. The instruction is then assembled into binary from the opcode and the specifiers, and is output to the object file. If a storage allocation declaration is found, the assembler outputs the initial values of the storage items to the object program.

The Program Debugger

Debugging assembly language programs can be difficult and frustrating. Of course, as in all programming, the most important step is preventing bugs through careful design and reasoning about your program. Errors are inevitable, however, and locating them is aggravated by the low level of assembly language and the difficulty of producing formatted output through assembly language.

Figure 3.2   Assembler pass one

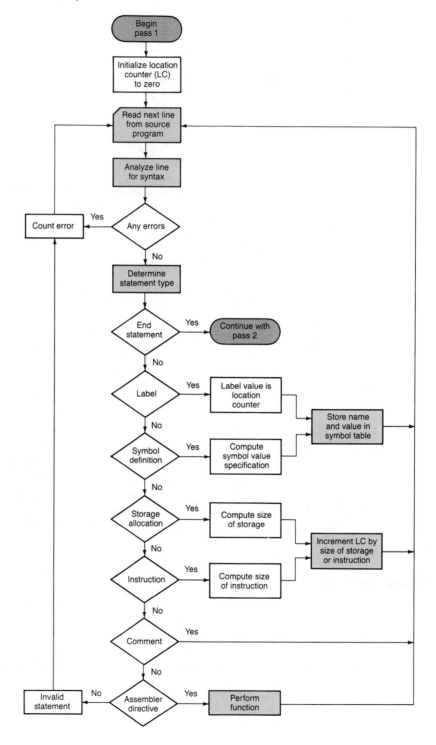

Figure 3.3   Assembler pass two

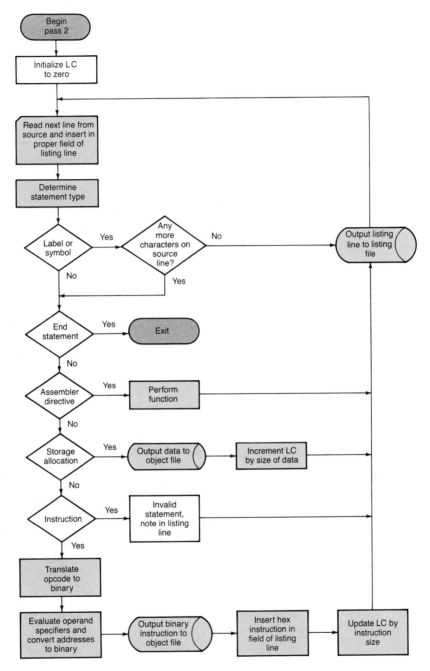

This section provides a brief overview of the VAX/VMS debugger, which can be used with high-level languages as well as assembly language. More details can be found in the *VAX/VMS Symbolic Debugger Reference Manual*. While some programmers survive without using a debugger, learning to use a debugger can greatly increase your productivity. More important, a debugger provides an interactive environment that allows you to experiment with your program while you learn assembly language.

Using the Debugger

The debugger is a powerful program that allows you to interactively control the execution of your program. Some of the facilities provided by most debuggers include the following:

- *State examination and modification.* You can examine variables and if needed, change their values. This saves debugging time, since you can manually change an incorrect variable in the middle of program execution and then allow the program to continue.

- *Execution control.* You can control the execution of the program in several ways. For example, you can execute the program one or more statements at a time (called *stepping* the program) to follow its execution and the results of its operations. Or you can modify the flow of execution, for example, by deciding to skip instructions, branching to different points in the program, or calling program procedures.

- *Breakpoints, watchpoints, and tracepoints.* You can define *breakpoints*, which are specific lines of source code or procedures of interest at which program execution should be stopped. When the breakpoint occurs, the user can examine program state and make modifications or continue. A *watchpoint* defines a variable of interest, perhaps one that is being incorrectly modified by some as yet unknown part of the program. The debugger can "watch" the variable and stop execution whenever that variable is about to be modified. A *tracepoint* defines an instruction or event whose execution causes the debugger to print a message. This produces a record of events that may be useful for debugging without stopping program execution following each event.

An important feature of the debugger is that it allows you to use the symbolic names you specified in your program for variables and labels. Since this symbol information is not typically stored with object files, a program must be assembled specially so that the symbol table is available to the debugger. The debugger itself is just a program that must be linked with the program to be debugged. So if you want to run the program MYPROG.MAR on VAX/VMS, you assemble, link, and run it as

```
$ MACRO/DEBUG MYPROG
$ LINK/DEBUG MYPROG
$ RUN MYPROG
```

After the RUN command is entered, the debugger will prompt the user at the terminal for commands (its prompt is DBG>).

The following descriptions include some of the most common commands and examples of their use. In these examples, commands are in uppercase for emphasis. They can be entered in either uppercase or lowercase and can be abbreviated.

Examining and Depositing

A common use of the debugger is to examine the values of program variables, locations in memory, and processor registers. The EXAMINE command is used for this purpose and takes as a parameter the symbolic or numeric address of the location to be examined. The debugger assumes that any parameter starting with a letter is a symbol and that any parameter starting with a number is a value. It also assumes that all values are in hexadecimal unless otherwise specified. Thus, the commands

```
EXAMINE ABC
EXAMINE 91FC
```

display the contents of the longwords at locations ABC and 000091FC, respectively. Note that in the second case, while VAX addresses are 32 bits (8 hexadecimal digits), the debugger simply appends zeros to the high-order part of the address. To display the contents of a location whose hexadecimal address begins with one of the characters A through F, you must append a leading zero to tell the debugger that this is a value, not a symbol. For example, the command

```
EXAMINE ABC,91FC,0A772,0D,R3
```

displays the contents of five longwords: the longword at symbolic location ABC, the longwords at addresses 000091FC, 0000A772, and 0000000D, and the contents of register R3. The VAX registers have built-in symbolic names R0—R11, AP, FP, SP, and PC. You can also specify a range of either addresses or registers to be examined by separating the symbolic or number values by a colon, for example, 200:220 or R3:R6.

By default, the examined locations are displayed in hexadecimal, but you can have them displayed in various representations, for example,

```
EXAMINE/DECIMAL/WORD AWORD,ANOTHERWORD
EXAMINE/ASCII:length MYSTRING
EXAMINE/BINARY/OCTAWORD FILTER,003F,R4
EXAMINE/INSTRUCTION DOIT:DOIT+20
```

In addition to changing the representation (for example, from hexadecimal to binary or decimal), you can change the size of the information unit displayed (by specifying /BYTE,/WORD, /OCTAWORD, and so on). For ASCII, you can specify the length of the string if you want to see more than four characters. The /INSTRUCTION option is particularly useful. In the preceding example, the EXAMINE/INSTRUCTION command prints the symbolic instructions between label DOIT and DOIT+20 (hexadecimal). Thus, you can ask the debugger to show you some section of your program.

You use the debugger DEPOSIT command to modify a variable, a location in memory, or a register. DEPOSIT assumes the same defaults as EXAMINE, which again can be changed by options to the command. The command

```
DEPOSIT/WORD HERE = 1234
```

deposits the value 1234 (hexadecimal) into the 16-bit word at the location specified by the symbol HERE. To deposit decimal 1234, you can override the default radix by specifying the radix converters, %BIN, %OCT, %DEC, or %HEX, for example,

```
DEPOSIT/WORD HERE = %DEC 1234
DEPOSIT R8 = %BIN 01011100
```

When you use these commands, the debugger always remembers the location most recently examined or deposited. That location is referred to as ".", which can be used as an abbreviation. For example, the sequence

```
EXAMINE MYVAR
DEPOSIT . = %DEC 10
EXAMINE .
EXAMINE
```

first examines the contents of location MYVAR, deposits decimal 10 in that longword location, and then examines it again. The final EXAMINE with no parameter displays the contents of the longword *following* MYVAR; that is, an EXAMINE command with no parameter increments the current location to the next longword.

Basic Control Flow

The basic program control operations are provided by GO and STEP. Initially, GO tells the debugger to begin execution of the program at its entry point (main program). Following any breakpoints, GO tells the debugger to continue execution from the current instruction. GO can also be used to continue execution at a specific location. For example,

```
GO NEXTLOOP
```

transfers control to the instruction at label NEXTLOOP.

The STEP command is used to "single-step" the program, one instruction at a time. When you give a STEP command, the debugger executes a single instruction and then prints the next instruction to be executed. You can STEP through multiple instructions by specifying as a parameter an integer number of instructions to be executed. Another important option is the behavior of STEP at a VAX CALL instruction. STEP/OVER will execute that procedure and stop at the next instruction following the CALL. STEP/INTO will execute the call and stop at the first instruction inside the called procedure. In addition, the options STEP/BRANCH and STEP/CALL will continue execution until the next branch or call instruction, respectively.

Setting Breakpoints, Watchpoints, and Tracepoints

Breakpoints tell the debugger to stop when a specific point in the program is reached. The commands

```
SET BREAK LOOPSTART
SET BREAK 0FD2
```

set breakpoints at the instruction at label LOOPSTART and at the instruction at address 00000FD2. You can examine breakpoints with SHOW BREAK and can cancel them with CANCEL BREAK. Using the DO clause, you can also supply a list of commands to be executed when the breakpoint occurs, for example,

```
SET BREAK LOOPEND DO ( EXAMINE I,J ; DEPOSIT K = 0 )
SET BREAK 0300 DO ( STEP ; GO )
```

A watchpoint tells the debugger to notify you and to stop execution when a specific location is modified. Like breakpoints, a simple SET WATCH command specifies the symbolic or numeric name of the location to watch. Watchpoints are examined with SHOW WATCH and cancelled with CANCEL WATCH.

A tracepoint follows execution of your program through specified instructions or events. SET TRACE sets a tracepoint at a particular program instruction. When that instruction is reached, the debugger prints a message and continues execution. Tracepoints are examined with SHOW TRACE and cancelled with CANCEL TRACE. Tracepoints can also be used to trace specific instructions. As a useful example, the command

```
SET TRACE/CALL
```

will print a message at the execution of every call instruction, showing the address at which the call occurs.

Using the Screen

The VAX/VMS debugger has a nice ability to divide the terminal or workstation screen into multiple windows. These windows can show a symbolic decoding of the instructions being executed, the current values of the registers, the user's commands, and the debugger's responses. To use the multiple-window debugger, type SET MODE SCREEN after running the program, and type DISPLAY REG to get a window with current register values. As you step through your program, the debugger highlights those registers whose values change.

First Program Example: Simple Output

As previously stated, one problem with debugging assembly language programs is the difficulty, compared to high-level languages, of performing input and output. This section presents our first complete programs, both to show the form of a complete program and to introduce some simple library routines for writing to the terminal. The material you need to understand these programs fully is covered later in the book. For now the goal is to allow you to imitate these programs to perform your own input and output.

The first program, shown in Figure 3.4, outputs two ASCII strings to the terminal. The strings are defined using the .ASCID directive, because the parameter to the terminal output procedure LIB$PUT_OUTPUT must be the address of a string descriptor. The program is actually a procedure called by the operating system when the program is run. The .ENTRY statement defines the name of the procedure, START, and the zero indicates that no registers need to be saved, since this is the main program.

The body of the program is simply two calls to the procedure LIB$PUT_OUTPUT. In a high-level language, you would simply write

```
LIB$PUT_OUTPUT("hello there");
```

and the compiler would generate this code for you. In assembly language, you must build the string descriptor explicitly and issue the call. On the VAX, procedure parameters are passed through the program's stack, as we shall see in Chapter 6. In this example, the PUSHAQ (push address of quadword) instruction pushes the address of the single parameter on the parameter-passing stack. The choice of the PUSHAQ instruction reflects the fact that the string descriptor is a 64-bit quadword. The parameter in this case is the string descriptor for the string to be output. The CALLS instruction calls the library procedure: the #1 indicates that there is only

Figure 3.4 Simple string output program

```
          .TITLE First Example Program

; First program to output a simple string to the terminal

HIMSG:  .ASCID \hello there\  ; initial message descriptor
BYEMSG: .ASCID \bye now\       ; final message descriptor

; All Main Procedure entry points are defined
; with a.ENTRY statement.

          .ENTRY START,0        ; main entry point
                                ; ..saves no registers

; Output the initial message to the terminal.

          PUSHAQ HIMSG          ; push descr. address on stack
          CALLS  #1,G^LIB$PUT_OUTPUT ; call output routine

; Output the final message to the terminal.

          PUSHAQ BYEMSG         ; push descriptor address
          CALLS  #1,G^LIB$PUT_OUTPUT ; call output routine
          RET                   ; don't forget to return
                                ; ..from the main program

          .END   START
```

one parameter, while the G^ tells the assembler that the addressing of this procedure will be resolved by the linker.

Finally, notice that the main program ends with a RET (return) instruction, as does any procedure. The .END assembler directive tells the assembler both that the program definition is complete and that the main program is called START. When we run this program, the operating system will transfer control to the address specified by the .END directive, which in this case is START.

Figure 3.5 is an extension of the simple program in Figure 3.4. In addition to the two strings, it prints the integers 10 through 0 in decreasing order. This program calls another library procedure, OTS$CVT_L_TI, which is an object-time system routine that converts a binary longword to an ASCII integer. The routine takes two parameters and in a high-level language would be called as OTS$CVT_L_TI (integer, string), where the ASCII value of the integer would be placed in the string. In this example, we must build a string descriptor, BUFDSC, to tell the procedure the size and the address of the string in which it can write the result. The addresses of the two parameters are pushed onto the stack before the call using the PUSHAQ and PUSHAL instructions. Note that the

Figure 3.5   Simple integer printing program

```
                .TITLE Second Program

        ;     Program to print integers from 10 down to 0.
        HIMSG:  .ASCID \hello there\   ; initial message
descriptor
        BYEMSG: .ASCID \bye now\       ; final message descriptor

        COUNTER:.LONG  10              ; init integer counter to
                                       10

        ; Build a string descriptor for the buffer in which
        ; to hold the ASCII value of the integer for output.

        BUFSIZE=10
        BUFDSC: .WORD  BUFSIZE         ; descriptor length field
                .WORD  0               ; descriptor type (unused)
                .ADDRESS BUFFER        ; descriptor address field
        BUFFER: .BLKB  BUFSIZE         ; allocate buffer space

        ; All procedure entry points are defined
        ; with a .ENTRY statement.

                .ENTRY START,0         ; main entry point
                                       ; ..saves no registers

        ; Output the initial message to the terminal.

                PUSHAQ HIMSG             ; push descr. address on stack
                CALLS  #1,G^LIB$PUT_OUTPUT ; call output routine

        ; Loop to process integers. On each pass a procedure is
        ; called to convert the integer to printable ASCII
        ; representation. The ASCII string is then output.

        10$:    PUSHAQ BUFDSC            ; push descriptor address
                PUSHAL COUNTER           ; push value to convert
                CALLS  #2,G^OTS$CVT_L_TI ; convert to integer ASCII
                PUSHAQ BUFDSC            ; now push dsc for output
                CALLS  #1,G^LIB$PUT_OUTPUT ; call output routine
                DECL   COUNTER           ; decrement integer
                                         counter
                BGEQ   10$               ; stop when counter < 0

        ; Output the final message to the terminal.

                PUSHAQ BYEMSG            ; push descriptor address
                CALLS  #1,G^LIB$PUT_OUTPUT ; call output routine
                RET                      ; return from main program

                .END   START
```

parameters are pushed onto the stack from last parameter to first parameter. Also, the CALLS instruction for OTS$CVT_L_TI specifies that there are two parameters.

For now, these examples will show you how to perform output of strings and integers. Table 3.5 describes some other library routines that you can use in a similar fashion; others can be found in the *VAX/VMS Run-Time Library Reference Manual*. For reading from the terminal, we use the routine LIB$GET_INPUT, which takes three parameters: the address of a string descriptor for a buffer into which the characters are read, the address of a string descriptor for an output string with which to prompt the user at the terminal, and the address of a word into which LIB$GET_INPUT stores the number of characters read from the terminal. We demonstrate the use of this procedure in Figure 3.6, a program that simply prompts the user to enter a string and then echoes that string at the terminal.

To get started, we suggest that you type in and execute one of these programs. Assemble and link the program with the debugger option and

Table 3.5 Some Useful VMS Library Procedures

Name and Parameters	Function
OTS$CVT_L_TB(longword,descriptor)	Converts a longword integer into binary representation in an ASCII string.
OTS$CVT_L_TI(longword,descriptor)	Converts a signed integer to a decimal ASCII string.
OTS$CVT_L_TZ(longword,descriptor)	Converts an unsigned integer to a hexadecimal ASCII string.
OTS$CVT_TI_L(descriptor,longword)	Converts the ASCII text string representation of a decimal number to a signed longword.
OTS$CVT_TZ_L(descriptor,longword)	Converts the ASCII text string representation of a hexadecimal value to a longword.
LIB$PUT_OUTPUT(descriptor)	Writes a string to the output device.
LIB$GET_INPUT(buffer_dsc,prompt_dsc,length)	Prompts the user with prompt_dsc, reads a string from the input device into buffer_dsc, and returns the number of characters read into length.

Figure 3.6 Simple terminal reading program

```
            .SBTTL Program to read input
    ;
    ; This program simply prompts the user for a string
    ; and then echoes the string
    ;
    INBUFSIZE = 100                 ; max. input size

    INDSC:  .WORD   INBUFSIZE       ; descriptor for
            .WORD   0               ; reading input
            .LONG   INBUF

    INBUF:  .BLKB   INBUFSIZE       ; input buffer itself
    INLEN:  .WORD   0               ; number of chars read

    IN_MSG: .ASCID \enter a string (exit with "$"): \
    OUT_MSG:    .ASCID \you typed the string: \

            .ENTRY START,0          ; main entry point
                                    ; saves no registers
    ; Program exits when user types a "$".
    ; Prompt the user for next input, read the user's
    ; input into INBUF

    10$:    MOVW    #INBUFSIZE,INDSC    set buffer size for input
            PUSHAW INLEN        ;       push addr. of ret. length
            PUSHAQ IN_MSG       ;       push addr. of prompt msg.
            PUSHAQ INDSC        ;       addr. of buffer for read
            CALLS   #3,G^LIB$GET_INPUT  ; read user input

    ; The user's string has been read into INBUF, and
    ; INLEN contains the number of characters read. Copy
    ; INLEN into the length field of INDSC so we can write
    ; out the string that has been read.

            MOVW    INLEN,INDSC     ; insert number of chars read
            PUSHAQ OUT_MSG          ; address of string descriptor
            CALLS   #1,G^LIB$PUT_OUTPUT     ; print output message
            PUSHAQ INDSC            ; addr. of user's input
            CALLS   #1,G^LIB$PUT_OUTPUT     ; print string user typed

    ; Check if user wants to exit

            CMPB    #^A/$/,INBUF    ; did user type a $?
            BNEQ    10$             ; continue if not
            RET                     ; else exit program
            .END START
```

get a listing file. In VMS, your program actually starts at memory address 200 hexadecimal, so you will have to add 200 hexadecimal to the addresses on the listing when specifying addresses. For example, if a variable appears at address 4F on your listing (all addresses are listed in hexadecimal), to examine it you would type EXAMINE 24F.

Use the debugger to set breakpoints or step through the program to see how it operates and what information you can learn from the debugger. You can use the debugger to experiment with instructions if you are not sure how they work. Once again, when pushing parameters for these procedures, the parameters are pushed in reverse order, that is, the last parameter listed in the high-level description is pushed first. Because these procedures use call by reference, it is always the address of the parameter that is pushed.

Conventions for Writing Programs

As you become comfortable with a new machine or language, you will develop a personal style of programming. This style is exhibited in several areas, including

- the way you structure programs

- the algorithms you use to solve common problems

- the instructions or language constructs you choose

- the format of the source program

- the language you use in commenting the program

Library shelves are filled with computer science books that teach you how to structure or format programs and what language constructs to use and avoid. Since this information is readily available, it is not repeated here. We will, however, make some general comments about assembly language programming.

Few assembly language programs are written now except for teaching purposes and for a small number of systems programs. Whether the program is used for a class or for systems programming, the programmer should have the following goals in mind:

1. The program must solve the problem at hand.

2. The program must communicate both the solution technique and the implementation details to the reader.

3. The program must be easy to understand and modify.

These goals require that the program be clearly documented and described. On a machine with a rich instruction set, such as the VAX, a number of different instructions are typically suitable for a given situation. Luckily, the simplest solution to a problem is usually the easiest to understand and the most efficient. Thus, you should try to select instructions and solution methods that are straightforward and easily comprehended. Also, to simplify debugging, we recommend that you do not try to optimize storage. For example, always use longwords to contain integers where possible, even if you know that the numbers you will manipulate will fit in shorter data types. In this way, you are less likely to use the wrong instruction to manipulate your data. Performance for byte, word, and longword is identical, so it won't cost anything in terms of run-time speed, and memory is cheap.

The comments are as much a part of the program as the instructions. It is not the number of comments that is important (particularly in assembly language, in which every line is usually commented) but the content of the comments. Each instruction should be followed by a comment that describes the logical operation or, perhaps, the reason for performing the instruction. The comment explains how the instruction fits into the problem solution.

Block comments can describe the flow or the logical function of a series of instructions and to break up a complicated section of code into smaller, more comprehensible pieces. Form good programming habits now, and you will be rewarded the first time you try to modify your own programs.

Exercises

1. Give an example of a simple high-level language statement and its assembly language equivalent.

2. Why are special symbols used, such as ":" and ";", in writing an assembly language statement?

3. What happens when the following code segment is executed by the VAX computer?

```
A:   .LONG   1948
B:   .LONG   13
C:   .LONG   1640
      .
      .
      .
ADDL    A,B
ADDL3   B,C,A
ADDL    A,B
```

4. What occurs when

```
ADDL3   A,A,A
```

is executed? What occurs when the two-statement program

```
HERE: ADDL3   A,A,A
      JMP     HERE
```

is executed?

5. Suppose three longword memory locations are defined as follows:

```
Address        Assembly Statement

 308        X:   .LONG  20
 30C        Y:   .LONG  9
 310        Z:   .LONG  10
```

Show the contents of X,Y,Z following the execution of the following instructions or groups of instructions. Assume for each case that the same initial contents of X,Y, and Z apply (that is, X is 20, Y is 9, and Z is 10).

```
a.   MOVL Y,X
b.   MOVAL Y,X
c.   SUBL Y,X
d.   SUBL X,Y
e.   SUBL3 Y,X,Z
f.   INCL Y
     SUBL3 Y,X,Z
g.   MOVAL X,X
     MOVAL Y,Y
     MOVAL Z,Z
h.   SUBL Z,X
     DECL X
     MOVL X,Y
```

6. Why can't a symbol begin with a digit? What's the advantage of equating a value to a symbol (for example, SIX = 6)? Which of the following takes more bytes of storage:

```
a. SIX:  .BYTE
b. SIX = 6
```

7. What hexadecimal numbers are stored in memory for the following statement?

```
.LONG  156,^D128,^A.12,3.,^X29,,^01234,3*5/4
```

8. Show what will be stored in memory starting at location 100 if the following is assembled. Assume that HERE is at location 100. Also list all symbols defined by these directives and their values.

```
HERE:    .LONG 102
THERE    = 104
THIS:    .BLKL 1
         .BLKB 4
THING =  200
ANOTHER: .LONG 12,34
```

4 Instruction and Addressing Fundamentals

Armed with the basic information presented in the previous chapters, we can now expand our instruction repertoire to write assembly language solutions for typical computer problems. But an understanding of the instruction set alone is not enough to write sophisticated assembly language programs and to understand how digital computers function. Along with the instruction set, we need to become familiar with the various techniques for addressing memory. Once we have a firm grasp of addressing and instruction formation, we can examine the encoding of instructions and learn how instructions are represented in memory. The examples and techniques presented here are all based on the VAX.

This chapter introduces simple programming examples and builds on them to demonstrate more advanced techniques. Thus, the first examples may seem awkward in retrospect. As the instruction set is developed, however, more efficient operations are explained and contrasted to the earlier examples.

VAX Instruction Characteristics

An important consideration in evaluating an architecture is the correspondence between a machine's basic data types and the operations (or instructions) that can be performed on those data types. For example, if a machine has byte, word, and longword integers, it should have an add instruction that operates on each of these data types in a uniform and consistent manner. If a longword can contain an integer or an address, these two objects may need to be treated differently so that addresses can be evaluated at run-time. These are some of the issues one needs to consider when examining a particular machine. Chapter 10 considers general issues in instruction set design and examines several instruction set architectures.

The VAX has a complete set of instructions that both perform generic operations on the primitive data types and allow for conversion from one data type to another. In addition, the VAX provides different instructions for manipulating numeric data types and addresses. Finally, there are the testable results of instruction execution that can be used to determine the effect of an instruction. In this way, we can change the order of execution of a sequence of instructions and cause different instruction streams to be executed for different data.

Generic Operations

The VAX has a relatively symmetric instruction set with respect to byte, word, and longword integers. That is, the general instructions can operate on any of these VAX data types. Instruction names are formed by taking generic operations, like MOV or ADD, and appending the data type of the operands, such as B, W, or L for byte, word, and longword integers, respectively. While integer arithmetic instructions are available on byte, word, and longword data types, quadword and octaword arithmetic are not fully supported.

Some instructions also exist in both two- and three-operand forms. We denote the two- and three-operand forms by appending a 2 or a 3 to the instruction name following the data type specifier. For the Add instruction, which has both two- and three-operand forms, we can construct the instructions

```
ADDB2
ADDB3
ADDW2
ADDW3
ADDL2
ADDL3
```

Because the two-operand forms are used more frequently, the VAX/VMS assembler allows us to drop the suffix 2 on these instructions.

Table 4.1 shows some of the general integer arithmetic and data manipulation instructions. Note which data types are available for each instruction and how many operands can be used. The Move and Clear instructions can operate on quadword and octaword elements, as well as bytes, words, and longwords.

Some of these instructions are familiar from Chapter 3. You have also seen Branch instructions which change program control flow. At this point it is appropriate to look at the branching mechanism in more detail.

Control Flow

Perhaps the single most powerful feature of any computer is its ability to make decisions. By "decisions," we mean the ability to perform different functions or to execute different program sections depending on conditions in the program. Generally, the computer does this simply by determining whether the result of an operation is positive, negative, or zero. The *conditional branch* instructions transfer control to a different program section based on these results.

The symbolic format of a VAX conditional branch instruction is

```
Bcondition destination
```

Table 4.1 VAX Generic Integer Instruction Set

Operation	Mnemonic	Data Types	Number of Operands
Move data from one location to another.	MOV	B,W,L,Q,O	2
Clear location (set to zero).	CLR	B,W,L,Q,O	1
Move negative: moves negated value of the first operand to second operand.	MNEG	B,W,L	2
Move complemented: moves the logical NOT of the source to the destination. This is the one's complement of the source, i.e., the values of all bits complemented.	MCOM	B,W,L	2
Increment location: adds one to a data element.	INC	B,W,L	1
Decrement location: subtracts one from a data element.	DEC	B,W,L	1
Add operands together: in the two-operand form, the result is stored in the second operand. In the three-operand form, the first two operands are added and stored in the third operand.	ADD	B,W,L	2,3
Subtract operands: in the two-operand form, the first operand is subtracted from the second, and the result is stored in the second operand. In the three-operand form, the first operand is subtracted from the second and the result is stored in the third operand.	SUB	B,W,L	2,3
Multiply operands.	MUL	B,W,L	2,3
Divide second operand by first operand.	DIV	B,W,L	2,3

where condition is a mnemonic that indicates for what. conditions a branch to the destination is made. For the conditional branches to operate, status information must be saved following each instruction so that the succeeding instruction(s) can examine it. On the VAX, there are four bits of status information, called the condition codes, that reflect the outcome of the last instruction executed. These bits are part of the program status word (PSW), which is the low word of the processor status longword (PSL) register. Instructions such as Branch examine the condition codes to determine what action to take.

The condition codes and their functions are as follows:

- N (*Negative Bit*). The N bit is set if the result of an instruction is negative; it is cleared if the result is positive or zero. For example, following a decrement instruction, the N bit is set if the decremented value is less than zero.

- Z (*Zero Bit*). The Z bit is set when the result of an instruction is exactly zero; otherwise it is cleared. For instance, the Z bit is set following a decrement instruction if the location decremented contains a one before the instruction is executed.

- V (*Overflow Bit*). The V bit is set following arithmetic operations if the result of the operation is too large to be represented in the data type used.

- C (*Carry Bit*). The C bit is set following arithmetic instructions in which a carry out of or a borrow into the most significant bit occurred.

The difference between overflow and carry is not always obvious. Overflow indicates that the result of an operation was too large for the data type and that the destination operand contains an incorrect number. It is used only for *signed* arithmetic. For example, in an integer add, if the operands are of the same sign but the result is of a different sign, then overflow occurred. In that sense, overflow destroys the sign bit. Suppose we want to add the following *signed* 4-bit numbers:

```
  7        0111
 +6        0110
 17        1101
```

When interpreted in two's-complement form, the value of the signed 4-bit result is −3, so overflow occurred. The addition of two positive numbers yielded a negative result.

Carry, which is used for *unsigned* arithmetic, is (in the case of ADD) a carry out of the high-order bit. Suppose we now add two unsigned 4-bit numbers:

```
 11        1011
 +6        0110
 17    1   0001
          ↑
          └─Carry
```

There is a one-bit carry out of the most significant bit, so the C condition code would be set. This condition can be used to implement multiprecision arithmetic and serves as input to the instructions Add With Carry (ADWC) and Subtract With Carry (SBWC).

For cases in which the programmer or the compiler needs to check explicitly for overflow or carry, there are four VAX instructions to test for the two possible states of these two possible condition codes: Branch on Carry Set (BCS), Branch on Carry Clear (BCC), Branch on Overflow Set (BVS), and Branch on Overflow Clear (BVC). Thus, following an arithmetic instruction, you can check explicitly for overflow:

```
ADDL    R0,R1
BVS     HANDLE_OVF
 .
 .
```

The VAX programmer's card provided as an appendix shows how each instruction affects condition codes. Some instructions set or clear condition codes based on the last arithmetic or logic result, some set or clear them unconditionally, and some leave them unaffected.

Because each byte, word, or longword can represent either a signed or an unsigned integer, you must be careful to use the correct conditional branch instruction following a comparison or an operation on integer quantities. Consider the following two bytes, A and B:

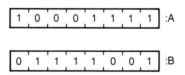

Which is larger? It depends, of course, on whether these bytes are being used to represent signed or unsigned 8-bit numbers. If the bytes are signed, then A is negative and B is larger. If the bytes are unsigned, A is larger.

Table 4.2 describes the two sets of conditional branches for signed and unsigned operands. It lists the instruction mnemonics and the conditions on which the branches are taken. For example, the BLSS instruction branches if the N bit is equal to one; the BLSSU instruction branches if the C bit is equal to one; the BGTR instruction branches if the logical OR of the N and Z bits is equal to zero, in other words, if *both* N and Z are zero.

The conditional branch instructions are the only place in the VAX architecture where the difference between signed and unsigned integers is visible. In particular, this difference is *not* visible to arithmetic instructions, such as ADDL; the ADDL instruction produces the correct result whether you intend its operands to be signed or unsigned. That is, when adding two two's-complement integers, the binary two's-complement

Table 4.2 VAX Conditional Branch Instructions

Operation	*Mnemonic*	*Branch Condition*
Signed Branches		
Branch on Equal	BEQL	Z = 1
Branch on Not Equal	BNEQ	Z = 0
Branch on Less Than	BLSS	N = 1
Branch on Less Than or Equal	BLEQ	(N OR Z) = 1
Branch on Greater Than	BGTR	(N OR Z) = 0
Branch on Greater Than or Equal	BGEQ	N = 0
Unsigned Branches		
Branch on Equal Unsigned	BEQLU	Z = 1
Branch on Not Equal Unsigned	BNEQU	Z = 0
Branch on Less Than Unsigned	BLSSU	C = 1
Branch on Less Than or Equal Unsigned	BLEQU	(C OR Z) = 1
Branch on Greater Than Unsigned	BGTRU	(C OR Z) = 0
Branch on Greater or Equal Unsigned	BGEQU	C = 0

result is the same whether the operands are being interpreted as signed or unsigned. If the operands are being used as signed integers, the result, when interpreted as a signed integer, will have the correct sum. If the operands are being used as unsigned integers, the result, when interpreted as an unsigned integer, will have the correct sum.

But when comparing two integers, you must specify which conditional branch to use so that the branch instruction examines the correct condition code bits. If you are using signed integers, the branch instruction examines only the Z and N bits; the C bit is ignored. If you are using unsigned integers, the branch instruction examines only the Z and C bits; in this case, the N bit is ignored.

The Compare and Test instructions specifically set the condition codes for program decision making and are usually followed by a conditional branch instruction. Each instruction can be used to test one item or compare two items of byte, word, longword, or floating-point data types.

It is important to be careful using conditional branches because different instructions affect the condition codes in different ways. When you use a Branch instruction following a Compare instruction, you are clearly testing the relationship between two data items. For instance, in the sequence

```
CMPL    A,B
BGTR    TARGET
```

the branch to TARGET is taken if A > B when A and B are treated as signed integers. In the sequence

```
CMPL    A,B
BGTRU   TARGET
```

the branch to TARGET is taken if A > B when A and B are treated as unsigned integers.

However, in the sequence

```
SUBL    A,B
BGTR    TARGET
```

the branch to TARGET is taken if *the result of the operation B−A is greater than zero* (assuming that A and B are signed integers). Following an arithmetic instruction, the branches test the relationship of the result to zero. Therefore, the following three sequences are all identical in effect:

```
1. SUBL  A,B
   CMPL  B,#0
   BGTR  TARGET

2. SUBL  A,B
   TSTL  B
   BGTR  TARGET

3. SUBL  A,B
   BGTR  TARGET
```

In example 1 above, the notation #0 means the value zero; # allows us to specify the operand *value* in the instruction instead of its *address*. From this, we see that the Test instruction (TSTL) simply compares an operand to zero. Following most arithmetic instructions, the test is superfluous because the condition codes are already based on the result. Therefore, the Test instruction is normally used to evaluate a data item that is *not* the result of the previous instruction (otherwise the test would be superfluous).

As an example, Figure 4.1 is a simple program that reads an integer from the terminal and tells the user whether it is positive, negative, or zero. Note that the branch instructions do not affect the condition codes, so several branches may follow an instruction that sets the condition codes.

In addition to the conditional branches already examined, several other branches appear in Figure 4.1. The Branch Byte (BRB) instruction is an *unconditional* branch instruction; that is, it always branches to the destination. There is also a Branch Word (BRW) instruction. The difference, between these two instructions is simply one of encoding efficiency. Branch Byte can only branch a small distance within the program, while Branch Word can branch a greater distance.

Figure 4.1   Branching program example

```
                .SBTTL Program to test for positive, negative, or zero

        ;
        ; This program reads an integer from the terminal
        ; and prints "positive", "negative", or "zero"
        ; depending on the value of that integer.
        ;
INBUFSIZE = 12
INDSC:  .WORD    INBUFSIZE          ; descriptor for
        .WORD    0                  ; reading integer
        .LONG    INBUF
INBUF:  .BLKB    INBUFSIZE          ; input buffer
INLEN:  .WORD    0                  ; number of chars read
VALUE:  .LONG 0                     ; binary input value
POS_MSG: .ASCID \input is positive\
NEG_MSG: .ASCID \input is negative\
ZER_MSG: .ASCID \input is zero\
USR_MSG: .ASCID \enter an integer: \
ERR_MSG: .ASCID \error in input\

        .ENTRY   START,0            ; main entry point
                                    ; saves no registers
        ; Program is an infinite loop.
        ; Prompt the user for next input, read the user's
        ; input into INBUF, and then call routine to
        ; convert the ASCII input to an integer.

10$:    MOVW     #INBUFSIZE,INDSC ; init inbuffer size
        MOVAW    INLEN,-(SP)        ; push addr. of ret. length
        MOVAQ    USR_MSG,-(SP)      ; push addr. of prompt msg.
        MOVAQ    INDSC,-(SP)        ; buffer for read
        CALLS    #3,G^LIB$GET_INPUT ; read user input
        MOVW     INLEN,INDSC        ; insert length read into.

        MOVAL    VALUE,-(SP)        ; space to return int.
        MOVAQ    INDSC,-(SP)        ; ascii integer
        CALLS    #2,G^OTS$CVT_TI_L ; convert ascii to int.
        BLBS     R0,20$             ; continue if no error
        MOVAQ    ERR_MSG,-(SP)      ; input error occurred
        CALLS    #1,G^LIB$PUT_OUTPUT ; print error msg
        BRB      10$                ; back for more input

        ; VALUE now has the 32-bit signed integer. Check to
        ; see what it is.

20$:    MOVAL    ZER_MSG,R0         ; assume it's zero
        TSTL     VALUE              ; what do we have?
        BEQL     40$                ; branch if zero
        BGTR     30$                ; branch if positive
        MOVAL    NEG_MSG,R0         ; else it's negative
        BRB      40$                ; go print message

30$:    MOVAL    POS_MSG,R0         ; positive message address
```

```
; R0 contains the address of correct message to print.

40$:      PUSHL    R0                     ; push message address
          CALLS    #1,G^LIB$PUT_OUTPUT ; write the message
          BRB      10$                    ; and go back for more
          .END START
```

The Branch on Low Bit Set (BLBS) instruction checks bit zero of a longword and branches to the destination if that bit is a one. The reason for using this instruction following certain system calls is that some procedures return a status value in R0 following a call. In VAX/VMS, status codes are defined so that if the status value is even (bit zero is zero), an error occurred, but if the value is odd (bit zero is one), the procedure succeeded. This makes it simple to test for failure or success.

Operand-Addressing Techniques

Memory addresses on the VAX are 32 bits in size. However, even though addresses are 32 bits, there are other methods for specifying operand addresses besides 32-bit values. These other methods, known as *addressing modes*, allow for more efficient representations of addresses within instructions. Addressing modes also simplify the manipulation of common data structures.

However an address is specified, the CPU must be able to locate or calculate the 32-bit operand address from the specification. This process is known as *effective address calculation*, and the result is the *effective address* of the operand.

This section examines the various addressing techniques for the VAX and the method of effective address calculation associated with each. Along with the instructions already examined, these techniques will be used to demonstrate the solutions to common programming problems.

Simple Addressing

Chapter 3 discussed simple symbolic address specification using symbolic labels. In that direct addressing mode, the operand is specified by a symbolic name that represents the address of the operand. In programming, we often say that the operand specifier "points to" the operand, or that the operand specifier is a *pointer*. This is shown diagrammatically in Figure 4.2, where the operand specifier is the address of the operand. If we assume an instruction such as

```
CLRW    ABC
```

then the *operand specifier* is the address ABC, and the operand itself is the *contents* of the symbolically referenced location ABC.

For the first example of addressing, consider an array-manipulation problem: to form the sum of two integer arrays, producing a third array.

Figure 4.2   **Simple symbolic address**

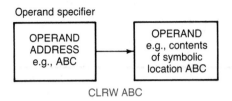

CLRW ABC

This summation could be expressed with a loop in a high-level language, such as Pascal, as shown in Figure 4.3.

Each of the three arrays for our assembly language example, labeled A, B, and C in Figure 4.4, is composed of fifty 32-bit integer elements. Instead of using a loop, as in the code in Figure 4.3, we first present a simple linear solution to the problem in Figure 4.5.

The program demonstrates a solution in which fifty three-operand Add Longword instructions are used to sum the elements of A and B into C. Since the elements added are longwords, we address every fourth byte. Notice that this introduces a typical programming problem: what is the address of the last element in an array of length N? Since the first element is at address $A + 0$, the last element is at $A + 4 \times (N - 1)$ for 4-byte longwords. That is, when the first symbolic address is zero, the last address is one less than the number of elements, times the number of bytes per element. You must be careful to account for both endpoints.

Notice also that the VAX memory is byte addressable. Each longword is specified by the address of its low-order byte. Had the example in Figure 4.5 used an array of bytes instead of longwords, the following Add Byte instructions would be used:

```
ADDB3     A,B,C
ADDB3     A+1,B+1,C+1
ADDB3     A+2,B+2,C+2
          .
          .
          .
```

Figure 4.3   **High-level integer array summation**

```
const n = 50;
var i:  integer;
    A:  array[1..n] of integer;
    B:  array[1..n] of integer;
    C:  array[1..n] of integer;

begin
    for i := 1 to n do
        C[i] := A[i] + B[i] ;

end;
```

Figure 4.4   Longword array

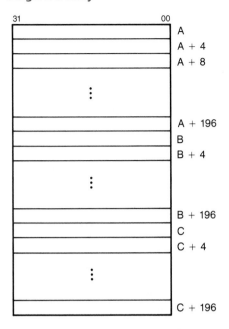

Figure 4.5   Simple linear array sum example

```
A:      .BLKL    50       ; define array A of 50 longwords
B:      .BLKL    50       ; define array B
C:      .BLKL    50       ; define array C
          .
          .
          .
        ADDL3    A,B,C     ; C(1) = A(1) + B(1)
        ADDL3    A+4,B+4,C+4
        ADDL3    A+8,B+8,C+8
          .
          .
          .
        ADDL3    A+196,B+196,C+196   ; C(50) = A(50) + B(50)
          .
          .
          .
```

For a 16-bit word array, the following Add Word instructions would be used:

```
ADDW3    A,B,C
ADDW3    A+2,B+2,C+2
ADDW3    A+4,B+4,C+4
  .
  .
  .
```

In other words, the increment between array elements depends on the data representation and is a multiple of the base-addressable unit, the byte. It is important to choose the appropriate Add instruction from the generic set of all Add instructions.

Immediate Mode

Programmers frequently need to specify constants in instructions. For example, there may be a need to add integer 5 to a longword or to store the character A in memory. One way to do this is to allocate storage containing the constant, as follows:

```
VALUE:   .LONG   5            ; constant value 5
         .
         .
         .
         ADDL    VALUE,A      ; add five to A
         .
         .
         .
```

Here the constant 5 is stored in memory at symbolic address VALUE. However, a more convenient and efficient notation is to use a literal in the instruction.

A *literal* is a constant or expression used in the instruction and stored as a part of the instruction rather than in a separate data location. The format for specifying a literal is #*value*, where value can be an expression (as in symbol definitions, the expression must be an assembly-time constant). For example, to add 5 to the longword A, we can now write

```
ADDL    #5,A
```

This is known as *immediate mode addressing* because the operand itself, not the operand address, is specified in the instruction. The number sign (#) indicates to the assembler that what follows is the immediate operand for the instruction. Figure 4.6 shows that the first operand specifier is the operand itself for the instruction CMPW #100,R0.

Figure 4.6 **Immediate mode addressing**

Operand specifier

```
┌─────────┐
│ OPERAND │
│ e.g., 100 │
│         │
└─────────┘
```

CMPW #100,VALUE

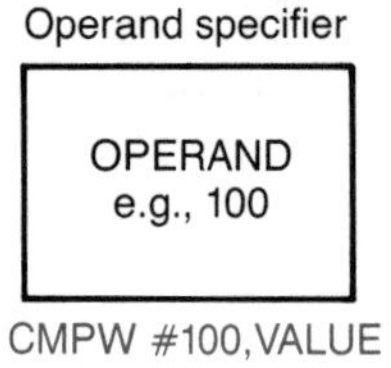

Figure 4.7   Loop array summation

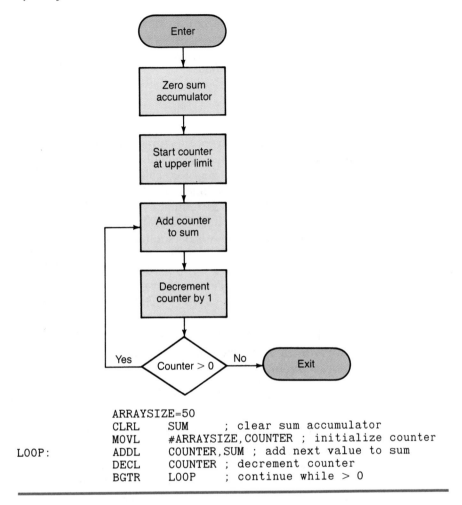

```
          ARRAYSIZE=50
          CLRL     SUM       ; clear sum accumulator
          MOVL     #ARRAYSIZE,COUNTER ; initialize counter
LOOP:     ADDL     COUNTER,SUM ; add next value to sum
          DECL     COUNTER ; decrement counter
          BGTR     LOOP    ; continue while > 0
```

Figure 4.7, a program to form the sum of the integers between 1 and 50, further illustrates the use of literals. Instead of a linear solution, it uses a loop to generate the values to be added.

Notice that the loop counts downward from 50 instead of upward from 0. This technique recognizes the fact that the DECL instruction set the condition codes, informing the control unit about the results of the last arithmetic operation just as the CMP instruction does. By performing the additions in reverse order so that COUNTER counts down rather than up, it is not necessary to use a CMP instruction to test for the upper limit. Instead, the program can test whether COUNTER is greater than zero after each iteration and continue to loop as long as COUNTER is positive.

The assembler assumes that a literal is a decimal (base 10) number unless it is told otherwise. Assembler directives can be used to change the radix or representation used, for example:

```
MOVL    #^XFFFF0000,STATUS
MOVW    #^A/HI/,MSGBUF
MOVF    #^F2.5,MYFLOAT
```

General-Purpose Registers

A register is a high-speed storage location that can be used for arithmetic, addressing, and, as we will see, for indexing arrays. Some early machines had only one register, called the *accumulator*, in which all arithmetic was done. Machines were structured that way because both memory and logic were extremely expensive. Since there was only one register, it was an implied operand in instructions. To perform the high-level statement A:=A+B on such a machine would require the steps

```
LOAD    A               ; load accumulator with A
ADD     B               ; add B to accumulator
STORE   A               ; store accumulator result
                        ; ...back in A
```

On machines like the VAX, all operations can be performed either in memory or in registers; the preceding steps can thus be written in memory-to-memory form as

```
ADDL    B,A             ; add B to A
```

There are still several good reasons for including registers in these machines. First, registers on most current computers are used to supply a limited amount of high-speed storage. On the VAX, for example, two-operand ADD instructions like the one just shown execute several times faster if both operands are in registers, as in

```
ADDL    R0,R1           ; add register 0 to register 1
```

If a storage location is to be used for a large number of arithmetic operations within a routine, it may pay to first load its contents into a register, perform all the operations on it, then move it back to memory. In fact, one of the most important (and difficult) tasks for a compiler is determining what variables to keep in registers.

A second advantage of registers is that they simplify the addressing of data structures such as arrays, as subsequent discussion will show. The third important feature of registers is that, because there are few of them, they can be addressed using fewer bits. On the VAX, for instance, there are sixteen 32-bit registers called R0, R1, ..., R15. Because there are only sixteen registers, each can be addressed in only 4 bits, compared to 32 bits that may be required to represent a memory address. This reduction in the size of operand addresses means a further increase in performance, since fewer bytes are fetched from memory to interpret the instruction.

Not all sixteen VAX registers are general purpose; four of them have special uses and should not be used for general programming. These four registers also have special names:

1. R12, known as the *argument pointer* (AP) is used in the subroutine-calling facility, described in Chapter 6.

2. R13, the *frame pointer* (FP), is also used in the subroutine-calling facility.

3. R14, the *stack pointer* (SP), is used to access the program's stack, a data structure described in Chapter 6.

4. R15 is the *program counter* (PC). On the VAX, the program counter is one of the general-purpose registers. As we will discuss later, this simplifies the encoding of some addressing modes.

The remaining twelve registers, R0 through R11, are available for general programming use and can be used as operands in place of memory locations in almost all VAX instructions.

Let us now reexamine the program shown in Figure 4.7. Instead of using memory locations for COUNTER and SUM, we use the registers R0 and R1, as shown.

```
        ;
        ; use R0 as SUM, R1 as loop COUNTER
        ;
                ARRAYSIZE=50
                CLRL    R0              ; clear sum accumulator
                MOVL    #ARRAYSIZE,R1   ; initialize counter
        LOOP:   ADDL    R1,R0           ; add next value to sum
                DECL    R1              ; decrement counter
                BGTR    LOOP            ; loop while counter > 0
```

A careful inspection of this code reveals that replacing the memory locations with registers reduces the number of memory references by two orders of magnitude.

A set of two adjacent VAX registers can be used as a 64-bit operand in a quadword instruction, or a set of four adjacent registers can be used as a 128-bit operand in an octaword instruction. The adjacent registers are specified by the low-order register number. For instance, the instruction

```
MOVQ     R3,R6
```

replaces the following two-instruction sequence:

```
MOVL     R3,R6
MOVL     R4,R7
```

Language compilers and assembly programmers often use this property as an optimization technique. For example, the Clear Quadword (CLRQ) instruction can be used to set two adjacent registers to zeros; Clear Octaword (CLRO) will set four adjacent registers to zero.

Indirect Mode

Besides being used for arithmetic, registers, as well as memory locations, can be used to hold addresses of operands. Referencing an element through a register or memory location is called *indirect addressing*. This *deferred* mode of addressing can be combined with other modes, described later, to provide sophisticated addressing techniques.

Indirect addressing can be used in many ways. For example, it can help the programmer to pass arguments to subroutines or to create linked data structures. These capabilities exist because indirect addressing specifies the "address of the address of the operand" rather than the "address of the operand." Figure 4.8 indicates how indirect addressing implies that the operand is the "address of the address" by including another operand box to point to the actual operand. Assembler syntax for indicating deferred addressing is the at sign (@) preceding a memory address for indirect addressing through a memory location, and parentheses surrounding a register name for indirect addressing through a register. This is shown pictorially in Figure 4.8 for the instruction

```
CLRW     @PABC
```

where it is assumed that the address of the symbolic location ABC is held in a memory longword labeled PABC.

Indirect addressing is used in the following program segment to clear the contents of the longword at location TARGET:

```
POINTER:    .ADDRESS TARGET    ; contains address of TARGET
TARGET:     .LONG    1234      ; contents of TARGET
              .
              .
              .

            CLRL     @POINTER   ; clear operand indirectly
              .
              .
              .
```

Figure 4.8 Indirect addressing

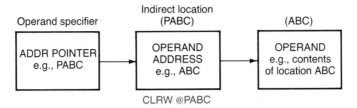

CLRW @PABC

Using a register to hold the address of the item to be cleared, we can use the following sequence:

```
POINTER:   .ADDRESS TARGET      ; contains address of TARGET
TARGET:    .LONG    1234         ; contents of TARGET
           .
           .
           .


           MOVL     POINTER,R2   ; load address of TARGET in R2
           CLRL     (R2)         ; clear longword at TARGET
```

The MOVL instruction loads R2 with the address of the operand to be cleared. The notation (R2) indicates that R2 *contains* the operand address.

Because the loading of addresses occurs frequently, the VAX has a Move Address instruction that loads the address of a specified element into a longword. Using the Move Address Longword (MOVAL) instruction, we no longer need the POINTER longword:

```
TARGET:   .LONG    1234         ; contents of TARGET
          .
          .
          .


          MOVAL    TARGET,R2    ; load address of TARGET in R2
          CLRL     (R2)         ; clear longword at TARGET
```

The operation of clearing a memory location can be applied to clearing an array of memory locations. The logical flow of operations to be performed is shown by the program segment in Figure 4.9. In this example, the MOVAL instruction is used to initialize R1 to the address of the first item in array A. R1 is advanced each time to point to the next element in the array.

It is possible for some computers to utilize multilevel indirect addressing if the location indirectly addressed is itself the address of another location to be indirectly referenced. Multilevel indirect addressing requires that each location referenced have a bit that specifies whether the location is an address to be used directly or indirectly.

Figure 4.9   Indirect addressing example

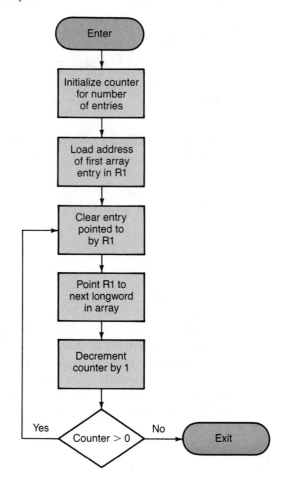

```
;
; Program to zero array of N longwords.
;

        N = 50                  ; define array size
A:      .BLKL    N              ; define array
         .
         .
         .
START:  MOVL     #N,R0          ; initialize loop count
        MOVAL    A,R1           ; load array A base address
LOOP:   CLRL     (R1)           ; clear entry pointed to by R1
        ADDL     #4,R1          ; point to next longword
        DECL     R0             ; decrement loop count
        BGTR     LOOP           ; continue while R0 > 0
```

The choice between multilevel and single-level indirect addressing is based on user convenience and cost. On a typical machine, every bit must be utilized efficiently, and multi-level indirect addressing is not provided. The reason is an economic one: multi-level indirection reduces the size of the address space by a factor of two.

Register Autoincrement and Autodecrement Modes

In Figure 4.9, the constant 4 was added to R1 during each loop iteration to advance it to the next longword in the array. Indexing forward or backward through an array occurs so frequently that some machines have built-in hardware to increment or decrement the contents of registers automatically.

The register *autoincrement* and register *autodecrement* addressing modes of the VAX provide for automatically stepping a register through the sequential elements of a table or array. This mode assumes the contents of the selected general register to be the address of, or pointer to, the operand. Thus, the pointer is stepped through a series of addresses so that it always points to the next sequential element of a table. And since the VAX recognizes the data type being addressed, it knows whether to increment the register by 1, 2, 4, 8, or 16 for byte, word, longword, quadword, or octaword operands, and by 4, 8, or 16 for F, G, or H floating-point formats, respectively.

In autodecrement mode, written as −(R), the contents of the register are decremented *before* being used as the address of the operand. In autoincrement mode, written (R)+, the contents of the register are incremented *after* being used as the address of the operand.

With this addressing mode, Figure 4.9 can be recoded as shown in Figure 4.10. Following each CLRL instruction at LOOP, the contents of R1 are automatically incremented by 4. If the instruction were

```
CLRW    (R1)+
```

then the value of R1 would be incremented by 2 since this instruction operates on word-sized data elements. If the instruction were

Figure 4.10   Use of autoincrement addressing

```
              .
              .
              .
    START:  MOVL    #N,R0    ; initialize loop count
            MOVAL   A,R1     ; load array base address
    LOOP:   CLRL    (R1)+    ; clear entry and advance
                             ; ...pointer to next entry
            DECL    R0       ; decrement loop counter
            BGTR    LOOP     ; continue until done
```

```
CLRB      (R1)+
```

then the value of R1 would be incremented by 1.

Figure 4.11 shows symbolically how autoincrement addressing is performed. In this figure it is assumed that register 8 contains the operand address ABC.

These addressing modes can be illustrated with the following example. Suppose the contents of the registers and memory are shown as follows. The table shows the contents of the longword beginning at each memory location.

Memory Address	Memory Contents	Register	Contents
200	1 3 0 F F 0 1 D	R0	200
400	0 0 1 3 7 0 1 3	R1	400
600	9 1 E B 0 8 1 0	R2	602
800	0 0 1 1 2 3 4 5	R3	802

Following execution of the two instructions

```
ADDB      (R0)+,(R1)+
ADDW      (R2)+,-(R3)
```

the contents of the registers and memory will be

Memory Address	Memory Contents	Register	Contents
200	1 3 0 F F 0 1 D	R0	201
400	0 0 1 3 7 0 3 0	R1	401
600	9 1 E B 0 8 1 0	R2	604
800	0 0 1 1 B 5 3 0	R3	800

Now suppose we wish to rewrite Figure 4.10 using autodecrement

Figure 4.11   Autoincrement addressing

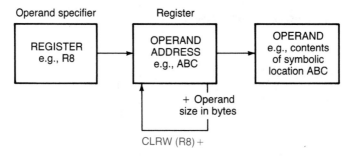

CLRW (R8)+

addressing. We begin by loading R1 with the address of the longword *following* array A since the decrement is done before the operation is performed:

```
BEGIN:  MOVL    #N,R0           ; initialize loop count
        MOVAL   A+<4*N>, R1     ; load address of longword
                                ; ...following array A
LOOP:   CLRL    -(R1)           ; clear previous entry
        DECL    R0              ; decrement loop counter
        BGTR    LOOP            ; continue until done
```

In the previous autoincrement example, following each execution of the CLRL instruction at loop, R1 points to the *next* element to be cleared. Following the execution of the CLRL instruction in this autodecrement example, R1 points to the *last* element cleared.

Looking back at Figure 4.3, we can now rewrite using a loop and autoincrement addressing:

```
START:  MOVL    #N,R0               ; initialize loop count
        MOVAL   A,R1                ; get address of array A
        MOVAL   B,R2                ; get address of array B
        MOVAL   C,R3                ; get address of array C
LOOP:   ADDL3   (R1)+,(R2)+,(R3)+   ; form C := A+B
        SOBGTR  R0,LOOP             ; loop until done
```

Here we have also introduced an instruction provided specifically for loops such as this. The Subtract One and Branch on Greater Than Zero instruction (SOBGTR) subtracts 1 from the loop counter (R0) and branches to the supplied address (LOOP) if the counter is still greater than 0. Otherwise, control continues at the next instruction. The SOBGTR implements a Pascal *for i:=N downto 1* loop. It replaces the DECL and BGTR instructions in previous examples. A companion instruction, Subtract One and Branch on Greater than or Equal to Zero (SOBGEQ), implements a *for i:=N downto 0* loop, replacing a DECL and BGEQ pair. More loop instructions appear in a forthcoming section.

Operand Context

Each operand in a VAX instruction has an implied *context* that defines the type of data element on which it operates. For the more sophisticated addressing modes such as autoincrement and indexed (yet to be discussed), it is important to understand the context to be certain how the registers will be used or modified. In the examples in the previous section, the context of the operand (R)+ was determined by the instruction; R1 was handled differently for CLRL than for CLRW.

It is sometimes possible for different operands of an instruction to have different contexts. For example, the Move Address instruction, used to store the address of a data element in a specified longword, has two operands:

1. The first operand, or *source operand*, provides the address specification of the data element. Its context is specified by the instruction, for example, MOVAB, MOVAW, MOVAL, MOVAQ, and MOVAO for byte, word, longword, quadword, and octaword elements, respectively.

2. The second operand, or *destination operand*, provides the address of a longword to receive the calculated 32-bit effective address. Its context is *always* longword, because effective addresses are always 32 bits.

For example, assume that the variable TEMP is stored at memory location 200, that R0 contains 300, and that R1 contains 400. For the instruction

```
MOVAW    TEMP,R0          ; R0 <- address of TEMP
```

the 32-bit address of the word TEMP is moved to R0. Following this instruction, R0 will contain 200—the address of TEMP. Had the instruction been

```
MOVAQ    TEMP,R0          ; R0 <- address of TEMP
```

the result would be the same. Here, context is unimportant because there is no ambiguity about how to evaluate the address of TEMP, and there are no side effects on registers (for example, autoincrementing). The *address* of TEMP is the same regardless of whether TEMP refers to the word beginning at address 200 or the quadword beginning at address 200; hence, whether a MOVAW or MOVAQ instruction is used does not affect the outcome. The programmer can choose one form over the other to enhance readability and to indicate the size of the operand.

In contrast, for the instruction

```
MOVAW    (R0)+,(R1)+
```

the difference is critical. In this instruction, the address of a *word* pointed to by R0 is moved into the *longword* pointed to by the contents of R1. Following the execution of this instruction, R0 will be incremented by 2 (a word increment), while R1 will be incremented by 4 (a longword increment). Given the initial values, the longword at memory address 400 would contain 300 following execution of the instruction, R0 would contain 302, and R1 would contain 404. Had we instead executed the instruction

```
MOVAQ    (R0)+,(R1)+
```

the longword at location 400 would still contain the value 300 and R1 would still contain 404, but R0 would contain 308.

Note that Move Address simply removes a level of indirection in the evaluation of the first operand. Typically, we calculate the effective address of an operand and then move the operand. With Move Address, we calculate the effective address of an operand and then move the address itself. Thus, the instructions

```
MOVL    R0,R2
```

and

```
MOVAL   (R0),R2
```

are equivalent. Both copy the contents of R0 to R2. In the first case, the copy is obvious. In the second case, the indirect addressing mode adds a level of indirection in specifying the operand address, while the Move Address instruction removes a level of indirection.

As another example of operand context, consider the instruction Move Zero-Extended Byte to Longword (MOVZBL). This instruction copies a byte to a longword, filling the top 24 bits of the longword with zeros. It can be used when copying a byte into a register to ensure that the upper 3 bytes of the register are zero, as in

```
MOVZBL    MYCHAR,R1
```

For this instruction, the first operand has byte context and the second operand has longword context. Therefore, the instruction

```
MOVZBL    (R2)+,(R3)+
```

adds 1 to R2 and adds 4 to R3 following the access of each operand.

For every instruction, each operand has a specific context that defines the data type of the operand. When you use addressing modes with side effects, such as autoincrement or autodecrement, you must be certain of the context of the operands being addressed. For instructions such as ADDL3, the context may be obvious: in this case, all three operands are longwords. However, with instructions such as Move Address and Move Zero-Extended, different operands may have different contexts. The VAX instruction card included in Appendix B shows the operand context for the operands of all VAX instructions.

Displacement Mode

Another common addressing requirement is to be able to address elements in *record* data structures. Such elements are addressed as offsets from the base of the structure. *Displacement mode*, whose format is

```
displacement(R)
```

is provided for this purpose. The displacement is a signed integer offset, that is, it can be positive or negative. As shown in the following code segment, displacement mode is similar to indirect register mode except that the effective address is computed by adding an integer displacement to the contents of the register. Figure 4.12 assumes that R2 contains the address of LIST in the instruction CLRW 4(R2). In the figure, two components of the operand specifier are shown: the register and the displacement.

An example to help us better understand the use of displacements is contained in the following data structure:

```
USRDATA:
        .BLKQ   1               ; user's first name
        .BLKQ   1               ; user's last name
        .BLKB   1               ; user's age
        .BLKB   1               ; user's height
        .BLKW   1               ; user's weight
        .BLKW   1               ; user's social security number
```

which can be pictured in memory as

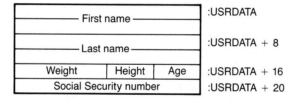

This could be the format of one entry in a large table of entries for many users of a system. To access any field for a particular table entry, we load the base address of the entry into a register and address each element by its *offset in bytes* from the base. For example, we can define symbolic offsets into the data structure as

```
Q_FIRSTNAME=0
Q_LASTNAME=8
B_AGE=16
B_HEIGHT=17
W_WEIGHT=18
L_SOC_SEC=20
```

where each symbol is the offset in bytes from the start of the structure to the given field. Notice that the offset names have been chosen to indicate the element size as well as the contents. This is a good convention to use

Figure 4.12   Displacement addressing mode

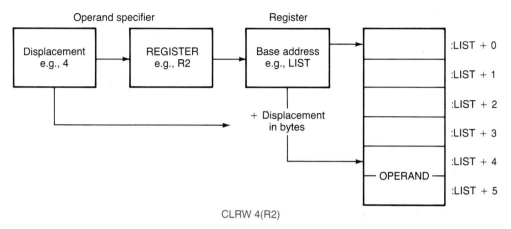

CLRW 4(R2)

when you are handling fields of different sizes. Given these symbol definitions, we could use displacement mode to access the needed field:

```
        .
        .
        .
MOVAL   USRDATA,R1              ; load table address
MOVL    L_SOC_SEC(R1),TEMP1     ; get SS number
MOVB    B_AGE(R1),TEMP2         ; get user's age
MOVQ    Q_LASTNAME(R1),TEMP3    ; get user's name
        .
        .
        .
```

In this example, notice the advantage of displacement mode for addressing variable-length data elements from a fixed address.

VAX also supports a *deferred displacement* addressing mode. In this mode, specified as

```
@displacement(R)
```

the displacement is added to the contents of the register to form the address of the operand address. A graphical representation of this addressing mode would be similar to that for displacement addressing (Figure 4.12) except that the operand now contains the address of the operand, instead of the operand itself.

The deferred displacement addressing mode is useful for accessing a data element whose address is stored in a data structure being accessed with displacement mode addressing. For example, if the contents of R6 and the memory locations are as shown:

Memory Address	Memory Contents	Register	Contents
208	0 0 1 F D A 1 0	R6	208
20C	1 3 A B F 0 1 0		
210	0 0 0 0 0 8 1 0		
810	0 F 1 D 0 2 3 4		

then, following execution of the instruction,

```
CLRW    @8(R6)
```

the contents of the register and memory will be

Memory Address	Memory Contents	Register	Contents
208	0 0 1 F D A 1 0	R6	208
20C	1 3 A B F 0 1 0		
210	0 0 0 0 0 8 1 0		
810	0 F 1 D 0 0 0 0		

Index Mode

One of the most powerful addressing features of the VAX is the ability to use an *index register* to specify the index of an array entry. The index register specifies which element of the array (for example, first, second, or third) is being addressed.

The format for index mode addressing is

```
base_address[R]
```

where base_address is a general address specification for the first element in the array and register R contains the index of the desired element. Because the array may be composed of byte, word, longword, quad-word, or octaword entries (or any of the floating-point data types), the index value must be multiplied by the appropriate size—1, 2, 4, 8, or 16—before being added to the base address. The VAX CPU selects the multiplier based on the context of the operand. The specification of the base address can use any addressing mode encountered so far, forming instructions such as

```
MOVL    ARRAY[R1],R2    ; displacement indexed
MOVAW   (R0)[R1],R2     ; register deferred indexed
MOVB    -(R0)[R1],R2    ; autodecrement indexed
```

The effective address of the operand is calculated by first computing the address of the base of the array or table. Then the value of the index register is multiplied by 1, 2, 4, 8, or 16, depending on the data type of the

Figure 4.13 Indexed addressing mode

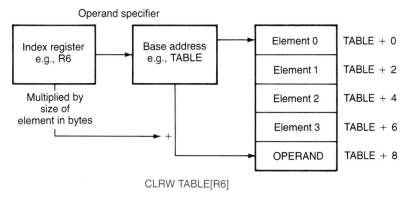

CLRW TABLE[R6]

operand, and added to the base address. As with autoincrement or autodecrement, the *context* of the operand affects the value of the register.

In Figure 4.13, we index into element 4 of the array called TABLE using the instruction CLRW TABLE[R6] (i.e., the contents of R6 is 4). Each element in the array TABLE is 2 bytes long.

We can illustrate this technique further by considering the instruction

```
MOVW    2(R1)[R2],2(R1)[R3]
```

Suppose the initial values of the registers and memory are

Memory Address	Memory Contents	Register	Contents
452	F7	R1	450
453	24	R2	2
454	6C	R3	3
455	10		
456	56		
457	0D		
458	98		
459	73		

ARRAY [0]		:452
ARRAY [1]		:454
ARRAY [2]		:456
ARRAY [3]		:458

This instruction moves the contents of the third element to the location of the fourth element of a word array (remember that the first index is zero). First, we must compute the address of the base of the array, which is specified by 2(R1). This means that the array base address is 2 bytes past the address contained in register R1, or at address 452. Next, because this is a word-sized array, we compute the offset to the element by multiplying the value in the index register R2 by 2. Thus, the element is 4 bytes (2 × 2) past the array base, or at address 452 + 4 = 456. The destination address is evaluated in the same manner, giving effective address 458 for the operand (this is the adjacent word in the array, since the array indices were 2 and 3). Following the execution of this instruction, the registers and memory look like this:

Memory Address	Memory Contents	Register	Contents
452	F7	R1	450
453	24	R2	2
454	6C	R3	3
455	10		
456	56		
457	0D		
458	56		
459	0D		

Returning to the Pascal example in Figure 4.3,

```
for i := 1 to 50 do
C[i] :=A[i] + B[i] ;
```

we can now "compile" this higher-level code into VAX assembly code using index mode addressing:

```
      CLRL    R0                      ; start at index 0
LOOP: ADDL3   A[R0],B[R0],C[R0]   ; add elements
      AOBLSS  #50,R0,LOOP ; loop while R0 < 50
```

Few machines could translate this Pascal loop into so few machine instructions. Notice that another looping instruction has been introduced, called Add One and Branch Less Than (AOBLSS). On each execution, 1 is added to the index operand (in this case, R0) and the incremented index is compared with the limit operand (in this case, 50). If the index is less than the limit operand, a branch is taken to LOOP, the destination. Otherwise, execution continues at the next instruction.

A Simple Example

As a simple example of the use of several addressing modes, let's examine the following code segment. The task is to search an employee data base to find the average third-year salary of every employee who has worked in the company for at least three years.

Assume we have a collection of employee records. Each employee record has five fields: a 16-byte name field, a longword employee ID number, a department number, the length of employment in years, and a pointer to an array containing the employee's salary at the start of each year of employment. The symbolic names of the record fields might be:

```
O_NAME = 0             ; 16-byte employee name string
L_ID = 16              ; employee ID number
L_DEPT = 20            ; employee department number
L_YEARS = 24           ; employment length in years
L_SALARY_POINTER = 28  ; pointer to array of salaries
```

The main program has an array that contains the pointers to each of the employee records, as well as some other variables, such as

```
NUM_EMPLOYEES=50    ; number of current employees
EMP_LIST: .BLKL NUM_EMPLOYEES ; array of record pointers
TOTAL:     .LONG 0   ; accumulator of total salaries
COUNT:     .LONG 0   ; count of employees accumulated
```

The data structure that exists at run time will resemble Figure 4.14. Figure 4.15 shows part of the program to compute the average third-year salary. This demonstrates the use of immediate, autoincrement, displacement, and displacement deferred indexed addressing modes. This last addressing mode, used for the first operand of the ADDL instruction, is somewhat complicated. We want to access the third entry of an array of salaries, the entry whose index is 2. Register R3 contains the base address of the employee record, while the record entry L_SALARY_POINTER has the address of the array of salaries. Therefore, we can use the specifier @L_SALARY_POINTER(R3) to reference the base address of the salary array. @L_SALARY_POINTER(R3)[R1] addresses the third array entry, since we have preloaded R1 with the correct index value.

Figure 4.14   Employee record data structure

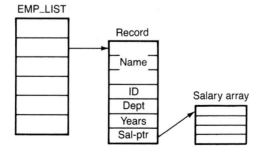

Figure 4.15 Employee record search example

```
;
;   Compute average 3rd-year salary
;
;   R0 keeps track of the number of records examined
;   R1 contains the constant integer 2 to be used to
;       index the (zero-origin) salary array
;   R2 has the address of the current pointer in EMP_LIST
;   R3 has the base address of the current record
;
GET_AVERAGE:
        CLRL    COUNT               ; initialize variables for
        CLRL    TOTAL               ; ...computing average
        MOVL    #NUM_EMPLOYEES,R0   ; number of records to check
        MOVL    #2,R1               ; load constant index
        MOVAL   EMPL_LIST,R2        ; first record pointer address
        BRB     20$                 ; start at end of loop
10$:
        MOVL    (R2)+,R3            ; get record address and
                                    ; ...advance to next pointer
        CMPL    L_YEARS(R3),#3      ; here 3 years?
        BLSS    20$                 ; skip this record if not
        ADDL    @L_SALARY_POINTER(R3)[R1],TOTAL ; add 3rd-year salary
        INCL    COUNT               ; another employee added
20$:
        SOBGEQ  R0,10$              ; continue if more records
```

Exercises

1. Describe the operation of the condition codes.

2. What are the contents of A and B following the execution of the instructions below?

```
    A:.LONG 5
    B:  .LONG -5
```

Assume for each case that the same initial contents of A and B apply (that is, A is 5 and B is -5).

```
    a.              CMPL    A,B
                    BLSS    NEXT
                    INCL    A
            NEXT:   INCL    A

    b.              CMPL:   A,B
                    BLSSU   NEXT
                    INCL    A
            NEXT:   INCL    A
```

```
        c.              SUBL   B,A
                        BGTR   NEXT
                        INCL   A
                NEXT:   INCL   A
```

3. Suppose you want to hand translate the FORTRAN arithmetic IF into VAX code, that is:

```
IF (K) 10,20,30
```

What would you write? Assume K is stored as a 32-bit integer.

4. Generally speaking, which do you think requires more memory space, immediate or simple addressing?

5. What are the contents of Y, Z, R0, and R1 following the execution of the following instructions? As before, assume the same initial contents for the variable for each instruction.

```
Address      Assembly  Statement    Register    Contents

532          Y:        .LONG 12     R0          532
536          Z:        .LONG 532    R1          536
```

```
a.   MOVAL  Z,Y
b.   MOVAL  Z,Y
c.   MOVL   @Z,Y
d.   MOVAL  @Z,Y
e.   MOVAL  @Z,@Z
f.   MOVL   R0,R1
g.   MOVL   (R0),R1
h.   MOVAL  (R0),R1
i.   MOVAL  (R0),(R1)
j.   MOVL   (R0),(R1)
k.   MOVL   Y+4,R0
l.   MOVAL  Y+10,(R0)
```

6. Rewrite the program of Figure 4.7, which forms the sum of the first 50 integers, to count upward from 1 to 50.

7. What is the difference between one level of indirect addressing and the use of general-purpose registers for addressing?

8. Using autoincrement addressing, write the instructions to initialize a ten-element longword array A to the values 0 through 9. Perform the same task using autodecrement addressing.

9. For each instruction below, what is the operand context for R1, and by what value will R1 be incremented following the execution of the instruction?

```
a.   CLRB   (R1)+
```

```
b.  MOVW    ABC,(R1)+
c.  MOVW    #1,(R1)+
d.  MOVAW   ABC,(R1)+
e.  MOVAW   (R1)+,ABC
f.  MOVAB   (R1)+,(R1)+
```

10. What is the effect on R2 and R3 after the execution of the instruction

```
. MOVAB  -(R3),(R2)+
```

11. Which of the following are legal VAX instructions? For any illegal instructions, say why they are illegal.

```
a .  CLRL   -(R1)
b .  CLRL   -(R1)[R4]
c .  CLRL   (R1)+[R4]
d .  CLRL   (R1)[R4]+
e .  CLRL   +(R1)
f .  CLRL   XYZ(R4)
g .  CLRL   (R1)(R2)
h .  CLRL   ARRAY[R7]
i .  CLRL   ARRAY[XYZ]
j .  CLRL   10(R1)
k .  CLRL   10(R1)[R2]
l .  CLRL   XYZ+10
m.   CLRL   (R1+10)
n .  CLRL   10(R4)+
o .  CLRL   R1[R4]
```

12. By what value will R1 be multiplied to compute the array index in the following instructions?

```
a.  CRLB    ARRAY[R1]
b.  MOVAW   TEST,(R0)[R1]
c.  MOVAW   (R0)[R1],TEST
```

13. Explain the uses of the following addressing modes and write a short code segment to demonstrate the use of each.

    a. Register deferred mode
    b. Displacement mode
    c. Index mode

5

VAX Instruction Encoding

Two features of its architecture make the VAX an interesting machine to examine. First is the variety of instructions and addressing modes, which allow the programmer or compiler to express complicated constructs in only a few machine-language instructions. Second is the instruction encoding, which allows these instructions to be represented efficiently in memory. This chapter discusses what an instruction looks like when it is assembled and stored in the memory of a computer.

General Instruction Format

In some machines, instructions are encoded as a series of words, where each word is divided into a number of fields. These fields are used to describe the operation code and the operand specifiers. Word-based instructions often consume more space than needed because they must be represented as an integral number of words.

The VAX instruction set was designed to be both general and highly memory-efficient. The result is a variable-length instruction format in which instructions are represented as a series of bytes. The first byte of each instruction is the opcode (some instructions actually have two-byte opcodes). Following the opcode are from zero to six operand specifiers. Each operand specifier can be from one to nine bytes long, with the first byte describing the addressing mode. Figure 5.1 shows this general format.

In the execution of an instruction, the CPU examines the first byte of the instruction, which contains the opcode. The opcode determines how

Figure 5.1 VAX instruction format

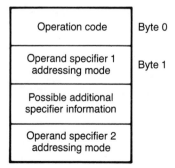

many operand specifiers follow. For each operand specifier, the CPU examines the first byte to determine the addressing mode for that specifier. Depending on the addressing mode used, the CPU may need to examine more bytes to compute the effective address of the operand. This process continues until all the specifiers have been evaluated. The operands are then fetched, and the operation is performed.

Encoding an Instruction

Every instruction consists of an opcode and from zero to six operand specifiers. The first byte of each operand specifier always indicates the addressing mode. Usually, this byte is broken into halves, one specifying the addressing mode, the other specifying the register to be used for addressing.

For example, in *register mode*, in which the operand is contained in a general register, the format of the operand specifier is

```
07      04 03      00
+---------+----------+
|    5    | Register |
+---------+----------+
```

where the high-order four bits specify that this is register mode (mode 5) and the low four bits specify which register is to be used.

Let us consider the instruction

```
ADDL    R0,R1
```

which adds the contents of register 0 to register 1. The opcode for the ADDL instruction is C0 hex. The operand specifiers for R0 and R1 are 50 and 51 hex, respectively, where the 5 indicates register mode. Each one-byte specifier would appear as:

```
R0 Register Mode              R1 Register Mode
07      04 03      00         07      04 03      00
+---------+----------+        +---------+----------+
|    5    |    0     |        |    5    |    1     |
+---------+----------+        +---------+----------+
```

Stored at address 200, this instruction appears in memory as follows:

Memory Address	Memory Contents	Interpretation
200:	C0	ADDL opcode
201:	50	R0 register mode
202:	51	R1 register mode

Suppose that one operand is autoincrement mode, such as

```
ADDL   R3,(R8)+
```

The operand specifier format for autoincrement mode is

Autoincrement Mode

07	04 03	00
8	Register	

The instruction thus appears in memory as

Memory Address	*Memory Contents*	*Interpretation*
200:	C0	**ADDL** opcode
201:	53	R3 register mode
202:	88	(R8)+ autoincrement mode

Now let us examine a slightly more complex addressing mode, displacement addressing. In displacement addressing, the register contains a base address to which a byte, word, or longword displacement is added to determine the operand address. The displacement follows the addressing mode in the instruction. Thus, depending on the size of the displacement, there are really three displacement addressing modes. Their representations are shown in Figure 5.2.

The displacements in the figure are signed integers. As a result, byte and word displacements are sign-extended and then added to the base register. If the operand is within ± 127 bytes from the base register address, byte displacement is used. If the operand is within ± 32,767 bytes from the base register address, word displacement is used. Whenever possible, the assembler or compiler chooses the most efficient addressing mode. Because displacements are often small, byte displacement is

Figure 5.2 Displacement address encoding

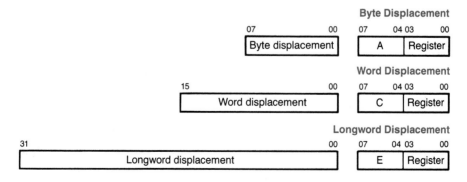

frequently used, saving up to three bytes in instruction length. As an example, look at the following three-operand Add instruction:

        ADDL3   8(R6),(R7)+,R8

This instruction would be assembled in memory as follows:

Memory Address	Memory Contents	Interpretation
200:	C1	ADDL3 opcode
201:	A6	byte displacement (R6)
202:	08	8 (byte displacement)
203:	87	(R7)+
204:	58	R8

Finally, let us examine an indexed mode example, in which two registers are required to specify the addressing mode. In index mode, both the index register and the base address specification must be included. Therefore, an index mode (mode 4) specifier must be at least two bytes long:

Index Mode

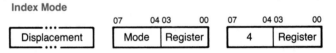

The first byte specifies that this is index mode, with the index register number contained in the low four bits. The following byte or bytes specify the base address. For instance, the instruction

        INCB   8(R2)[R3]

would be assembled as

Memory Address	Memory Contents	Interpretation
200:	96	INCB opcode
201:	43	[R3] index mode
202:	A2	byte displacement (R2)
203:	08	8 (byte displacement)

Or, the two-operand instruction

        MOVAL   (R1)[R5],(R2)[R5]

would be assembled as

Memory Address	Memory Contents	Interpretation
200:	DE	MOVAL opcode
201:	45	[R5] index mode
202:	61	(R1) indirect register
203:	45	[R5] index mode for second operand
204:	62	(R2) indirect register

Program-Counter Relative Addressing

We have yet to discuss how simple symbolic addresses are represented. Addressing memory in this way is actually quite similar to displacement mode addressing, but it involves a unique feature of the PDP-11 and VAX family architecture—the use of the program counter as a general register. Although we described the symbolic name as a representation for the 32-bit operand address, the assembler actually uses a more compact encoding. Called *relative addressing*, this mode represents the data element by its displacement or position relative to the program counter value, as shown in Figure 5.3.

Like displacement mode, in relative addressing a signed byte, word, or longword offset is added to a register to form the operand address. In this case, however, the register used is the program counter (R15 or PC). The effective address of the operand is formed by adding a byte, word, or longword displacement to the value of the program counter when the instruction is being decoded. That is, memory is addressed by its distance from the instruction referencing it. The format of relative mode is shown in Figure 5.4.

This style of addressing is useful for two reasons. First, it is efficient because most operands are relatively close to the instructions that reference them, and the offset can be specified in 8 or 16 bits. Second and more important is the fact that relative mode addressing is *position independent*. As long as the distance relationship between the instruction and the operand remains fixed, the program can be loaded anywhere in memory and will still execute correctly without modification. If the instruction contained an actual 32-bit address instead of a relative address, the data

Figure 5.3 PC relative addressing

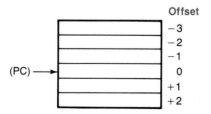

Figure 5.4   PC relative address encoding

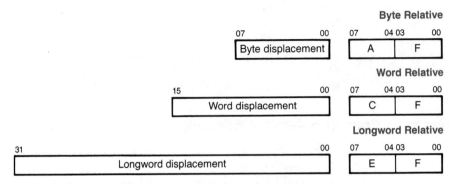

item would always have to be loaded at the same base address. Position independence becomes important in a multiprogramming system, in which several programs share a single routine. If the routine is position independent, it can be loaded in any place within each user's memory space, giving the system more flexibility in arranging routines.

As an example of relative addressing, consider how the instruction

```
MOVW     MYDATA,R1
```

would be assembled. Suppose the instruction is located at address 600 in memory and the word **MYDATA** is stored at address 804. Memory would appear as follows:

Memory Address	Memory Contents	Interpretation
600:	B0	MOVW opcode
601:	CF	word relative mode
602:	00	displacement
603:	02	...is 200 hex
604:	51	R1, register mode
.		
.		
.		
804:	05	MYDATA first byte
805:	14	MYDATA second byte

Effective
operand address =   604   (program counter)
                 + 200   (word displacement)
                    804

To understand how the effective address of the operand is calculated, consider the following. As the opcode and operand specifiers are fetched and evaluated, the PC is advanced over them to the next operand specifier or instruction. When the first operand specifier is fetched, the PC is incremented to the next operand specifier at address 604. The relative displacement, 200 hex, is added to the updated PC, giving address 804 for the operand MYDATA. The second operand is then evaluated, and the word at MYDATA is moved to R1.

If this routine is moved so that it is loaded at address 1024 instead of 600, the contents of memory would be

Memory Address	Memory Contents	Interpretation
1024:	B0	MOVW opcode
1025:	CF	word relative mode
1026:	00	displacement
1027:	02	...is 200 hex
1028:	51	R1, register mode
.		
.		
.		
1228:	05	MYDATA first byte
1229:	14	MYDATA second byte

Effective
operand address =   1028   (program counter)
                               + 200   (word displacement)
                               ────
                               1228

Notice that even though the instruction and the datum have been moved, the instruction still executes properly without change because the relative distance between the instruction and the operand remains constant.

Negative displacements are calculated similarly. For example, suppose the MOVW instruction is at location 600 but the word MYDATA is stored at location 400. Our example then becomes

Memory Address	Memory Contents	Interpretation
400:	05	MYDATA first byte
402:	14	MYDATA second byte
.		
.		
.		
600:	B0	MOVW opcode
601:	CF	word relative mode
602:	FC	displacement

(continued)

Memory Address	Memory Contents	Interpretation
603:	FD	...is FDFC hex (−204 decimal)
604:	51	R1, register mode

Effective
operand address =   604   (program counter)
                       +FDFC   (word displacement)
                        400

A common but more complicated example involves the use of relative addressing to specify the base of an array, for example,

```
TSTL    MYLIST[R4]
```

where the relative addressing specifier follows the indexed mode specifier in the instruction stream. This is shown below:

Memory Address	Memory Contents	Interpretation
1024:	D5	TSTL opcode
1025:	45	[R4] indexed mode
1026:	CF	word relative mode
1027:	FF	displacement is
1028:	01	...01FF hex
1029		next opcode

.
.
.

| 1228: | | MYLIST first byte |

When an operand is addressed using an indirect memory reference, such as

```
MOVW    @MYDATA,R1
```

relative deferred mode addressing is used. This is similar to relative mode except that the effective address calculated is the address of a longword containing the operand address rather than the operand itself.

Immediate Addressing

When an immediate operand is specified in an instruction, such as

```
MOVW    #^X200,R3
```

immediate mode addressing is used. It is similar to autoincrement mode except that the PC is used as the general register. In other words, as the operand is decoded, the PC points to the literal (constant value) in the instruction stream. The PC is incremented over the operand as the operand is fetched. The format for immediate mode is

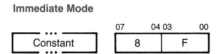

Immediate Mode

For the preceding Move Word instruction, the memory format would be

Memory Address	Memory Contents	Interpretation
. . .	B0	MOVW opcode
. . .	8F	immediate mode
. . .	00	word
. . .	02	...constant
. . .	53	R3 register mode

When the first byte of the operand specifier is fetched, the PC points to the 16-bit constant. The constant is then fetched, and the PC is incremented by the size of the constant in bytes. It is the context of the operand that specifies how big the constant must be; in the preceding instruction, since the first operand had word context, the processor knew that the constant was 2 bytes long. If the instruction had been

```
MOVO     #^X200,R3     ; initialize octaword
```

then the constant in the instruction would have to be 16 bytes long, that is, 0000000000000200! Obviously this may not be a space-efficient means for initializing the octaword to hex 200.

In fact, because many literals used in programs are small, the VAX has a special addressing mode called *short literal*. In this mode, the constant is held in the operand specifier itself. The format of a short literal specifier is

Literal Mode

In other words, any operand specifier in which the high two bits are zeros contains a literal constant in the low six bits. Because the literal is

Figure 5.5   Comparison of short literal and register mode encoding

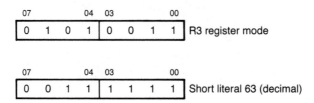

unsigned, integer values from 0 through 63 can be represented, avoiding the need for immediate mode addressing. For example, the instruction

        MOVL   #8,R5

would be assembled as

Memory Address	Memory Contents	Interpretation
. . .	D0	MOVL opcode
. . .	08	short literal
. . .	55	R5

This is four bytes shorter than immediate mode.

We can see how this works if we look at the encoding of the largest short literal (63) compared to a register mode specifier, as shown in Figure 5.5. Notice that register mode has a nonzero bit in the upper two bits of the operand specifier. All addressing modes other than short literal have nonzero bits in the upper two bits of the operand specifier because all of them have mode codes greater than or equal to 4. Codes 0, 1, 2, and 3—the only ones with two high-order zero bits—have been reserved for short literal.

Absolute Addressing

On occasion, instructions must reference an *absolute address*, that is, a location fixed in the address space. This is usually a location defined by the operating system to be constant for all processes in the system. For absolute mode addressing, the actual 32-bit address is contained in the instruction stream. This mode is the same as autoincrement deferred, but again the PC is specified as the general register. The format for absolute mode is

Absolute Mode

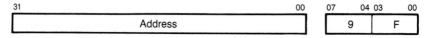

The assembler syntax for absolute addressing is *@#address*, for example,

```
TSTL      @#^X1234
```

This instruction tests the longword at address 00001234 regardless of where the instruction is located in memory. The instruction would be assembled as

Memory Address	Memory Contents	Interpretation
. . .	D5	TSTL opcode
. . .	9F	absolute mode
. . .	34	32-bit
. . .	12	...operand
. . .	00	...address
. . .	00	...is 00001234

Branch Addressing

The last addressing mode we will examine is *branch addressing*. The coding of a conditional branch instruction, shown in Figure 5.6, differs from the modes previously discussed in that there is no operand specifier. Each conditional branch consists of a one-byte opcode followed by a one-byte signed displacement. The signed displacement is used in a fashion similar to relative addressing and is added to the program counter to form the branch destination address. This different addressing choice was made because branches are frequent and most conditional branch instructions specify a destination within a short distance. Also, very few branches require advanced addressing modes.

For example, the instruction sequence

```
        TSTL    R0      ; check for R0 zero
        BEQL    NILL    ; branch if so
        INCL    R0      ; else add one
NILL:   .
        .
        .
```

would appear in memory as

Figure 5.6 Conditional branch encoding

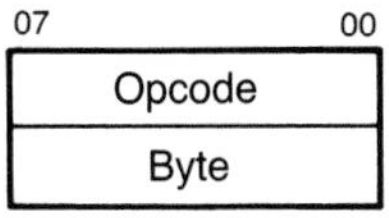

Memory Address	Memory Contents	Interpretation
200:	D5	TSTL code
201:	50	R0 register mode
202:	13	BEQL opcode
203:	02	byte displacement
204:	D6	INCL opcode
205:	50	R0 register mode
206:		<next instruction>

Branch	204	(program counter)
destination	+ 02	(byte displacement)
address =	206	

Because of this addressing mode, a conditional branch can be used only if the branch target is within ± 127 bytes from the instruction. If the branch target is farther away, the code sequence must be changed. Suppose the location NILL in the preceding example was actually at address 600, so that the conditional branch instruction BEQL would not reach. We could then recode the instruction as follows:

```
          TSTL      R0        ; check for R0 zero
          BNEQ      NOTNILL   ; branch if not zero
          BRW       NILL      ; branch to NILL if zero
NOTNILL:  INCL      R0        ; add one
              .
              .
              .
```

Here, the condition of the branch has been reversed, and an unconditional Branch with Word Displacement (BRW) instruction has been inserted. As one might expect, the BRW instruction consists of a 1-byte opcode followed by a 16-bit signed displacement. This technique is used often when the target of a conditional branch is more than 127 bytes away. For short-distance unconditional branches, there is also a Branch with Byte Displacement (BRB) instruction.

Summary

This chapter focused on the encoding of VAX instructions and operand specifiers in memory. All the VAX addressing modes, except for short literal and branch addressing, use at least one register to specify the operand address. The programmer can specify the register explicitly, as in the register deferred example, INCL (R5), or the assembler can use a register to encode the effective address of an operand or a literal. For example, in the instructions

```
    TSTL      VAR1
```

and

```
MOVL    #100,R6
```

the assembler uses the program counter as a general register to point to the operand address displacement or the operand itself within the instruction. In this way, almost all references on the VAX are position independent.

The indexed addressing modes use two registers, one for the index register and one for the specification of the base address of the array. The base address of the array can be specified using any mode except for literal, indexed, and register.

Tables 5.1, 5.2, 5.3, and 5.4 contain descriptions of all the VAX addressing modes. The notations B^, W^, and L^ indicate byte, word, and longword values, respectively. Notice the variety of addressing that is provided using only 4 bits of encoding within an operand specifier. The flexibility comes from the indexed addressing mode and from the use of the program counter as a general register.

Table 5.1   VAX General Register Addressing Modes

Name of Mode	Assembler Notation	Hex	Description
Short literal	#literal	0–3	The literal value is contained in bits 0 through 5 of the operand specifier.
Index	base[Rx]	4	The effective address of the operand is formed by first calculating the effective address of the array base and then adding the value of the index register multiplied by the size in bytes of each array element.
Register	Rn	5	The register contains the operand.
Register deferred	(Rn)	6	The register contains the address of the operand.
Autodecrement	−(Rn)	7	Register is decremented by the size of the operand in bytes and then used as the address of the operand.
Autoincrement	(Rn)+	8	Register is used as the address of the operand and then incremented by the size of the operand in bytes.
Autoincrement deferred	@(Rn)+	9	Address in register is a pointer to the effective address of the operand. Register is incremented by 4 after being used to access the effective address.

Table 5.2   VAX Displacement Addressing Modes

Name of Mode	Assembler Notation	Hex	Description
Byte displacement	B^Disp(Rn)	A	Displacement is sign-extended to 32 bits and added to the register to form the effective address.
Byte displacement deferred	@B^Disp(Rn)	B	Displacement is sign-extended to 32 bits and added to the register to form a pointer to the effective address.
Word displacement	W^Disp(Rn)	C	Displacement is sign-extended to 32 bits and added to the register to form the effective address.
Word displacement deferred	@W^Disp(Rn)	D	Displacement is sign-extended to 32 bits and added to the register to form a pointer to the effective address.
Long displacement	L^Disp(Rn)	E	Displacement is added to the register to form the effective address.
Long displacement deferred	@L^Disp(Rn)	F	Displacement is added to the register to form a pointer to the effective address.

Table 5.3   VAX Program Counter Addressing Modes

Name of Mode	Assembler Notation	Hex	Description
Immediate	#literal	8	Literal operand follows the operand specifier in the instruction stream. Assembled addressing mode is $(PC)+$.
Absolute	@#address	9	The address of the operand follows the operand specifier in the instruction stream. Assembled addressing mode is $@(PC)+$.
Relative	address	A,C,E	Operand is located at specified address. The effective address is formed by adding the contents of the updated PC to the byte, word, or longword offset that follows the operand specifier in the instruction stream. The assembled addressing mode is *Displacement(PC)*.

(continued)

VAX Program Counter Addressing Modes

Name of Mode	Assembler Notation	Hex	Description
Relative deferred	@address	B,D,F	The effective address of the operand is located at specified address. The effective address of the pointer is formed by adding the updated PC to the byte, word, or longword offset that follows the operand specifier in the instruction stream. The assembled addressing mode is *@Displacement(PC)*.

Table 5.4   VAX Indexed Addressing Modes

Name of Mode	Assembler Notation	Description
Register deferred indexed	(Rn)[Rx]	The index register is multiplied by the size of the operand in bytes, forming the adjusted index. The result is added to the contents of Rn to form the operand address.
Autoincrement indexed	(Rn)+[Rx]	Same as register deferred indexed except that Rn is incremented after the operand address is calculated.
Autodecrement indexed	−(Rn)[Rx]	Same as register deferred indexed except that Rn is decremented before the operand address is calculated.
Displacement indexed	D(Rn)[Rx]	The base address, formed by adding the byte, word, or longword displacement to the contents of the register, is added to the adjusted index to form the operand address.
Displacement deferred indexed	@D(Rn)[Rx]	The displacement is added to Rn to form the address of a pointer to the base address. The base address is then fetched and added to the adjusted index to form the operand address.
Autoincrement deferred indexed	@(Rn)+[Rx]	Rn contains the address of a pointer to the base address. The base address is fetched and added to the adjusted index to form the operand address. Rn is then incremented by 4.

Exercises

1. "Reassemble" the following machine instructions into the symbolic assembly instructions from which they were generated. (Bytes are shown right to left. Use the programmer's card in Appendix B to find the opcodes and addressing modes.)

   ```
   Byte  4   3   2   1   0

    a.                50  D4
    b.            56  65  D0
    c.        57  65  45  DE
    d.    82  43  51  60  C1
    e.            50  05  D0
   ```

2. Write an assembly language program segment to compute

   ```
   for i := 2 to 49 do
   A[i]  := A[i-1] + A[i+1]
   ```

3. Translate the assembly language program solution for exercise 2 into its hexadecimal equivalent VAX machine code.

4. Explain the difference between PC-relative and absolute addressing. Why is PC-relative preferable in most addressing applications?

5. In a machine such as the VAX, with both indirect and immediate addressing, what is the meaning of an indirect immediate operand?

6. Write a program to inclusively sum all of the positive longwords between the addresses held in the longwords FIRST and LAST. For example, the beginning and ending of the program might look like

   ```
   FIRST:   .ADDRESS THIRD
   SECOND:  .LONG 1123
   THIRD:   .LONG -54A3
   FOURTH:  .LONG 177D
   FIFTH    .LONG -1122
   SIXTH    .LONG 9A9
   LAST     .ADDRESS FIFTH
   START:   .
            .
            .
   ```

7. Explain how short literal addressing mode works. In particular, why is it that no separate operand specifier byte is required for short literal?

8. Assemble the following instructions into hexadecimal VAX machine code.

Assume that each instruction is assembled at address 500 and that the symbols
LONGA and LONGB are at addresses 400 and 600, respectively.

a.	MOVL	LONGB,R0
b.	MOVAL	LONGB,R0
c.	MOVL	400,R0
d.	MOVL	#400,R0
e.	MOVL	#4,R0
f.	MOVL	LONGA[R0],LONGB[R1]
g.	BRW	LONGA+20
h.	MOVL	255(R1),R2
i.	MOVL	256(R1),R2
j.	MOVL	10(R1)[R2],R3
k.	MOVL	@#LONGB,R0

6

Advanced Control Structures

Chapter 4 presented the basics of VAX programming. There are other techniques that facilitate good programming in assembly language, and these demand additional VAX instructions. This chapter introduces new VAX instructions and, more important, it describes the procedure-calling facility that permits modular programming and supports high-level languages. It also discusses macro facilities that allow the programmer to extend the instruction set.

The Jump Instruction

Elementary branching and looping were illustrated in Chapter 4. Two types of conditional branches were given, signed and unsigned. The two unconditional branches, Branch Byte (BRB) and Branch Word (BRW), transfer to locations within 8-bit or 16-bit offsets, respectively, from the branch instruction. Although the unconditional branches are efficiently encoded, they do not allow the use of sophisticated addressing modes and are incapable of transferring control outside the range of the 16-bit offset. For requirements such as these, the Jump instruction (JMP) is provided. Unlike Branch instructions, in which the destination is a displacement to be added to or subtracted from the PC, the destination of a JMP instruction can be specified by any of the legal addressing modes. The target location can be any location within the address space of the user's program. What follows are some examples of legal JMP instructions:

```
JMP     CONTINUE        ; transfer to location CONTINUE
JMP     @NEXTADDR       ; NEXTADDR contains target
                        ; ...address
JMP     (R1)            ; R1 contains target address
JMP     @(R4)+          ; R4 points to a longword
                        ; ...containing the target
                        ; ...address.  Fetch the target
                        ; ...address, increment R4
                        ; ...by 4 and jump to the
                        ; ...destination.
```

A common use of the generalized addressing capability of the JMP instruction is for taking a specified action based on a numeric code. The computed GOTO of FORTRAN is one example in which transfer of control is made to one of several labelled statements, based on the value of the

Figure 6.1   Jump table problem

```
              .
              .
              .
TABLE     .ADDRESS ADD,SUB,MUL,DIV ; addresses of simulated ops
              .
              .
DISPATCH:
          MOVL    CODE,R1         ; load the routine indicator
          BLSS    ERROR           ; error if CODE < 0
          CMPL    CODE,#MAXCODE   ; is CODE too large?
          BGTR    ERROR           ; error if CODE > MAX
          MOVL    TABLE[R1],R1    ; get routine address
          JMP     (R1)            ; jump to appropriate routine
ADD:          .                   ; process ADD operation
              .
              .
          JMP     HERE            ; return to common exit
SUB:          .                   ; process SUB operation
              .
              .
          JMP     HERE            ; return to common exit
              .
              .
              .
HERE:                             ; all routines jump here
                                  ; when done
```

variable INDEX, as in

```
GOTO (100,200,300,400,...),INDEX
```

Another example might be found in writing a machine simulator, in which transfer of control is made to the Add, Subtract, Multiply, or Divide routines based on the value of the variable CODE. If the addresses of these routines are placed in a table, an indirect jump could be used to transfer control to the appropriate arithmetic routine. For instance, suppose codes of 0 through 3 indicate ADD, SUB, MUL, and DIV, respectively. The dispatching code might appear as in Figure 6.1.

This example again illustrates the use of indexing on the VAX. If the value of CODE is 3, for instance, the MOVL instruction will load the longword at TABLE+12 (the address of the DIV routine) into R1. The JMP then transfers control to that routine.

Case Statements

The problem of dispatching to a routine based on the value of a variable occurs frequently enough that some high-level languages include special constructs to handle it, such as the computed GOTO in FORTRAN and the Case statement in Pascal. Because of this, the VAX instruction set includes a Case instruction so that such control structures can be represented efficiently. Not only does Case handle the transfer of control, it also handles the initialization and bounds checking for the INDEX variable. The general form of the VAX Case statement is

```
            CASE    SELECTOR,BASE,LIMIT
     TABLE: displacement 0
            displacement 1
                  .
                  .
                  .
            displacement n-1
     OUTOFBOUNDS:
                  .
                  .
                  .
```

The objective of the Case statement is to transfer control to one of n locations based on the value of the integer SELECTOR operand. The BASE operand specifies the lower bound for SELECTOR. Following the CASE instruction is a table of word *displacements* for the n branch locations. The entries in the table are displacements and not addresses so that CASE can be position independent in the same way that other conditional branches are position independent. Just as the displacements in branch instructions are added to the PC to give the branch destination, these word displacements are added to the address of the *first* displacement (TABLE, in this example) to form the Case branch destinations.

The instruction subtracts BASE from SELECTOR, producing a zero-origin index into the table of branch locations. This index is compared with LIMIT to check that it is in the table range. Therefore, the LIMIT operand specifies the largest legal value of SELECTOR − BASE and is one less than the number of branch displacements.

Although the explanation of this statement is somewhat complex, we can represent the instruction with the following description:

```
     if SELECTOR = BASE+0 then GOTO (TABLE+displacement 0)
     if SELECTOR = BASE+1 then GOTO (TABLE+displacement 1)
     if SELECTOR = BASE+2 then GOTO (TABLE+displacement 2)
            .
            .
            .
     if SELECTOR = BASE+LIMIT then GOTO (TABLE+displacement n-1)
     otherwise
          GOTO OUTOFBOUNDS
```

In other words, if the SELECTOR operand is between BASE and BASE + LIMIT, then the value of SELECTOR − BASE is used to select a table entry with which the branch destination is computed. If the SELECTOR is *not* between BASE and BASE + LIMIT, the SELECTOR is out of bounds; in this case, execution continues at the instruction *following* the Case table. Therefore, immediately following the table there must be instructions to handle an index-out-of-bounds error.

A simple example of the use of the Case statement is the computed FORTRAN GOTO of the last section

```
GOTO (100,200,300,400,500),INDEX
```

which branches to one of the statement labels based on the value of INDEX. We can also represent this example using the Pascal Case statement

```
case INDEX of
  1:      <statement for INDEX=1>;
  2:      <statement for INDEX=2>;
  3:      <statement for INDEX=3>;
  4:              .
  5:              .
end;
```

In VAX assembly language, we would code this as

```
          CASEL    INDEX,#1,#4      ; range is from 1 to 5
CASETABLE:
          .WORD    L100-CASETABLE   ; if INDEX = 1, go to L100
          .WORD    L200-CASETABLE   ; if INDEX = 2, go to L200
          .WORD    L300-CASETABLE   ; if INDEX = 3, go to L300
          .WORD    L400-CASETABLE   ; if INDEX = 4, go to L400
          .WORD    L500-CASETABLE   ; if INDEX = 5, go to L500
          BRW      ERROR            ; if INDEX > 5 or < 1,
                                    ; ...go to ERROR
L100:     .                         ; code for INDEX = 1
          .
          .
          .
L200:     .                         ; code for INDEX = 2
          .
          .
```

It is important to observe that displacements are used rather than actual addresses. Thus, to form the displacement, the difference between the branch address and the base address of the Case table is computed and stored. Since the branch table elements are differences, the Case instruction is position independent. In addition, notice that the Case instruction specifies the data type of the SELECTOR operand, so there are three possible forms: CASEB, CASEW, and CASEL. In the previous example, CASEL was used because the variable INDEX is a longword. The branch displacements are *always* 16-bit words, independent of the data type of the SELECTOR. (The Jump table example in Figure 6.1 can be recoded similarly to use the Case statement. This is left as an exercise.)

Case is most useful when the possible values of the SELECTOR are relatively compact. If the value space of SELECTOR is sparse, then the table becomes large and many elements are wasted. For example, suppose we want to jump to one of four places based on the value of the variable INDEX, and its possible values are 3, 4, 20, and 21. In this case, we would need a table following the Case with nineteen entries, fifteen of which would contain the branch displacement to an error routine. Depending on whether we value space or time, we might still choose to use the Case, or we might instead use a series of Compare and Branch instructions.

A more serious problem with these techniques for transferring control is that there is no automated way for the code at the destination to return to the main line following dispatch. Subsequent sections will consider more generalized subroutine facilities on the VAX. However, before looking at these advanced programming techniques, let us examine additional methods of constructing loops for the VAX.

Loops

Chapter 4 introduced several looping examples in the context of sample programs, including the Subtract One and Branch and the Add One and Branch instructions. There are two versions of each instruction, depending on the desired end conditions. Thus, these instructions implement the following high-level language equivalents:

```
SOBGEQ  INDEX,LOOP      ; for index = initial down to 0 do
SOBGTR  INDEX,LOOP      ; for index = initial down to 1 do
AOBLEQ  LIMIT,INDEX,LOOP ; for index = initial to limit do
AOBLSS  LIMIT,INDEX,LOOP ; for index = initial to limit-1 do
```

The flow of control for these instructions is similar. We can demonstrate it with the flowchart in Figure 6.2 when the conditions are replaced by the appropriate operation for each instruction.

The use of the AOB instructions is exemplified in the construction of a typical bubble sort routine. If LIST is the array of values to be sorted and SIZE is the number of elements in the array, then the Sort algorithm in Pascal could be expressed as

```
for i := 0 to SIZE-2 do
begin
        for j := i+1 to SIZE-1 do
        if LIST[i]  > LIST [j] then
        begin
                TEMP := LIST [i] ;
                LIST[i] := LIST[j] ;
                LIST[j] := TEMP ;
        end ;
end ;
```

Figure 6.2   VAX loop instructions

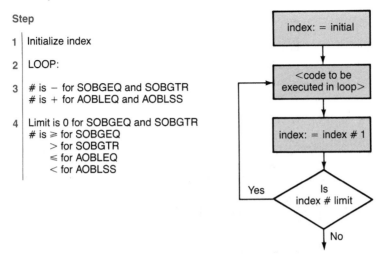

Step

1 | Initialize index

2 | LOOP:

3 | # is − for SOBGEQ and SOBGTR
    # is + for AOBLEQ and AOBLSS

4 | Limit is 0 for SOBGEQ and SOBGTR
    # is ≥ for SOBGEQ
        > for SOBGTR
        ≤ for AOBLEQ
        < for AOBLSS

In VAX assembly language, we can code this routine as shown in Figure 6.3. Notice that the VAX assembly language and Pascal routines are not equivalent if size ≤ 1.

Even more interesting are the Add Compare and Branch (ACB) generic instructions that efficiently implement the general FOR or DO loops found in higher-level languages. The ACB—which uses a word branch displacement and can be used with byte, word, longword, F_floating, D_floating, G_floating, and H_floating operands—allows the programmer to construct loops with increasing or decreasing index values.

The execution of the instruction

```
ACBL    LIMIT,INCR,INDEX,LOOP
```

first adds the increment value INCR to the index value INDEX. A test is then made to determine whether the LIMIT has been reached; if it has not, a branch is taken to the branch address LOOP. If INCR is negative, the loop continues while INDEX ≥ LIMIT; if INCR is positive, the loop continues while INDEX ≤ LIMIT. For example, to implement the FORTRAN DO-loop

```
        DO 30 LCV=10,0,−2
            .
            .
            .
30      CONTINUE
```

which loops six times while LCV takes on the values 10, 8, 6, 4, 2, and 0,

Figure 6.3   Bubble sort flowchart and routine

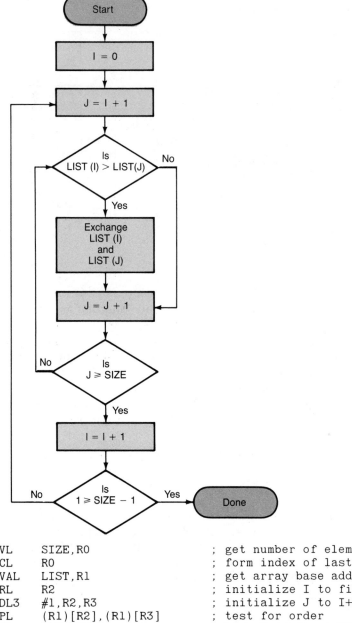

```
            MOVL    SIZE,R0                 ; get number of elements
            DECL    R0                      ; form index of last entry
            MOVAL   LIST,R1                 ; get array base address
            CLRL    R2                      ; initialize I to first index
OUTER:      ADDL3   #1,R2,R3                ; initialize J to I+1
INNER:      CMPL    (R1)[R2],(R1)[R3]       ; test for order
            BLEQ    CONTINUE                ; branch if first LEQ second
            MOVL    (R1)[R2],TEMP           ; save LIST(I)
            MOVL    (R1)[R3],(R1)[R2]       ; exchange LIST(I)
            MOVL    TEMP,(R1)[R3]           ; ...and LIST(J)
CONTINUE:
            AOBLEQ  R0,R3,INNER             ; update J
            AOBLSS  R0,R2,OUTER             ; update I
```

the ACBL equivalent instruction would be

```
         MOVL  #10,LCV  ; initialize loop control value
DO_LOOP: .
         .
         .
         ACBL  #0,#-2,LCV,DO_LOOP ; increment and test LCV
```

The Stack

Before proceeding to more advanced control structures, we will examine one of the most important data structures in both systems and applications programming: the *stack*. A stack is an area of memory, that is, an array of contiguous data cells, used to store temporary data and subroutine invocation information. Data items are dynamically added to or removed from the stack in *last-in, first-out* (LIFO) fashion. When we remove or *pop* an entry from the stack, it is always the last item that was added or *pushed* onto the stack.

Imagine a stack to be like a spring-loaded cafeteria tray holder in a school cafeteria, where the trays are the data items to be saved. If we want to save several items, we place (push) them onto the stack (of trays). To get them back, we simply pick them up in reverse order, remembering that the last we placed onto the stack is the first one we get back.

For any stack, a variable called the *stack pointer* always points to the last entry pushed onto the stack, as shown in Figure 6.4. This last entry is referred to as the top of the stack.

On the VAX, a register can be used as a stack pointer. The autoincrement and autodecrement addressing modes are convenient for pushing entries on or popping them off a stack. By convention, stacks on the VAX grow in the negative direction, toward memory location zero. To push a new entry onto the stack, we use the autodecrement addressing mode, subtracting the element size from the stack pointer and moving the element to memory. An example of a stack (containing longwords) is shown:

Address (hex)	Memory	Stack Pointer
100	?	
104	?	
108	?	
10C	?	
110	20	←R6

R6 is being used as a stack pointer for a stack that has one entry. The current top of the stack is location 110, which contains the value 20. Question marks (?) indicate that we do not know or care about the values

Figure 6.4   Stack pointer

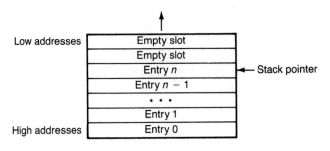

above the stack pointer. Suppose the location at ITEM contains the value 65. The instruction

```
MOVL    ITEM,-(R6)              ; save ITEM on R6 stack
```

moves the pointer to the next location and inserts the value of ITEM there, leaving the stack as follows:

Address (hex)	Memory	Stack Pointer
100	?	
104	?	
108	?	
10C	65	←R6
110	20	

We remove an item from the stack using the autoincrement address-ing mode. Executing the instruction

```
MOVL    (R6)+,R8   ; pop stack to R8
```

moves the top entry in the stack to R8 and changes the stack pointer to point to the previous top of the stack. The stack now appears as follows:

Address (hex)	Memory	Stack Pointer
100	?	
104	?	
108	?	
10C	?	
110	20	←R6

The stack pointer now points at the first entry, exactly where it was before the push and pop operations. Of course, we know that there is still a 65 at location 10C, but it will be overwritten by the next Push instruction.

On the VAX, register 14 is reserved for a stack pointer. R14 is denoted as SP, for stack pointer, by the assembler. When a program is loaded, the operating system automatically allocates a block of memory in the user's address space and loads SP with the address of the block. Some instructions implicitly use SP and the user's stack. For example, the instruction

```
PUSHL      R5
```

pushes the contents of R5 onto the stack pointed to by SP. This instruction is equivalent to

```
MOVL       R5,-(SP)
```

but is shorter because the −(SP) is implied. Likewise, we can write

```
POPL       R3
```

to remove the top entry from the stack and store it in R3. (The VAX does not actually have a POPL instruction because, as we shall see, there are a number of mechanisms for removing items from the stack automatically. However, the assembler recognizes "POPL Destination" and generates "MOVL (SP)+,Destination" instead.)

As an example of how the stack can be used to store temporary variables, we will use the three-instruction exchange in the sorting routine from the previous section:

```
   .
   .
   .
MOVL      (R1)[R2],TEMP          ; save LIST(I)
MOVL      (R1)[R3],(R1)[R2]      ; exchange LIST(I)
MOVL      TEMP,(R1)[R3]          ;...and LIST(J)
   .
   .
   .
```

Instead of using the variable TEMP to hold LIST[I] during the exchange, we easily could have used the stack and written:

```
PUSHL     (R1)[R2]               ; save LIST[I] on stack
MOVL      (R1)[R3],(R1)[R2]      ; replace LIST[I]
POPL      (R1)[R3]               ; restore LIST[J]
```

This is shorter because we need not represent the address of TEMP in the instruction stream. It also allows the use of reusable storage space, that is, stack space that any routine can use. The destinations of the push and the pop are implied by the register SP.

The stack is also commonly used to save registers. Often we need to use registers for a section of code, but we want to save their current values for later use. In the following section of code, registers 4, 5, and 6 are saved and then restored from the stack:

```
PUSHL   R6                  ; save R6
PUSHL   R5                  ; save R5
PUSHL   R4                  ; save R4
    .
    . (instructions that
    .  modify R4–R6)
    .
POPL    R4                  ; restore R4
POPL    R5                  ; restore R5
POPL    R6                  ; restore R6
```

Notice that the registers are restored in opposite order since the stack is last-in, first-out.

Registers are saved and restored so frequently that the VAX has special Push and Pop Registers instructions to store and retrieve multiple registers from the stack. The operand to these instructions is a 16-bit mask with 1 bit corresponding to each register in the VAX register set. The assembler syntax ^M<Ra,Rb,...,Rn> automatically generates the mask with the proper bits set for the registers to be saved or restored. For example, the preceding example can be replaced with the following sequence:

```
PUSHR   #^M<R4,R5,R6>        ; save three registers
    .
    .  (instructions that
    .   modify R4–R6)
    .
POPR    #^M<R4,R5,R6>         ; restore three registers
```

The Push Registers instruction pushes the registers in high-to-low order, while the Pop Registers instruction restores them in low-to-high order. This is done so that contiguous registers will be stored in increasing memory addresses on the stack. Registers are pushed and popped in this order regardless of the order in which they are specified. Thus, the Push Registers instruction will copy the registers as shown in Figure 6.5.

As we shall see, the stack is often used to contain arguments for a subroutine being called. Since addresses as well as values are passed to subroutines, the VAX also has Push Address instructions to store addresses on the stack. The instruction

```
PUSHAL  ITEM
```

Figure 6.5   Stack following PUSHR #^M<R4,R5,R6>

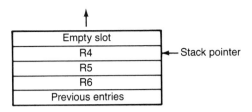

pushes the address of ITEM onto the stack. This is the same as writing

```
MOVAL     ITEM,-(SP)
```

but shorter. There are Push Address instructions for all VAX data types: PUSHAB, PUSHAW, PUSHAL, PUSHAQ, PUSHAO, PUSHAF, PUSHAD, PUSHAG, and PUSHAH. Each instruction pushes a 32-bit address onto the stack. The data type indication is used to evaluate context-dependent addresses, as in the instruction

```
PUSHAW    ARRAY[R3]
```

in which the word-context indication is needed to evaluate the effective address. As in the Move Address instruction, the context of the operand is determined by the data type specified in the instruction, while the context of the implied second operand (that is, the top of stack) is always longword.

We conclude this section with a short code segment that uses the stack. This example, shown in Figure 6.6, takes an integer and uses the routine LIB$PUT_OUTPUT to write the characters one at a time.

The stack is used because the algorithm extracts the digits from least significant to most significant, although we read numbers in the opposite order. When a digit is extracted in binary, the ASCII equivalent is computed by adding the value of ASCII zero to the number. This example also introduces a new instruction, Extended Divide (EDIV), which divides a 64-bit dividend by a 32-bit divisor, producing a quotient and a remainder of 32 bits each. The format of EDIV is

```
EDIV      divisor,dividend,quotient,remainder
```

EDIV sets the condition codes based on the quotient produced. Because we are using all longword values, the upper half of the quadword dividend is cleared before the loop begins. In addition, the CLRQ instruction, when given a register operand, clears two consecutive registers.

For example, suppose NUMBER contains the value 35. Following the

Figure 6.6   Integer-to-ASCII conversion code

```
;
; Output an integer in ASCII representation.
;
; Input:
;
;       NUMBER contains value to be evaluated
;
; Output:
;
;       ASCII value output by LIB$PUT_OUTPUT
;
; Register usage:
;
;       R2 = number to be evaluated
;       R3 = upper 32 bits of quadword (64-bit) number
;       R4 = number of digits to be output
;
CHARBUF:.BLKB    16                      ; output character buffer
CHDSC:  .LONG    16                      ; output string descriptor
        .ADDRESS CHARBUF


OUTASC:
        PUSHR    #^M<R2,R3,R4>           ; save registers to be modified
        CLRL     R3                      ; zero R3 (upper dividend bits)
        MOVL     #1,R4                   ; we'll get at least 1 digit
        MOVL     NUMBER,R2               ; get number to be evaluated
10$:    EDIV     #10,R2,R2,-(SP)         ; push low order decimal digit
                                         ; ...on stack, R2 gets quotient
        BEQL     20$                     ; branch if zero quotient
        INCL     R4                      ; count one more digit
        BRB      10$                     ; continue for next digit

;
; The digits have been pushed on the stack in reverse order.
; Now pop them off, converting each to ASCII and placing it in
; the next position in CHARBUF.  When done, CHARBUF will have
; the ASCII string to be output.
;


20$:    MOVL     R4,CHDSC                ; set length in descriptor
        MOVAL    CHARBUF,R0              ; R0 <- buffer address
30$:    ADDL3    #^A/0/,(SP)+,R1         ; R1 <- digit
        MOVB     R1,(R0)+                ; insert digit in buffer
        SOBGTR   R4,30$                  ; continue until done
        PUSHAQ   CHDSC                   ; now output the buffer
        CALLS    #1,G^LIB$PUT_OUTPUT
        POPR     #^M<R2,R3,R4>           ; restore registers
```

execution of the EDIV instruction at LOOP1, the stack appears as

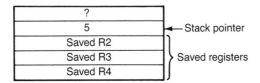

The second time through the loop, the stack appears as

3	← Stack pointer
5	
Saved R2	
Saved R3	
Saved R4	

In LOOP2, the characters are popped off the stack and are converted to ASCII.

Subroutines and Procedures

The best way to write a program to solve a problem is to subdivide the problem into manageable pieces. Experience has shown that large, monolithic programs are difficult to debug and maintain. Building programs in smaller units that can be debugged independently allows productivity, reliability, and maintainability to be substantially increased. (Of course, dividing a program into small pieces does not itself guarantee that the program will be productive, reliable, or maintainable.)

In addition to making programs easier to maintain, subroutines save on program space. When a single function must be performed several times within a program, the function is made into a subroutine so that the same code is not duplicated at each point where it is needed. However, it is not required that a routine be called more than once from a program. An instruction sequence should be made into a subroutine whenever doing so simplifies coding or comprehension of the program.

One of the more important aspects of dividing a program into subprograms is defining the routine interfaces and the standards followed for transferring both data and control. A good subroutine facility must include the following properties:

1. The subroutine must be able to be invoked from many different places in the program. This is known as "calling" the subroutine.

2. The subroutine must be able to return to the caller without knowing explicitly where it was called from.

3. There must be a simple and unambiguous mechanism for transmitting arguments between the calling routine and the called procedure.

4. The subroutine must be able to operate without knowledge of the environment in which it is called or the state of the variables in the outside program, except for the information passed explicitly in the calling sequence.

If a subroutine is specified in such a way that it receives its input arguments and output arguments explicitly and has no knowledge of the outside world, then it will be able to be debugged independently. A special test program may easily be written that simply passes arguments to the subroutine and examines the results. Both input arguments and results are passed via the calling mechanism—neither party has global knowledge. Subroutines written in this way can be used without change as part of other programs that need the same function. This reusability reduces work tremendously because commonplace functions need be written only once. A well-defined interface also makes the calling program independent of the implementation of the function provided by the subroutine. If a sorting procedure is too slow, for example, the algorithm can be changed without requiring any modification to the calling program.

Invoking routines and transmitting arguments are so important in programming that the VAX instruction set contains some high-level mechanisms to deal with them. Indeed, the VAX has two forms of the subprogram call: the procedure call and the subroutine call. The significant difference between these two forms is in the linkage mechanism. The procedure call, which is discussed first, is much more powerful in its handling of the arguments. Several of the sixteen general-purpose registers have been reserved for the procedure-calling facility, and the stack is heavily used to automate the transfer of control and the passing of arguments. On the other hand, the subroutine call, while still using some of the registers, is simpler and faster.

The VAX general procedure-calling facility is provided by the Call instruction. The Call mechanism provides the four following features:

1. Arguments are passed uniformly and consistently. The called routine can determine the number of arguments passed and can address them as offsets from a fixed pointer called the argument pointer (AP).

2. Registers are saved so that the called procedure can use registers without modifying values left there by the caller.

3. The called procedure can allocate local storage on the stack and address local variables as offsets from a fixed pointer called the frame pointer (FP).

4. Returning is done uniformly and consistently. The called procedure can return at any time. Any values pushed on the stack will be popped off, the saved registers will be restored, and control will be returned to the instruction following the Call, all automatically.

The following sections examine how these features are implemented.

Argument Lists and Call Instructions

For the VAX, arguments are transmitted to a called procedure in an *argument list*. A VAX argument list is an array of longwords in which the first longword contains a count (in the first byte) of the number of arguments to follow. The general format is shown in Figure 6.7.

Each entry in the list can be a value or an address. Passing data to a procedure by address is known as *call by reference*, while passing immediate values in the argument list is known as *call by value*. The argument list can be allocated in static memory or can be pushed onto the stack prior to the call. Consequently, there are two forms of the Call instruction.

The General form, CALLG, takes as operands the address of an argument list anywhere in memory and the address of the procedure to call. For example, suppose we want to invoke the routine MYPROC and pass it two arguments whose values are 600 and 84. The following code shows the allocation of the argument list and the Call instruction:

```
          ; Define Argument list for call to MYPROC

ARGLIST:  .LONG 2                   ; argument count
          .LONG 600                 ; first argument
          .LONG 84                  ; second argument
             .
             .
             .
BEGIN:       .
          <code section>
             .
             .
          CALLG   ARGLIST,MYPROC    ; call procedure MYPROC
             .                      ; with...argument list
             .                      ; ARGLIST
             .
```

Figure 6.7   VAX call argument list

	n
Argument 1	
Argument 2	
.	
.	
Argument n	

If a second call to MYPROC is needed with different values for the arguments, the main procedure could use a different argument list or could dynamically move the values into the list starting at label ARGLIST.

The second form of the call instruction is the Stack form, CALLS, in which the argument list is pushed onto the stack; that is, the stack is used as space in which to dynamically construct the argument list immediately before the call. The following example shows the invocation of MYPROC using the CALLS instruction:

```
        .
        .
        .
        PUSHL   #84             ; push second argument
        PUSHL   #600            ; push first argument
        CALLS   #2,MYPROC       ; call procedure MYPROC
        .
        .
        .
```

There are two important details about the use of CALLS. First, the arguments are pushed in *reverse order* because the stack grows toward lower addresses. Second, the first operand of CALLS is the count of the number of calling arguments; the CALLS instruction itself pushes the argument count onto the stack before transferring control. When the called procedure terminates by executing a return (RET) instruction, the argument list is automatically removed from the stack if a CALLS instruction was used. Execution of a RET instruction by the procedure returns control to the instruction following the Call that invoked it. Thus, following the return from the call, the calling routine does not have to remove its arguments from the stack, since the stack pointer is restored to its state before the arguments were pushed.

There are a number of tradeoffs between the use of CALLS and CALLG. CALLG makes sense where the number of arguments and the value of each argument are fixed. CALLG is usually faster because the argument list is allocated at the time the calling routine is compiled. No instructions need to be executed to push arguments onto the stack. Depending on the number of calls used in the program, either form could be more space-efficient. On the VAX, the instruction to push a value onto the stack is often shorter than the storage required for the value itself because of short literal addressing. For example, the instruction to push the integer 1 onto the stack takes 2 bytes, while a longword argument containing the integer 1 takes 4 bytes.

CALLG is used by older languages, such as FORTRAN. All modern languages use CALLS because it is more dynamic, allows for nested routine invocations, and permits recursion and reentrancy (to be discussed later). In this book, procedure calls are coded using CALLS.

The Argument Pointer

Before transferring control to the procedure, the Call instruction loads register 12, the argument pointer (AP), with the address of the argument list either in memory (for CALLG) or on the stack (for CALLS). The procedure can access arguments as fixed offsets from AP. The first longword that AP points to always contains the number of arguments to follow. For instance, procedure MYPROC could access its calling arguments with the following code:

```
MYPROC:    .
           .
           .
           MOVL    (AP),R0       ; get argument count
           MOVL    4(AP),R1      ; get first argument
           MOVL    8(AP),R2      ; get second argument
           .
           .
           .
           RET                   ; return to caller
```

Note that MYPROC cannot tell (and should not care) whether it was called by a CALLS or a CALLG instruction. In either case, MYPROC begins execution with register AP pointing to the argument list.

Saving Registers

The CALLS and CALLG instructions transfer control to the procedure at the address specified by the second operand. To make it simple to save registers, the first word of the called procedure always contains a save mask similar to the one used in the PUSHR and POPR instructions. The Call instruction examines the mask and saves on the stack the registers corresponding to the bits set in the mask. By convention on VAX/VMS, all registers used in a procedure must be preserved by that procedure with the exception of R0 and R1, which are used to return values to the caller, and R12 through R15 (AP, FP, SP, and PC), which are special registers. The calling routine, then, does not have to worry about saving or restoring registers across procedure calls. The execution of a RET instruction restores the saved registers before returning control.

Each procedure that is called has the same basic format:

```
PROC:    .WORD   ^M<Ra,...,Rn>     ; registers to save
         .
         .
         .
         <routine code>
         .
         .
         .
         RET                       ; return to caller
```

The VAX hardware always interprets the first word of a called procedure as a register mask, so the mask must not be omitted. Because of this, the VMS assembler has a special format for declaring procedures. The .ENTRY directive declares the start of a procedure and defines both the entry point name and the save mask. For example, using .ENTRY we would code the previous procedure as

```
.ENTRY   PROC,^M<Ra,...,Rn> ; procedure PROC
   .
   .
   .
<routine code>
   .
   .
   .
RET                          ; return to caller
```

If we leave out the second argument to .ENTRY, the directive will simply place a zero-valued mask as the first word of the procedure, causing no registers to be saved.

As already mentioned, procedures do not specify the saving of R12 through R15, since these are special and are saved automatically by the procedure-calling mechanism, as will soon be discussed. Also, R0 and R1 are not saved by convention, since they are used to return results to the calling procedure. This convention is enforced by the assembler, which will not allow R0 and R1 in the call mask, although the hardware would permit these bits to be set in the mask.

The format of the 16-bit mask for procedure calls is actually as follows:

15	14	13	12	11	00
DV	IV	0	0	Registers	

Bits 0 through 11 specify the registers to be saved. Bits 12 and 13 are always zero. Finally, bits 14 and 15 can be used to set the PSW bits indicating whether integer overflow (IV) and decimal overflow (DV) should be enabled within the called procedure. This is to permit some procedures to easily ensure that they always execute in the same environment with respect to overflow.

Note that when we use a register mask as an argument in a PUSHR or POPR instruction, we typically use immediate mode addressing for the mask; thus, it must be preceded by a #, for example,

```
PUSHR    #^M<R1,R2,R4>
```

However, when used in the .WORD or .ENTRY declaration, the mask is not preceded by a # since we are just specifying the mask as a data value in a data allocation directive.

An Example Procedure

Now that we have seen how arguments are transmitted, how registers are saved, how control is transferred with the Call instruction, and how control is returned with RET, we will use the sorting example from the discussion of loops to build a callable procedure. The Sort procedure will be called with an argument list containing two arguments: the address of an array of longwords to be sorted and the address of the number of elements in the array. This example also shows the style we will use for documentation within the program. Normally, procedure values are returned in R0 and R1; therefore, these registers are not saved and restored by the called procedure.

```
        .SBTTL SORT - Procedure to Sort a Longword Array
;++
;
; FUNCTIONAL DESCRIPTION:
;
;       This procedure arranges an array of signed longword integers
;       into increasing numerical order.
;
; CALLING SEQUENCE:
;
;       Called with CALLS or CALLG to Sort.
;
; INPUT PARAMETERS:
;
;       ARRAY(AP) - the address of the array of longwords to be sorted
;       ARRAYSIZE(AP) - the address of the number of longwords in ARRAY
;
; OUTPUT PARAMETERS:
;
;       None
;
; COMPLETION CODES:
;
;       None
;
; SIDE EFFECTS:
;
;       All registers except R0 and R1 are preserved.
;--
        ARRAY=4                         ; offset to array address
        ARRAYSIZE=8                     ; offset to array length


;
; The following implements a bubble-up sort, where the smallest values
; are "bubbled" up to the top of the list.
;

        .ENTRY  SORT,^M<R2,R3>          ; procedure SORT, save 2 regs
        SUBL3   #1,@ARRAYSIZE(AP),R0    ; subtract 1 from array size
                                        ; ...to form last entry index
```

```
          BLEQ    40$                      ; done if 1 entry or less
          MOVL    ARRAY(AP),R1             ; get array base address
          CLRL    R2                       ; I is index of first entry
10$:      ADDL3   #1,R2,R3                 ; initialize J to I = 1
20$:      CMPL    (R1)[R2],(R1)[R3]        ; is first LEQ second?
          BLEQ    30$                      ; branch if so

;
; Found larger number before smaller one, exchange them.
;

          PUSHL   (R1)[R2]                 ; save LIST(I)
          MOVL    (R1)[R3],(R1)[R2]        ; exchange LIST(I)
          POPL    (R1)[R3]                 ; ...and LIST(J)
30$:
          AOBLEQ  R0,R3,20$                ; update J
          AOBLSS  R0,R2,10$                ; update I
40$:      RET                              ; return to caller
```

One of the changes made to this code sequence is the introduction of local labels. As mentioned before, a local label is a symbol of the form *integer$* that replaces alphanumeric labels. Since a local label is defined only within the local symbol block in which it appears, the definition of another alphanumeric symbol begins a new block in which local symbols using the same number can be defined. In other words, a routine following Sort can also use local labels 10$, 20$, 30$, and 40$. Since another routine cannot transfer to Sort at any place except its entry point, local symbols enforce the isolation of routines.

The Call Frame

On execution of a RET instruction by a procedure, the following four functions are performed automatically:

1. Anything pushed onto the stack by the procedure is removed.

2. The registers saved on entry are restored.

3. If the procedure was invoked by a CALLS, the argument list is removed from the stack.

4. Control is returned to the instruction following the Call statement.

In other words, the state of the main routine is restored except for any output results that may have been written within the procedure (or values returned in registers R0 or R1).

The RET instruction can perform these functions and remember all the work being done because, once more, the stack is a convenient mechanism for maintaining information. When a CALLS instruction is executed, a data structure known as a *call frame* is built on the user's stack. The call frame contains the state information needed by the RET instruction to restore the registers, restore the stack, and return control. Register 13, the frame pointer (FP), is loaded with the address of the call frame. Therefore, the RET instruction simply uses FP to locate the call frame and restore the previous state.

The structure of the call frame is shown in Figure 6.8. The components of the call frame are:

1. A longword condition handler address. Here, the calling routine may store the address of an error-handling routine to be called if an exceptional error condition arises in the procedure.

2. The saved program status word (PSW) of the calling routine. The PSW contains enable bits that indicate how to handle arithmetic-error conditions. The condition codes, also part of the PSW, are stored as zero and are not preserved over the call.

3. A copy of the register save mask found at the call site. This mask is saved so that the RET instruction knows which registers are to be restored from the call frame.

4. A single bit that indicates whether this call was the result of a CALLS or a CALLG. If a CALLS was used, RET removes the argument list from the stack and examines the argument count in the first longword of the list to determine the number of arguments.

5. A two-bit field called stack pointer alignment (SPA). The Call instruction always aligns the call frame on a longword boundary. Therefore, if the stack is not aligned at the time of the call, up to 3 spare bytes may

Figure 6.8   VAX call frame

31	30 29 28 27		16 15 14	05 04	00	
Condition handler (initially 0)						(FP)
SPA	S 0	Mask	Z	PSW<14:5>	0	
Saved AP						
Saved FP						
Saved PC						
Saved R0 (...)						
Saved R11 (...)						

(0 to 3 bytes specified by SPA)

S = Set if CALLS; clear if CALLG.
Z = Cleared by CALL. Set by software to force a reserved operand call on RET.

be skipped before the first entry in the frame (the highest-numbered register saved) is pushed. SPA is used to remember how many bytes were skipped so that the stack can be restored when the call frame is removed.

6. All registers specified by the save mask, with the highest-numbered register saved first, as in the PUSHR instruction.

To see what might happen to the stack on a procedure call, consider the following example. Suppose that the following code is used to call the procedure Sort:

```
LISTSIZE:
          .LONG    20              ; size of array
AGELIST:
          .BLKL    20              ; array of 20 elements
          .
          .
          .
MAIN:   <code sequence>
          .
10$     PUSHAL   LISTSIZE          ; push address of array length
        PUSHAL   AGELIST           ; push address of array
        CALLS    #2,SORT           ; call Sort routine
20$     .
          .
          .
```

Assuming the stack is aligned on a longword before the PUSHAL instruction at location 10$, the state of the stack following the call is shown in Figure 6.9. Although the called procedure may use the stack and the

Figure 6.9   Stack following CALLS to Sort routine

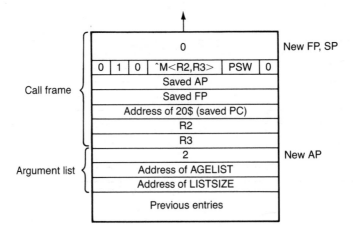

value of SP changes accordingly, FP remains fixed. Thus, the call frame can always be found.

Local Variables

Another advantage of having a fixed FP register for the duration of a call is that the procedure can allocate local variables on the stack and address them as fixed offsets from FP. The following procedure has two local variables, A and B, which are allocated on the stack. The example shows the allocation and the addressing of these locals:

```
A = -4                              ; offset to local A
B = -8                              ; offset to local B
    .
    .
    .
.ENTRY  PROC,  ^M<R2,R3,R8,R10>     ; registers to save
SUBL    #8,SP                       ; make room for 2 longwords
                                    ; ...on the stack
    .
    .
MOVL    R0,A(FP)                    ; store R0 in A
MOVL    R1,B(FP)                    ; store R1 in B
    .
    .
RET                                 ; return to caller
```

At entry to this procedure, FP and SP both point to the top of the stack, which is the top longword in the new calling frame. FP will remain fixed for the duration of the call. In the code, the SUBL instruction allocates space for two longwords on the stack by subtracting 8 from the stack pointer. The stack pointer now points to the first of two longwords on the stack preceding the call frame, as shown in Figure 6.10. Had we wanted to initialize this local storage to zero, we could have used a Clear instruction instead of the Subtract, that is,

Figure 6.10 **Stack following allocation of locals**

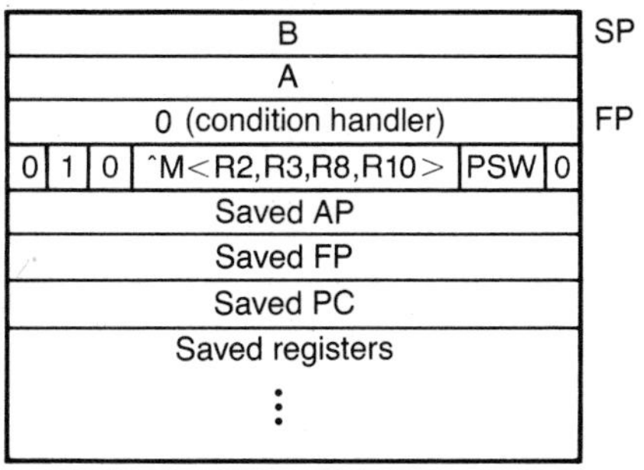

B	SP
A	
0 (condition handler)	FP
0 1 0 ^M<R2,R3,R8,R10> PSW 0	
Saved AP	
Saved FP	
Saved PC	
Saved registers	
⋮	

```
CLRQ    -(SP)
```

also adjusts the stack pointer and zeros the two locals on the stack.

The important point to note is that once these locals are allocated, they are addressed as fixed offsets from FP, *not* from SP. After locals are allocated at the start of the procedure, the stack can continue to be used for local computations without affecting addressing of the locals. If the start of the procedure stack is not fixed at FP, we must manually keep track of the changing offset between SP and local storage. This can become a problem when one procedure calls another. Another advantage of fixing FP, illustrated previously, is that the RET instruction automatically deallocates the temporary storage for A and B.

Let's look again at the integer-to-ASCII output code shown in Figure 6.6. In Figure 6.11, we have converted that code into a procedure. As part of the conversion, the local parameters CHARBUF, a 16-byte buffer, and CHDSC, a quadword string descriptor, are both stack-allocated as dynamic local storage.

Fast Linkages

The procedure call is used as the standard interface between routines written in all languages. Consequently, it is possible for a FORTRAN routine, for instance, to call a Pascal or assembly language routine.

In assembly language, however, it is sometimes desirable to call a short procedure, known in VAX terminology as a subroutine, without invoking the overhead of the general Call facility. Compilers could also use this linkage for internal subroutines. In this quick linkage, input and output arguments are usually transmitted in general registers. There is no automatic saving of registers or restoring of the stack. The called subroutine must take care of those tasks explicitly.

Branch Subroutine Byte and Branch Subroutine Word (BSBB and BSBW) instructions are used to invoke such short subroutines. Just like Branch instructions BRB and BRW, these instructions transfer to subroutines within byte or word offsets from the current location. When a BSBB or BSBW is executed, it simply pushes the PC (the address of the instruction to return to) onto the stack and branches to the subroutine. To return, the subroutine executes a Return from Subroutine (RSB) instruction, which merely pops the return address from the stack and returns. Because BSB instructions do not use a frame pointer, the subroutine must be sure to save and restore registers and to restore the stack to its original condition before an RSB is executed.

In the code sequence on p. 144 using the BSB instruction, the problem is to compute the value of

$$ARRAY\,(0)^0 + ARRAY\,(1)^1 + ARRAY\,(2)^2 + \cdots + ARRAY\,(n)^n$$

Figure 6.11   Integer-to-ASCII output procedure

```
;
; OUTASC -- Procedure to output an integer in ASCII representation.
; Called with CALLS or CALLG
;
; Input:
;
;       NUMBER(AP) contains value to be evaluated
;
; Output:
;
;       ASCII value output by LIB$PUT_OUTPUT
;
; Register usage:
;
;       R2 = number to be evaluated
;       R3 = upper 32 bits of quadword (64-bit) number
;       R4 = number of digits to be output
;


            NUMBER  = 4                 ; offset to input parameter
            BUFSIZE = 16                ; size of buffer
            CHARBUF = -BUFSIZE          ; offset to start of buffer
            CHDSC   = CHARBUF-8         ; offset to string descriptor

            .ENTRY  OUTASC,^M<R2,R3,R4> ; OUTASC entry point
            ADDL    #CHDSC,SP           ; allocate space for locals
                                        ; (remember, CHDSC is negative)
            CLRL    R3                  ; zero R3 (upper dividend bits)
            MOVL    #1,R4               ; at least one digit of output
            MOVL    NUMBER(AP),R2       ; get number to be evaluated
10$:        EDIV    #10,R2,R2,-(SP)     ; push low-order decimal digit
                                        ; ...on stack, R2 gets quotient
            BEQL    20$                 ; branch if zero quotient
            INCL    R4                  ; count one more digit
            BRB     10$                 ; continue for next digit


;
; The digits have been pushed onto the stack in reverse order.
; Now pop them off, converting each ASCII and placing it in
; the next position in CHARBUF.  When done, CHARBUF will have
; the ASCII string to be output.
;


20$:        MOVL    R4,CHDSC(FP)        ; set length in descriptor
            MOVAL   CHARBUF(FP),R0      ; R0 <- buffer address
            MOVL    R0,CHDSC+4(FP)      ; init address in descriptor
30$:        ADDL3   #^A/0/,(SP)+,R1     ; R1 <- ASCII digit
            MOVB    R1,(R0)+            ; insert digit in buffer
            SOBGTR  R4,30$             ; continue until done
            PUSHAQ  CHDSC(FP)           ; now output the buffer
            CALLS   #1,G^LIB$PUT_OUTPUT
            RET                         ; return to caller
```

given the address of **ARRAY**, the number of elements, n, and the address into which to write the result. A subroutine is used to raise each entry to the necessary power.

```
        .SBTTL   COMPUTE - Calculate Sum of Array[i]**i
;++
;
; FUNCTIONAL DESCRIPTION:
;
;       This routine computes the sum of Array[i]**i
;
; CALLING SEQUENCE:
;
;       CALLS OR CALLG
;
;  INPUT PARAMETERS:
;
;       ARRAY(AP) - address of the array
;       SIZE(AP) - number of elements in array
;       RESULT(AP) - address of longword to receive computed result
;
; OUTPUT PARAMETERS:
;
;       RESULT(AP) - longword pointed to receives computed value
;
; SIDE EFFECTS:
;
;       None
;--

        ARRAY  = 4                      ; offset to array address
        SIZE   = 8                      ; offset to array size
        RESULT = 12                     ; offset to address of result
                                        ; longword


;
; Register Usage:
;
;       R1 = value of current array entry
;       R2 = address of next array entry
;       R3 = power to which value will be raised
;       R4 = sum accumulator
;

        .ENTRY   COMPUTE,^M<R2,R3,R4>   ; COMPUTE entry point
        MOVL     ARRAY(AP),R2           ; get first element address
        CLRQ     R3                     ; zero R3 (first power)
                                        ; ...and R4 (accumulator)
10$:    MOVL     (R2)+,R1               ; get next array entry
        BSBB     POWER                  ; compute to proper exponent
        ADDL     R0,R4                  ; add this element to sum
```

```
        AOBLSS  SIZE(AP),R3,10$          ; continue with next entry
                                         ; ...and power
        MOVL    R4,@RESULT(AP)           ; store result
        RET                              ; return to caller


;
; Subroutine to raise element to a given power.
;
; CALLING SEQUENCE:
;
;       BSBB or BSBW
;
; INPUT PARAMETERS:
;
;       R1 = value
;       R3 = power to raise value to
;
; OUTPUT PARAMETERS:
;
;       R0 = (R1)**R3
;

POWER:
        MOVL    #1,R0                    ; assume result is 1
        PUSHL   R3                       ; save register
        BLEQ    30$                      ; branch if power LEQ 0
        MOVL    R1,R0                    ; copy value for first power
        BRB     20$                      ; begin loop at end
10$:    MULL    R1,R0                    ; compute next power
20$:    SOBGTR  R3,10$                   ; continue until done
30$:    POPL    R3                       ; restore saved register
        RSB                              ; return to main routine
```

The BSBB and BSBW instructions, like the BRB and BRW instructions, can transfer to locations within reach of an 8- or 16-bit offset from the current location. If that range is insufficient, the Jump to Subroutine (JSB) instruction is used. Like JMP, JSB can use any of the addressing modes to specify its target destination; for example, you can specify a Jump to Subroutine indirectly through a register. Routines invoked by JSB still return with the RSB instruction.

Recursion

It is often useful for a routine to be able to call itself. Such routines, known as recursive routines, simplify the expression of many mathematical and syntactical algorithms. Recursive routines may not have any static storage (that is, variables allocated with .LONG, .BLK, and so on). *All* local variables must be allocated on the stack so that the variables from one call are not modified by another recursive call. Here is another reason why the

Figure 6.12 Recursive call frames

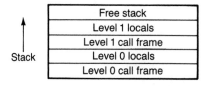

call frame is so useful. As Figure 6.12 shows, if we look at the stack after several levels of recursive calls, we will see the state information for each level.

The classic example of recursion is in the calculation of N factorial, denoted by $N!$. N factorial is the product of all of the numbers from 1 through N inclusive:

$$N! = N \times (N-1) \times (N-2) \times \cdots \times 1$$

The value of zero factorial is defined as 1, so we can write the recursive definition of $N!$ as

$$N! = \begin{cases} N \times (N - 1)! & N > 0 \\ 1 & N = 0 \end{cases}$$

Because most FORTRAN compilers use static variable allocation rather than stacks and call frames, they are not capable of executing recursive routines. In Pascal, however, we could code the recursive $N!$ routine as follows:

```
function FACTORIAL (n: integer): integer;
begin
      if N < 1 then FACTORIAL :=1
      else  FACTORIAL := n * FACTORIAL (n-1)
end;
```

There are two ways to represent this in VAX assembly language, depending on whether the CALLS or BSB instruction is used for linkage. Either instruction will work because each uses the stack to store the return information and each uses R0 to return the value of $N!$. The CALLS version receives N through the call frame, while the BSB version receives N through R0 (see Figure 6.13).

Although the recursive definition of $N!$ is notationally nice, it may not be a good way to implement the computer calculation. In this case, the straightforward solution shown at the top of p. 148 is much faster and shorter, as well as making better use of stack space.

Figure 6.13   Recursive N! routine using CALLS and BSB

```
        .ENTRY  START,0         ; main program entry
        PUSHL   N               ; number to compute factorial
        CALLS   #1,NFACT        ; call factorial routine
        RET                     ; return with result in R0

;
; Recursive routine to compute N!.

        .ENTRY  NFACT,^M<R2>    ; factorial entry point, save
                                ; ...R2 on recursive call
        MOVL    #1,R0           ; assume N is 0, return 1
        MOVL    4(AP),R2        ; copy N
        BEQL    10$             ; exit if N=0

;
; Build call frame with N-1 for next invocation to
; compute (N-1)!.
;

        SUBL3   #1,R2,-(SP)     ; push N-1 on stack
        CALLS   #1,NFACT        ; recursive call
        MULL    R2,R0           ; compute N*(N-1)!
10$:    RET                     ; return to caller
```

a. CALLS

```
;
; Recursive subroutine to compute N!.  N is passed to the
; subroutine in R0.  At each level, N is saved in R1, and N-1
; is passed to the recursively called subroutine to calculate
; (N-1)!.
;

NFACT:  PUSHL   R1              ; save R1
        MOVL    R0,R1           ; copy N
        BNEQ    10$             ; continue if N not 0
        MOVL    #1,R0           ; N is 0, return 1
        BRB     20$             ; exit
10$:    DECL    R0              ; compute N-1
        BSBB    NFACT           ; recursive call
        MULL    R1,R0           ; compute N*(N-1)!
20$:    POPL    R1              ; restore R1
        RSB                     ; return to caller
```

b. BSB

```
NFACT:   MOVL    #1,R0          ; initialize factorial
         TSTL    N              ; test N
         BEQL    20$            ; N is 0, return 1
         MOVL    #1,R1          ; initialize counter
10$:     MULL    R1,R0          ; compute N*(N-1)
         AOBLEQ  N,R1,10$       ; continue until done
20$:     RSB                    ; return to caller
```

One problem with recursive routines, then, is that they can require a tremendous amount of stack space for the nested call frames and variables. As another example, in Figure 6.14 we once again present the integer-to-ASCII conversion routine seen earlier; however, this time we use recursion to accomplish the same result.

Reentrant Routines

With recursion, we have seen that several simultaneous invocations of a routine can exist, each in its own stage of execution. This is possible because each invocation has its own local-state information maintained by the call frame and local storage. Whenever a recursive call is made, a new state is created by building a new call frame on the stack, thereby preserving the state of the calling routine.

On multiprogramming systems, it is particularly advantageous if commonly used programs can be shared. It is desirable for several user processes to be able to execute a routine without each needing a private copy. This sharing can save memory space, allowing more users to fit in memory and thus increasing performance. The biggest gain comes from sharing utilities such as editors, compilers, and linkers. Although many people may be editing at any time, there need be only one copy of the editor code in memory.

Programs or routines that can be shared among many users are known as *reentrant*. Several different user processes can be in some stage of execution at different places within a reentrant routine. For a routine to be reentrant, it must consist of pure code and data. In other words, no part of the routine can be modified by its execution. Any variables that are modified must be part of the private state information belonging to each user, such as the registers and stacks. Since each user process has its own program counter, stack pointer, general register set, and stack, several user programs may be in the process of executing the same code section. If one user is interrupted and another begins executing the same code sequence, no problems occur because the modified data is unique in each user's private state area.

For example, consider the procedure *A*:

```
.ENTRY  A
MOVL    4(AP),R0
MULL    #2,R0
RET
```

Figure 6.14   Integer-to-ASCII recursion routine

```
;
; Procedure to output an integer in ASCII representation.
; Called with CALLS or CALLG
;
; Input:
;
;       NUMBER(AP) contains value to be evaluated
;
; Output:
;
;       ASCII value output by LIB$PUT_OUTPUT
;
; Register usage:
;
;       R2 = number to be evaluated
;       R3 = upper 32 bits of quadword (64-bit) number

        NUMBER  = 4                     ; offset to input parameter
        BUFSIZE = 16                    ; size of buffer
        CHARBUF = -BUFSIZE              ; offset to start of buffer
        CHDSC   = CHARBUF-8            ; offset to string descriptor

        ENTRY   OUTASC,^M<R2,R3,R4+    ; OUTASC entry point
        ADDL    #CHDSC,SP              ; allocate space for locals
                                       ; (remember, CHDSC is negative)
        CLRL    R3                     ; clear R3 (upper dividend bits)
        MOVL    NUMBER(AP),R2          ; get number to be evaluated
        CLRW    CHDSC(FP)             ; zero descriptor length
        MOVAL   CHARBUF(FP),R0        ; R0 <- buffer address
        MOVL    R0,CHDSC+4(FP)        ; init address in descriptor
        BSBB    PUTNUM                ; call recursive routine
        PUSHAQ  CHDSC(FP)             ; output the buffer
        CALLS   #1,G^LIB$PUT_OUTPUT
        RET                           ; return to caller


;
; Recursive routine to output a number in ASCII.  Each level extracts a
; low-order digit and makes a recursive call if the result is not a 0.
; When the last digit is reached, a return is made winding back through
; the levels and writing the digits in high to low order.
;
; During each recursive call, R4 is used to hold the current digit.
;

PUTNUM:
        PUSHL   R4                    ; save old R4
        EDIV    #10,R2,R2,R4          ; stack low order digit
        BEQL    10$                   ; branch if done
        BSBB    PUTNUM                ; recursive call for next digit
10$:    ADDL3   #^A/0/,R4,R1          ; R1 <- ASCII digit
        MOVB    R1,(R0)+              ; insert next digit
        INCW    CHDSC(FP)            ; count one more character
        POPL    R4                    ; restore saved register
        RSB                           ; return to caller
```

This procedure accepts a single parameter and returns in R0 that parameter multiplied by 2. The procedure is reentrant because all computation is done using the stack and the registers. Because each user process has its own stack and registers, several processes can be in some state of execution of this procedure without interfering with each other, since each executes the instructions of the procedure on their local registers and stack. Suppose, on the other hand, that the procedure had been written as

```
X:      .LONG   0
        .ENTRY  A
        MOVL    4(AP),X
        MULL    #2,X
        MOVL    X,R0
        RET
```

In this case, the procedure is not reentrant because it uses a statically allocated variable. If several users tried to execute this procedure, they could get inconsistent results. For example, if one user begins executing procedure *A* and is interrupted before the MULL instruction, the next user who begins execution of *A* will destroy the first user's value stored in *X*.

In general, all operating system procedures are reentrant. In VAX/VMS, all processes in the system share the operating system implicitly, and many of them can execute operating system routines at the same time.

Macros

Subroutines and procedures are usually called *closed* routines. They consist of self-contained code that performs a specified function. Only one copy of the routine is required, and it can be invoked from many places within the program. Control is passed to the site of the routine by a Call and is returned to the instruction following the Call upon completion. In contrast, a routine embedded at the place of invocation in such a way that no linkage mechanism is required to pass values or control is an *open* routine.

Assembly language programmers often find that certain instruction sequences occur frequently within their code. The VAX/VMS assembly language *macro* capability allows the programmer to define a sequence of statements to be substituted for the macro name wherever it is used within the program. A macro defines an open routine in that the source statements are placed in line at each site where the macro is used.

For example, we frequently need to zero the registers R0 through R5. Defining the macro CLRREGS, we can simply write CLRREGS in the program as if it were a machine instruction:

```
.MACRO  CLRREGS
CLRQ    R0                        ; clear R0 and R1
```

```
     CLRQ    R2                          ; clear R2 and R3
     CLRQ    R4                          ; clear R4 and R5
     .ENDM   CLRREGS
```

Macros such as this give us a shorthand notation. At each occurrence of
CLRREGS within the program, the assembler substitutes the three instructions contained in the macro. Called macro expansion, this is a simple
character-string substitution process that allows the programmer to specify one set of character strings (the macro body) to be substituted for
another character string (the macro name).

A macro must be defined before it is used. The pseudo-operation
.MACRO begins the definition of the macro; .ENDM indicates to the macro
assembler that this is the end of the source text to be included in the macro
expansion. When the assembler encounters a .MACRO directive, it adds
the macro name to its macro name table and stores the source text for
future use. Normally, macro expansions are not printed in the assembly
listing unless the special .LIST directive includes the macro expansion
argument (ME).

Each time the macro CLRREGS is used, it generates exactly the same
instructions. It is sometimes useful to write macros that contain parameters so that slightly different sequences can be produced. This can be done
by using formal arguments with the macro definition. When the macro is
expanded, any occurrences of the formals are replaced by the actual
arguments specified when the macro is invoked. For instance, using a
formal argument, we can write a general macro to push a quadword onto
the stack:

```
     .MACRO  PUSHQ    ITEM
     MOVQ    ITEM,-(SP)
     .ENDM   PUSHQ
```

Whenever the macro is invoked, the actual argument specified replaces
the formal argument, ITEM, in the expanded macro. A code sequence
containing

```
     PUSHQ   ARRAY2[R4]
```

generates the instruction

```
     MOVQ    ARRAY2[R4],-(SP)
```

In this way, macros are used to create an extended instruction set.

When several arguments are needed, they are separated by commas
(,). In this case, the actual arguments must be specified in the same order
as the formals. By using keywords, however, the arguments can be
specified in any order. A keyword is a formal argument name along with its
default value. The general format for a macro definition with keywords is

```
.MACRO macro_name keyword1=default1,keyword2=default2,...
    .
    .  macro body
    .
.ENDM   macro_name
```

When the user codes a keyword macro, the actual argument is specified as *keyword* = *actual*. If no actual argument is given for a formal argument, its default value is used. For example, if the macro PUSHQ is frequently used to push R0 and R1, it could be recoded with this default as

```
.MACRO   PUSHQ    ITEM=R0
MOVQ     ITEM,-(SP)
.ENDM    PUSHQ
```

Now just coding PUSHQ without arguments produces MOVQ R0,−(SP). Using the macro with an actual argument, we could write

```
PUSHQ    ITEM=ARRAY2[R4]
```

Of course, keywords are more useful in macros with many arguments, because the arguments can be written in any order.

Creating Local Labels

Having labels in macros is often useful. Although the programmer can specify labels in the macro definition, the labels can be unintentionally duplicated in the source code that surrounds the macro call, thereby causing errors. Furthermore, each invocation of the macro produces the same label. To avoid duplication, the assembler has the ability to create unique local labels in the macro expansion.

To illustrate this point, let us consider the macro that implements the new instruction JUMPIFZERO. The macro definition might be given as

```
       .MACRO   JUMPIFZERO     A,TARGET
       TSTL     A                       ; is A 0?
       BNEQ     X                       ; continue if not
       JMP      TARGET                  ; else jump to target
X:
       .ENDM    JUMPIFZERO
```

(Note that macros can contain comments.) Each time the macro is expanded, the label *X* will be redefined, causing an error. While it is possible to make the label one of the parameters of the macro definition, a better solution is to use a created local label. Local labels created by VAX assembly language start at 30000$ and range up to 65535$. Each time the assembler generates a new local label, the number part of the label is incremented by 1. Consequently, a unique label is generated each time that should not interfere with user-defined local labels.

Using this facility, the JUMPIFZERO macro can be written as

```
        .MACRO   JUMPIFZERO A,TARGET,?X
        TSTL     A                        ; is A 0?
        BNEQ     X                        ; continue if not
        JMP      TARGET                   ; else jump to target
X:
        .ENDM    JUMPIFZERO
```

Placing a question mark (?) in front of a formal argument name specifies a created local label. When the macro is expanded, the assembler creates a new local label if the corresponding actual argument is blank. If the corresponding actual argument is specified, the assembler substitutes the actual argument for the formal argument. If JUMPIFZERO is invoked twice,

```
JUMPIFZERO        FIRST,HERE
JUMPIFZERO        SECOND,THERE
```

the resulting code is

```
        TSTL     FIRST
        BNEQ     30000$
        JMP      HERE
30000$:
        TSTL     SECOND
        BNEQ     30001$
        JMP      THERE
30001$:
```

Macro Calls within Macro Definitions

To build more complex macros, it is often convenient to use one macro within the definition of another. In other words, if a macro has been defined previously, it can be called by another macro as if it were part of the basic instruction set. Consider the simple macros to push and pop quadwords:

```
.MACRO   PUSHQ   A              .MACRO   POPQ   A
MOVQ     A,-(SP)                MOVQ     (SP)+,A
.ENDM    PUSHQ                  .ENDM    POPQ
```

These macros can now be used to write a more complex macro that allows the contents of two quadwords to be exchanged:

```
.MACRO   SWAPQ   A,B
PUSHQ    A
MOVQ     B,A
POPQ     B
.ENDM    SWAPQ
```

An interesting generalization of this "complex" macro would be to allow it to work for either longwords or quadwords. PUSHL and POPL instructions already exist in the basic VAX instruction repertoire (POPL is actually an assembler-defined macro). Having defined PUSHQ and POPQ, it is a simple matter to modify the macro definition so that one of the arguments is the data type. We do so by using argument concatenation. That is, we form the operation name by combining the string PUSH with the value of a parameter containing the type indicator L or Q. This operation of constructing a single string from two strings is concatenation.

Argument Concatenation

The argument-concatenation operator, the apostrophe ('), concatenates a macro argument with some constant text. Apostrophes can precede or follow a formal argument name in the macro source. If a formal argument name in the macro definition is preceded (or followed) by an apostrophe ('), the text before (or after) the apostrophe is concatenated with the actual argument when the macro is expanded. The apostrophe itself does not appear in the macro expansion.

Turning to the SWAP macro, we generalize it by including the TYPE formal argument:

```
.MACRO SWAP      A,B,TYPE
PUSH'TYPE        A
MOV'TYPE         B,A
POP'TYPE         B
.ENDM            SWAP
```

This macro exchanges two longword or quadword arguments, using the stack for temporary storage. Coding the two lines

```
SWAP     X,Y,L
SWAP     R,S,Q
```

expands into the instructions

```
PUSHL    X
MOVL     Y,X
POPL     Y
PUSHQ    R
MOVQ     S,R
POPQ     S
```

Repeat Blocks

A programmer occasionally needs to create a table of values. Although every line could be typed individually, it is far easier to write a macro to generate the entire table. The repeat-block directive, specified by the .REPT and .ENDR pseudo-operations, provides the necessary function.

For example, to build a table of ten entries, each entry containing the integer five, we can write

```
.REPT   10
.BYTE   5
.ENDR
```

A more interesting example consists of generating ten entries containing the integers 1 through 10, each of which is labelled uniquely (for example, L1 to L10). To do this, we must pass numeric values as arguments.

When a symbol is specified as an actual argument in a macro, the name of the symbol (the character string), not its value, is passed to the macro. It is possible, however, to pass a value provided that a backslash (\) precedes the symbol name. The macro assembler then passes the decimal value of the symbol.

To generate the 1 through 10 list, we first create the TABLE macro, which generates the label and storage for each integer:

```
        .MACRO   TABLE    VALUE
L'VALUE:
        .BYTE    VALUE
        .ENDM    TABLE
```

To generate the ten-element labelled storage, the TABLE macro is included in the following REPEAT block:

```
COUNT=1
    .REPT   10
    TABLE   \COUNT
COUNT=COUNT+1
    .ENDR
```

The symbol COUNT is used within the assembler REPEAT loop to generate the integers from 1 through 10.

Of more general purpose use is the indefinite repeat block. Indefinite repeat allows a list of arguments to be specified. The block is repeated once for each argument in the list. The general format is

```
.IRP    symbol,<argument list>
 .
 .
 .
.ENDR
```

Each time the block is repeated, *symbol* is replaced by successive actual arguments. The actual argument list must be enclosed in angle brackets (<>) and separated by commas.

For example, the following indefinite repeat block pushes a number of longwords onto the stack:

```
.IRP    ITEM,<VALUE,R0,FROG,SQUAREROOT>
PUSHL   ITEM
.ENDR
```

The assembler expands this repeat loop as

```
PUSHL   VALUE
PUSHL   R0
PUSHL   FROG
PUSHL   SQUAREROOT
```

A more sophisticated example, in which the list is passed as an argument to a macro, occurs in generating a Case statement. The CASE macro automatically generates the Case table from a list of branch destinations and calculates the index limit. This macro can be coded as

```
.MACRO  CASE    SOURCE,DISPLIST,TYPE=B,BASE=#0,?TABLE,?ENDTABLE
CASE'TYPE       SOURCE,BASE,#<<ENDTABLE-TABLE>/2>-1
TABLE:
        .IRP    DESTINATION,<DISPLIST>
        .WORD   DESTINATION-TABLE
        .ENDR
ENDTABLE:
        .ENDM   CASE
```

The CASE macro uses several of the techniques already described, namely,

- concatenation to form either a CASEB, CASEW, or CASEL instruction

- use of defaults, so that the default instruction is CASEB (that is, TYPE=B) and the default base is 0

- computation of the expression

  #<<ENDTABLE-TABLE>/2>-1,

  producing the limit operand based on the number of elements in DISPLIST

- use of the indefinite repeat to produce the table of offsets following the Case instruction

- use of created local labels

  For example, the statements

```
                CASE      APPLE,<A,B,C>,TYPE=W
                            .
                            .
                            .
      A:        MOVL      TYPE1,R0
                BRB       HERE
      B:        MOVL      TYPE2,R0
                BRB       HERE
      C:        MOVL      TYPE3,R0
      HERE:       .
                  .
                  .
```

cause the following code to be generated:

```
                CASEW     APPLE,#0,#<<30001$-30000$>/2>-1
      30000$:
                .WORD     A-30000$
                .WORD     B-30000$
                .WORD     C-30000$
      30001$:
                  .
                  .
                  .
      A:        MOVL      TYPE1,R0
                BRB       HERE
      B:        MOVL      TYPE2,R0
                BRB       HERE
      C:        MOVL      TYPE3,R0
      HERE:       .
                  .
                  .
```

Conditional Assembly

A final example of controlling the assembly process involves conditional assembly. Although not strictly a function of a macro assembler, conditional directives are usually used within macro definitions.

The value of conditional code lies in its use in the modification and, hence, "customization" of the assembly code generated. Different final code can be produced, depending on symbol values or environment conditions in the program. For example, some early versions of the PDP-11 did not have hardware Multiply and Divide instructions. Conditional assembly was often used to generate either Multiply and Divide instructions or calls to routines to simulate these instructions, depending on a symbol in the program specifying the machine version.

Conditional assembly should be used with caution. Many programs with large amounts of conditional assembly are never fully debugged, because so many possible versions can be generated.

The format for the conditional assembly block directive is

```
.IF      condition argument(s)
  .
  . <conditional statements>
  .
.ENDC
```

If the specified condition is met, the assembler generates statements contained within the block. If the condition is not met, the statements are not generated. The condition codes are shown in Table 6.1.

The blank and identical tests can be used only within the body of a macro. All others can be used anywhere within the assembly program. There are other forms of conditional code, but we will not examine them here.

As an example of the use of conditional assembly, the following macro implements a general procedure call. Arguments to the macro consist of the procedure to call and as many as ten longword parameters for the procedure. The parameters are pushed onto the stack in reverse order. Since the macro can have a variable number of arguments, the not-blank operator (NB) is used to avoid pushing arguments that are not specified.

```
.MACRO CALL      ROUTINE,P1,P2,P3,P4,P5,P6,P7,P8,P9,P10
ARGCOUNT=0                         ; no arguments pushed yet
.IRP    NEXTARG,<P10,P9,P8,P7,P6,P5,P4,P3,P2,P1>
.IF NB  NEXTARG                    ; if argument is there, then
PUSHL   NEXTARG                    ; ...push longword argument
ARGCOUNT=ARGCOUNT+1                ; count argument pushed
.ENDC                              ; end of conditional
.ENDR                              ; end of indefinite repeat
CALLS   #ARGCOUNT,ROUTINE          ; call ROUTINE
.ENDM   CALL                       ; end of MACRO
```

The symbol ARGCOUNT keeps track of the number of arguments pushed for the CALLS instruction. Arguments are checked in reverse order by the .IRP loop and pushed if they are supplied. For example, the statement

```
CALL    FIZZ,R0,ARRAY2[R3],PEANUT,#5,@INDR
```

generates the following code sequence:

```
PUSHL   @INDR            ; push longword argument
PUSHL   #5               ; push longword argument
PUSHL   PEANUT           ; push longword argument
PUSHL   ARRAY2[R3]       ; push longword argument
PUSHL   R0               ; push longword argument
CALLS   #ARGCOUNT,FIZZ   ; call FIZZ
```

When the CALLS is assembled, the symbol ARGCOUNT will have the value 5.

Table 6.1   Condition Tests for Conditional Assembly Directives

Condition Tests*

Positive	Complement	Format	Condition that Assembles Block
EQ	NE	.IF EQ expression	Expression is equal to 0 (or not equal to 0).
GT	LE	.IF GT expression	Expression is greater than 0 (or less than or equal to 0).
LT	GE	.IF LT expression	0 Expression is less than (or greater than or equal to 0).
DF	NDF	.IF DF symbol	Symbol is defined (or not).
B	NB	.IF B macro_argument	Argument is blank (or not).
IDN	DIF	.IF IDN argument 1, argument 2	Arguments are identical (or different).

*VAX assembly language also allows long forms for these condition tests such as EQUAL for EQ and NOT_BLANK for NB.

Summary

This chapter covered many important concepts in program control. We saw how the Loop and Case instructions provide capabilities similar to those available with high-level languages. We also examined the procedure-calling mechanisms. Although somewhat complex, the existence of these mechanisms helps achieve better program structuring. Even more important, the implementation of a procedure call in the architecture creates a standard for VAX language compilers. Therefore, a program can call procedures written in several different languages.

We also examined the stack and the useful properties that come with using a stack for linkage. The next chapter examines other data structures and their manipulation by the VAX.

Exercises

1. Recode the Jump table problem of Figure 6.1 to use the Case statement.

2. Rewrite the sort example in Figure 6.3 to arrange the list in decreasing order.

3. Rewrite the sort example in Figure 6.3, but this time replace the AOB instructions with SOB instructions. Next, replace the AOB instructions with ACB instructions.

4. The VAX macro routine in Figure 6.3 to sort numbers is not equivalent to the Pascal bubble sort. How can the macro routine be rewritten to be equivalent?

5. Code a routine to sum all the numbers between 0 and 100 that are divisible by three.

6. Suppose that the code segment shown in Figure 6.6 to convert an integer to ASCII begins with (R2)=1578. Show the state of the stack at each execution of the statements at 10$ and 30$.

7. Code a routine to convert a numeric ASCII string to binary. Assume that the routine receives three input parameters: the number of digits in the string, the address of the string, and the address of a longword in which to return the binary value. For example, the calling sequence could be as follows:

```
SIZE:    .LONG   3               ; number of digits in string
STRING:  .ASCII  /154/           ; the string to be converted
VALUE:   .BLKL   1               ; place to hold returned value
         .
         .
         .
         PUSHAL  VALUE           ; address of returned value
         PUSHAB  STRING          ; address of string
         PUSHL   SIZE            ; size of string
         CALLS   #3,CVT_TO_BINARY ; call convert procedure
```

8. For the previous problem (conversion to binary routine), show what the stack looks like after the procedure has been called by a CALLS instruction. Show what the stack looks like after the procedure has been called by a CALLG instruction.

9. Suppose we have an application that requires the use of two stacks that grow at different rates. To make the maximum use of our memory of size N longwords, we want to implement both stacks so that if one has less than $N/2$ elements, the other can have more than $N/2$ elements. The stacks can be built so that they grow from opposite ends of the memory block toward the middle, as shown in Figure 6.15.

Write routines PUSHA, POPA, PUSHB, and POPB to push and pop longwords from the stacks A and B. Also write a routine INITSTACKS to initialize the stack pointers. Assume the stacks use the array at address STACK that contains N longwords.

10. Write the procedure call for the procedure in Figure 6.6. Show what the call frame would look like after the procedure is invoked.

Figure 6.15 *Data instructions for problem 9*

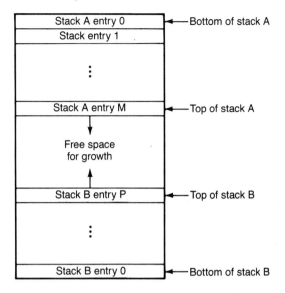

11. What is the advantage of reserving one register as a frame pointer? What is the advantage of a reserved argument pointer? Suppose we didn't have a reserved frame pointer and argument pointer. What difference would it make in our code?

12. What are the advantages and disadvantages of using the CALL instruction instead of the BSB instruction? When would you use one over the other?

13. Write a multiply subroutine that computes the product of two 32-bit values held in registers R0 and R1. The 64-bit result should be left in R2 and R3.

14. Show the contents of the stack at each execution of the statement at NFACT for both recursive factorial routines in Figure 6.13. Assume that the value of N is 4.

15. What is the difference between a macro and a subroutine?

16. Code a macro to initialize a table of longwords to the values 0 through 9. Modify the macro to accept the table size, lower bound, and upper bound as parameters.

17. Write a macro to copy N words from the array A to the array B (for example, COPY A,B,N). Next write a macro using COPY that switches the contents of the arrays A and B using the stack (for example, SWITCH A,B,N).

7

More VAX Data Types

Previous chapters have presented many of the VAX information units and data types. This chapter takes a closer look at some of those data types and the instructions that manipulate them. In particular, it examines single-bit and bit-field instructions, string instructions, floating-point instructions, and instructions to convert between data types.

Bits and Bit Fields

Bit-manipulation instructions were more meaningful in earlier mini-computers, in which memory size and instruction sets were limited. Under these conditions, it was often necessary to manipulate individual bits within a word or a byte (hence the designation of such a programmer as a "bit hacker") to conserve space or to mask out individual bytes within a word for computers without byte-manipulation instructions. With the 32-bit address space of the VAX and the large primary memories present on modern systems, programmers do not have to be as concerned with bit efficiency. However, because of the VAX I/O architecture inherited from the PDP−11, these instructions are still needed to test and set individual bits contained within I/O device registers.

Bit-manipulation instructions can be divided into three classes. The first includes instructions that perform logical functions on bits contained within a byte, a word, or a longword. The second class covers instructions that test a single bit within a longword to determine if a branch is to be taken. The third class consists of instructions that deal with arbitrary bit strings.

Logical Bit Instructions

Bit Set (BIS), Bit Clear (BIC), Bit Test (BIT), and EXCLUSIVE OR (XOR) are the generic set of logical operations that manipulate byte, word, and longword data. These instructions are defined in Table 7.1.

When using these instructions, we usually think of the first operand as being a mask whose bits are applied to the second operand according to the instruction. A *mask* is a sequence of bits used in a logical operation to test, set, or clear the corresponding bits of an operand in a bit-manipulation instruction. For example, the instruction

Table 7.1   VAX Logical Bit Instructions

Operation	Mnemonic	Data Types	Number of Operands
Bit Set (logical OR). In the two-operand form, set all bits in the second operand corresponding to bits set in the first operand. In the three-operand form, the the result is written to the third operand.	BIS	B,W,L	2,3
Bit Clear. Clear all bits in the second operand corresponding to bits set in the first operand.	BIC	B,W,L	2,3
Bit Test. Test the condition of the bits in the second operand to determine if they correspond to the bits set in the first operand. The destination is not affected, but the condition codes are set based on the logical AND of the mask and second operand.	BIT	B,W,L	2
EXCLUSIVE OR. Form the EXCLUSIVE OR of the two operands.	XOR	B,W,L	2,3

```
BICB     #3,R4
```

or alternatively

```
BICB     #^B00000011,R4
```

masks, or clears, bits 0 and 1 in R4. These are the bits set in the mask operand. Other bits in the destination are unaffected. The Bit Set instruction

```
BISB     #3,R4
```

sets bits 0 and 1 in R4 to 1. Such instructions are frequently used to zero part of an integer. One way to zero the high-order 16 bits of R1 would be with the instruction

```
BICL     #^XFFFF0000,R1
```

which uses a mask with the upper 16 bits set.

The Bit Test instruction tests whether any of the bits set in the mask are also set in the destination operand. Neither operand is changed, but the condition codes are set based on the result of the logical AND of the two operands. As an example, suppose we want to test whether all the odd-numbered bits in the byte MY_BITS are zero. This could be done with the sequence

```
BITB    #^B01010101,MY_BITS
BEQL    ALL_ZERO
```

If any of the odd-numbered bits in MY_BITS are set, the result of the logical AND will be nonzero, the Z condition code will be cleared, and the branch instruction will fail. If all the odd-numbered bits are zero, the result of the BITB will be zero, the Z condition code will be set, and the branch will succeed. In either case, MY_BITS will remain unchanged.

It is worth noting that the VAX does not have a logical AND instruction. If we want to form the logical AND of two longwords, we would have to do it with a multiinstruction sequence, for example,

```
MCOML   LONG1,R0   ; form complement mask
BICL    R0,LONG2   ; "AND" them together
```

Here, the Move Complement Longword (MCOML) instruction builds a mask in R0 of the one's complement of the bits in LONG1. Those bits are then used as a mask in the Bit Clear Longword instruction. Thus, to perform the logical AND, we are building a mask from LONG1 that allows us to turn off (zero) all bits in LONG2 corresponding to zero bits in LONG1.

Single-Bit Instructions

The VAX has a number of instructions that test the condition of one bit or that test and modify the bit in a single operation. As we will see, this second form is particularly useful for synchronizing several processes. Both types of instructions are listed in Table 7.2.

A special case of the Bit Test instructions is covered by the Branch on Low bit (BLB) pair of instructions. BLBC and BLBS test the least significant bit, bit 0, of a longword and branch if it is clear or set, respectively. Together with the TSTL instruction, BLBC and BLBS enable you to test either the most significant bit (MSB) or the least significant bit (LSB) of any longword. These instructions were provided specifically for examining values returned from subroutines. In the VAX/VMS operating system, for example, all system routines return a code in R0 that indicates the final status of the routine. The values of these codes are defined such that all error codes are even (bit 0 is 0) and all success codes are odd (bit 0 is 1). You can easily test for the success or failure of a routine with the BLBC and BLBS instructions.

The Branch on Bit instructions and the Branch on Bit and Modify instructions allow you to test and set a bit within an arbitrary bit field. In each case, the single bit specified by the position and base operands is

Table 7.2   *VAX Single-Bit Instructions*

Operation	Mnemonic	Operands
Branch if Low Bit Clear	BLBC	source,branch_destination
Branch if Low Bit Set	BLBS	source,branch_destination
Branch if Bit Set	BBS	position,base,branch_destination
Branch if Bit Clear	BBC	position,base,branch_destination
Branch if Bit Set and Set Bit	BBSS	position,base,branch_destination
Branch if Bit Set and Clear Bit	BSC	position,base,branch_destination
Branch if Bit Clear and Set Bit	BBCS	position,base,branch_destination
Branch if Bit Clear and Clear Bit	BBCC	position,base,branch_destination
Branch if Bit Set and Set Interlocked	BBSSI	position,base,branch_destination
Branch if Bit Clear and Clear Interlocked	BBCCI	position,base,branch_destination

tested. If it is in the state tested for, a branch is taken to the destination. If the instruction so specifies, the tested field is set or cleared regardless of the initial state of the bit. The bit is located by specifying the address of a byte (base operand) and the offset to the bit to be tested (position operand). For example, the following two sequences are equivalent:

```
BBC    #3,R0,NOTSET        BITB   #8,R0
                           BEQL   NOTSET
```

Both test whether the fourth bit in R0 (bit number 3) is zero and branch if so. Note that the BBC instruction takes a bit position while the BITB instruction takes a mask.

The last two instructions included in Table 7.2, BBSSI and BBCCI, are identical to BBSS and BBCC except that the memory location under examination is *interlocked*. These instructions are provided so that if more than one VAX processor or I/O device are cooperatively accessing memory, only one at a time will be able to test and modify the given bit.

Designers of operating systems will recognize these instructions as useful for implementing Dijkstra's *P* and *V* operations. For those unfamiliar with those operations, a simple example demonstrates how two bit fields can be used to coordinate or synchronize two processes within a computer.

Suppose two processes share a resource that only one process can access at a time. The Bit Test and Set Interlocked instructions can be used to ensure unique access. First, we define a flag bit in memory shared between the processes. When this flag is set, the resource is free. Before accessing the shared resource, each process tests the bit and branches to its code if the flag is set. If the flag is not set, the process continues to loop until the bit becomes set. When a process finds the bit set, it clears the bit until it is finished with the resource. This coordination is coded as follows:

```
FLAGS:  .LONG 1                 ; flag initially 1 (free)
        .
        .
        .
;
; Code for first process
;


;
; Start of unique access code for first process
;
WAIT1:  BBCCI   #0,FLAGS,WAIT1  ; loop until bit is set
                                .
GO_ON1:                         .
        <access shared resource>
                                .
        BISL    #1,FLAGS        ; restore flag bit
                                .   ; continue processing
                                .
;
; Code for second process
;


;
; Start of unique access code for second process
;
WAIT2:  BBCCI   #0,FLAGS,WAIT2  ; loop until bit is set
                                .
GO_ON2:                         .
        <access shared resource>
                                .
        BISL    #1,FLAGS        ; restore flag bit
                                .   ; continue processing
                                .
                                .
```

Both processes wait for the flag bit. The first process to find the flag bit set is allowed to fall into its main body of code. The other process continues to clear the already clear flag bit until it is (re)set to 1. Of course, a coordination mechanism like this should be used only when the code section to be used exclusively is extremely short. Typically, synchronization is accomplished through operating system calls that queue a waiting process until the unavailable resource becomes available.

It is important to note that on all VAX single-bit and variable-length bit-field instructions, the bit-position operand is interpreted as a signed longword offset from the base address. That is, the selected bit can be in the range of -2^{31} to $2^{31}-1$ bits from the base address. Therefore, the upper 29 bits of the position operand contain a signed byte offset from the base address to the byte containing the selected bit. The low three bits of the position operand contain the bit number within the selected byte.

A good demonstration of the use of this feature is shown in the following Sieve of Eratosthenes program for producing prime numbers. The program uses a string of N bits to represent the integers from 0 through $N-1$, where the bit position of each bit represents an integer (for example, bit 6 in the string represents integer 6). The program begins with the prime number 2 and marks off all multiples of 2 by setting the bits whose position number is a multiple of 2. These cannot be prime, because they are evenly divisible by 2. The program then searches for the next zero bit in the string. This bit represents a prime number since it is not a multiple of any lower number. As each prime is found, all of its multiples are marked off, and a search is made for the next zero bit. For writing the primes, we use the OUTASC procedure shown previously in Figure 6.11.

```
;
; Sieve of Eratosthenes routine for producing prime numbers.
;

        SIEVESIZE = 10000            ; find all primes < 10000
SIEVE:  .BLKB   SIEVESIZE/8          ; produce initial table of
                                     ; ...SIEVESIZE bits (zeroed)
        .ENTRY  PRIMES,^M<R2,R3>     ; routine entry point
        MOVL    #2,R2               ; start with prime 2
10$:    PUSHL   R2                  ; output the primes
        CALLS   #1,OUTASC           ; write it
        MOVL    R2,R3               ; use R3 to form multiples

;
; Set all bits that are multiples of the prime just found.
;

20$:    BBCS    R3,SIEVE,30$         ; eliminate next multiple
30$:    ACBL    #SIEVESIZE-1,R2,R3,20$ ; form next multiple
;
; Search for the next zero bit in the string.
;

40$:    BBC     R2,SIEVE,10$         ; check for next prime
        AOBLSS  #SIEVESIZE,R2,40$    ; continue looking for bit
        RET                          ; return to caller
```

Having considered instructions operating on single bits, we next consider instructions that operate on bit strings.

Variable-Length Bit Fields

The VAX also has instructions to extract, insert, and compare bit strings up to 32 bits long. The bit string is described by three arguments: its base address, the position of the first byte relative to the base, and the size in bits of the string. When extracting a bit field, the bit string, specified by the position, size, and base operands, is moved right-justified into the longword destination operand. The upper bits of the destination can be sign-extended from the field or zeroed, depending on the instruction. When inserting a field, the low-order "size" bits of the source are moved to the bit field specified by the base and position operands. The bit field instructions are listed in Table 7.3.

Table 7.3   VAX Bit Field Instructions

Operation	Mnemonic	Operands
Extract Field. Move the specified field into the destination, right-justified and sign-extended to 32 bits.	EXTV	position,size,base, destination
Extract Zero-Extended Field. Move the specified field into the destination, zero-extended to 32 bits.	EXTZV	position,size,base, destination
Compare Field. Compare the sign-extended field with the source operand, setting the condition codes.	CMPV	position,size,base, source
Compare Zero-Extended Field. Compare the zero-extended field to the source operand, setting condition codes.	CMPZV	position,size,base, source
Insert Field. The size operand specifies the number of low-order bits to be moved from the source to the field described by position, size, and base.	INSV	source,position,size, base
Find First Set. Locates the first 1 bit in the specified field.	FFS	position,size,base, findposition
Find First Clear. Locates the first zero bit in the specified field. If a zero bit is found, findposition is replaced by the position of the bit and the Z condition code is cleared. Otherwise, Z is set and findposition is replaced by the position (relative to the base) of the bit one position past the specified field.	FFC	position,size,base, findposition

The following example shows the use of the Extract Zero-Extended (EXTZV) instruction to print the ASCII hexadecimal value of a 32-bit longword. The field instruction is used within a loop to extract the eight 4-bit digits from left to right. We assume that there is a procedure OUTCHAR that prints a single ASCII digit. On each execution of the EXTZV, a 4-bit field is extracted from R0 and placed, right-justified and zero-extended, into R2. R1 specifies the starting bit position for the string.

```
;
; Print hexadecimal ASCII representation of a longword.
;
;     R0 - contains longword to be evaluated
;     R1 - position of the 4-bit field to be extracted
;

HEXDIGITS:                              ; ASCII names for hex digits
      .ASCII   /0123456789ABCDEF/
         .
         .
         .
PRINTHEX:
      MOVL     NUMBER,R0        ; get binary number to output
      MOVL     #<<4*8>-4>,R1    ; begin with last hex digit
10$:  EXTZV    R1,#4,R0,R2      ; R2 <- next binary digit
      MOVZBL   HEXDIGITS[R2],-(SP) ; push the ASCII repr.
      CALLS    #1,OUTCHAR       ; print the digit
      ACBL     #0,#-4,R1,10$    ; continue left to right
```

To reverse this process, we can use the Insert Field (INSV) instruction. The following code assumes that we have in HEX_ASCII the 8-character ASCII hexadecimal representation of a 32-bit value, including leading zeros. This instruction sequence takes the ASCII digits and reproduces the 32-bit binary value in R0. It relies on the fact that the ASCII values for the decimal digits are close to the uppercase letters in the ASCII sequence.

```
;
; Produce binary value from 8-character ASCII Hexadecimal
; string
;
HEX_ASCII:
      .BLKB    8                   ; space for ASCII Hex digits
;
; The following table has the binary values for the 16 hex
; digits in their ASCII sequence.  The 7 blanks are for the 7
; characters between "9" and "A" in the ASCII code.
;
HEXVALUES:
      .BYTE    0,1,2,3,4,5,6,7,8,9
      .BLKB    7
      .BYTE    10,11,12,13,14,15
```

```
        .
        .
        .
GETBINARY:
        MOVL    #<<4*8>-4>,R1    ; begin with last hex digit
        MOVAB   HEX_ASCII,R2     ; load address of ASCII string
        CLRL    R3               ; ensure upper part of R3 is zero
10$:    SUBB3   #^A/0/,(R2)+,R3  ; get distance from ASCII "0"
        MOVZBL  HEXVALUES[R3],R3; get digit's binary value
        INSV    R3,R1,#4,R0      ; insert proper R0 bits
        ACBL    #0,#-4,R1,10$    ; continue left to right
```

The Find First Set and Find First Clear bit instructions are included in Table 7.2 because they also deal with bit fields. However, these instructions are used to locate the first 0 or 1 bit in a string of length 0 to 32 bits. The instructions return the position of the first bit found in the specified state and clear the Z condition code. If a bit is not found in the specified state, the instructions return the position of the bit following the field and set the Z condition code. For example, the instruction

```
    FFS     #0,#32,ENTRY,R0
```

will cause R0 and Z to be set to the following values, given the specified decimal contents of ENTRY:

Contents of ENTRY	R0	Z
1	0	0
4	2	0
8	3	0
9	0	0
0	32	1

As noted in the previous section, the starting-position argument can be greater than 32 bits from the base address. This is useful for searching long bit strings. The string can be searched 32 bits at a time; if the specified bit is not found, the findposition argument will contain the position of the next 32-bit field to search. We could have used this feature in the Sieve of Eratosthenes. At the end of the procedure, a Branch on Bit Clear instruction was used within a loop to locate the next zero bit.

```
40$:    BBC     R0,SIEVE,10$       ; check for next prime
        AOBLSS  #SIEVESIZE,R0,40$  ; continue looking for bit
```

Using the Find First Clear instruction, we could rewrite this loop to scan 32 bits at a time. Following each FFC instruction, we check the Z bit to see if we should scan the next 32 bits or process the found bit. The code is more complicated because we must now check explicitly to see if R0 is out of range. Furthermore, we must make sure that the loop at 40$ does not go out of bounds; we do this by placing a longword of ones following SIEVE.

```
;
; Sieve of Eratosthenes routine for producing prime numbers.
;

            SIEVESIZE = 10000        ; find all primes < 10000
SIEVE:  .BLKB   SIEVESIZE/8          ; produce initial table of
                                     ; ...SIEVESIZE bits (zeroed)
        .LONG   ^XFFFFFFFF           ; ensure search terminates

        .ENTRY  PRIMES,^M<>          ; routine entry point
        MOVL    #2,R0               ; start with prime 2
10$:    PUSHL   R0                  ; output the primes
        CALLS   #1,OUTASC           ; write it
        MOVL    R0,R1               ; use R1 to form multiples

; Set all bits that are multiples of the prime just found.

20$:    BBCS    R1,SIEVE,30$        ; eliminate next multiple
30$:    ACBL    #SIEVESIZE-1,R0,R1,20$ ; form next multiple

; Search for the next zero bit in the string.

40$:    FFC     R0,#32,SIEVE,R0     ; look for next zero bit
        BEQL    40$                 ; not found, go back again
        CMPL    R0,#SIEVESIZE       ; are we done?
        BLSS    10$                 ; no, go process this bit
        RET                         ; else exit
```

Converting Integer Data Types

It is often necessary to convert an item of one data type to another, whether it is to be stored in a field of a different size, loaded into a register, or used in an arithmetic operation. The VAX makes data conversion simple with two instructions, Convert and Move Zero-Extended.

The Convert instructions allow us to move a signed byte, word, or longword datum to a field of a different size. The six signed-integer Convert instructions are shown in Table 7.4.

When a shorter data type is converted to a longer data type, a sign extension is performed. That is, the high-order bit, which is the sign bit, is duplicated in the high-order bits of the longer destination, and the low-order bits are copied. Consider the following byte-to-word conversion:

```
A:      .BYTE   ^B11010011          ; byte of binary data
B:      .WORD   0                   ; word to receive
                                    ; sign-extended byte
        CVTBW   A,B                 ; extend byte to word
```

Table 7.4 VAX Integer Convert Instructions

Operation	Mnemonic	Operands
Convert Byte to Word	CVTBW	byte_datum, word_datum
Convert Byte to Longword	CVTBL	byte_datum, longword_datum
Convert Word to Byte	CVTWB	word_datum, byte_datum
Convert Word to Longword	CVTWL	word_datum, longword_datum
Convert Longword to Byte	CVTLB	longword_datum, byte_datum
Convert Longword to Word	CVTLW	longword_datum, word_datum

Following execution of the Convert instruction, the contents of A and B would be

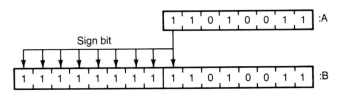

Notice that the low-order seven bits of byte A, the magnitude, have been copied directly into the low-order seven bits of word B. The sign bit of byte A has been extended left to fill the high byte of word B.

On a conversion from a longer to a shorter data type, the larger number is *truncated* to fit in the smaller datum. Truncation is illustrated in the following conversion:

```
A:    .BYTE   0                       ; byte to receive truncated
                                      ; ...word
B:    .WORD   ^B1111111111001111      ; binary word
      .
      .
      CVTWB   B,A                     ; convert word to byte
```

Following this instruction, the contents of A and B are

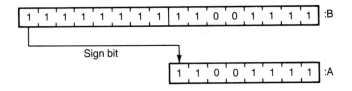

In this case, only the least significant eight bits of B are preserved in A.

If the upper byte was not all ones as shown, integer overflow would occur. In using the convert instruction, you must be careful when the destination field is smaller than the source field. Integer overflow will occur unless *all* the upper bits of the source (the bits truncated) are the same as the resulting sign bit of the destination field.

A frequent use of these instructions, particularly smaller-to-larger conversions, is movement of a byte or word datum to a register in order to perform arithmetic. If the datum is moved to the register with a Move instruction, the high-order bits of the register retain their old values.

To extend an unsigned data type, there are three Move Zero-Extended instructions that zero-extend bytes to words (MOVZBW), bytes to long-words (MOVZBL), and words to longwords (MOVZWL). These are also frequently used to move a short datum to a register, where we prefer the high-order bits of the register to be zeroed first. If we declare

```
A:      .BYTE   5                ; the data byte
```

then instead of coding

```
        CLRL    R0               ; clear register
        MOVB    A,R0             ; move byte to R0<7:0>
```

we can write

```
        MOVZBL  A,R0             ; move zero-extend
                                 ; ...byte to register
```

The context of the operand is always determined by its data type. Thus, in the instruction Move Zero-Extended Byte to Longword (MOVZBL), the first operand has byte context and the second has longword context. Following the execution of the instruction

```
MOVZBL  (R0)+,(R1)+
```

the value of R0 is incremented by 1, while R1 is incremented by 4.

The Move Zero-Extended instructions can also be used to save space, although this is a minor issue. The instructions

```
MOVL    #20,R0           MOVZBL  #20,R0
```

are equivalent: both move the value 20 decimal into R0, and both take 3 bytes to encode because the literal 20 can be encoded as a short literal. On the other hand, if we had written

```
MOVL    #200,R0          MOVZBL  #200,R0
```

then, although the effects of the operation are identical, the MOVZBL instruction is shorter to encode. The reason is that 200 is too large for a short literal but small enough to be represented in a byte. Both instructions will encode the 200 as an immediate operand, but because of the different *contexts* of the first operand, MOVL will store 200 as a 32-bit literal and MOVZBL will store it as an 8-bit literal.

Character Strings

As we have seen, bytes can be used to hold 256 different numerical values (00 to FF hex). We can assign representations to these numbers to allow us to manipulate characters, decimal numbers, special symbols, and so on. Although we could choose any representation we like for the characters, we use the ASCII code to allow the connection of computers and peripherals made by different manufacturers.

On some machines that are not byte addressable, handling characters is a complex task because several characters can be packed into the smallest unit. On the VAX, character handling is aided by the fact that each character is uniquely addressable and by the existence of a full set of instructions that manipulate strings of characters. These instructions move, compare, and search strings of characters up to 65,535 (64K) bytes in length. In descriptions of these instructions, the terms "byte" and "character" are equivalent because the instructions deal with strings of bytes independent of the representations used. However, the instructions are called *character string* instructions because they are usually used with character text strings.

A character string on the VAX is specified by the string length in bytes (the length is contained in a word, hence the 64K maximum string length) and the address of the first character of the string. The string instructions use from two to six of the general registers, R0 through R5, to hold temporary values and to return updated string pointers. In other words, regardless of what registers are specified as operands to the instructions, some of the low-numbered registers will be modified to contain values returned by the instructions. These are the first instructions we have seen that have such a side effect. It is important to set up the registers carefully when using string instructions or to save and restore low-numbered registers that contain useful information. Therefore, the PUSHR and POPR instructions can be used effectively to preserve registers that are modified by the character string instructions.

As an example, look at the string instruction MOVC3. This instruction moves a byte string from one location to another, that is, it copies a block of memory. The three operands are the length of the string to be moved, the address of the source string to move, and the address of the destination to receive the string. Thus, the format of the instruction is

```
MOVC3   length,srcaddress,dstaddress
```

Following the execution of MOVC3, the registers have the following values:

- R0, R2, R4, and R5 = 0

- R1 = the address one byte beyond the source string

- R3 = the address one byte beyond the destination string

Consider the following example, in which there are three message strings, including one that will be moved to the block of memory at OUTBUFFER depending on the value contained in R6. Each of the three strings is stored as a counted ASCII (.ASCIC) string; in other words, the first byte contains the length of the string, not including the count byte. If R6 contains a zero, the first message will be moved; if it contains a one, the second message will be moved; and so on.

```
          MAXMSG = 2                          ; maximum message number
MSGADDRS:                                     ; addresses of the messages
          .ADDRESS MSG1
          .ADDRESS MSG2
          .ADDRESS MSG3
MSG1:     .ASCIC   /THIS IS THE FIRST MESSAGE/
MSG2:     .ASCIC   /THIS IS THE SECOND MESSAGE/
MSG3:     .ASCIC   /THE THIRD MESSAGE IS HERE/
OUTBUFFER:                                    ; 100-byte output buffer
          .BLKB    100
            .
            .
            .
          CMPL     R6,#MAXMSG                  ; validate range of msg number
          BGTRU    ERROR                       ; error if too large
          MOVL     MSGADDRS[R6],R8             ; get address of ASCIC
                                               ; ...string to be moved
          MOVZBL   (R8)+,R7                    ; R7 <- length of string
                                               ; R8 now points to first char.
          MOVC3    R7,(R8),OUTBUFFER           ; move string to output buffer
            .
            .
            .
```

The MOVC5 instruction copies a block of memory in which the source and destination strings can differ in length. If the source is longer than the destination, only the number of characters specified by the destination length is copied (that is, the string is truncated). If the source is shorter than the destination, the remainder of the destination is filled with copies of a "fill" character specified as one of the operands. The format for MOVC5 is

```
MOVC5    srclength,srcaddress,fillchar,dstlength,dstaddress
```

Following MOVC5, the registers are the same as for MOVC3 except that R0 contains the number of characters not moved if the source was longer than the destination. In addition, the condition codes are set based on the comparison of the source length and the destination length. MOVC5 is the preferred way to fill a block of memory with any one character because a source length of zero causes the entire destination to be filled with the fill character. For instance, the instruction

```
MOVC5    #0,(R0),#0,#512,OUTBUF
```

causes the 512-byte buffer OUTBUF to be zeroed. Note that the source operand pointed to by R0 is never referenced; therefore, R0 need not contain a valid address.

Table 7.5 describes some of the other string instructions. More can be found in the *VAX Architecture Reference Manual*.

Table 7.5 VAX String Instructions

Operation	Mnemonic	Operands
Compare two strings. These instructions do a byte-by-byte comparison, setting the condition codes based on a comparison of the first bytes, if any, that do not match.	CMPC3 CMPC5	length,src1address, src2address src1length,srcaddress, fillchar, src2length, src2address
Locate a character in a given string. Following this instruction, R1 contains the address of the located character or one byte past the string if the character was not found. R0 contains the number of bytes left in the string.	LOCC	character,srclength, srcaddress
Skip over all consecutive occurrences of a character in a given string. This is like LOCC except the test is for inequality instead of equality. The registers are set in a manner similar to LOCC.	SKPC	character,srclength, srcaddress
Find a substring within a string. The string specified by src1length and src1address is searched for a substring matching the one specified by src2length and src2address. Following execution, if a match was found, R0 contains the number of bytes remaining in string one, including the substring; R1 contains the address of the located substring. On no match, R0 contains zero and R1 points one byte past string one.	MATCHC	srclength,src1address, src2length,src2address

As a final example, the routine in Figure 7.1 checks an input buffer to see whether it contains the name of a chess piece. Leading blanks are first removed from the input buffer, and the string is then checked against the names of chess pieces stored at NAMES. If a match is found, a variable is returned indicating which piece it was. On return, R0 indicates whether a match was found.

Figure 7.1   Subroutine to validate name of chess piece

```
        .SBTTL  VALIDATE – Validate Name of Chess Piece

;++
; FUNCTIONAL DESCRIPTION
;
;       This routine locates the next string in a buffer and checks to
;       see if it is the name of a chess piece.
;
; CALLING SEQUENCE
;
;       CALLS OR CALLG
;
; INPUT PARAMETERS:
;
;       BUFLEN(AP) – length of the buffer to be checked
;       BUFADR(AP) – address of the buffer
;       RETKEY(AP) – address of a longword to receive the piece number
;
;
; OUTPUT PARAMETERS:
;
;       RETKEY(AP) = if name is valid, address pointed to receives the
;                    piece number with the encoding
;                    0 = king, 1 = queen, 2 = bishop, 3 = knight,
;                    4 = rook, 5 = pawn
;
; RETURN VALUE:
;
;       R0 = 0 if no match, 1 if valid name is found
;
;--


        BUFLEN = 4                      ; offset to length argument
        BUFADR = 8                      ; offset to address argument
        RETKEY = 12                     ; offset to return address


;
; List of counted string names for pieces.  Zero length terminates the
; list.
;

NAMES:
        .ASCIC /KING/
        .ASCIC /QUEEN/
        .ASCIC /BISHOP/
```

```
        .ASCIC /KNIGHT/
        .ASCIC /ROOK/
        .ASCIC /PAWN/
        .BYTE  0                        ; terminate list

        .ENTRY VALIDATE,^M<R2,R3,R4,R5,R6> ;entry, registers to save
        SKPC   #^A/ /,BUFLEN(AP),@BUFADR(AP)  ; skip leading
                                            ; ...blanks
        BEQL   30$                      ; exit if nothing there
        MOVQ   R0,R4                    ; save input length and
                                        ; ...address in R4 and R5
        CLRL   R6                       ; zero piece indicator
        MOVAL  NAMES,R1                 ; get address of piece list
10$:
        MOVZBL (R1)+,R0                 ; R0 <- length of piece name
                                        ; R1 <- address of first char.
        BEQL   30$                      ; exit if table is exhausted
        CMPC5  R0,(R1),#^A/ /,R4,(R5)   ; strings match?
        BEQL   20$                      ; exit if strings match
        ADDL   R0,R1                    ; form address of next ASCIC
                                        ; ...string to check
        INCL   R6                       ; note next piece number
        BRB    10$                      ; continue loop

;
; Piece was located, return success and piece number.
;

20$:

        MOVZBL #1,R0                    ; success return code
        MOVL   R6,@RETKEY(AP)           ; return piece number
        RET
;
; Valid name not found, return error code.
;

30$:
        CLRL   R0                       ; error code
        RET
```

Packed Decimal String Instructions

For some languages, such as COBOL, it is often more convenient to treat the computer as a decimal machine rather than a binary machine. Consequently, many machines have implemented decimal arithmetic as well as binary. The internal representation of a number for decimal arithmetic is the packed decimal string. This string is a contiguous sequence of 4-bit digits, each representing a decimal digit from 0 to 9, with the low digit representing the sign. A decimal string is described by its length in digits (not bytes) and the address of the low-order byte. The assembler directive .PACKED is used to store one packed decimal string of variable length up to 31 digits in multiple consecutive bytes.

Corresponding to the set of binary arithmetic instructions, the packed decimal instruction set includes Move Packed (MOVP), Compare Packed (CMPP), Add Packed (ADDP), Subtract Packed (SUBP), Multiply Packed (MULP), and Divide Packed (DIVP). The decimal string instructions always treat the decimal strings as integers, with the decimal point immediately to the right of the least significant digit of the string. If the result of a decimal instruction is to be stored in a string that is larger than the result, the most significant digits are filled with zeros. Thus, the only difference between these instructions and the binary arithmetic instructions is that a length operand is required, since packed decimal strings can be of varying length. The formats for these instructions are presented in Table 7.6.

The setting of the condition codes for packed decimal arithmetic is similar to that for binary arithmetic instructions, with decimal overflow resulting when the destination string is too short to contain all the nonzero digits of the result. If overflow occurs, the destination string is replaced by the correctly signed least significant digits of the result.

Table 7.6   VAX Packed Decimal String Instructions

Operation	Mnemonic	Operands
Move source string to destination.	MOVP	length,srcaddress,dstaddress
Compare source string to destination string.	CMPP	length,srcaddress,src2address
Add source string of length ADDLENGTH to destination string of length SUMLENGTH.	ADDP	addlength,addaddress,sumlength, sumaddress
Subtract source string from destination string.	SUBP	sublength,subaddress,diflength, difaddress
Multiply multiplier by multiplicand and place result in product.	MULP	mulrlength,mulraddress,muldlength, muldaddress,prodlength,prodaddress
Divide dividend by divisor and store result in quotient.	DIVP	divrlength,divraddress,divdlength, divdaddress,quolength,quoaddress
Convert packed decimal string to longword integer.	CVTPL	srclength,srcaddress,dstaddress
Convert longword integer to packed decimal.	CVTLP	srcaddress,dstlength,dstaddress

The VAX instruction set includes instructions for converting from packed decimal to other formats. Thus, the representation of a number can be chosen for a particular application and converted, as necessary, to a different internal representation for manipulation. In general, however, the decimal string instructions are used by language compilers for COBOL and other business languages and are rarely used at the assembly level.

Multiple-Precision Integer Arithmetic

Handling large numbers in earlier 16-bit minicomputers or microprocessors required the programmer to use multiple-precision arithmetic. With the advent of minicomputers and microprocessors having longer word lengths, multiple precision is not used as frequently. Still, a corollary to Murphy's Law holds that whatever the available precision, some programmers want more.

For VAX double-precision arithmetic, several adjacent longwords are used to hold an arithmetic value. With 32-bit arithmetic on the VAX, the range of signed integers is from $-2,147,483,648$ to $2,147,483,647$; for 64-bit arithmetic, the range is extended from -2^{63} to $2^{63}-1$, almost beyond imagination.

Multiple-precision addition and subtraction are performed using the Carry bit, along with the instructions Add with Carry (ADWC) and Subtract with Carry (SBWC). To add two 64-bit numbers takes two instructions, one to add the low-order 32 bits and another to add the high-order 32 bits and any carry from the first addition.

For instance, if we have two longwords containing the double-precision operand A and two containing the double-precision operand B, we perform a double-precision Add, as follows:

```
A:      .LONG   4321        ; least significant bits of A
        .LONG   8765        ; most significant bits of A
B:      .LONG   1212        ; least significant bits of B
        .LONG   7878        ; most significant bits of B
          .
          .
          .
        ADDL    A,B         ; adds least significant bits
                            ; ...of A and B together
        ADWC    A+4,B+4     ; adds most significant bits of
                            ; ...A and B with Carry bit
                            ; ...from previous instruction
```

For greater precision, additional ADWCs can be appended.

In addition to its support for 32-bit integer Multiply (MUL) and Divide (DIV) instructions, the VAX has two additional instructions specifically for handling multiplication and division of larger integers. Extended Multiply (EMUL) multiplies two 32-bit values, producing a 64-bit product, and also adds another 32-bit value to the result. The format of EMUL is

```
EMUL    multiplier,multiplicand,addend,product
```

Extended Divide (EDIV) divides a 64-bit number by a 32-bit number, producing a 32-bit quotient and a 32-bit remainder. The format of EDIV is

```
EDIV    divisor,dividend,quotient,remainder
```

This instruction is often used when the remainder of a division is required because the integer divide instructions produce only the quotient.

Finally, there are shift instructions for moving bits within longwords and quadwords, as shown in Table 7.7. These complementary instructions allow the programmer to shift the bits within longwords (ASHL) and quadwords (ASHLQ) using the Arithmetic Shift and to rotate bits within longwords (ROTL) using the Rotate Long. Both instructions are capable of shifting bits both left and right, depending on the *count* operand.

The difference between Rotate and Shift is their treatment of the sign bit. The Rotate instruction, as the name implies, rotates the longword either left or right. On a rotate to the left, for example, each bit shifted out to the left becomes the new low-order bit of the longword. Rotate is a "logical" instruction because it assumes that the longword does *not* contain a signed data type, that is, it does not treat bit 31 specially.

Arithmetic Shift, on the other hand, assumes a signed data type. If the source is shifted n bits to the left, n zero bits are fed into the low-order n bits of the information unit. Overflow will occur if any of the bits shifted into the sign bit position are not identical to the sign bit. On arithmetic shift of n bits to the right, the low-order n bits are shifted out and lost, while the sign bit is replicated in the high-order n bits that were moved. Arithmetic Shift was often used on machines without multiply and divide to multiply or divide by a power of two. Each bit shifted left is a multiply by 2 while each bit shifted right is a divide by a power of 2. Thus, to multiply a signed longword in R3 by 8, we could write either

Table 7.7 VAX Shift Instructions

Operation	Mnemonic	Operands
Arithmetically shift the source operand into the destination field. The number of bits shifted is given by the count field. A positive count is a left shift; a negative count is a right shift, with the bit sign replicated. Destination value sets N and Z bits.	ASHL ASHQ	count,source, destination
Rotate logically the source operand into the destination field. A positive count rotates to the left, a negative count to the right. Destination value sets N and Z bits.	ROTL	count,source, destination

```
        ASHL    #3,R3,R3
```

or

```
        MULL    #8,R3
```

The shift might be faster, depending on the implementation, but the multiply is more obvious and is a shorter instruction because it has one fewer operand.

Floating-Point Arithmetic

Early minicomputers did not include any real floating-point hardware. Rather, software was used to manipulate the signs, exponents, and fractions, as well as any required normalization associated with floating-point values. As hardware became cheaper and instruction sets were expanded, floating-point instructions were added but were often incompatible with existing instruction sets. The PDP-11 series, for example, had several different instruction sets using two-word and four-word formats to manipulate the same floating-point values. The problem of compatibility arose in part because floating-point was added after the basic architecture was frozen. As a result, the set of unassigned opcodes was not large enough to implement this new set of instructions gracefully.

Fortunately, the VAX was planned to allow for orderly growth of instructions, and floating-point instructions were a part of the basic instruction set. Two new formats, G_floating and H_floating, were added to the VAX several years after its introduction and were easily integrated into the architecture because of the availability of two-byte opcodes and the general orthogonality of the instruction set. Table 7.8 lists the floating-point instructions. Note that the four floating-point formats simply add four more data type qualifiers to the standard instruction set. The F, D, G, and H data types are appended to the generic arithmetic instructions to handle floating-point values.

Handling floating-point values on the VAX is relatively easy because of the existence of a complete set of conversion instructions to convert both between the various floating-point data types and also between signed integers and floating-point values. The assembly programmer can thus use floating-point variables without knowing the details of the floating-point format. These instructions are listed in Table 7.9.

There are three types of conversions, as shown in Table 7.9: exact conversions, truncated conversions, and rounded conversions. During conversion from an integer to a floating-point data type (for example, Convert Longword to G_Floating, CVTLG), or from a smaller floating-point format to a larger floating-point format (for example, Convert G_Floating to H_Floating, CVTGH), sign extension takes place. Here the source data type can be represented exactly in the destination data type.

Table 7.8   VAX Floating-Point Instructions

Operation	Mnemonic	Data Types	Number of Operands
Move source operand to destination field. Set condition codes N and Z.	MOV	F,D,G,H	2
Move address of floating operand.	MOVA	F,D,G,H	2
Zero floating-point destination field. Clear N bit and set Z bit.	CLR	F,D,G,H	1
Move negated source to destination, setting N and Z bits.	MNEG	F,D,G,H	2
Compare floating operands.	CMP	F,D,G,H	2
Test floating operand.	TST	F,D,G,H	1
Add floating operands.	ADD	F,D,G,H	2,3
Add Compare and Branch. The addend, index, and limit are all of the specified floating-point data type.	ACB	F,D,G,H	4
Subtract operands.	SUB	F,D,G,H	2,3
Multiply operands.	MUL	F,D,G,H	2,3
Divide operands.	DIV	F,D,G,H	2,3
Extended multiply and integerize. (See *VAX Architecture Reference Manual* for detailed description.)	EMOD	F,D,G,H	5
Evaluate polynominal.	POLY	F,D,G,H	3

Some other conversions, particularly from floating point to signed integer, are done by truncating the fraction. Finally, a third class of conversion is performed not by truncating but by rounding up or down as appropriate. Conversions from floating point to longword are available in both truncated and rounded forms: Convert G_Floating to Longword (CVTGL) truncates the fraction while Convert Rounded G_Floating to Longword (CVTRGL) rounds to the nearest integer.

One interesting VAX floating-point instruction is POLY, which provides polynomial evaluation used in calculation of math functions such as SINE and COSINE. POLY takes three operands: a floating-point *argument* (X), an integer *degree* of the polynomial to be evaluated, and a table of floating-point *coefficients* (C(0) through C(n)). The polynomial instruction computes the value of the function:

$$C(0) + C(1) \times X + C(2) \times X^2 + \cdots + C(n) \times X^n$$

Table 7.9   VAX Floating-Point Conversion Instructions

Exact Conversion	Truncated Conversion	Rounded Conversion
CVTBF	CVTFB	CVTLF
CVTBD	CVTFW	CVTDF
CVTBG	CVTFL	CVTGF
CVTBH	CVTDB	CVTHF
CVTWF	CVTDW	CVTHD
CVTWD	CVTDL	CVTHG
CVTWG	CVTGB	CVTRFL
CVTWH	CVTGW	CVTRDL
CVTLD	CVTGL	CVTRGL
CVTLG	CVTHB	CVTRHL
CVTLH	CVTHW	
CVTFD	CVTHL	
CVTFG		
CVTFH		
CVTDH		
CVTGH		

There are four POLY instructions to support coefficients and arguments in the four floating-point data types.

Exercises

1. Write a short sequence of instructions to test if bits 15, 12, 3, and 1 are set in a word. Write a single instruction to invert all the bits in a longword.

2. A common data structure used in operating systems is the bit map. A bit map is a contiguous string of bits that indicates which blocks of a fixed-size multiblock data structure are in use. For example, a disk composed of 1000 512-byte disk blocks (discussed in more detail in the next chapter) can have a 1000-bit bit map in which a 1 in bit position N indicates that block N is in use. A 0 in bit N indicates that the corresponding block is free for use.

3. Write instruction sequences to set the odd-numbered bits in a byte using (1) the BIS instruction, (2) the BBC instructions (i.e., BBCC, BBSS, etc.), and (3) the INSV instruction.

4. Using the Find First Bit instructions, write a routine to locate a free block from a data structure of N blocks using an N-bit bit map. The routine inputs the address of the first byte of the bit map and its size in bits and outputs the position (number) of the first free block. The routine should set the bit for the block being allocated to note that it is in use. It should return an error code if no free block is found.

5. Extend your routine to locate the first free collection of M contiguous blocks.

6. One of the convert instructions, Convert Longword to Quadword, does not exist in the VAX instruction set. Write a macro to perform this operation.

7. Code a macro or subroutine to duplicate the EDIV instruction using only 32-bit arithmetic.

8. A simple encoding technique is to translate alphanumeric text into shifted text. This is done by writing the alphanumeric characters twice, one string above the other, with the second string shifted by one or more characters, for example,

```
A  B  C  D  E  F .....  0  1  2  3 .....  !  @  $
@  $  A  B  C  D .....  Y  Z  0  1 .....  %  &  !
```

A word is encoded then by replacing its representation on the first line by the second, for example, CAFE becomes A@DC. Write a procedure to perform this encoding using all of the ASCII alphanumeric characters including space.

9. The Move Characters instructions were described in some detail. The MOVC5 instruction has five operands: source length, source address, fill character, destination length, and destination address. Following the execution of MOVC5, the registers are

```
R2,R4, and R5 = 0
R1 = Number of unmoved bytes in the source string
R3 = Address 1 byte beyond the last byte moved in the
     source
R4 = Address 1 byte beyond the destination
```

and the condition codes are set based on the comparison of the source length and destination length, that is,

```
N <-- Source length LSS destination length
Z <-- Source length EQL destination length
V <-- 0
C <-- Source length LSSU destination length
```

Code a routine to emulate the MOVC5 instruction without using character-string instructions.

10. Modify the routine of Figure 7.1 to validate chess piece names to allow for one-character abbreviations of the names. The routine should also accept N for Knight and K for King, but still allow KN or KI as valid abbreviations.

11. Write a subroutine to convert packed decimal strings to longwords, but do not use the convert instructions.

8

Linked Data Structures

An important aspect of program design is the definition of the data structures to be manipulated. Proper data structuring can make the difference between simple and difficult implementation or between superior and mediocre performance. For many applications, writing code is nearly automatic once the data structures are defined, because the instructions merely move data between the structures. The ease of coding depends on the thought given to the data design. This is especially true for operating systems, for which an examination of the data structures often tells more about the system than the code itself.

Among the benefits of high-level languages is the ability to define abstract data types. The compilers for these languages can also check to see that we use the data types properly. To simplify the generation of code by such languages, some computers include more complex data types and data structures in their basic instruction sets.

This chapter examines the manipulation of some more complex data types with the VAX instruction set. In particular, it concentrates on linked structures, lists, queues, and trees.

Multi-Element Structures and Records

Collections of data items that must be manipulated as a group occur frequently in programming. Arrays, lists, queues, and trees are typical multi-element data structures commonly used in both high-level and assembly language programming. These data structures are alike in that they are homogeneous collections of data elements.

Other multi-element data structures are not homogeneous. Collections of data items are called *records*, and a collection of records is called a *file* in COBOL, a *structure* in PL/I, and a *record structure* in Pascal. Each record is actually a logical data item, with its own characteristics of size, type, and initial value, conveniently grouped to form a composite data structure.

Records and files are logical entities that must be manipulated based on a knowledge of their structure. Therefore, different sequences of instructions, offsets, and pointers may be needed to access the elements of different records. For example, we found in the discussion of displacement mode in Chapter 4 that it is necessary to provide the offsets for the different elements that make up the structure. In contrast, when we deal with arrays, the indexed form of addressing is sufficient to step through the elements of the array sequentially.

Arrays

The simplest implementation of an *array* is nothing more than a contiguous collection of identical memory elements. In this form, accessing individual elements is performed by computing an address based on the size of the element—byte, word, longword, and so on—and the relative position (index) of the element in the array. For example, the assembly language code to perform the FORTRAN statement

```
J = A*K+B(I)
```

in VAX assembly language would be

```
MOVL    I,R1            ; place subscript in register
CVTLF   K,R0            ; convert integer K to floating
MULF2   A,R0            ; for A*K as floating value
ADDF2   B[R1],R0        ; add in B to form A*K+B(I)
CVTFL   R0,J            ; store integer result in J
```

When multidimensional arrays are used, the problem of accessing a particular element becomes one of the mapping of a multidimensional array into the linear or one-dimensional form on the computer's memory. For instance, arrays in FORTRAN are stored by column. The two-dimensional array

1   2

3   4

is stored in memory by the compiler as

1

3

2

4

To access the element $A(I,J)$, we must compute the index to the column and then to the elements within the column. This requires knowledge of the bounds of the array indices.

To make it easier for compilers to address arrays, the VAX instruction set contains an Index instruction. This instruction calculates an index for an array of fixed-length data types, both integer and floating, and even for arrays of bit fields, character strings, and decimal strings. The format of the Index instruction is

```
INDEX    subscript,lower_limit,upper_limit,size,index_in,
         index_out
```

We will not examine this instruction in too much detail. Its main value is verification of the subscript range, that is, that

$$lower\_limit \leq subscript \leq upper\_limit$$

If the condition is false, Index causes a trap. Because the instruction traps on an illegal subscript (to be handled by a special trap-handling procedure), a compiler can calculate the proper array index and implicitly check the subscript at the same time. The arithmetic performed is

$$index\_out = (subscript + index\_in) \times size$$

For example, suppose we have a 3x4 array of integers such as

```
X: array [0:2,0:3] of integer;
```

and we want to zero X[I,J]. We can use two Index instructions to compute the correct index and also to perform the bounds check on I and J. Assuming that the array is stored in row major form, we might use the following instructions:

```
INDEX    I,#0,#2,#4,#0,R0 ; R0 gets index to proper row
INDEX    J,#0,#3,#1,R0,R0 ; R0 gets index to proper entry
CLRL     X[R0]            ; zero the entry
```

The first instruction forms the index to the start of row I in memory, while the second instruction forms the index to entry J in that row. Multiple Index instructions can be cascaded to handle arrays of any dimension. If either I or J had been out of bounds, an exception would have been generated.

Circular Lists

One common application of a list is in the implementation of a circular queue or ring buffer, illustrated in Figure 8.1a, which passes information between two or more routines. One routine is usually a producer, the other a consumer. The first feeds information to the list, while the latter removes and processes information.

Figure 8.1   Circular list

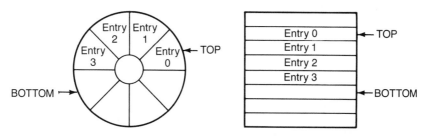

a. Logical structure   b. Physical structure in memory

Two pointers, TOP and BOTTOM (see Figure 8.1b), point to the next element to remove and the next slot to insert data, respectively. When the producer has data, it places the data in the array slot pointed to by BOTTOM and updates BOTTOM to point to the next slot. When the consumer wants to process data, it removes the entry pointed to by TOP and updates TOP to point to the next entry. Since the circular buffer is implemented in linear memory, the routines check for the end of the list when updating pointers. If a pointer is updated past the end of the list, it is reset to point to the first list entry, producing a circular effect. The only restriction is that the producer must not insert faster than the consumer is able to remove. Otherwise, the buffer overflows and data is lost.

What follows are routines for inserting and removing characters from a character ring buffer. Such routines might be used by a terminal handler that accepts complete lines from a remote terminal and passes those lines to the operating system command interpreter for processing.

```
        .SBTTL   Circular Buffer Management Routines


;
; Storage for the buffer and pointer variables.
; The variable COUNT keeps the number of entries in the buffer so that
; it is easy to check for empty or full conditions.
;
        BUFSIZE = 100            ; define size of buffer
BUFFER: .BLKB   BUFSIZE         ; define character ring buffer
COUNT:  .LONG   0               ; initial count is 0


;
; The pointers TOP and BOTTOM contain indices to the current first and
; last data items in the list.
;

BOTTOM: .LONG   0               ; start bottom at 0
TOP:    .LONG   0               ; start top at 0

        .SBTTL   INSBUF - Routine to Insert In Circular Buffer
```

```
;++
; ROUTINE DESCRIPTION:
;
;        This routine inserts a byte into the circular buffer.
;
; CALLING SEQUENCE:
;
;        CALLS or CALLG
;
; INPUT PARAMETERS:
;
;        CHAR(AP) - the low byte of the first argument contains the
;                   character to be inserted
;
; OUTPUT PARAMETERS:
;
; None
;
; RETURN VALUES:
;
;        R0 =
;                0 -> buffer is full
;                1 -> character successfully inserted
;
;--
        CHAR = 4                    ; offset to first argument

        .ENTRY  INSBUF,^M<>         ; save no registers
        CLRQ    R0                  ; assume full-buffer error
                                    ; ...and zero R1 for EDIV
                                    ; ...instruction
        CMPL    #BUFSIZE,COUNT      ; is buffer full?
        BEQL    10$                 ; exit with error if so
        MOVL    BOTTOM,R0           ; get last entry index
        MOVB    CHAR(AP),BUFFER[R0] ; insert char. in buffer
        INCL    COUNT               ; note one more in buffer
        INCL    R0                  ; update bottom pointer
        EDIV    #BUFSIZE,R0,R1,BOTTOM   ; wrap pointer by using
                                    ; ...MOD (pointer, bufsize)
                                    ; ...and restore it to
                                    ; ...memory
        MOVZBL  #1,R0               ; insert success code
10$:    RET                         ; return to caller


        .SBTTL REMBUF - Routine to Remove from Circular Buffer

;++
; ROUTINE DESCRIPTION:
;
;        Remove the next character from the front of the circular list.
;
; CALLING SEQUENCE:
;
;        CALLS or CALLG
```

```
;
; INPUT PARAMETERS:
;
;       CHARADR(AP) - address of byte to receive the removed character
;
; OUTPUT PARAMETERS:
;
;       Removed character is stored in address pointed to by
;       CHARADR(AP).
;
; RETURN VALUES:
;
;       R0 =
;               0 -> buffer is empty
;               1 -> character removed successfully
;--

        CHARADR = 4             ; offset to address
                                ; ...argument

        .ENTRY  REMBUF,^M<>     ; save no registers
        CLRQ    R0              ; assume buffer empty
        TSTL    COUNT           ; is buffer empty?
        BEQL    10$             ; exit with error if so
        MOVL    TOP,R0          ; get top entry index
        MOVB    BUFFER[R0],@CHARADR(AP) ; return character to
                                        ; ...caller
        DECL    COUNT           ; note one less entry
        INCL    R0              ; point to next entry
        EDIV.   #BUFSIZE,R0,R1,TOP  ; wrap pointer if needed
                                    ; ...and return to memory
        MOVZBL  #1,R0           ; insert success code
10$:    RET                     ; return to caller
```

EDIV is used in these routines to implement a Modulus function, automatically wrapping the pointer back to the beginning of the list when it reaches the end. This occurs whenever the pointer reaches BUFSIZE, because the remainder on division is zero. Otherwise, the remainder is the same as the original index.

Linked Lists

We have already seen examples of more advanced data structures: arrays, stacks, and circular lists. Implementation of these structures on the VAX is aided by the instruction set and the addressing modes. We now turn to some more complex linked data structures.

A *linked* data structure can be conceptualized as an array in which the elements do not occupy consecutive locations in memory. To find the array element n or to move from element n to $n + 1$, we must have a pointer to that element, namely, its address. In the simplest scheme, in Figure 8.2, there is a fixed-length table of pointers that gives the location of each element in the data structure. The elements may be of fixed or

Figure 8.2   Pointer table array

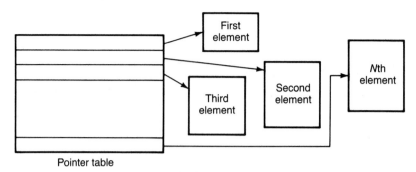

Pointer table

variable length. A zero in one of the pointer table entries may indicate that there is no associated data element.

By setting up such a data structure, we have simply added a level of indirection to the array addressing. This allows us to remove the restriction that the data elements be fixed in length and contiguous in memory. We can also now allocate array elements as we need them, which may be beneficial if they are large. The pointer table itself must be of fixed allocation, however, so we must know the maximum number of entries to allocate. The cost, then, is one pointer, or 4 bytes, per entry.

One way to solve the problem of preallocating the pointer table is to include the pointer within each data entry, as in Figure 8.3. A list *head* is needed to locate the first data element, which then points to the next, and so on. The last data entry contains a zero pointer indicating that no entries follow, that is, it is the end or *tail* of the list.

This structure is known as a *singly linked list*. It sacrifices the ability to address or locate an entry directly by its position because we must search through the chain of links. However, with a singly linked list, it is easy to move from one entry to the next.

Insertion in a singly linked list is simple. We first locate the entry that the new element will follow. If the new element is to be at the head of the list, it follows the list header. Figure 8.4 shows a linked list before and after the element X is inserted following block 1. On the VAX, the instruction sequence is straightforward because indirect addressing modes may be used. The instructions of Figure 8.5a will insert a new entry in a list,

Figure 8.3   Singly linked list

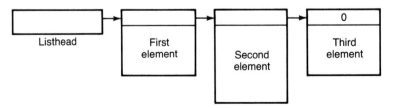

Figure 8.4   Insertion in singly linked list

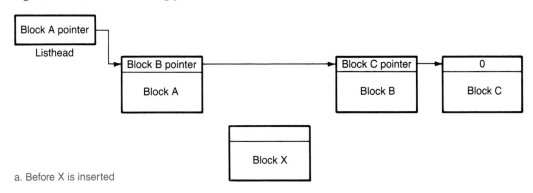

a. Before X is inserted

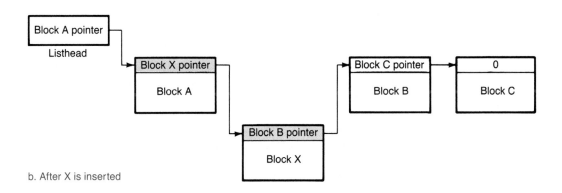

b. After X is inserted

Figure 8.5   Inserting/removing an entry in a singly linked list

```
        ;
        ;  Insert entry in singly linked list.
        ;

                MOVL     (R0),(R1)       ; link new entry to next one
                MOVAL    (R1),(R0)       ; insert new entry
```

a. Inserting instructions

```
        ;
        ;  Remove entry (address in R1) from previous entry (address
        ;  in R0).
        ;

                MOVL     (R1),(R0)       ; link previous to following
```

b. Removing instructions

assuming that R1 contains the address of the new entry and that R0 contains the address of the entry that the new one is to follow. The removal of a block is even shorter, as shown in Figure 8.5b.

The use of a singly linked list is exemplified in the management of a dynamic memory pool. In an operating system, one large pool of memory may be shared by many programs and users. When a routine needs to allocate a block of memory for a dynamic data structure, it calls the pool manager and requests a block of the needed size. When the program is finished with the block, the block is returned to the pool manager. Dynamic allocation saves memory space on the system, because it is not necessary for each routine to preallocate storage that is used only occasionally.

The scheme shown in Figure 8.6 is used within the VMS operating system. The free memory pool is maintained as a list of memory blocks. The first two longwords of each block contain the size of the block and a pointer to the next block. When the system is initialized, there is only one large block. As users begin to allocate and return memory, the pool becomes fragmented and contains many discontiguous pieces of different sizes, as shown in Figure 8.7. If memory returned to the pool is adjacent to a block already there, the two are joined to form one larger block. If all the blocks are returned, the list reverts to the state shown in Figure 8.6. To make the consolidation of blocks easier, the list is kept in memory address order.

The routine in Figure 8.8, which is also flowcharted in Figure 8.9, allocates a block of memory of variable size from the pool. It scans the list for a block of sufficient size. If it finds a block of exactly the right size, that block is removed from the chain and returned to the caller. If it finds a larger block, that block is split into two pieces, one the size requested and

Figure 8.6   Initial dynamic list

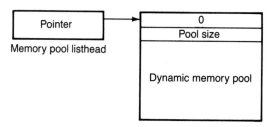

Figure 8.7   Fragmented memory list

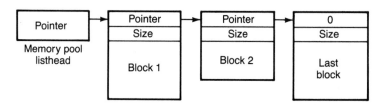

Figure 8.8   Allocate dynamic memory procedure

```
          .SBTTL ALLOCATE - Routine to Allocate Dynamic Memory
;++
;
; FUNCTIONAL DESCRIPTION:
;
;         Allocate a block of memory from the dynamic pool list. (Blocks
;         requested must be at least 8 bytes long.)
;
; CALLING SEQUENCE:
;
;         CALLS or CALLG
;
; INPUT PARAMETERS:
;
;         SIZE(AP) - size of block requested
;
; OUTPUT PARAMETERS:
;
;         RETADR(AP) - address of longword to receive address of allocated
;                       block
;
; RETURN VALUES:
;
;         R0 = 0 if no block found, 1 if block returned
;--

          SIZE = 4                  ; offset to size argument
          RETADR = 8               ; offset to return address

          .ENTRY  ALLOCATE,^M<R2,R3> ; registers to save
          MOVAL   LISTHEAD,R0      ; get memory listhead address
          MOVL    SIZE(AP),R1      ; get size of requested block
10$:      MOVL    R0,R2            ; save previous block address
          MOVL    (R2),R0          ; get next block address
          BEQL    30$              ; exit with error if zero
          CMPL    R1,4(R0)         ; this block large enough?
          BGTRU   10$              ; if not, try next block
          BEQL    20$              ; if EQL, exact size found
;
; Block of memory was found which is larger than amount needed. Return
; size requested and form new block from remainder.
;
          ADDL3   R0,R1,R3         ; compute address of new piece
          MOVL    (R0)+,(R3)+      ; copy forward link from old
                                   ; ...piece to new piece
          SUBL3   R1,(R0),(R3)     ; store size of new piece in
                                   ; ...second longword
          MOVAL   -(R3),-(R0)      ; move address of new piece to
                                   ; ...top of old block
20$:      MOVL    (R0),(R2)        ; link new piece to previous
                                   ; ...block
          MOVL    R0,@RETADR(AP)   ; return allocated block address
          MOVL    #1,R0            ; note success
          RET
30$:      CLRL    R0               ; error exit, note error
          RET                      ; return to caller
```

Figure 8.9   Flowchart for dynamic memory pool allocation

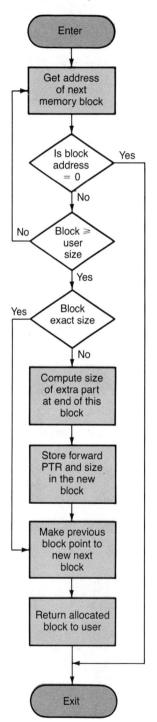

one the remainder of the larger block. The requested block is returned to the caller, and the remainder is linked into the list with its new size.

This routine makes good use of the indirect, autoincrement, and autodecrement addressing modes to manipulate the list and associated pointers. The memory deallocation is left as an exercise at the end of this chapter.

Doubly Linked Lists

Although singly linked lists are convenient for many applications, there are some applications in which such lists are not efficient. These applications require scanning both backward and forward in the list or inserting at the tail of the list. Inserting at the tail can be made more efficient simply by keeping a pointer to the last entry as well as the first. To efficiently scan backward, however, a *doubly linked list* is needed.

A doubly linked list has both backward and forward pointers in each list element, as shown in Figure 8.10. Such a doubly linked list is often used to implement a queue, that is, a linear list in which elements are added to the end of the list and removed from the beginning of the list. On the VAX, each queue element is linked through a pair of longwords; the first longword is the forward link, and the second the backward link. A queue is described by a queue header, which is simply a pair of longwords. A queue header for an empty queue appears in Figure 8.11.

Note that both the forward and backward links point to the head at location H. Figure 8.12 shows the structure of the queue following the insertion of queue elements at locations N and P. The forward pointer of the last entry always points back to the queue header.

Figure 8.10   Doubly linked list

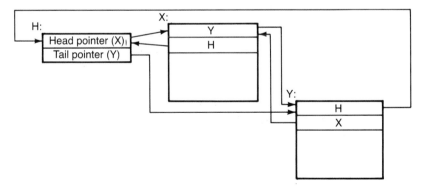

Figure 8.11   Empty queue header

H:	H	Forward link
H + 4:	H	Backward link

Figure 8.12   *Queue insertion*

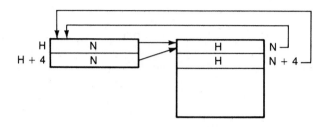

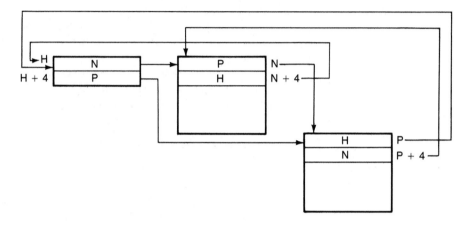

Inserting and removing entries from a queue requires a little more work than from a singly linked list, because three elements with pointers must be modified: the element to be inserted or removed, its predecessor, and its successor. The steps for inserting an entry are

1. Store the address of the successor in the new entry's forward link field.

2. Store the address of the predecessor in the new entry's backward link field.

3. Store the address of the new entry in the predecessor's forward link field.

4. Store the address of the new entry in the successor's backward link field.

The steps for removal of an entry are

1. Store the forward link of the entry to be removed in the forward link field of its predecessor.

2. Store the backward link of the entry to be removed in the backward link field of its successor.

An element can be removed from a doubly linked list given only the address of the element. However, a removal from a singly linked list requires the address of the previous element.

Queue operations are used so frequently that the VAX architecture contains the instructions INSQUE and REMQUE to insert and remove entries from doubly linked lists. These are provided mainly for the operating system, which maintains almost all of its dynamic data structures as queues. The formats of these instructions are

```
INSQUE  entry,predecessor
REMQUE  entry,destination
```

INSQUE inserts the element specified by *entry* into the queue following the element *predecessor*. Both *entry* and *predecessor* are addresses of the two-longword queue headers within the specified elements. REMQUE removes the entry from the queue and places its address in the operand specified by *destination*.

To illustrate this, we return to the insertions pictured in Figure 8.11. To insert entry N at the head of the list, we use the instruction

```
INSQUE  N,H              ; insert element N following
                         ; ...header, that is, at head of
                         ; ...queue
```

Then, to insert element P at the tail of the list, we write

```
INSQUE  P,@H+4           ; insert element P following
                         ; ...last entry, that is, at tail
                         ; ...of queue
```

The specification H+4 uses the tail pointer in the queue header to reference the address of the last element as the predecessor for the insertion. Had we known that the last element was at T, we could have written

```
INSQUE  P,T              ; insert element P following
                         ; ...element T
```

with the same effect. However, insertions at the tail of a queue normally use the pointer in the queue header.

For removing entries, the instruction

```
REMQUE  @H,TEMP          ; remove element at head
```

removes the first entry in the queue, loading its address into the longword TEMP. The instruction

```
REMQUE   @H+4,TEMP         ; remove element at tail
```

removes the tail entry, also loading its address into **TEMP**.

INSQUE sets the Z condition code if the entry inserted was the first in the queue. REMQUE sets the Z condition code if the entry removed was the last one or the queue was already empty. The V bit is set if there was no entry to remove. The programmer can thus easily test for special queue conditions.

One important property of the queue instructions is that they cannot be interrupted. Queues are often used for communication or synchronization among several processes. If several steps were required to insert and remove entries, it would be possible for a process to be interrupted before the operation was completed, leaving queue pointers in an inconsistent state. Because queue manipulation is done with single, uninterruptable instructions, cooperating processes do not have to worry about interrupts, as long as they insert or delete from the head or tail.

The routine that follows is an example of the use of queues by two cooperating processes. The first process collects experimental data and inserts it into a buffer. Because the data arrives quickly, the process does not want to take time to write the buffer to disk. Consequently, it queues the buffer for a second process that writes the data to the disk. There is also a queue of free buffers. When the collection process fills a buffer, it takes a new buffer from the free queue. When the writing process empties a buffer, it puts it back on the free queue for the use of the collection process.

The writing process dequeues buffers and writes them to disk. When the process finds the queue empty, it suspends, or "goes to sleep." The collection process wakes it up when a new buffer is placed on the full queue. These processes must share the memory that contains the queue headers and the data buffers.

Three routines are shown: an initialization routine that sets up the queues, queue headers, and associated variables; the data collection routine; and the writing routine from the second process.

```
.SBTTL — Common Data Shared by Both Processes

;
; The data buffers are initially allocated from a shared pool.
; Assume that a routine (ALLOCATE) can be used to allocate them.
; The variables below describe the number and size of the
; buffers.
;       Note that the double == and :: are used to define variables that
;       are global, that is, known outside of a particular module.
```

```
            BUFSIZE == 512                     ; size of buffers to allocate
            NUMBUFS == 10                      ; number of buffers to get


;
; These are shared variables.  The three current pointers describe the
; buffer currently being filled with data.
;
CURBUF::
            .BLKL   1                          ; address of current buffer
CUREND::
            .BLKL   1                          ; address of end of buffer
CURPTR::
            .BLKL   1                          ; address to put next data item
                                               ; ...in buffer


;
; Following are the queue headers for the free and full buffer queues.
;

FREELST::
            .BLKQ   1                          ; free list head
FULLST::
            .BLKQ   1                          ; full list queue

            .END

            .TITLE - Collection and Initialization Module
            .SBTTL - Initialization Routine
;++
;
; FUNCTIONAL DESCRIPTION:
;
;       This routine allocates buffers and initializes the queues, queue
;       headers, and pointers.
;
; CALLING SEQUENCE:
;
;       CALLS or CALLG
;
; INPUT PARAMETERS:
;
;       None
;
; IMPLICIT INPUTS:
;
;       FREELST, FULLST, CURBUF, CURPTR, CUREND, BUFSIZ, NUMBUFS
;
; OUTPUT PARAMETERS:
;
;       None
;
;--

            .ENTRY  INIT, ^M<R2>              ; main entry point
```

```
;
; Initialize queue headers.
;

        MOVAL       FREELST,FREELST         ; initialize empty free queue
        MOVAL       FREELST,FREELST+4       ; ...header
        MOVAL       FULLST,FULLST           ; initialize empty full queue
        MOVAL       FULLST,FULLST+4         ; ...header

;
; Allocate buffers and place them on a free queue. Assume that routine
; ALLOCATE allocates a buffer of the given size and returns its address
; in the longword passed.
;

        MOVL        #NUMBUFS,R2             ; number of buffers to get
10$:    PUSHAL      -(SP)                   ; save space for buffer addr.
        PUSHL       #BUFSIZ                 ; parameter for routine to
        CALLS       #2,ALLOCATE             ; ...allocate a buffer
        BLBC        R0,ERROR                ; check error status
        INSQUE      @(SP)+,FREELST          ; insert buffer on free queue
        SOBGTR      R2,10$                  ; continue until done

;
; Pull one buffer off the queue and set up pointers for data collection.
; The first data item is stored at 8 bytes past the start of the buffer
; since the first two longwords are used as the queue pointer links.
;

        REMQUE      @FREELST,CURBUF         ; take one from current buffer
        ADDL3       #8,CURBUF,CURPTR        ; compute address to store
                                            ; ...first data item
        ADDL3       #512,CURBUF,CUREND      ; remember buffer end addr.
        RET                                 ; return to caller


        .SBTTL COLLECT - Data Collection Routine

;++
;
; FUNCTIONAL DESCRIPTION:
;
;       This routine collects 32-bit data items and stores them in a
;       buffer.  When the buffer is full, it is queued for another
;       process to write.
;
; CALLING SEQUENCE:
;
;       CALLS or CALLG
;
; INPUT PARAMETERS:
;
;       None
;
; IMPLICIT INPUTS:
```

```
;
;         FREELST, FULLST, CURPTR, CURBUF, CUREND
;
; OUTPUT PARAMETERS:
;
;         None
;--

        .ENTRY  COLLECT,^M<>              ; entry point, save no regs

;
; Assume that GETDATA returns the 32-bit data item in R0.
;

        CALLS   #0,GETDATA                ; get 32-bit datum
        MOVL    CURPTR,R1                 ; place to store value
        MOVL    R0,(R1)+                  ; store datum in buffer
        CMPL    R1,CUREND                 ; is buffer full?
        BLSSU   10$                       ; branch if not full

;
; Buffer is full.  Queue on the end of the full queue, and pull off
; another buffer for data collection.
;

        INSQUE  CURBUF,@FULLST+4          ; queue at end of full queue
        CALLS   #0,WAKEPROCESS            ; wake buffer writing process
        REMQUE  @FREELST,R1               ; get next free buffer
        BVS     NOBUFFER                  ; error if no buffer
        MOVL    R1,CURBUF                 ; save current buffer address
        MOVAB   BUFSIZ(R1),CUREND         ; store buffer and address
        MOVAB   8(R1),R1                  ; address for next datum
10$:
        MOVL    R1,CURPTR                 ; save new data pointer
        RET                               ; return to caller

        .SBTTL OUTBUF - Routine to Write Buffer

;--
;
; FUNCTIONAL DESCRIPTION:
;
;         This routine removes buffers from a queue and outputs them to
;         disk.  It then sleeps until awakened by the collection process.
;
; CALLING SEQUENCE:
;
;         CALLS or CALLG
;
; INPUT PARAMETERS:
;
;         None
;
; IMPLICIT INPUTS:
```

```
;
;          FREELST, FULLST
;
; OUTPUT PARAMETERS:
;
;          None
;
;--

          .ENTRY   OUTBUF, ^M<R2>              ; OUTPUT entry point


;
; Following is an infinite loop to remove and process entries.
;

10$:      REMQUE   @FULLST,R2                  ; remove from full queue head
          BVC      20$                         ; continue if we got one
          CALLS    #0,SLEEP                     ; else go to sleep
          BRB      10$                         ; try again when wakened
20$:


;
; Assume routine OUTPUT writes a buffer to disk with call
;
;          OUTPUT (BUFFERADDRESS, LENGTH)
;
;


          PUSHL    #BUFSIZ                      ; push length argument
          PUSHAL   (R2)                         ; push buffer address
          CALLS    #2,OUTPUT                    ; write to disk
          INSQUE   (R2),@FREELST+4              ; insert on free queue
          BRB      10$                          ; look for more buffers

          .END
```

Self-Relative Queues

The previous section described the VAX INSQUE and REMQUE instructions and the doubly linked structures they manipulate. These instructions operate on queue elements that contain a two-longword field for storing the forward and backward links, as shown in Figure 8.10. Such queues are known as *absolute queues* because the forward and backward link fields are stored as 32-bit absolute addresses.

As the preceding programming example indicates, queues can be shared by several processes, and the instructions cannot be interrupted. As long as insertions and deletions are made from the head or the tail, the queue will remain consistent. There are, however, two problems with absolute queues:

1. Because queue link fields are absolute addresses, each process sharing a queue must see all queue entries at the same addresses. Or,

to look at it another way, absolute queues cannot be easily relocated in memory; that is, they are not position independent.

2. While absolute queue instructions cannot be interrupted, they still pose a problem if queues are shared between processes running on different processors of a shared-memory multiprocessor. In this case, it is possible for two processors to be executing insert or remove operations simultaneously on the same queue entry.

To solve both of these problems, a new queue format and new queue instructions were added to the VAX architecture. This format is known as *self-relative queues*. Self-relative queue addressing is similar to PC-relative addressing. Instead of containing an absolute address, each forward and backward link is stored as a 32-bit *displacement*. The forward link is stored as the displacement of the next queue entry to the current entry; the backward link is stored as the displacement of the previous entry to the current entry. This is shown in Figure 8.13.

Four instructions manipulate self-relative queues: Insert Entry into Queue at Head, Interlocked (INSQHI), Insert Entry into Queue at Tail, Interlocked (INSQTI), Remove Entry from Queue at Head, Interlocked (REMQHI), and Remove Entry from Queue at Tail, Interlocked (REMQTI). As you might guess, self-relative queues can be accessed only at the head or the tail. In addition, the self-relative queue headers must be aligned on a quadword boundary (addresses evenly divisible by 8).

Figure 8.13 **Self-relative queue format**

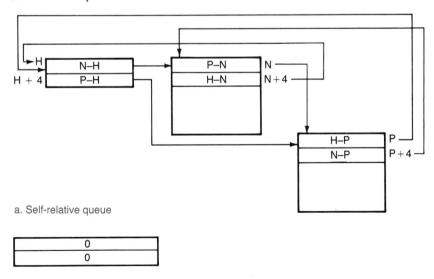

a. Self-relative queue

b. Empty self-relative queue header

The reason for the boundary restriction is that, to ensure that only one processor accesses a queue at a time, bit zero of the queue header is used as an interlock. When a self-relative queue instruction is executed, it checks bit zero of the header. If this bit is set, another processor is already accessing the entry, so the instruction terminates after setting the C condition code. If the bit is clear, the instruction sets the bit and then performs the insert or remove operation. Therefore, programs that use these instructions must explicitly check the C bit and reexecute the instruction if the bit is set. For example, if we were to use self-relative queues in procedure COLLECT in the previous shared-queue example, the queue manipulate code would be changed to

```
;
; Buffer is full.  Queue on the end of the full queue, and pull off
; another buffer for data collection.
;

2$:     INSQTI   CURBUF,FULLST           ; queue at end of full queue
        BCS      2$                      ; repeat if queue is locked
        CALLS    #0,WAKEPROCESS          ; wake buffer writing process
4$:     REMQHI   FREELST,R1              ; get next free buffer
        BVS      NOBUFFER                ; error if no buffer
        BCS      4$                      ; repeat if queue is locked
        MOVL     R1,CURBUF               ; save current buffer address
        MOVAB    BUFSIZ(R1),CUREND       ; store buffer and address
        MOVAB    8(R1),R1                ; address for next datum
10$:
```

Note that the operands for self-relative queue instructions are specified differently than for absolute queues. For example, while REMQUE specifies as an operand *the address of the element to be removed*, REMQTI and REMQHI specify the address of the queue header, and the opcode specifies whether to remove the first or the last entry. Similarly, INSQHI and INSQTI specify the address of the queue header and the opcode indicates whether to insert at the head or tail. Therefore, the formats are

```
        INSQHI   entry,header
        INSQTI   entry,header
        REMQHI   header,destination
        REMQTI   header,destination
```

Trees

The final linked data structure we will examine is the tree. A *tree* is simply a linked structure in which there is one special element called the root, whose function is analogous to the queue header in a linked list. The root points to from zero to n elements, each of which is itself a tree. Figure 8.14 shows a simple tree structure.

The relationships between elements, or *nodes*, of a tree are often described using family tree terminology—parent, sibling, offspring, and

Figure 8.14 Simple tree

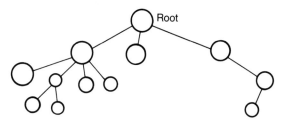

so on. The terminal nodes are known as leaves. The tree in Figure 8.14 is drawn with the root at the top, but this is not the only possible graphic representation. Since relationships such as left and right, up and down are used to describe tree elements, one must be careful to draw trees in a consistent manner.

Trees are often useful for storing representations of alternatives, particularly in game playing, where each path represents the possible moves or actions. For instance, following each move in a tic-tac-toe game, one subtree describes the remaining possible moves. Searching down the tree, we can examine the possible moves and choose one that results in a win or a draw. Of course, for more complicated games, it is almost impossible to enumerate or search the entire tree.

One common tree species is the *binary tree*, in which each node can have from zero to two offspring. A binary tree is usually ordered. For example, the tree can be maintained so that for the value (N) stored at each node, all descendant nodes with values less than N are to the left in the tree, and all nodes with values greater than N are to the right. Binary trees are often used to maintain tables of names because the ordering allows for easy searching and alphabetical listing.

Suppose we want to build a binary tree to store the following names: John, Paul, George, Ringo, Groucho, Chico, Harpo, Zeppo, Othello, Hamlet, and Richard III. If we begin with John at the root and insert each subsequent name so as to maintain the right or left alphabetical relationship, the tree will appear as shown in Figure 8.15.

Figure 8.15 Alphabetical binary tree

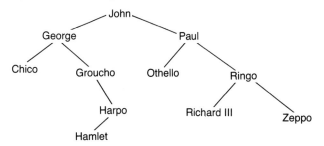

The following routine inserts an element in a binary tree. Each element is a five-longword block in which the first two longwords are used to point to the two offspring, left and right, and in which the last three longwords contain a 12-byte name string. The routine searches down the tree until it finds a terminal node after which the new entry can be inserted. A zero pointer indicates that there is no offspring.

```
        .SBTTL INSTREE - Routine to Insert Element in Binary Tree

;--
;
;
; FUNCTIONAL DESCRIPTION:
;
;       This routine inserts a 5-longword block containing an ASCII
;       name string into a binary tree.  The longword ROOT contains the
;       address of the root node.
;
; CALLING SEQUENCE:
;
;       CALLS or CALLG
;
; INPUT PARAMETERS:
;
;       BLOCK(AP) contains the address of the 5-longword node to be
;               inserted, structured as follows:
;
;
;               +-----------------------+
;               |        LEFT LINK      |
;               +-----------------------+
;               |        RIGHT LINK     |
;               +-----------------------+
;               |  12-byte              |
;               +                       +
;               |      name             |
;               +                       +
;               |        string         |
;               +-----------------------+
;
;
; OUTPUT PARAMETERS:
;
;       None
;
; RETURN VALUES:
;
;       R0 = 1 if node inserted successfully
;       R0 = 0 if name already exists in tree, duplication error
;--

        BLOCK = 4                               ; offset to argument
```

```
;
; Offsets into tree element.
;

        LEFT = 0                        ; define left link offset
        RIGHT = 4                       ; define right link offset
        NAME = 8                        ; define name string offset

        .ENTRY  INSTREE,^M<R6,R7,R8>    ; INSTREE entry point
        PUSHL   #0                      ; push error code, assume
                                        ; ...duplicate
        MOVL    BLOCK(AP),R6            ; get input block address
        MOVAL   ROOT,R8                 ; get address of root element
        BRB     20$                     ; check if root exists

;
; Check if new entry is <, > or = to current block.  If < or >, then
; continue scanning tree or insert new entry if no successor to current
; node.  If =, then return error indication.  As tree is scanned, R6
; contains the address of the new entry to insert. R7 contains the
; address of the node in the tree being examined.
;

10$:    MOVAL   LEFT(R7),R8             ; get pointer to < (left) side
        CMPC3   #12,NAME(R6),NAME(R7)   ; compare new name to node
                                        ; ...value
        BEQL    40$                     ; branch if same, return error
        BLSS    20$                     ; continue if < current node
        MOVAL   RIGHT(R7),R8            ; else get pointer to >
                                        ; ...(right) side

;
; R8 now contains address of the left or right pointer in the current
; node, depending on whether the new name is < or > than the name in this
; node.
;

20$:    TSTL    (R8)                    ; any offspring in this node?
        BEQL    30$                     ; insert new entry here if not
        MOVL    (R8),R7                 ; else get offspring address
        BRB     10$                     ; ...and continue tree scan

;
; Found the place to insert new node.  R8 contains address of pointer
; in new parent.
;

30$:    CLRQ    (R6)                    ; zero both pointers in new
                                        ; ...entry
        MOVL    R6,(R8)                 ; link new node to parent node
        PUSHL   #1                      ; push success code
40$:
        POPL    R0                      ; get return code from stack
        RET                             ; return to caller
```

Summary

This chapter examined a number of data structures and how the VAX instruction set manages them. We can see how the instruction and addressing techniques have evolved to efficiently support the needs of compilers and operating systems.

In one way or another, most operating systems use all data structures and manipulation techniques described here. In fact, most of the code in an operating system is there to manipulate queues, lists, records, and other data structures. The manipulated data elements are usually called *control blocks*. A control block is a data structure composed of a number of elements of different sizes that describes a resource or a physical or logical entity in the system. For example, there may be control blocks to describe each device, each user program, each file, and each I/O request. These control blocks are knit together to form a complex web that describes the state of the system at any time.

Figure 8.16 shows a small section of a simple operating system I/O data base. Each box is a control block that contains state information

Figure 8.16   Sample I/O data base organization

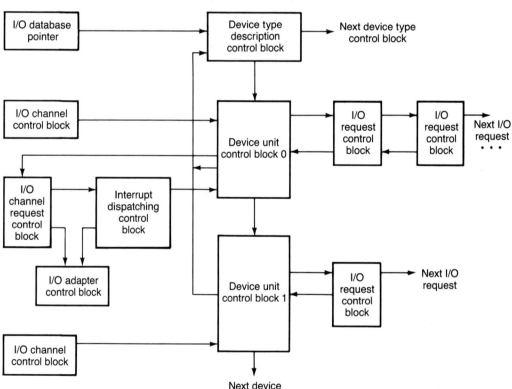

about one resource: a device unit, a device controller, a bus or data path, or an input or output request. The arrows show which control blocks contain pointers to others. Some control blocks are queued to others, while some are members of several queues at once.

With this number of components to manipulate, the design of the data structures can clearly have a significant impact on the complexity and performance of a system. Careful, detailed analysis is required to ensure that data structures can be manipulated efficiently.

Exercises

1. Write the Dynamic Memory Deallocation routine corresponding to the Allocate Dynamic Memory routine in Figure 8.9. When a block of memory is returned, the deallocation routine should check whether it can be combined with any adjacent memory blocks.

2. Suppose the VAX did not have queue instructions to manipulate doubly linked lists. Produce INSQUE and REMQUE macros that insert and delete entries from doubly linked lists without using the queue instructions. What are the differences between using the instructions and using the macros?

3. Figure 8.13 shows the format of a VAX self-relative queue. Write procedures to insert and remove entries in a self-relative queue without using the VAX self-relative queue instructions.

4. Suppose you have a singly linked list where each 64-bit list element contains a 32-bit forward link followed by a 32-bit data element that contains four ASCII characters. Write a procedure that is called with two parameters, the address of the list header and a 32-bit longword containing four ASCII characters. Your procedure will remove the list element whose four-character data field matches that specified on the call. If a match is not found, your procedure should return an error indication.

5. Using a recursive method, write a procedure that descends through a binary rooted tree and prints the value of each leaf.

9

Analysis of the VAX Instruction Set

Previous chapters have described the characteristics of the VAX instruction set—its operations, data types, addressing modes, and so on. The VAX is one of the more complex instruction sets. It is complex first because of the number of operations and addressing modes; the VAX has over 300 opcodes and over 20 addressing modes. Second, it is complex because of the generality with which the addressing modes can be applied: any addressing mode can be used for any operand specifier. This leads to a very flexible variable-length encoding of instructions. However, this format is more difficult for the hardware to execute than would be a fixed-length format. The next chapter discusses these tradeoffs.

Now that you understand the VAX and the possible options for instructions and addressing, it is interesting to examine how the VAX architecture is used in actual applications. This might give you some intuition into architecture design. In fact, the VAX design grew out of a similar examination of applications on the PDP−11.

Several studies have measured the dynamic operation of the VAX under various workloads. There are a number of techniques that are typically used to evaluate an architecture:

- The most common technique is to build an instruction trace program that executes a target program one instruction at a time, collecting interesting data as each target instruction is executed. Such a program can be simplified with proper hardware support; for example, the VAX has a trace trap bit in the PSL that, when set, causes a trap following the execution of the next instruction. As the trace program executes the target program, it can easily calculate instruction frequencies, addressing mode frequencies, and so on. It cannot, however, make judgments about real-time properties of the program, because it changes the environment in which the program runs. Also, it typically cannot trace the operating system.

- Hardware monitors can be used for measurement. A hardware monitor is an external device that is connected through probe wires to interesting signals on the target machine. Because the monitor is passive, it does not change the environment in which the target programs are run, and it can measure operating systems as well as user programs. Hardware monitors are expensive and often require the construction of special hardware to capture or regenerate needed signals. The hardware monitor needs to be faster than the target CPU, since it must both capture and process signals at the same rate at which they're generated.

- Measurement can be made by modifying the machine itself to collect data. This has been done in some cases with the VAX and is simplified by the fact that the VAX is microcoded. We will examine microcode later, but basically, the VAX instruction set is actually interpreted by a lower-level *microprogram* executing on the actual hardware. This microprogram can be modified to collect data.

The first two techniques were used by studies reported in 1982. First, Douglas Clark and Henry Levy (1982) used a hardware monitor to gather instruction opcode data on a VAX−11/780. The importance of using a hardware monitor was to determine both the *frequency* with which opcodes were used and the *time* spent executing various opcodes. Because of the range of complexity of VAX instructions, there is a wide variance in instruction execution times. It is interesting to know which instructions are most frequent and which account for most of the execution time. To optimize the implementation of an architecture, the execution time data is crucial.

For example, Table 9.1 shows the data accumulated by the hardware monitor during the execution of the VAX/VMS FORTRAN compiler. First, we notice that the most frequent instructions are MOVL and BNEQ. In general, over a number of architectures, simple moves have been found to be the most frequent operations and control instructions such as branch the next most frequent. Second, we notice the difference between frequency and time. While MOVL accounts for 12.36 percent of the instructions executed, it accounts for only 6.76 percent of the time. On the other hand, CALLS, which accounts for only 2.54 percent of the instructions, accounts for 21.59 percent of the time! So in the FORTRAN compiler, over a fifth of the time is spent executing CALLS and almost a third of the time is spent in CALLS and RET combined. CALLS consumes so much time because it requires many memory writes to build the procedure activation record. Information such as this was useful in determining which parts of the VAX to optimize, and newer VAXes have more highly optimized CALL and RET instructions. Therefore, if the same measurements were run on different implementations of the VAX, the frequency order would be identical but the time order would be different on each implementation.

For comparison, Table 9.2 shows opcode data for the Whetstone benchmark, which is often used to compare the floating-point performance of various machines. There are two things to notice about these

Table 9.1   Instruction Distributions for VMS FORTRAN Compiler

Rank	Frequency Order		Time Order	
	Instruction	Frequency (%)	Instruction	Time (%)
1	MOVL	12.36	CALLS	21.59
2	BNEQ	8.72	RET	9.46
3	MOVAB	5.56	MOVL	6.76
4	CMPL	5.34	BBC	6.32
5	BEQL	4.49	MOVC5	4.86
6	BBC	4.05	BNEQ	3.70
7	ADDL2	4.03	MOVAB	3.02
8	MOVZWL	3.10	EXTZV	2.70
9	MOVZBL	3.01	CMPL	2.64
10	PUSHL	2.93	MOVZWL	2.41
11	CMPW	2.71	MOVZBL	2.35
12	CALLS	2.54	CMPW	1.88
13	RET	2.52	PUSHL	1.86
14	BRB	2.33	BEQL	1.46
15	CMPB	2.21	MOVW	1.23

Table 9.2   Instruction Distributions for Whetstone Benchmark

Rank	Frequency Order		Time Order	
	Instruction	Frequency (%)	Instruction	Time (%)
1	MOVL	21.99	CALLG	13.01
2	ADDF3	7.15	MOVL	12.81
3	MULF3	6.42	RET	9.94
4	AOBLEQ	5.08	CALLS	6.55
5	MOVAL	3.74	DIVF3	6.28
6	RET	3.55	MULF3	6.04
7	ADDF2	3.54	AOBLEQ	4.63
8	DIVF3	2.79	POLYF	4.41
9	CMPL	2.60	ADDF3	4.39
10	SUBL3	2.47	EMODF	2.97
11	CALLG	2.12	MULL3	2.13
12	MULL3	1.95	ADDF2	2.11
13	BLEQ	1.75	SUBL3	1.61
14	MULF2	1.54	MOVAL	1.53
15	RSB	1.54	MULL2	1.39

results. First, we see some different opcodes appearing in the top fifteen. So, different programs use the VAX instruction set in different ways. Second, while this is a benchmark to measure floating-point performance, notice that CALL and RET still account for about one-fifth of the program's execution time.

Cheryl Wiecek (1982) used the trace method to measure the dynamic execution of several VAX/VMS compilers. Compilers are interesting because they are examples of some of the largest application programs, and typical compilations of even simple programs can execute millions of instructions. In addition to instruction frequencies, Wiecek was able to determine frequencies for addressing modes. For example, Table 9.3 shows the frequencies of the various addressing modes for executions of the VAX/VMS FORTRAN and PL/I compilers. Not surprisingly, the most frequent addressing mode is register. Second in line among all the compilers measured is literal addressing mode; this indicates the importance of having instruction-stream literals (and short literals) in the VAX. These literals reduce the number of required data fetches.

Table 9.4, also from Wiecek's study, shows the distribution of memory references among each of the VAX information units. The data is classified by the type of operation: read, write, or modify (a modify operand is an operand that is read and rewritten during the instruction, for example, R1

Table 9.3   VAX Addressing Mode Frequencies

Addressing Mode	FORTRAN	PL/I
Register	41.0	42.2
Literal	18.2	10.9
Byte Displacement	13.6	11.2
Register Deferred	9.1	2.5
Autoincrement	4.1	4.4
Index	5.6	8.8
Long Displacement	5.5	3.5
Word Displacement	1.5	13.9
Autodecrement	0.5	0.3
Autoincr. Deferred	0.3	0.0
Long Displ. Deferred	0.0	0.1
Word Displ. Deferred	0.0	0.1

Table 9.4   VAX Operand Accesses by Data Type

Data Type	Reference Type		
	Read (%)	Write (%)	Modify (%)
Byte	16	4.4	31.4
Word	17.7	5.8	17.5
Longword	65.8	88.4	51.1
Quadword	0.5	1.3	0.0
Octaword	0.0	0.1	0.0

in the instruction INCL R1). It is not surprising that most operations occur on longwords, but the distributions are different for the different types of operations. Wiecek points out that about 70 percent of data references occur to the stack; this would include the procedure activation records, dynamically allocated locals, and other stack storage. Only 30 percent of data references are to static memory.

Wiecek found other interesting statistics that help us to understand the behavior of the "average" VAX instruction. For example, the average instruction is 3.8 bytes long and has 1.8 operand specifiers. Also, on the average, the PC is changed due to a branch every 3.9 instructions. Another study by Clark (1983) gives us a good characterization of the execution of the average VAX instruction on the VAX−11/780. On that machine, the average instruction takes between 10 and 12 cycles; VAX−11/780 cycles are 200 nanoseconds, so the average instruction takes about 2 microseconds to execute. Of that time, about 75 percent is spent actually computing, that is, performing the operation, address arithmetic, and so on. The remaining 25 percent is spent waiting either for instruction or memory data to arrive in the CPU. Finally, Clark found that the average instruction does one memory access, with reads twice as likely as writes.

It is important to remember that with the complex architecture of the VAX there is a large variance in the work done for each instruction. The preceding statistics were averaged over tens of millions of instructions. Finally, you must be extremely cautious when you use measurements of any kind to compare different architectures. For example, vendors frequently quote the performance of their machines in MIPS: millions of instructions per second. During the 1980s, the VAX−11/780 became the standard of comparison and is known as a 1−MIP machine. In fact, as we can see by the average instruction time on the 780, a VAX−11/780 executes at about 1/2 MIPS. However, because of the high level of VAX instructions, a VAX executing 1/2 MIPS can do as much work as a simpler architecture executing 1 or 2 MIPS, depending on that architecture. Therefore, MIPS is not a good unit for comparing different architectures, although it is fine for comparing implementations of the same architecture.

Exercises

1. What are other common units beside MIPS that are used to describe computer performance?

2. Why is it useful to collect instruction usage statistics on computer instruction sets? Why is it important to consider both time and frequency order when examining instruction usage in a computer instruction set?

3. Suppose that you had to redesign the VAX to use only four addressing modes. Which four would you choose? Why?

4. Table 9.4 shows the distribution of memory references among each of the VAX information units, giving the reference type (read, write, modify) as well. For longwords, most accesses are writes, while for bytes, reads and modifies greatly outnumber writes. Can you give any possible explanation for this?

5. What useful measurements allow one member of the VAX family to be compared to another? Can these same measurements be used to compare a VAX to a completely different architecture?

10 *Comparative Architectures*

The preceding chapters have focused on the user-visible architecture of the VAX. In the course of those chapters, you became familiar with addressing techniques, the instruction execution process, and the formation of instructions. However, with the knowledge of only one computer, you have little basis on which to evaluate its architecture.

This chapter examines four other instruction set architectures: the IBM 360/370, the CDC Cyber series, the Intel 80386, and the Berkeley RISC. Each of these systems had different design goals, so different tradeoffs were made by the designers. Of course, systems evolve, and computers such as the VAX and RISC were designed with the knowledge of the successes and shortcomings of previous architectures.

It is not our intention to describe these architectures completely. Rather, we hope that this material will broaden your perspective and solidify the material already covered.

General Issues in Instruction Set Design

Before presenting the instruction sets, let's consider some general issues in instruction set design. In particular, there are three attributes of instruction sets that are often discussed. The first attribute is *generality*. By generality, we mean that various aspects of an instruction architecture can be used in a general (as opposed to a restrictive) fashion. As an example, let's consider the CPU registers. In an architecture that supports generality, each register could be used for any data type and for any function. In contrast, some architectures restrict various registers. The Motorola 68000 series has separate registers for addresses and data; pointers must be kept in address registers. The IBM 360 has separate registers for floating-point operands. The Intel 8086 microprocessor has eight registers, but almost every one is dedicated to a specific function. On the VAX, twelve of the general-purpose registers are truly general purpose, but four have predefined functions. Such restrictions reduce the generality of the registers and consequently reduce the number of effective registers, since the machine has predetermined how they will be used.

The second attribute is *orthogonality*. We say that a machine is highly orthogonal if every operator can be applied to every data type. The VAX is orthogonal with respect to byte, word, longword, and floating-point data types. That is, nearly all operations are available on all of these data types. On the other hand, the VAX is not orthogonal with respect to some of the larger data types, such as quadword, which is not fully supported. Orthogonality simplifies compiler implementation because there are fewer special cases to remember; operations can be applied in straightforward fashion to any data type.

The third attribute is *symmetry*. Symmetry is related to generality and is often used to describe the way in which operands can be specified. For example, some machines permit register-to-register or memory-to-register arithmetic but not memory-to-memory or register-to-memory. Or suppose we have a subtract instruction in which the minuend can use any addressing mode, but the subtrahend can use fewer addressing modes. This would again add complexity to a compiler, which may need to generate additional instructions compared to a compiler for a more symmetric instruction set.

Of course, attributes such as generality, orthogonality, and symmetry are frequently traded off to reduce instruction size or machine complexity. Where to make the tradeoff depends on the requirements for the machine and its implementation, as well as the available compiler technology. However, these are useful concepts to keep in mind as you examine different instruction set architectures.

The IBM System 360/370

The IBM System 360/370 (S/370) family, introduced in the mid−1960s, is probably the most widely used computer architecture and has enjoyed a long life in many implementations. The instruction set has been copied by vendors manufacturing S/370 plug-compatible CPUs, and has been carried forth by IBM in the 4300 series. This section briefly describes the S/370 instruction set architecture and addressing. Our objective is to examine some alternatives to the addressing and instruction representation to the VAX.

The S/370, like the VAX, is a byte-addressable computer that operates on information units that are multiples of the 8-bit byte. The main S/370 information units are the 8-bit byte, the 16-bit halfword, the 32-bit word, and the 64-bit doubleword, as shown in Figure 10.1. On the S/370, bits are numbered from left to right, making bit 0 the most significant bit.

The S/370 has sixteen 32-bit general registers, numbered from 0 to 15. The even-odd pairs can be used as double registers. For example, registers 2 and 3 can be used to contain a doubleword, but registers 3 and 4 cannot. There are also four 64-bit floating-point registers for floating-point operations, numbered 0, 2, 4, and 6. The adjacent floating-point registers 0, 2, 4, and 6 can be used to contain extended floating-point operands.

Although the original S/360 was a 32-bit system in that it operated

Figure 10.1   *S/370 information units*

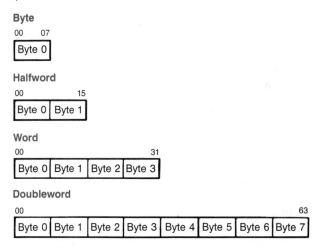

primarily on 32-bit quantities, program addresses were 24 bits in length. When a register was used for addressing, the high-order 8 bits (0-7) were ignored in the effective address calculation. Therefore, a program could address 2^{24} or 16,777,216 bytes of memory. This restriction was eliminated with the S/370 extended architecture, which provides addressing of 2^{31} bytes.

Address computation on the S/370 is simpler than on the VAX because there are fewer options. A memory address is generally formed as the sum of the contents of a general register (known as the base register, B) and a 12-bit integer (known as the displacement, D). This is shown symbolically as D(B) and is similar to displacement addressing on VAX.

The second method of address specification uses an index register (shown as X) in addition to the base and the displacement. The index register can be used to address an element of an array pointed to by the base register. The displacement is summed with the contents of the base and index registers, yielding the effective operand address. This is shown as D(X,B) and is similar to displacement indexed addressing on the VAX, except that the index register is not multiplied by the array element size. Therefore, to step through an array of 32-bit entries, the index register must be incremented by 4 following each step.

These two modes provide the only method of memory-address specification in an S/370 instruction. To address an item in memory, then, a base register must always be used. Since displacements are 12 bits, a base register can address a memory block of 4096 bytes. In general, one of the sixteen general-purpose registers must be reserved as a base register to address each 4096-byte segment of contiguous data or code. However, if the segments are not in use simultaneously, a single base register can be

loaded with the address for a new segment whenever that segment needs
to be referenced.

On the VAX, the instruction opcode specifies the size, type, and
number of operands. In general, each operand specifier contains 1 byte to
indicate the addressing mode used. On the S/370, the opcode specifies the
addressing mode of the operand specifiers in addition to the size and type
of the operands. This reduces the space required for operand specifiers,
since the addressing mode is implicit. With this approach, a large number
of opcodes would be required if many types of addressing are desired, but
as we have stated, the S/370 has chosen to limit the number of addressing
modes in favor of bit efficient instructions.

System 370 instructions are 2, 4, or 6 bytes in length. There are five
instruction formats, allowing for five forms of source and destination
specification. We will examine each form briefly.

1. Register-to-register (RR) format. In register-to-register format, both
   operands are contained in registers.

```
00                   07 08     11 12     15
┌──────────────────────┬─────────┬─────────┐
│       Opcode         │   R1    │   R2    │
└──────────────────────┴─────────┴─────────┘
```

The assembler syntax for RR instructions is

```
OPCODE R1,R2
```

For example, the Add Register (AR) instruction to sum the contents of
two registers,

```
AR   4,5
```

adds register 5 to register 4, leaving the sum in register 4. (Note that
the meaning of source and destination operands is the reverse of that
used by the VAX, that is, the first operand is the destination.)

2. Register-with-indexing (RX) format. In register-with-indexing format,
   the first operand is contained in a register, the second is a memory
   location specified by base, index, and displacement.

```
00                   07 08    11 12    15 16    19 20                     31
┌──────────────────────┬────────┬────────┬────────┬──────────────────────┐
│       Opcode         │   R1   │   X2   │   B2   │          D2          │
└──────────────────────┴────────┴────────┴────────┴──────────────────────┘
```

The assembler syntax for an RX instruction is

```
OPCODE R1,D2(X2,B2)
```

The opcode determines which is the source and which is the destination. For example, the memory-to-register Add instruction

```
A  R,D(X,B)
```

adds the contents of the memory location to the register, R, leaving the result in the register, while the Store instruction

```
ST  R,D(X,B)
```

stores the contents of the register in the specified memory location.

3. Register-to-storage (RS) format. The register-to-storage format shown has three operands: two registers and one memory location specified by a base register and displacement.

| 00 | 07 | 08 | 11 | 12 | 15 | 16 | 19 | 20 | 31 |

| Opcode | R1 | R3 | B2 | D2 |

The assembler syntax for RS instructions is

```
OPCODE R1,R3,D2(B2)
```

For example, the Store Multiple (STM) instruction

```
STM   Ra,Rb,D(B)
```

stores the registers Ra through Rb at consecutive memory locations beginning with the effective address base + displacement.

4. Storage immediate (SI) format. In this format, an 8-bit immediate operand and a memory location are specified.

| 00 | 07 | 08 | 15 | 16 | 19 | 20 | 31 |

| Opcode | I2 | B1 | D1 |

The assembler syntax for an SI instruction is

```
OPCODE  D1(B1),I2
```

For example, the Move Immediate (MVI) instruction

```
MVI   12(7),6
```

moves the value 6 to the memory location specified by the sum of the contents of base register 7 and the displacement 12.

5. Storage-to-storage (SS) format. The storage-to-storage format is used only for string operands. The address of each operand is specified by a base register and displacement. There are two storage-to-storage formats, one where a 4-bit length is specified for each operand, and one where a single 8-bit length is specified for both operands. The machine formats for SS instructions are as follows:

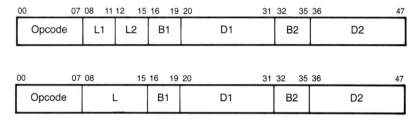

The assembler syntax for SS instructions is

```
OPCODE D1(L1,B1),D2(L2,B2)
```

or

```
OPCODE D1(L,B1),D2(B2)
```

For example, the Move Character String instruction

```
MVC  0(64,4),16(5)
```

moves the 64-byte character string from the location specified by base register 5 and displacement 16 to the location specified by base register 4 and displacement 0.

The S/370 supports both register-to-register and memory-to-register arithmetic, but not register-to-memory or memory-to-memory. Therefore, an intermediate register must be used to add two storage locations. To add memory locations A and B, one must code:

```
L         R2,A          load A into R2
A         R2,B          add B to R2
ST        R2,B          store result in B
```

All three instructions are RX format instructions. Notice, however, that the positions of source and destination are specified by the opcode. To specify symbolic operands such as A and B, the assembly programmer tells the assembler which register is to be used as a base register, and the assembler computes the displacement.

The S/370 instruction set also does not have instructions for all of its information units. For instance, there are five integer Add instructions:

1. Add two signed 32-bit registers (AR).

2. Add a signed 32-bit storage location to a register (A).

3. Add a signed 16-bit storage location to a signed 32-bit register (AH, for Add Halfword).

4. Add two unsigned 32-bit registers (ALR, for Add Logical Registers).

5. Add an unsigned 32-bit storage location to an unsigned 32-bit register (AL, for Add Logical).

Although this examination of the S/370 has been brief, we can make the following observations:

1. The S/370 architecture has less generality in its instruction encoding than VAX, but the equivalent addressing modes have more compact representations.

2. Memory addressing on the S/370 requires a base register that can address a block of 4096 bytes. Since a full 31-bit address cannot be directly contained in an instruction, random addressing of large arrays is not as convenient as it is on the VAX.

3. The S/370 has index registers similar to the VAX, although the index register must be manually incremented by the size of each array element. However, the S/370 has instructions for incrementing index registers and testing for upper limits that simplify index-register handling.

4. The S/370 general registers cannot be used for floating-point operations, and only the even-odd pairs can be used as extended registers. There is no concept of autoincrement or autodecrement.

5. The S/370 does not have memory-to-memory arithmetic. Tradeoffs were made to reduce the size of instructions and to simplify instruction encoding. Thus, S/370 instructions are kept short, from 2 to 6 bytes in length, whereas VAX instructions can be very long. It is difficult to compare this with the VAX architecture, because several S/370 instructions can be required to represent a single VAX instruction.

6. Because of the compactness of instruction representation, there is no indirection on the S/370.

The CDC Cyber Series

The Control Data Corporation (CDC) Cyber series is the successor to the 6000 series introduced in the early 1960s. It was built initially as a scientific processor for Atomic Energy Commission installations. Because of its speed and powerful floating-point instructions, it found wider acceptance in other computing communities, particularly among academic institutions. The architecture is unusual because the Cyber is a multiprocessor system with one high-speed central processor and multiple peripheral processors. Our interest lies not in that feature of the architecture, but rather in the information units, instruction set, and addressing modes of the central processor. While there are several processors, only the central processor can be used directly by the programmer.

The Cyber, unlike the VAX and the S/370, is not a byte addressable computer. Rather, its only information unit is the 60-bit word shown in Figure 10.2. This word can hold a 60-bit floating-point data type or a 48-bit integer value. Indeed, the length of the word was chosen to support floating-point values that were common to the type of scientific computing expected to be performed on the Cyber.

The numbering of the bits, as shown in Figure 10.2, is like that of the VAX, going from right to left, with bit 59 as the most significant bit. Instructions, addresses, and data are all stored within a word, which is the basic addressable unit.

The central processor contains twenty-four operating registers. These registers are divided into three eight-register groups: the operand, or X registers; the address, or A registers; and the increment, or B registers. They are usually referred to as the X, A, and B registers in assembler syntax. Figure 10.3 shows these registers and their interaction with the arithmetic unit and central memory.

Addresses for the Cyber are 18-bit quantities. This nominally limits program addresses to 2^{18}, or 262,144, words of memory. Effective address computation is even simpler for the Cyber than for either the S/370 or the VAX. However, since this is basically a register machine, the style of memory addressing is rather unusual.

Figure 10.3 shows that the X register set is 60 bits wide, but the A and B registers are only 18 bits wide. This is because all instructions operate on 60-bit data words or 18-bit address or index operands. There are no special registers for floating-point values as in the S/370. Since the 60-bit floating-point value that can be stored in a word has sufficient range, there

Figure 10.2 **Cyber information units**

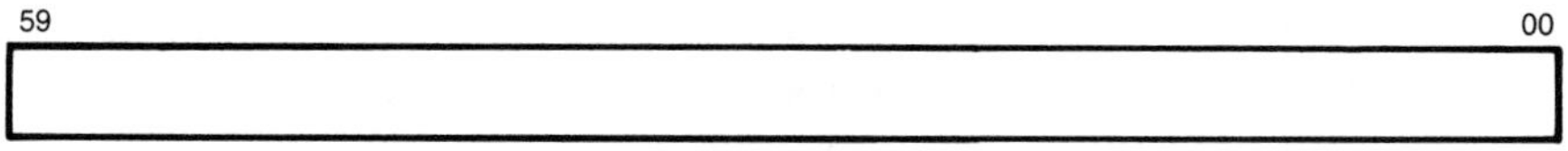

59   00
```
┌────────────────────────────────────────────────────────────────────────────┐
│                                                                              │
└────────────────────────────────────────────────────────────────────────────┘
```

Figure 10.3 Cyber organization

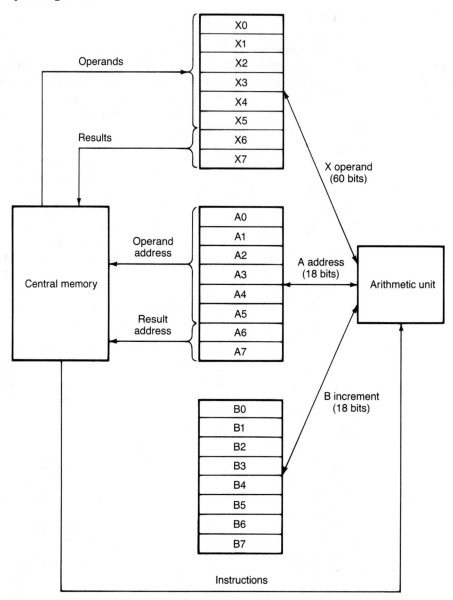

is no double precision. Double-precision values, while computed (that is, the product of two single-precision floating-point values), are not normally saved. Instead, truncation is performed to save only the most significant bits of the product (or quotient).

Figure 10.4 Pass filling instruction

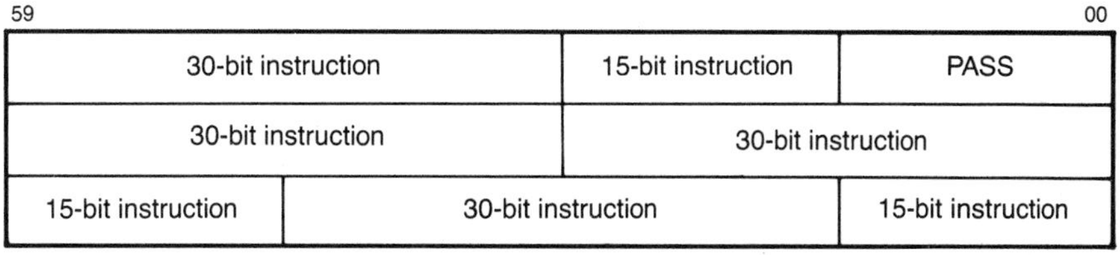

59			00
30-bit instruction		15-bit instruction	PASS
30-bit instruction		30-bit instruction	
15-bit instruction	30-bit instruction		15-bit instruction

To fetch a word from the central memory, one must load the memory address into one of the first six A registers (A0 to A5). The memory reference cycle then automatically causes the memory contents to be placed in the corresponding X register. To store a value in memory, the value is first placed in X register 6 or 7 (X6 or X7). Then the memory address to which the value is to be stored is placed in the corresponding A register, causing the memory write to occur. Thus, the reading from and writing to memory is a side effect of loading an address into an A register. Before giving examples of Cyber instructions, we will first examine how addresses are formed.

A memory address can be contained within an instruction, just as an absolute address is held in a VAX instruction. Alternatively, a memory address can be computed and/or indexed using a B register. There is no indirect addressing in the machine, no autoincrement or autodecrement, and no displacement addressing. Immediate values can be stored as address constants that are not used to reference memory. That is, any 18-bit value that is part of an instruction and not used to load an A register can be used as an immediate value to be added to or subtracted from a B or X register.

Instructions are either 15 or 30 bits in length, and from two to four instructions can be stored in a word. However, if a 15-bit instruction is between two 30-bit instructions, a Pass or Loop instruction can be necessary to fill a word (see Figure 10.4). That is, 30-bit instructions cannot be split over two 60-bit words.

Generally speaking, a 15-bit instruction contains a 6-bit opcode and three 3-bit register fields, while a 30-bit instruction contains a 6-bit opcode, two 3-bit register fields, and one 18-bit constant, as shown.

15-bit Instruction

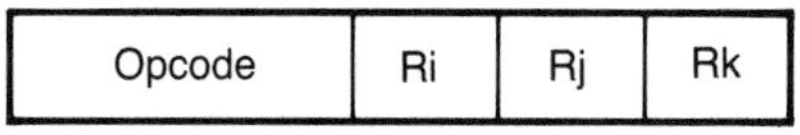

Opcode	Ri	Rj	Rk

30-bit Instruction

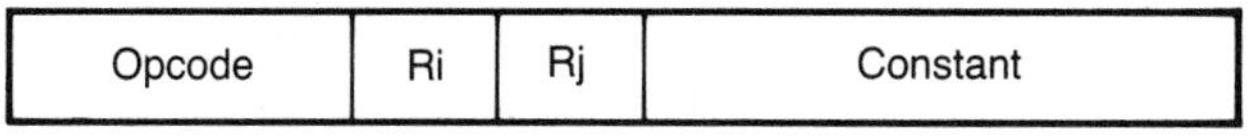

Opcode	Ri	Rj	Constant

Symbolic opcodes specify the arithmetic, logical, floating-point, or address type of operation, along with the destination register. For example, to set X2 to 10, one would write

```
SX2      10
```

The actual instruction generated is

```
SX2      B0+10
```

because two registers are called for in the 30-bit instruction format. Fortunately, register B0 is hard-wired to contain a zero, and the assembler substitutes the correct form for the abbreviated instruction.

To move a word from one memory location to another on the Cyber requires several instructions, as it does for the S/370. On the VAX one might write

```
MOVL     HERE,THERE
```

while for the Cyber, one would be forced to write

```
SA1      HERE
SX6      X1
SA6      THERE
```

This series of instructions causes the contents of memory location HERE to be placed in register X1 (by the Set Register A1 instruction); the logical or Boolean transfer of the contents of register X1 to register X6; and the storing of the contents of register X6 into the memory address THERE, which is Set into register A6. It is worthwhile repeating here that the first six A registers serve to read from memory while the last two serve to write to memory. That is why the transfer from X1 to X6 (the BX6 instruction) is required.

The split of six A registers for reading memory and two for writing memory relates to the number of memory fetches versus the number of memory writes. An analysis of typical programs would show that for every ten reads from memory there is usually only one write back to memory. The ten values read usually will be combined to form some new result, which is then stored. One might then argue that there should be a 7-to-1 split for the Cyber series. The reason that the 6-to-2 split was chosen was that the earlier 6600 computer with its multiple functional units was able to perform several operations in parallel, and there were occasions when even the two A registers were insufficient to allow all the units to operate simultaneously.

Another interesting example of programming the Cyber series is illustrated with the addition of two index array elements ARRAY(i) and

ARRAY(j), equivalent to the VAX instruction

```
ADDL     ARRAY[R1],ARRAY[R2]
```

which might be coded for the Cyber as

```
SA1      B1+ARRAY
SA2      B2+ARRAY
IX6      X1+X2
SA6      A2
```

This series of instructions illustrates several new points about the Cyber. First, it shows indexing where B registers contain the indices i and j, in the same way that the VAX registers R1 and R2 contain them. However, all data words are of the same length and the index does not need to be multiplied by the number of bytes in the operand type. Second, addition can be performed as the sum of two integer values, with the result stored in an X register ready for storing back into memory. Third, since the address at which the resultant value is to be stored is already in an A register, it can be copied from that register into an output A register.

Six classes of operations can be performed on the Cyber data types. Unlike the VAX and S/370 assemblers, where the opcode is distinct from the operands, the Cyber assembler format uses the first letter of the symbolic opcode to describe which hardware arithmetic unit and type of operation (for example, floating-point, logical shift) is to be performed. The actual operation, however, is given by the arithmetic operator between the two register operands. For example, a floating-point divide requires the multiply/divide unit and the first letter of the opcode is an F; the remaining part of the opcode specifies the destination register (say X5), and the actual divide operation is then given by writing X3/X1, where X3 and X1 specify the dividend and divisor operand. Symbolically, we write

```
FX5      X3/X1
```

Some of the first letters used to specify the arithmetic or logical unit that is to perform an operation are

A Perform arithmetic shift on an X register (shift unit).

B Perform logical operation on a pair of X registers (the Boolean unit).

C Count the number of ones in an X register (the divide unit).

D Perform double-precision arithmetic operation on a floating-point value held in two X registers and truncate the result into a single-precision value (the multiply and divide units).

F   Perform single-precision arithmetic operation on a floating-point value held in two X registers (the multiply and divide units).

I   Integer add and subtract (add unit).

J   Jump to indexed address formed as the sum of a B register and the constant field (the branch unit).

L   Perform logical shift on an X register (the shift unit).

N,P,Z   Jump on X value being negative, positive, or zero (the branch unit).

R   Round result of floating-point operation (the multiply and divide units).

S   Set an A, B, or X register (the increment unit).

We have already seen a few of the increment and Boolean unit instructions (SA1 and BX6) and one example of the add unit (IX6). Branch instructions on the Cyber must be combined with the appropriate test, since the machine has no condition codes in which to store state information on arithmetic results. For example, the Branch if Negative instruction

        NG   X4, THERE

branches to symbolic location THERE if the contents of X4 are negative.

Generally there is an adequate instruction set to perform all of the functions that could be performed by the VAX. However, it takes careful programming to fit 15- and 30-bit instructions into an instruction stream, without filling memory with a lot of Pass instructions.

Earlier versions of the Cyber series (the 6000 series) did not have character-manipulation instructions. Indeed, a byte on the Cyber was a 12-bit quantity, since this was the length of a peripheral processor word, although characters themselves were 6 bits, which allowed for the storing of ten characters per word. Later versions supported the ASCII character set, although not quite as gracefully as the VAX, and there were additional character-handling instructions.

Many VAX instructions used to assist the operating system or to perform I/O do not exist for the Cyber central processor. Rather, the monitor and all I/O capabilities reside with the peripheral processors. You might view the central processor as an attached computing engine fed by the peripheral processors.

The differences between the VAX and the Cyber series are so significant that it is difficult to compare them. The Cyber was optimized for arithmetic calculations using the relatively slow core memories available at the time the architecture was designed. Once a value was fetched into an X register (a relatively slow process), it could be manipulated much more quickly using the register-to-register instructions. By providing multiple arithmetic functional units in some versions of the Cyber series, along with a fast buffer memory to hold several instruction words to be executed, it was possible to overlap operations as well as memory reads and writes. In its day, the Cyber was a very fast computing machine.

The Intel 80386 Microprocessor

The Intel 80386 is an evolution of several generations of microprocessors from Intel, the originator of the microprocessor. Predecessors of the 80386 are the 8086 and the 80286, both of which are 16-bit processors, that is, they have 16-bit instructions, 16-bit addressing, and 16-bit words. The 80386 extends those addressing capabilities to 32 bits. The 80386 is designed to be compatible with its predecessors, so it has both a 32-bit mode and a 16-bit mode. The way in which these modes are implemented makes the 80386 somewhat complex; for example, there are two processor-state bits to indicate whether addressing is 16 or 32 bits and whether instructions are 16 or 32 bits. These defaults can even be overwritten on a per-instruction basis. This section examines only the 32-bit instruction mode of the 80386. More details on the 80386 can be found in the *80386 Programmer's Reference Manual* from Intel.

As previously stated, the 80386 is a 32-bit microprocessor with full 32-bit addressing and data types. The basic data types are the 8-bit byte, the 16-bit word, and the 32-bit doubleword; these can be treated as signed or unsigned entities. Instructions are available to deal with single bits, bit fields of one to thirty-two contiguous bits, and character strings up to four gigabytes in length. While the 80386 does not have on-chip floating-point support, a floating-point coprocessor (the Intel 80387) is available to handle 32-, 64-, and 80-bit floating-point data types. The bits in these various data types are numbered from the least significant bit on the right to the most significant bit on the left. The left-most bit is the sign bit. The 80386 is byte addressable, and a data type is addressed by its low-order byte.

Perhaps the biggest visible holdover from its predecessors is the fact that the 80386 has only eight registers. These registers are 32-bit versions of the eight 16-bit registers in the 8086. The eight registers have the names EAX, EBX, ECX, EDX, ESI, EDI, EBP, and ESP. In earlier Intel microprocessors, each of these registers was dedicated more or less to specific purposes. On the 80386, they are somewhat more general purpose in function, although ESP is used as a stack pointer and EBP is used as a frame base pointer for procedure calls. The processor also contains a 32-bit program counter and a 32-bit flags register that contains some privileged and some nonprivileged state bits, such as the four condition code bits for overflow, carry, zero, and negative.

Several different memory management schemes are available on the 80386. At the simplest level, memory is divided into six different segments, where a segment is simply a logically contiguous string of memory bytes. A program has a code segment (CS), a stack segment (SS), and four data segments (DS, ES, FS, and GS). Six segment registers contain the base addresses for each of the six segments. As we shall see, different addressing modes explicitly specify particular segments. The program counter is actually an offset into the code segment, and the stack pointer is an offset into the stack segment. Instructions such as PUSH and POP automatically change ESP and move data to or from the stack segment.

The Intel 80386 supports a number of addressing modes for specifying operands. The simplest modes are *register mode*, in which the operand is in a register, and *immediate mode*, in which the operand is part of the instruction. There are several ways to specify an effective address, which is always interpreted as an offset into a particular segment:

1. *displacement*—A scalar displacement included in the instruction is the effective address of the operand.

2. *base*—A specified register contains the effective address of the operand.

3. *base + displacement*—A scalar displacement is added to the contents of a register to form the effective address.

4. *displacement + (index × scale)*—The contents of a register (called the index register) is scaled by the size of the operand (2, 4, or 8 bytes) and added to the displacement to produce the effective address.

5. *base + index + displacement*—The effective address is formed by summing the contents of the two registers (base and index) and the displacement.

6. *base + (index × scale) + displacement*—The effective address is formed by summing the contents of the base register, the scaled contents of the index register, and the displacement.

Figure 10.5 shows the general format of an 80386 instruction. Not all instructions have all these fields, since some of them depend on the opcode and addressing mode. The table in Figure 10.5 shows the field sizes if they are present. The encoding of some of these fields is often complicated. We will describe the meanings of the various fields and their encodings, although not in complete detail.

Figure 10.5   Intel 80386 instruction format

Immediate	Displacement	Scale	Mod R/M	Opcode		Prefixes

Field	Size (bytes)
Prefixes	1 each
Opcode	1 or 2
Mod R/M	1
Scale	1
Displacement	1, 2, or 4
Immediate	1, 2, or 4

Preceding an instruction can be one or more special instruction prefix bytes, which are opcodes used to override a default for a single instruction. For example, as previously mentioned, the 80386 has a 32-bit mode and a 16-bit mode. In 32-bit mode, operands can be either 8-bit bytes or 32-bit doublewords. In 16-bit mode, operands can be either 8-bit bytes or 16-bit words. Therefore, if you want a single instruction operating in 32-bit mode to manipulate a word, it must switch to 16-bit mode. This can be accomplished by prefixing that instruction with a 1-byte operand-size override prefix. Other override prefixes exist to change segments and to ensure locking for instructions that need to synchronize in a multiprocessor environment.

The opcode is an 8- or 16-byte field that indicates the operation to perform. Some opcodes contain a 1-bit field that indicates the data size of the operand. In 32-bit mode, as already described, this bit indicates whether the operand is 8 bits or 32 bits. Another 1-bit field present in some opcodes indicates the direction of the operation; this is needed because of the lack of symmetry. For example, a memory address specification is always the second operand of an instruction, which is typically the source of the instruction.

Following the opcode is a byte called *mod r/m*, which specifies the addressing mode and can indicate both the source and destination. The format of the mod r/m byte is

07	06 05	03 02	00

Mod	Reg	R/M

The mod r/m byte is composed of three fields. The center three bits (marked *reg*) specify the destination register. The 5-bit field formed by concatenating the mod field and the r/m field indicates one of thirty-two possible source addressing modes. The 2-bit mod field indicates whether the source is specified by a register, a register indirect, a register with 8-bit displacement, or a register with 32-bit displacement addressing mode. For each of these, the 3-bit r/m field indicates which register is to be used. If the mod field specifies an effective address (that is, not register mode), an r/m value of binary 100 indicates that this mode uses a scaled index register.

For cases that use scaling, a scale byte follows the mod r/m field. The format of the scale byte is

```
07  06 05    03 02    00
┌────┬──────┬──────┐
│ SS │ Reg  │ Base │
└────┴──────┴──────┘
```

where *ss* is the scale factor (1, 2, 4, or 8), *reg* is one of the eight registers to be used as an index register, and *base* specifies which segments are to be used and whether an 8-bit or 32-bit displacement is added to the effective address.

If a displacement is present, it follows the mod r/m or the scale byte if one is present. Any immediate data then follows last.

We will not discuss the 80386 in any more detail, but the preceding description should give you some intuition about the basic structure of 80386 instructions. In general, the 80386 is a complex machine. As an example of this complexity, the 80386 chip contains almost twice as many components as the CMOS VAX chip. This complexity is the result of compatibility, which is often required in the commercial microprocessor marketplace. At each generation, chip manufacturers limit their architectures based on the current chip technology. When technology changes, manufacturers are able to add more features, but they must do so in a way that retains compatibility with their existing products. In contrast, minicomputer manufacturers are not quite so limited by space as single-chip microprocessor manufacturers, so they have been able to design architectures for a longer lifetime.

Despite its complexity, the Intel 80386 is destined to become a successful product. The 80386 is the basis of a generation of personal computers and its performance has greatly increased the computing capabilities available to personal computer users. The 80386 has also been used as the basis of a multiprocessor computer system, the Symmetry, made by Sequent Corporation.

Reduced Instruction Set Computers

Over the past several years, an important trend has developed in computer architecture. This trend has led to a new generation of processors based on a philosophy of reduced instruction set computers (RISCs). As opposed to complex instruction set computers (CISCs), of which the VAX is possibly the major example, RISCs take a "less is more" approach. While there is debate over exactly what a RISC is, some of the basic properties of a hypothetical RISC might include the following:

- A small number of instruction operations. A RISC computer might have on the order of fifty different instructions.

- A simple-to-decode instruction format. A RISC would typically have fixed-length instructions, for example, all instructions could be 32 bits in length with fixed fields for the opcode and operand specifiers. This simplifies decoding when compared to the decoding of the variable-length instructions on the VAX.

- Direct hardware instruction execution. In contrast, most CISCs are microprogrammed (we will discuss microprogramming in some depth in a later chapter).

- A small number of addressing modes. A RISC would have only a few ways of specifying operand addresses.

- A load-and-store architecture, with arithmetic available only in register-to-register instructions.

- A small, fixed instruction cycle time. The objective is to make all instructions sufficiently simple that they can all execute in one short cycle. Making the cycle time as short as possible is one of the most important goals.

- An open-implementation philosophy. That is, a RISC architecture might choose *not* to hide some "messy" implementation features if they can be exploited to gain performance.

In fact, this approach resembles some of the simplest early computers, with instruction sets directly executed by the hardware. Many of the reasons for the change to more complex instruction sets, as well as for a swing back in the other direction, are technological. For example, when CPUs are much faster than memories, it makes sense to do more work per instruction; otherwise, the CPU would always be waiting for the memory to deliver instructions. This leads to more complex instructions that encapsulate what would otherwise be implemented as subroutines. If CPU and memory speeds are more balanced, then a simple approach can make more sense, assuming that the memory system is able to deliver one instruction and some data each cycle.

Another reason for simplifying computer architectures is the change from medium-scale to very-large-scale integrated circuits (VLSI). With VLSI, there is a tremendous cost for off-chip communication, so it pays to make the architecture simple enough to fit on a single chip. As chips become more dense, however, either instruction complexity (to avoid going off chip as frequently) or the amount of memory on chip will have to be increased. Most of the latest VLSI microprocessors have chosen to increase the amount of on-chip memory to buffer instructions and data.

Fundamentally, RISC advocates argue that adding a more complex instruction or addressing mode often affects the design of a computer by complicating, and thus slowing down, important stages of the instruction-execution process. While the addition of the complex function might make that function execute faster than an equivalent sequence of simpler instructions, it can lengthen the instruction cycle time. This could make all instructions slightly slower. Thus, the addition of a new function had better increase the *overall* performance of the processor enough to compensate for the decrease in instruction-execution rate. Compared to a CISC, a RISC needs to execute many more instructions to perform the same function; if the cycle time of the RISC is fast enough, however, it can buy back the time needed for the additional instructions.

The RISC philosophy has been used even within the realm of more complex machines. For example, the DEC MicroVAX II is a single-chip version of the VAX architecture. To ensure that the MicroVAX could be built on a single chip, DEC simplified the VAX architecture by removing many of the complex instructions (for example, commercial instructions), emulating them in software instead. A RISC philosophy has been used at the microlevel of the VAX 8800 family of machines, where the principal goal was a reduced microcycle time. This was achieved by simplifying the operations that the hardware can perform.

In any case, the design of an architecture involves many tradeoffs, both technical and marketing, and an architecture must span many different technologies and implementations. The current trend is certainly toward simplified architectures, but only time will tell whether that is a long-term or short-term trend.

The next section examines the Berkeley RISC II, a reduced instruction set microprocessor developed at University of California at Berkeley. We concentrate on some of the interesting architectural features of the RISC II and do not describe its VLSI implementation. If you are interested in RISCs and RISC processor design, refer to some of the sources in the bibliography, including the paper by Hennessy (1984). The best source on RISC II is the fine thesis by Manolis Katevenis, *Reduced Instruction Set Computer Architectures for VLSI*, which is published by MIT Press.

Berkeley RISC II

The Berkeley RISC II, as its name implies, is the second implementation of a RISC microprocessor at University of California, Berkeley. The RISC research project was probably most responsible for publicizing the advantages of designing microprocessors with simplified instruction sets. In the following discussion, RISC refers to the RISC II implementation, although in the aspects that we present, RISC I and RISC II are almost identical.

RISC is a 32-bit microprocessor; all instructions are 32 bits, and the basic data type is the 32-bit word. Each procedure executing on the RISC can address thirty-two 32-bit registers. While the basic data type is the word, RISC also supports 8-bit bytes and 16-bit halfwords. RISC is byte addressable, and addressing is similar to the VAX in that each information unit is addressed by its low-order byte. Bits are numbered right to left from least significant to most significant. Words and halfwords must be properly aligned in memory; that is, halfwords must begin at even addresses and words must begin at addresses evenly divisible by 4.

There are three interesting architectural features of the RISC that we will consider: its instructions, its register organization, and its branch instructions.

True to its name, the RISC instruction set consists of only 39 opcodes. There are only two instruction formats, called short-immediate and long-immediate. The opcode indicates which format is used. Short-immediate format is as follows:

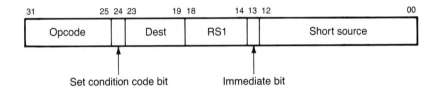

The interpretation of most of these fields is straightforward. The *opcode* specifies the operation to perform, *dest* is a destination register number, and *rs1* is a source register number.

A short-immediate instruction has two forms as indicated by bit 13, the immediate bit. If bit 13 is zero, then bits 0 through 12 contain a 13-bit immediate value. If bit 13 is set, then bits 0 through 4 of the instruction contain a second source register (rs2); in this case, bits 5 through 12 are unused. This second format permits three-operand instructions, where all operands are in registers.

The second instruction format, called long-immediate, is shown below:

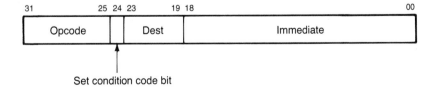

In this format, there is a single register (*dest*) and a 19-bit immediate value.

The RISC has four condition code bits: N, Z, V, and C. Instead of setting the condition codes automatically as a side effect following every instruction, the set condition code bit in each instruction indicates explicitly whether the condition codes should be set. This makes it possible to set the condition codes, execute several instructions, and then branch on the result of the instruction that set the condition codes.

RISC is a load-and-store machine, meaning that arithmetic operations can be performed only in registers. Register zero is special in that it always returns a value of zero. It can be written but a write to register zero has no impact. This fact reduces the number of opcodes. For example, there is no register move instruction, since a move is simply accomplished by adding register zero to a source register and storing the result in the destination register. Moving a register to itself or to register zero can be used to set the condition codes, that is, as a test instruction. Subtracting two registers and storing the result in register zero is a compare instruction.

RISC supports only twelve arithmetic and logic instructions:

- shift left logical, shift right logical, and shift right arithmetic

- logical AND, OR, and XOR

- add, subtract, and subtract inverse (all three are also available using the carry bit)

All twelve instructions are short-immediate format; when a 13-bit immediate is used it is always sign-extended to 32 bits. An inverse subtract is needed to permit both register minus immediate and immediate minus register.

Load and store instructions are used to move data between memory and registers. On a load instruction, the effective address can be specified in one of three ways:

- in short-immediate form as *register + register*,

- in short-immediate form as *register + 13-bit immediate*, or

- in long-immediate form as *PC + 19-bit immediate*.

The first two forms are called register-indexed and the last form is called PC-relative. There are ten load instructions to permit both register-indexed and PC-relative loads from words, and register-indexed and PC-relative loads from both signed and unsigned bytes and halfwords. Six Store opcodes are available to write bytes, halfwords, and words using the last two effective address formats shown.

The other major instruction group is for control transfer. The conditional jump instruction, available with both PC-relative and register-indexed addressing, uses instruction bits 19 through 22 to specify the condition to be tested. These four bits specify sixteen boolean functions of the condition codes for which a true result causes a branch; one of the values specifies "branch always" and provides the unconditional branch. There are also two subroutine call opcodes (for the two addressing formats) and a subroutine return.

An interesting feature of the RISC branch instruction—and a feature that is common to most reduced instruction set computers—is that all of the branches are *delayed branches*. Branch instructions cause a significant performance problem in computer implementations. On most computers, while one instruction is being executed the next sequential instruction is being *prefetched* so it will be available when the processor is ready. Otherwise, the processor would have to wait for memory to deliver each instruction. When a branch instruction succeeds, the prefetched instruction will not be the next instruction to be executed, and the processor must wait for the new target instruction to be fetched.

Delayed branches are one solution to this problem. On the RISC, the instruction *following* a conditional or unconditional branch is *always* executed. For example, if we have the sequence

```
ADD      R2,R3  (set condition codes)
JUMPEQ   P2
SUB      R4,R5
P1:         .
            .
            .
P2:         .
```

then the SUB R4,R5 executes whether or not the JUMPEQ instruction succeeds. If the conditional jump does succeed, the SUB executes followed by the instruction at P2. If the conditional jump fails, the SUB executes followed by the instruction at P1. In this way, the processor has work to do while the next instruction stream is fetched.

The success of a delayed branch mechanism depends on the ability of the high-level language compiler to find instructions that can be placed following branches. Basically, these must be instructions that can be executed whether or not the branch succeeds, and for which there are no dependencies before the branch. If the compiler cannot find such an instruction for a particular delayed branch, it simply follows the branch with a no-op.

Perhaps the most unusual architectural feature of the RISC is its register window mechanism, which is responsible for much of its performance gain. While register windows are implemented on the RISC, they are not really related to the reduced instruction set nature of Berkeley RISC and could be used equally well on a CISC.

The principal objective of the register window mechanism is to reduce the time for a procedure call. As discussed in Chapter 9, the VAX Call instructions take a significant portion of the execution time. Part of the reason for this is the number of memory writes needed to pass parameters and to save registers. These overheads are avoided on the RISC by using *overlapping* register windows, which work as follows. The RISC chip actually has 138 registers. Each procedure can address 32 registers, which are organized into four groups:

- Registers 0-9 are global registers, visible to all executing procedures in a program.

- Registers 10-15 are output parameter registers, used to write parameters to be passed to procedures to be called.

- Registers 16-25 are local registers, used to store local variables within a procedure.

- Registers 26-31 are input parameter registers, used by a procedure to receive inputs from its caller.

When a procedure has to call another procedure, it writes parameters for the procedure to be called into registers 10-15. When it executes a procedure call, the called procedure is allocated the next set of registers on the register stack. This is done in such a way that registers 10-15 of the *calling* procedure become registers 26-31 of the *called* procedure. Thus, the called procedure automatically sees its inputs in the input registers, and it is allocated sixteen new registers on the stack for its local variables and output parameters. Two special processor registers are used to indicate the current state of the register stack for the executing procedure. The general organization of the register stack is shown in Figure 10.6.

Register windows reduce the number of writes on procedure call because (1) parameters are passed in registers and (2) the called procedure does not have to save registers because it is allocated new local registers. This mechanism works well because most programs make frequent procedure calls, but the depth of procedure calls does not vary greatly. RISC has space for a call depth of eight procedures. When the eighth procedure attempts to call the ninth, a register stack overflow occurs and the operating system must migrate one or more register stack frames to main memory. As returns occur, an underflow eventually occurs and those frames will need to be brought back. Another problem with large register files is that the time to context switch between user processes increases as the amount of state to be saved increases.

Berkeley RISC is interesting for a number of reasons, including its streamlined instruction set, register windows, and delayed branch mechanism. Since Berkeley RISC, a number of reduced instruction set processors have appeared on the marketplace.

Figure 10.6 Berkeley RISC register window stack

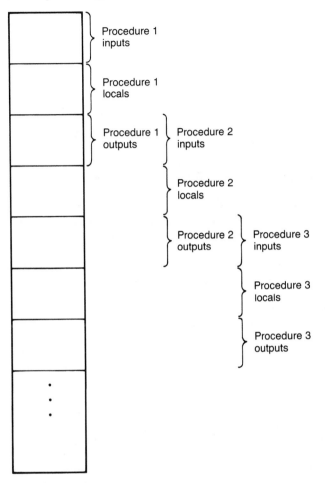

Summary

This chapter introduced the instruction set architectures of four computer systems. The instruction set for each machine was designed based on the goals and constraints of that system and on the available technology. The designers for each machine made different tradeoffs in addressing capabilities, instruction size, data types, and generality.

We have focused on the representation of addresses and the coding of instructions. This examination gives us a better basis for comparing computer systems and for evaluating the architecture of the VAX. Of course, the VAX has benefited from analysis of previous instruction sets, such as the IBM 360/370 and the PDP−11. Similarly, the RISC processors have benefited from analysis of the VAX.

Exercises

1. How are memory addresses represented in IBM 370 instructions? How can the CPU tell which addressing method is being used?

2. What information about the instruction is given by the opcode in a VAX instruction? In an S/370 instruction?

3. What is a System 370 base register? Why are base registers used?

4. What is the difference between index registers on the S/370 and index registers on the VAX?

5. Why do we say that the S/370 is a load-and-store machine?

6. The CDC Cyber series has a larger word size than any of the other machines we have examined. Why do you suppose that 60-bit words were chosen, as opposed to 32- or 16-bit words?

7. Why do we say that reading or writing memory is a side effect on the CDC Cyber computer?

8. What are some differences of memory addressing among the IBM System 370, the Intel 80386, and the VAX?

9. What is the major difference between the encoding of addressing modes on the VAX and the encoding of addressing modes on the Intel 80386? Why would you choose one over the other?

10. Discuss the advantages and the disadvantages of register windows as implemented on the Berkeley RISC. Suppose you had a choice of register windows or a single file of 128 registers, which would you choose and why?

11. What is a delayed branch? What would be the advantages and the disadvantages of having a delayed branch instruction that executes two instructions following the branch instead of one?

12. Describe an interesting feature of each of the architectures presented. Now that you have seen several other instruction sets, what features of the VAX do you think are most interesting in comparison? What things about the VAX would you change if you were able to modify the architecture?

11 *Physical Input and Output*

So far, we have concentrated on the environment visible to the machine language programmer, consisting mainly of the hardware instruction set, memory and its addressing, and the functions provided by the assembler. This and following chapters will begin to examine how the real hardware and the operating system software combine to provide each user with a simple, predictable, logical environment in which to create and execute programs.

On a single-user computer, all the physical resources are at the user's disposal: the processor, the memory, and the peripherals. Conceptually, the user should be able to access these resources directly. In general, even single-user computers must permit cooperation between several programs running simultaneously on that computer. Similarly, on a shared computer, resources must be divided equitably among the users so that each user receives a fraction of the total resources available. In addition, it is desirable for each program to be unaware of the others, that is, for each program to view memory and peripherals as if it were the only program in the system. To permit this, the operating system must transform the physical hardware resources into logical resources that the user manipulates.

The system printer, for instance, is a logical device that different users (or different programs on a single-user computer) share. Each user sees this logical device as being capable of printing program listings and other files on command. The printer automatically prints a header page identifying the user and the listing. The physical printer hardware, on the other hand, is not so elegant and must be programmed at a basic level. Some printers must be fed one character or a line at a time by a controlling program. If each user wrote directly to the printer, the output would consist of a mess of interspersed lines and characters from different users' files. Consequently, the operating system manages the physical printer, giving each user access to a logical printer while maintaining the integrity of the material being printed.

Even though the multiprogrammed operating system does not permit direct control of such devices by user programs, it is still valuable to examine how input/output (I/O) is performed. It is also useful to understand the physical characteristics of some typical devices and how they are controlled. In this way, we can more easily understand how software transforms physical devices into high-level logical devices that programmers can access.

I/O Processing

In requesting an I/O operation, the programmer normally specifies an operation to be performed (for example, read or write), the main memory address that is to receive data or that contains data to be output, and the amount of data to be moved. The operating system software initiates a data transfer between the device and memory. Early computers required that the processor control the entire I/O operation; the processor would execute an instruction to transfer the data and would be forced to wait until the operation was completed. During that time, thousands of instructions could have been executed. However, since the program would not continue until the I/O operation was completed, a significant amount of processor time was lost.

To take advantage of this idle processor time, new computers have *I/O controllers*, as shown in Figure 11.1. A controller contains special hardware to handle device operations. Once an operation has been accepted by the controller, the CPU is free to continue processing. In this sense, a controller is simply a slave computer that performs I/O at the request of the master CPU.

Controllers can control several devices simultaneously; once one device is started, the controller is free to start another device. A computer

Figure 11.1   Simple I/O structure

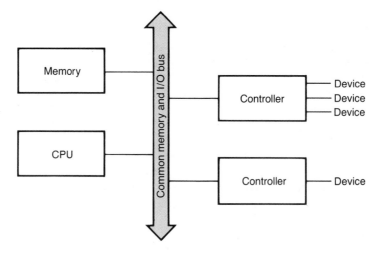

with several controllers can thus perform computation concurrent with I/O processing on multiple devices.

Instead of waiting in a loop for an operation to complete, some computers periodically *poll* all active devices to check their status. After finding a device that has completed an operation, the processor can initiate another operation and then process the data read or written. Because this still consumes a large amount of CPU processing, *interrupts* were introduced. An interrupt is a signal from a device controller to the processor that indicates that the device needs attention. The processor starts the operation, and the controller interrupts when the operation is done. On the VAX, an interrupt automatically saves the state of the running program and causes execution of an operating system routine to handle the interrupt. An interrupt is thus similar to a subroutine call initiated by the device controller asynchronously to the execution of the currently executing program.

By suspending execution of a program that is waiting for the completion of an I/O operation and starting another program to be executed, the processor resource can be shared and more efficiently utilized. Now, however, when an interrupt occurs, the state of the running program must be preserved while an operating system routine is run to handle the interrupt. This saving of the state is performed automatically on the VAX.

For VAX peripherals, there are two styles of I/O programming. The choice of style depends primarily on the speed of the device. For slow devices such as terminals, *programmed I/O* is used. In programmed I/O, the controller contains a special register, called a buffer register, that the processor loads with a single character to be written out. The device writes the character and then interrupts when it is ready for the next one. Or, on input, the device deposits a single character into a buffer register and interrupts the processor, which removes it. Although processing can be overlapped with the operation, the processor must move each byte to or from the controller.

For high-speed devices such as disks, the controller normally performs *direct memory access* (DMA) I/O, sometimes called *nonprocessor request* (NPR) I/O. In this mode, the controller performs a block transfer, in which large blocks of data are moved directly between the device and memory. The entire transfer occurs without processor intervention. To handle such an operation, the controller contains special registers that the CPU loads with information about the transfer. The controller must be told how many bytes to move, where the main memory buffer is located, what device unit and device location to operate on, and what operation to perform. The controller moves the specified amount of data and then interrupts when it is done.

Even though I/O devices can operate independently of the CPU, at times the CPU and the I/O devices contend for the use of main memory.

Controllers have internal memories, again called buffers, in which data is placed before being read or written. Because the controller needs to empty its buffer memory before incoming data overwrites its contents, the controller has precedence over the CPU when accessing main memory. The I/O controllers simply cause the CPU to pause while the data is transferred into memory. This process is called *cycle stealing*, because the I/O units steal cycles from the CPU. Cycle stealing works because I/O controllers make memory requests infrequently and tie memory up for only short periods of time.

Control and Status Registers and I/O Space

We have noted that VAX I/O controllers contain special registers for holding control information and for buffering data. These are known as *control and status registers* (CSRs) and *data buffer registers* (DBRs). Each I/O device controller contains a set of registers, which are assigned addresses in the physical address space (that is, addresses on the bus). The contents of these registers can be manipulated by standard VAX instructions. Therefore, the VAX, unlike many other computers, needs no special I/O instructions. For example, the following instruction could be used to store an output character in a device buffer register:

```
MOVB    CHAR,DEVICE_BUFFER_REGISTER
```

An I/O device driver, which is the software that controls the device, senses the status of the controller and commands the controller by reading and writing the control and status registers. In addition, the device driver reads from and writes to the data buffer registers to obtain input and to initiate output.

I/O device registers have fixed addresses in the upper half of the VAX *physical address space*. The physical address space consists of all the addresses that can be broadcast on the system memory bus. If the system memory bus has thirty address bits, then the system has a 30-bit physical address space. Physical addresses are different from the logical addresses used by programs, which are called *virtual addresses*. Virtual addresses (the addresses seen by the program) are translated by the processor into physical addresses (the addresses put on the bus to access real memory).

On the VAX, the lower half of the physical address space is used for primary memory, as shown in Figure 11.2. Thus, some memory references access physical memory locations, while others access device registers. The VAX hardware is capable of restricting the access to the I/O registers. Normally, user programs are not allowed to read or write CSRs. (For historical reasons, most VAX I/O registers must be accessed as 16-bit quantities using word context instructions.)

Figure 11.2 VAX physical address space

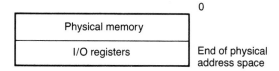

Low-Speed Devices

Low-speed peripheral devices include line printers, terminals, card readers, and some smaller disks. For most of them, device data transfers occur one byte at a time. The device driver writes to the device by moving a character into the output data buffer register of the controller; it reads by moving a character from an input data buffer register. One CSR is normally used to indicate errors and command completion.

The Line Printer

One of the simplest I/O devices is the line printer. For example, the model LP11 line printer controller has two 16-bit I/O registers—one control and status register and one data buffer register—in the physical address space. Figure 11.3 shows the format of these registers. The Error and Done bits of the status register are read-only bits. Software instructions cannot modify them, and they can be set or cleared only by the

Figure 11.3 Line printer I/O registers

Line Printer Status Register

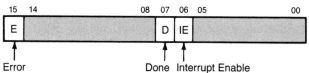

Error—The controller sets this bit when an error condition exists, such as line printer out of paper, printer off-line, or printer on fire.

Done—The controller sets this bit whenever the printer is ready to accept the next character to be printed.

Interrupt Enable—The software sets this bit to tell the controller to interrupt when either D or E is set by the device, that is, if an error occurs or the printer is ready for another character.

Line Printer Data Buffer Register

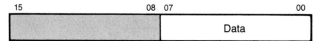

The software loads bits 0 through 7 with the ASCII character to be output.

controller. To output a character, the software moves an 8-bit ASCII character into the lower byte (bits 0 through 7) of the line printer data buffer register using a MOVB instruction of the form

```
MOVB    CHAR,LP_BUFFER_REGISTER
```

Although the LP11 controller requires that characters be moved one at a time into the data register, it contains some further internal buffering to reduce the number of interrupts. This buffering allows the controller to hold several characters at a time. Instead of writing one character to the printer and interrupting upon its completion, the controller holds several characters and interrupts only when the entire buffer is written to the printer. If internal buffer space is available when a character is moved to the data buffer register, the controller immediately copies the character into internal buffer storage and sets the Done bit. When the internal buffer is full, the Done bit remains clear until the controller is ready.

The following sample routine outputs a string of ASCII bytes to an LP11 line printer. The routine continues inserting characters until the controller fails to set the Done bit. It then waits for an interrupt before continuing.

```
;++
;
; ROUTINE DESCRIPTION:
;
;       This routine outputs a string of ASCII characters to an LP11
;       line printer.
;
; CALLING SEQUENCE:
;
;       BSB or JSB
;
; INPUT PARAMETERS:
;
;       R0 contains the number of characters to output
;       R1 contains the address of the string
;
; OUTPUT PARAMETERS:
;
;       None
;
; SIDE EFFECTS:
;
;       R0 and R1 are modified
;
;--

        LP_CSR= ...              ; define CSR address
        LP_DBR= ...              ; define DBR address
```

```
WRITEHELP:

        PUSHR   #^M<R2,R3>       ; save registers
        MOVAW   @#LP_CSR,R2      ; copy CSR address to R2
        MOVAW   @#LP_DBR,R3      ; copy DBR address to R3
10$:    CLRW    (R2)             ; clear Interrupt Enable bit

;
; Begin writing string.
;

        BRB     30$              ; start at end of loop
20$:    BITW    #^X8080,(R2)     ; test Error and Done bits
        BLEQ    40$              ; branch if Error set or Done
                                 ; ...clear (printer not ready)
        MOVB    (R1)+,(R3)       ; output character to printer
30$:    SOBGEQ  R0,20$           ; continue if more to output
        BRW     DONE             ; finish up if done

;
; Either an error exists or printer is not ready.  If not ready, then
; allow interrupts and wait.  R0 must be incremented because the SOBGEQ
; at 30$ decremented it without outputing a character.
;

        40$:    BLSS    ERROR            ; handle error if E set
                INCL    R0               ; update character counter
                BISB    #^X40,(R2)       ; set interrupt Enable
                  .
                <wait for interrupt after line is printed>
                  .
                BRB     10$              ; continue
                  .
                  .
```

Terminal Multiplexing

A typical controller for video and hard-copy terminals is more complicated than a printer controller, because it must handle simultaneous input and output. Users often type while output is still being delivered to the terminal. In addition, because terminals are among the slowest input devices due to human typing speeds, one controller on a VAX typically handles four, eight, or sixteen lines at a time, depending on the controller.

An early VAX terminal controller was the DZ11, shown in Figure 11.4. We use the DZ11 as an example because of its simple structure. The DZ11 is an eight-line terminal multiplexer that controls eight asynchronous lines for communications with terminals or other computers. Although a DZ11 controller contains nine I/O registers, we will examine only a few registers and fields to see how a multiplexer is controlled. The registers we will discuss are the Control and Status Register (CSR), the Transmit Buffer

Figure 11.4   DZ11 terminal multiplexer

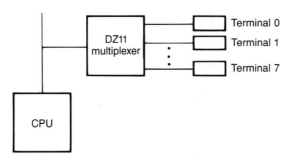

Register (TBUF), and the Receive Buffer Register (RBUF). These registers and their important control fields are shown in Figure 11.5.

Output on the DZ11 is similar to that on the line printer, except that the programmer must specify which terminal is to be selected. For each line, a single-character buffer holds the character being output. When a buffer for any line becomes empty, indicating that the terminal is ready to receive the next character, the controller loads the line number into the TLINE field of the CSR ands sets the TRDY bit. If transmit interrupts are enabled (that is, the TIE bit is set), an interrupt is generated. The software handling the interrupt must then move the next character for that terminal into TBUF. Writing the character to TBUF causes the controller to transmit the character to the specified terminal and to clear the TRDY bit in the CSR.

Because several terminals may be sending at once, the DZ11 contains a 64-word buffer for input characters called the SILO (for "service in logical order"). As each character is received, it is placed in the SILO with the line number on which it arrived. RBUF is actually the bottom of the SILO. As characters arrive, they are added to the top of the SILO; characters move toward the bottom as software removes characters from RBUF. Each time RBUF is read, the next character in the SILO is moved to RBUF. Whenever a new character is moved into RBUF, the controller sets RDONE in CSR and interrupts if receive interrupts are enabled.

Terminals can be run in either local-echo or remote-echo mode. In local-echo mode, the terminal itself displays each character as it is typed. In remote-echo mode, the character is merely sent to the computer. The computer must then output it again to make it appear on the screen, a process called echoing. Remote-echo allows for more complex terminal functions, particularly for editing, and shows the user that the correct character was received. The echoing can usually be done fast enough that the character appears instantaneously. Local-echo is sometimes useful when terminals are connected over slow long-distance lines in which the echo time is long.

Figure 11.5   DZ11 terminal multiplexer I/O registers

Control and Status Register (CSR)

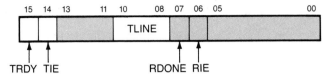

TRDY TIE   RDONE RIE

Receiver Interrupt Enable (RIE) — Software sets this bit to cause the controller to interrupt when a character is received.

Receiver Done (RDONE) — The controller sets this bit when a character becomes available in the read buffer. The bit is cleared when the character is read by software.

Transmitter Line Number (TLINE) — The controller loads this 3-bit field with the line number of the line that is ready for transmission of another character.

Transmitter Interrupt Enable (TIE) — Software sets this bit to cause the controller to interrupt when a line is ready for another character to transmit.

Transmitter Ready (TRDY) — The controller sets this bit when a line is ready to transmit a character.

Transmit Buffer Register (TBUF)

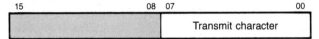

Software loads bits 0 through 7 of TBUF with the character to be transmitted to the terminal whose number is in the TLINE field of CSR.

Receive Buffer Register (RBUF)

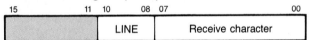

Bits 0 through 7 of RBUF contain the character received from the terminal whose number is in the 3-bit LINE field.

High-Speed Devices

High-speed devices include primarily magnetic disks and tapes. These are known as *mass storage devices*, because in comparison with primary memories, they have large capacities. A single magnetic disk pack can store up to 600 million bytes of data, which it can transfer at rates of over a million bytes a second. Disks are known as *direct* or *random-access* storage devices, because any location on a disk is directly addressable. In contrast, tapes are *sequential-access* storage devices, because they must be sequentially scanned to find a given location.

Magnetic Disks

A disk is a rotating, flat magnetic platter that resembles a phonograph record. Much like the grooves of a record, the surface of the platter is divided into concentric *tracks*, although the grooves do not spiral toward the center. Each track is again subdivided into *sectors* or *blocks*, as shown in Figure 11.6. The sector, typically the smallest addressable unit, holds a fixed amount of data. On the VAX, most disks have sectors of 512 bytes, referred to as *disk blocks*.

To read or write a sector, a magnetic read/write head senses or magnetizes the sequential stream of bits on the track passing beneath it. Most common disks are *moving-head disks*, with one read/write head per surface that must be mechanically positioned over the track to be accessed. The positioning of the head, called a *seek*, usually takes from 10 to 50 milliseconds. In applications in which performance is critical, *fixed-head disks*, which have one read/write head for every track, are used. With fixed-head disks, no seeks are required; however, fixed-head disks are prohibitively expensive.

Once the read/write head is positioned to the track, it must wait for the correct sector to pass by. Known as *latency time*, this rotational delay can be minimized by increasing the rotational speed of the disk. However, increases in speed are limited by physical tolerances in the balancing of the rotating mass. Most large disks spin at 3600 revolutions per minute.

The total transfer time for a disk read or write operation thus has three components:

$$total\ time = seek\ time + latency\ time + data\ transfer\ time$$

Two techniques are generally used to increase the storage per disk device. The number of bits stored on the surface can be increased either

Figure 11.6 Single-disk platter surface

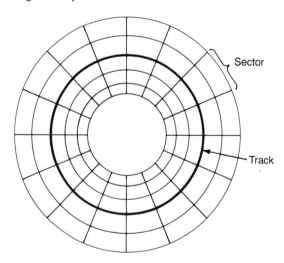

by storing more bits per inch around a track or by increasing the number of tracks. However, there is always a limit to how much information can be successfully stored and retrieved from a disk. As densities increase, so do error rates.

To increase the storage of each device, several platters are usually mounted together to form a disk pack, as shown in Figure 11.7. A separate read/write head is used for each surface of each platter. Another benefit of this arrangement is that more data can be read before the heads need to be moved. Indeed, for these multiplatter disks, the concept of a track gives way to that of a *cylinder*, formed by the logical grouping of all tracks at the same radius on each platter, as Figure 11.7 illustrates.

Most disks today are built with "Winchester" technology. These are sealed drives (that is, the disks are nonremovable), which keeps the operating environment cleaner. Alignment problems of heads and platters are reduced because one set of read/write heads operates with only one physical disk for its lifetime.

Table 11.1 compares performance characteristics of several disks commonly used on VAX systems.

Simplified Disk Control

Examining some of the I/O registers for a VAX disk device will help you better understand how software handles a disk. This section examines the RK07, which was one of the earliest and simplest of disks. Each RK07 disk drive is connected to an RK711 disk controller, which is capable of handling up to eight drives. The controller has DMA capability and can move up to 64K 16-bit words of data to or from the disk without processor intervention. The controller is also capable of initiating several simultaneous seek operations, although only one device can transmit at a time.

Figure 11.7 Multiplatter disk

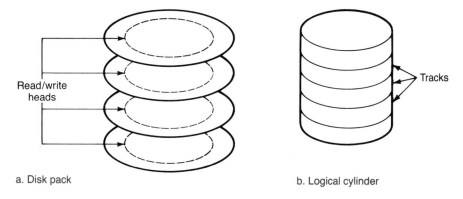

Read/write heads

a. Disk pack

Tracks

b. Logical cylinder

Table 11.1   Common VAX Disk Characteristics

Characteristic	*RX53 Floppy*	*RD54*	*RA70*	*RA81*	*RA82*
Form size	5.25	5.25	5.25	10.5	14
Bytes/pack	1.2M	160M	280M	456M	622M
Number of platters	1 (flex)	2	2	4	4
Cylinders/cartridge	160	1224	1507	1248	1423
Tracks/cylinder	2	15	11	14	15
Sectors/track	15	17	33	51	57
Bytes/sector	512	512	512	512	512
Rotational frequency, rpm	360	3600	3600	3600	3600
Average latency (1/2 revolution), ms	83	8.3	8.3	8.3	8.3
Average seek, ms	92	30	19.5	28	24
Peak transfer rate, bytes/s	512K	625K	1.4M	2.2M	2.4M

The RK711 has fifteen I/O registers, several of which are partially described in Figure 11.8. To perform a transfer to or from memory, the device driver performs the following steps:

1. It calculates the disk address of the first block of the transfer. The disk address is composed of three parts: cylinder number, track number, and sector number. The cylinder number is moved to the Desired Cylinder Register for head positioning.

2. It loads the Drive Select field in CSR2 with the number of the disk unit.

3. It loads the Function field in CSR1 with the code for a seek function.

4. It enables interrupts and sets the Go bit in CSR1 to execute the seek for the desired cylinder. The device interrupts when the seek is complete.

Figure 11.8   RK07 disk I/O registers

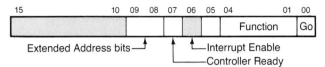

Go — The software sets this bit to cause the controller to execute the specified function on the selected unit.

Function — These bits specify the command to be performed by the controller, that is, read data, write data, seek.

Interrupt Enable — When this bit is set, the controller will interrupt when (1) a command completes, (2) a drive indicates an attention condition, or (3) any drive or the controller indicates the presence of an error.

Controller Ready — This bit is set by the controller when it is ready to process a new function.

Extended Bus Address — The controller transfers data into a memory buffer specified by an 18-bit address. The low 16 bits are loaded into the Bus Address Register, and the high 2 bits are loaded into this field.

Disk Control and Status Register 2 (CSR2)

Drive Select — Software loads this field with the unit number of one of eight possible drives on which to perform an operation.

Disk Desired Cylinder Register (DC)

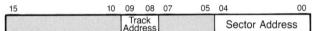

Cylinder Number — Software loads this field with the cylinder number of the first sector for the operation.

Disk Address Register (DA)

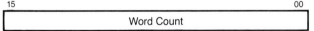

Sector Address — Software loads this field with the number of the desired sector on the selected track and cylinder.

Track Address — Software loads this field with the number of the desired track on the selected cylinder.

Disk Word Count Register (WC)

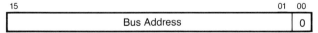

Word Count — Software loads this register with the two's complement of the number of data words to be transferred to or from memory. In other words, the negative word count is stored.

Disk Bus Address Register (BA)

```
15                                                01  00
┌─────────────────────────────────────────────┬─────┐
│              Bus Address                     │  0  │
└─────────────────────────────────────────────┴─────┘
```

Bus Address — Software loads this register with the low 16 bits of the 18-bit bus address for the main memory buffer. The low bit is always 0 because it must be the address of a word. The disk transfers only an even number of words.

5. When the seek completes, the device drive loads the track number and the sector number into the Disk Address Register and reloads the cylinder number in the Desired Cylinder Register, in case it has been overwritten by another concurrent disk operation.

6. It then loads the Word Count Register with the number of words to transfer and the Bus Address Register with the bus address of the main memory buffer.

7. It loads the Function field in CSR1 with the code for the operation, whether read or write.

8. Finally, it enables interrupts and sets the Go bit to start the operation. The device interrupts when the transfer completes or an error occurs.

The following simplified code sequence executes a function on the RK07. The routine is passed a control block containing a buffer address and length, a unit number, a disk function number, and a disk block number. The disk block number must be translated into cylinder, track, and sector address. The routine does no initialization or error checking, but merely loads the registers and starts the operation.

```
;++
;
; ROUTINE DESCRIPTION:
;
;        Routine to execute a specified function on the RK07 disk.
;
; CALLING SEQUENCE:
;
;        BSB or JSB
;
; INPUT PARAMETERS:
;
;        R0 =    address of a control block containing the following
;                fields:
;
;        BUFFER(R0)   =  address of the user's buffer (only 18
;                        bits are used)
;        BUFLEN(R0)   =  length of user buffer in words
;        BLOCKNUM(R0) =  logical block number of first disk
;                        block of the transfer if the disk is
;                        imagined as a contiguous array of disk
;                        blocks
;        UNIT(R0)     =  unit number of disk device
;        FUNCTION(R0) =  code number of disk function to perform
;
;--


;
```

```
; Define Disk I/O Register Addresses
;
        RK_CSR1 = ...                       ; define first CSR address
        RK_CSR2 = ...                       ; define second CSR address
        RK_WC = ...                         ; define Word Count Reg.
        RK_BA = ...                         ; define Bus Address Reg.
        RK_DA = ...                         ; define Disk Address Reg.
        RK_DC = ...                         ; define Desired Cylinder
;
; Define Offsets for Input Control Block Arguments
;

        BUFFER = 0                          ; offset to buffer address
                                            ; ...argument
        BUFLEN = 4                          ; offset to buffer length
        BLOCKNUM = 8                        ; offset to block number
        UNIT = 12                           ; offset to unit number
        FUNCTION = 16                       ; offset to Function code


;
; Define Disk Geometry Characteristics for Computing Disk Address
;
        CYLINDERS = 815                     ; number of cylinders on pack
        TRACKS = 3                          ; number of tracks per cylinder
        SECTORS = 22                        ; number of sectors per track
        BLOCKS_PER_CYLINDER = SECTORS * TRACKS ; just as it says


;
; Calculate the disk address parameters from the disk block number and
; load the appropriate registers.
;

RKDISK:
        PUSHR   #^M<R2,R3,R4,R5>            ; save registers
        MOVL    BLOCKNUM(R0),R1            ; get logical block number
        CLRL    R2                          ; clear next reg. for 64-bit
                                            ; ...divide
        EDIV    #BLOCKS_PER_CYLINDER,R1,R2 ;
                                            ; R1 <- cylinder number
                                            ; R2 <- sectors left on cyl.
        CLRL    R3                          ; clear next reg. for 64-bit
                                            ; ...divide
        EDIV    #SECTORS,R2,R2,R3          ; R2 <- track number on cyl.
                                            ; ...R3 <- sector num. on track
        MOVW    R1,@#RK_DC                  ; load cylinder register
        MULL    #256,R2                     ; shift track number left
        BISW3   R2,R3,@#RK_DA              ; load Disk Address Reg. with
                                            ; ...track and sector numbers
        MOVW    UNIT(R0),@#RK_CSR2         ; load unit number into CSR2
        MNEGW   BUFLEN(R0),@#RK_WC         ; load Word Count Register with
                                            ; ...2's complement of
                                            ; ...transfer size
        MOVW    BUFFER(R0),@#DK_BA         ; place low 16 bits of address
                                            ; ...in Buffer Address Register
```

```
;
; Construct a mask for CSR1 containing the Go bit, the Interrupt
; Enable bit, the Function code field, and the two high order
; address bits from the 18-bit bus address.  Load the CSR1 to
; initiate function.
;

        EXTZV   #16,#2,BUFFER(R0),R4    ; get two high bits of
                                        ; ...bus address
        MULL    #256,R4                 ; shift bits to bits <9:8>
        INSV    FUNCTION(R0),#1,#4,R4   ; insert Function code in
                                        ; ...bits <4:1>
        BISW3   #^X41,R4,@#RK_CSR1      ; enable interrupts, and
                                        ; ...execute the function
        .
        .
        .
```

This routine is a simplified example showing only the loading of some of the important device registers. A real device driver can be extremely complicated. The actual function execution is only a small part of the work to be done. On disk devices, more than half the driver code may be devoted to detecting and recovering from controller or disk unit errors, of which there are many varieties. Another large part of the driver is concerned with interfacing with the operating system and its data structures. However, examples like this do give some sense of the complexities involved in handling a real device.

Magnetic Tape

Magnetic tape is 1/2-inch mylar film with an iron oxide coating on one side. A standard 10 1/2-inch reel contains 2,400 feet of tape capable of storing up to 140 million characters of data at a density of 6,250 bits per inch, although some new cartridge drives can store close to 300 megabytes at higher densities of 10,000 bits per inch on a small, 5 1/4-inch cartridge.

Each data byte is written as 8 data bits plus one parity bit across the width of the tape, as shown in Figure 11.9. The parity bit is set or cleared to make an even number of ones in the 9-bit character. This is known as even parity. When the tape is read, if the character contains an odd number of ones, then a 1-bit error has occurred.

A tape with the format shown in Figure 11.9 is known as nine-track tape because there are nine data channels. Most drives are also capable of producing seven-track tape that uses six data bits and one parity bit. However, since ASCII characters are eight bits wide, nine-track tape is more useful on the VAX.

Data characters on tape are stored in variable-length blocks. Industry standards allow blocks to be from 18 to 2,048 characters long. Blocks can be partitioned into records. Unlike a disk device, which revolves continuously, a tape must be set in motion before it can be read or written.

Figure 11.9   Magtape format

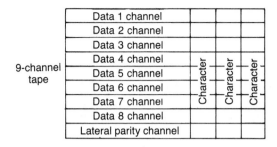

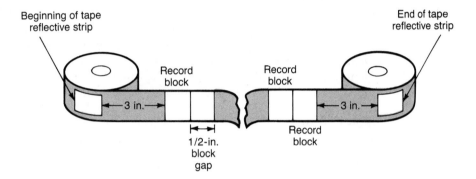

Because reaching the proper tape speed requires time, a 1/2-inch space, called the interblock gap, is left between blocks. Hence, the tape is better utilized if longer blocks are used or if the blocks are grouped together to reduce the amount of wasted space.

A tape controller normally handles several tape drives. Several drives at a time can be rewinding or spacing, although only one can transfer data at a time. The controller can execute functions to read in the forward or reverse direction, write, space forward or reverse, rewind, unload, or erase. Transfer to or from the tape are DMA. While the tape handles characters one at a time, the controller holds two characters for input or output. As a result, transfers between the controller and memory occur one word at a time.

Mass Storage Control Protocol

An earlier section showed an example of a disk interface and driver code to control it. One problem with control and status register interfaces on VAXes was the *ad-hoc* nature of such interfaces. That is, each new disk device would have a different interface and would require new driver software to be written for each operating system and computer to which that driver could be attached. The work involved in developing these new drivers was significant.

To attack this problem, Digital Equipment Corporation developed a standard message-oriented protocol for controlling disks and tapes, called the Mass Storage Control Protocol (MSCP). Each new disk controller developed for VAXes is required to implement this protocol, so from the disk driver's point of view, all devices have the same interface. Coding is simplified and time is saved.

MSCP works, in general, as follows. For each request to the disk, the disk driver builds a *command packet*, which is a data structure whose format is specified by MSCP. The packet contains several fields, including an operation code that tells the device what function to perform, device status information, and parameters required by the operation code. The command packet is placed on a *command queue* in memory, which is shared by both the disk driver software and the controller hardware. The controller copies the contents of the command packet to its own internal memory, examines it, and performs the function. The controller then uses the original command packet memory to build a *response packet*, which indicates whether the operation completed successfully. The response packet is placed on a *response queue* maintained by the VAX. The controller then interrupts the host processor to notify the driver that a response packet has been queued and the operation has completed.

There are several advantages to this scheme. The most obvious is that the differences in specific drives are transparent to host drivers. A disk can identify itself and indicate how many disk blocks it contains, but otherwise its interface is standardized. MSCP devices present a higher-level interface than did CSR-controlled disks; the driver does not worry about sectors and cylinders, but views the disk as a contiguous sequence of blocks. Furthermore, bad blocks can be handled by the controller transparently to the driver. The controller can replace a bad block with another block while making that new block appear to be in the location of the original one. In fact, most disks now have "extra" blocks that are available just for this purpose.

Another advantage of this scheme is that it presents the possibility of controlling disks remotely. That is, once a command packet is constructed, it is a simple matter to send the packet over a network to the device. With CSRs, the communication between the driver and the controller is based on shared memory. Moving to a message-oriented scheme greatly simplifies distribution, but there is a time penalty associated with the network. Another advantage is that the command-queue mechanism permits the device to examine several pending requests before choosing one. For example, a disk controller could queue commands internally and examine the command queue to optimize its use of the disk. The controller would order the I/O requests so as to choose next the request closest on the disk surface to the current head position.

Networks

A final type of I/O device we will consider is the network interconnect, which permits a CPU to talk to one or more other CPUs. In a network, each CPU is called a *node*.

Networked computers are called *loosely coupled* systems because they cooperate over a relatively slow medium and interact on a fairly coarse scale. Loosely coupled nodes share large objects such as files or programs rather than single bytes or words. It is usually possible, for example, to request execution of service programs on remote computers. Over networks, nodes communicate by sending either fixed-length or variable-size messages.

In contrast to networking, shared-memory multiprocessors, which we will consider in a later chapter, are said to be *closely coupled*, because processor interaction is through shared memory. In these systems, sharing of small amounts of data can be very rapid. Closely coupled programs can handle fine-grained interaction, for example, accessing one byte or word at a time. Because one CPU need only wait until another is through reading or writing a single data item, there is little performance degradation when data is shared in a multiprocessor.

Networks are complex structures and present many difficulties for system software. An international standard, the ISO model, describes a model of the multiple-layered software that is used to transfer programs and data between nodes. Because this detail is beyond the scope of this book, you should refer to a text specifically on networking for more information. This section simply examines some of the high-level alternatives in physical interconnection organization, that is, network topology.

Figure 11.10 shows several alternative network structures. Figure 11.10a is a conventional point-to-point network. In this organization, each cable connects two nodes. Such a network is often called a *store-and-forward* network, because intermediate nodes are responsible for receiving messages and forwarding them along the way to their destination. For example, a message from node D to node A must pass through nodes B and C. If B or C is unavailable, A and D would not be able to communicate. This could be solved by building a *fully connected* point-to-point network, that is, one in which each node has a direct point-to-point link with every other node. However, such a network is prohibitively expensive and complex for even a network of moderate size. Consider that it would require on the order of N^2 wires to fully connect N nodes.

Another networking alternative, a *star* configuration, is shown in Figure 11.10b. In this organization, all nodes are connected through either a central node or special-purpose central switch. The DEC CI (computer interconnect) bus is organized in this fashion. The advantage of this structure is that it is logically fully connected, and no failure of a processing node will interrupt communications between other nodes.

Figure 11.10   Network topologies

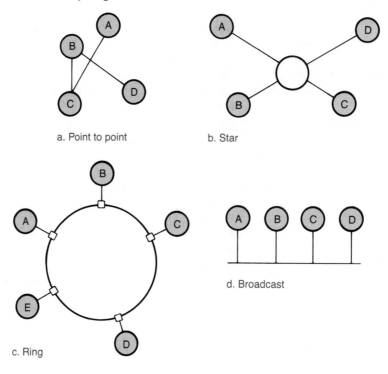

a. Point to point

b. Star

c. Ring

d. Broadcast

Also, the average node-to-node wiring distance is reduced compared to some other schemes. The obvious disadvantage is the potential complexity of the central switch, which must be extremely reliable for the network to function reliably.

A ring network, typically called a *token-passing ring*, is shown in Figure 11.10c. In this organization, a single cable in the shape of a circle passes through a ring interface connected to each of the nodes. Typically, bits circulate around the cable in slots of fixed size. The concept of slots is a result of the small and finite amount of time it takes for a data bit to traverse the ring from start to finish. Multiple data bits can be inserted into the ring until the first bit arrives back at the start. By dividing the stream of bits into blocks of n bits, we can arrive at a set number of slots each capable of holding the n bits.

In a token-passing ring, a special token within a slot travels around the ring to indicate a free slot. When a node sees this token and it wishes to transmit a message, it removes the token and places its message in the available slot or slots. The message contains the address of both the sender and the receiver, as well as the data to be transmitted. When the receiver's interface sees the message, it copies the message from the ring and replaces the token so that another node can use that slot. Or a message may continue around the ring until it arrives back at the original sender; the receiver can modify the message slot to indicate that the message has been read, so the sender has a definite acknowledgement.

Finally, Figure 11.10d shows a broadcast network. The most common broadcast network is the 10-megabit/second Ethernet, which is a standard developed jointly by Xerox, DEC, and Intel. In a broadcast network, all nodes sit on a long triaxial cable. When a node sends a message, that message is visible to all nodes on the cable. However, only the destination node sees its address in the message header and copies the message from the cable. By using a special predefined address, it is fairly easy in such a network to use the broadcast feature so that a message is received by all nodes. Other predefined addresses can be used to *multicast* to a subset of nodes that are listening for that particular multicast address.

One issue with broadcast cables is resolving contention, since all nodes could potentially try to send a message at once. The conventional scheme used to resolve contention is called Carrier Sense Multiple Access with Collision Detection, or CSMA/CD for short. In this scheme, each node has an interface that continually listens for messages. When a node wants to send a message, it first listens to see if there is a transmission in progress. If the cable is quiet, the node begins sending its message while continuing to listen. If two nodes sense that the network is available and try to transmit at the same time, a *collision* occurs and both nodes detect the collision as a change in the message being transmitted. Fortunately, a collision can occur only in the time it takes for the start of the message to propagate the length of the cable.

When a collision occurs, both sending nodes *back off*, that is, they stop transmitting. Each node waits a random interval and then tries again, first listening to see if another transmission is going on and then transmitting if it is not. The random interval is different for each node, therefore those two nodes will not collide again. If a node retransmits and collides again (this time with another node), the sending node once again backs off but waits a longer random interval. Multiple consecutive collisions indicate a busy network, and the back-offs become longer to try to reduce the network load. In typical Ethernet networks, however, the cable is rarely utilized more than a few percent of the time.

Broadcast, token-passing ring, and star networks are typically used to build *local area networks* (LANs). A LAN usually connects nodes located only a short distance apart, for example, 1,000 meters or less, typically the size needed to lay cable in a small building. These networks rely on full connectivity and low message-propagation time. By contrast, the point-to-point network structure is used to implement *long-haul networks*, that is, networks that connect systems that may be hundreds or thousands of miles apart. In this case, the point-to-point links may range from slow-speed dial-up telephone line to dedicated data line to satellite transmission.

Long-haul networks are typically more complex and have to deal with more complex failure modes, such as lost or duplicated message packets, network partitioning, unreliable interconnects, and so on.

The Initial Bootstrap Problem

We have examined the structure of I/O devices such as disks and buses and the logic needed to program them. One problem of any computer system is how it is started. Given a code required to read a disk, how is the machine "smart" enough to load the operating system from disk when it is first plugged in and powered on?

The procedure for bringing up the software from a bare machine is known as *bootstrapping* (booting), because the system is being "brought up by its bootstraps." The booting procedure usually has several stages. On some early minicomputers, a small program was loaded into memory by hand via switches on the front panel of the processor. This program, known as the *primary bootstrap*, was typically only ten or twenty instructions long. On most modern computers, the primary bootstrap is stored in a read-only memory (ROM) chip that can be activated by the push of a button.

Every system must have at least one mass storage device, called the *boot device*, which contains more code for starting the system. This code, called the *secondary bootstrap* program, is stored at a known place on the device, such as block zero of a disk. The purpose of the primary bootstrap is simply to load the secondary bootstrap into memory and transfer control. The secondary bootstrap program is large enough to contain logic for locating and loading the rest of the operating system.

Before loading or starting the bootstrap, the computer must be brought to a known state. The processor must be halted, devices must be initialized so that no transfers occur into memory, and memory management must be turned off. The primary and secondary bootstraps operate on a bare processor and physical memory. As more intelligence is loaded, devices are initialized, memory management is turned on, and the operating system takes control. Finally, users are allowed to access the system.

Summary

This chapter considered some of the characteristics of VAX input and output devices. We discussed the functions performed by I/O controllers, which control several devices concurrently and provide for the buffering of data between the device and memory. The differences between programmed I/O, where the CPU reads and writes data registers, and DMA I/O, where the device transfers directly to memory, were discussed in light of the speed of the data transfer. We looked at several typical I/O devices, their physical characteristics, their programming, and their operation.

The complexity of the devices and the need to share them among many users or processes precludes executing code that manipulates most I/O devices directly. Therefore, a controlling operating system is necessary to manage these and other resources. Subsequent chapters discuss how the VAX hardware facilitates the management of resources and examine the characteristics of operating systems in general. We will also take a closer look at one particular operating system, the VAX Virtual Memory System (VAX/VMS).

Exercises

1. Explain the concept of contention as it applies to I/O devices using main memory.
2. What is the difference between a device and a device controller?

3. Sketch out the logical flow for the receiving and the transmitting of characters for the DZ11 terminal controllers.

4. Explain the difference between a fixed-head disk and a moving-head disk.

5. Why is it best to make a disk a DMA-type device?

6. For disk and tape I/O devices, list the functions that should be performed by the device drivers.

7. List several advantages of using a message-oriented interface, such as MSCP, over a CSR-oriented interface.

8. Describe the topological alternatives for network interconnection and list some of the essential properties of each alternative.

9. One popular method of connecting terminals is through a network terminal controller and *concentrator*. The controller sits in a box to which the terminals connect. The box is not connected to a computer directly but sits on an Ethernet. Describe how such a concentrator might be used and what are its advantages and disadvantages.

12 *The Support of an Operating System*

Chapter 11 considered some of the physical characteristics of the VAX I/O system. The complexity of the I/O devices and the need to share them among many users and processes precludes the execution of code that can manipulate I/O devices directly. However, even if we could directly access the physical devices, most applications would find little utility in doing so. Accessing a disk sector is of as little use to the payroll program as it is to the Fourier transform program. These programs do not want to handle interrupts or errors from the printer controller or worry about sharing the printer. Instead, a controlling program, the operating system, is used to manage those and other physical resources.

The need for an operating system is really a matter of economics. Early computers were batch-processing systems. A single program, submitted on a deck of punched cards, was read into the computer memory and executed. When a program finished printing its results, the next program was loaded and run.

The main problem with this mode of processing was that a single program could not use all of the expensive resources of the computer system effectively. Some programs were small in size, and most of the memory sat empty while they were executed. Some programs were I/O intensive, and since the program had to wait for each I/O operation to complete, the processor remained mostly idle. Finally, some programs were totally compute-bound, leaving the I/O devices unused while they ran.

Efficiently utilizing expensive hardware resources required the sharing of the processor, memory, and I/O devices by several programs at a time. This sharing would allow one program to be computing while another waited for its I/O operations to complete. Several programs would be loaded into memory so that the processor could be quickly switched from one program to another if the current program requested an I/O operation or finished processing.

Sharing of resources was made possible by a *multiprogrammed* operating system. The multiprogramming system allows several programs to compete for computer resources, which are divided equitably among the programs. The multiprogramming system creates a logical environment for the programs, where each program operates as if it were the only one using the system. This ability to create a simple, logical environment for each program is a consequence of sophisticated software that allows such conveniences as named files instead of disk cylinders or sectors.

To provide these features, the operating system must deal with a number of complex issues. First, it must handle complex devices at the physical I/O level and be able to recover from unexpected device errors and conditions. Second, it must create an environment for each program, allowing the program to access shared resources but separating it from other programs. Since several programs share the hardware, they must be protected from each other. Third, the operating system must try to schedule resources in a way that provides fair service to each program while maintaining high utilization of the resources. This is a difficult decision-making process, since fair service and high utilization are often mutually exclusive.

One might argue that as hardware prices decline, the economics will no longer justify sharing as they have in the past. Already, it is possible for many users to have a stand-alone computer, either a personal computer or workstation. However, even a single-user computer needs an operating system to perform the myriad of complex physical housekeeping functions. In fact, single-user operating systems may be more complex because users' demands for new services are increasing quickly as prices decrease. In addition, the single-user computer must cooperate with other computers in a network to provide communications and informational and computational services.

This chapter examines how an operating system manages the sharing of the processor and memory. Then we look at how the VAX architecture supports the operating system by providing high-level operating-system features in the hardware.

Sharing the Processor

As we have said, the multiprogramming system must divide the available processor time among its users in a way that is equitable. The *scheduler* is the operating system module that selects the programs to be run on the processor and decides how long each should run. The general strategy is to subdivide each second of processor time into a number of units, called *time slices*. Each program in the system is given one time slice to execute, after which it is interrupted so that another program can run. This is shown in Figure 12.1. A new program is also started whenever a running program completes or waits for an I/O operation to finish. Thus, the scheduler attempts to deliver some fraction of the processor time to each program in the system.

In this way, each of the n programs in the system sees a processor with $\frac{1}{n}$ times the power of the actual CPU. From the point of view of the program, it executes continuously on a processor of speed $\frac{1}{n}$. However, a

Figure 12.1   *Division of processor time by the scheduler*

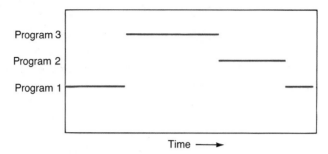

user at a terminal running a highly interactive program (that is, one that issues a large number of terminal I/O operations) may not be able to tell the difference, because the I/O operations are overlapped with the processing of the user's programs.

Sharing the Memory

Just as the operating system manages the sharing of the processor, it also manages the sharing of memory among several programs. Sharing of memory is more complex because programs address specific memory locations. Therefore, in addition to managing the physical division of memory among the programs, the operating system and the hardware must make each program believe that it is the only program in memory. The system must provide a logical environment for each program that allows the program to operate as if it had been loaded into contiguous physical memory.

This logical environment allows every program to be written for a contiguous, zero-based physical address space. However, since computers must run several programs concurrently to achieve high utilization, the operating system must provide the logical environment that the program expects.

There are several techniques for hiding from the program its physical location in memory. The simplest scheme for allowing several programs to coexist in memory is relocation through the use of a hardware base register. With this technique, each program is loaded into contiguous physical memory, as shown in Figure 12.2.

The CPU hardware contains two special registers: a base register and a length register. Before a program is started, these registers are loaded with the base physical address and the length of the program. When the program generates an address, the hardware first checks the length register to ensure that the program accesses only its memory. Then, the hardware adds the value of the base register to the program-generated address, producing the actual physical address. In this way, several

Figure 12.2 *Relocated programs in physical memory*

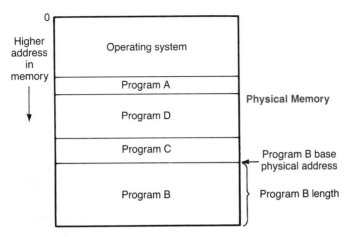

programs can reside in memory simultaneously. A program can be located anywhere in physical memory and still address memory as if it were loaded at physical address zero. Of course, there must be sufficient contiguous memory to contain the entire program.

Program-generated addresses are called *virtual addresses*, because they refer to the contiguous logical address space, not to the actual physical memory locations. The CPU hardware converts a program-generated virtual address into a *physical memory address* through the addition of the contents of a relocation register.

A slight extension of the relocation scheme is *segmentation*. Logically, users write programs and subprograms that can be conveniently thought of as segments into which a problem has been subdivided. Each program segment in the system is written as if it were loaded into a contiguons memory space, starting with memory address zero. To support segmentation, mapping hardware must include a base register and a length register for each possible segment, as shown in Figure 12.3. Address translation is more complex because the hardware must locate the appropriate base register for each memory reference. Segmentation does not require that the program be contiguous in physical memory. Since each segment is mapped separately, it could be loaded anywhere in memory.

The problem with the relocation and segmentation schemes is the complexity of memory management for the operating system. As programs exit or wait for the completion of an event, they are removed from memory, leaving odd-sized holes. Because of this *memory fragmentation*, unoccupied segments may not be large enough to hold new program segments that need to be loaded into memory. The operating system must move segments around to compact all free segments into a large contiguous space. This shuffling of memory is expensive and time consuming.

Figure 12.3 Program segmentation

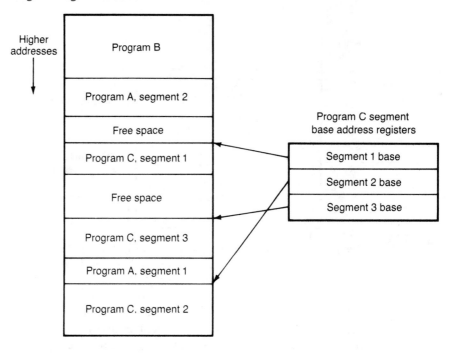

Since it involves moving resident segments, the base registers must be changed to reflect the new virtual-to-physical translation. Because running programs must be stopped to allow relocation, less useful work is accomplished.

Managing, compacting, and relocating odd-sized segments is time consuming. From the operating system viewpoint, a more uniform and more easily handled method of memory management is required. One solution is paging, which removes the need for the entire program to be in physical memory. Paging also solves the problems of fragmentation and compaction. In the paging scheme, the program is divided into equal-sized blocks called pages. Physical memory is also divided into pages. Because both programs and physical memory are divided into pieces of equal size, there is no problem fitting the pieces of a program into memory. Any program page will fit into any memory page. Since a page is usually smaller than a program, many pages are needed to hold the entire program. With paging there is no fragmentation problem. However, on the average, the last page of a program will be only half filled. This wasted space is known as *internal fragmentation*, as opposed to the *external fragmentation* caused by segmentation.

For each program there is a list of mapping registers called a *page table*. The elements in the page table are *page table entries* (PTEs), each containing the base physical address for one page. Each PTE also contains one bit, the Valid bit, that indicates whether the page is actually in physical memory. The presence of the Valid bit removes the restriction that all of the program must be in memory. If a reference is made to a nonresident or invalid page (that is, the Valid bit in the corresponding page table entry is 0), the hardware initiates an operating system routine that loads the page from disk. On a paging system with sufficient address space, the programmer need not worry about whether the program fits in physical memory. The programmer constructs the program for a large contiguous address space, and the operating system does the rest.

Figure 12.4 shows an example of the physical address computation for a paging machine with N-bit addresses and M-bit pages (i.e, 2^M bytes per page). The virtual address can be viewed as containing two logical components, a virtual page number and a byte offset within that page. The virtual page number, i, selects the ith page table entry, which contains the physical address of that page. The byte offset is appended to the physical page address to form the physical memory address of the referenced byte.

The difference between segmentation and paging is that segmentation is convenient for the user, while paging is convenient for the operating system. In a strict sense, segmentation is concerned with the logical allocation of the program, while paging is concerned with the physical allocation of the program. As with page table entries, it is possible for segment registers to contain a Valid bit; a segment fault would be generated on an attempt to access a segment not loaded in primary memory. With many segment registers (or more likely, with a segment table and many segment table entries), the program can be divided into many segments that can be scattered throughout physical memory. If the

Figure 12.4 *Address translation in a typical paging system*

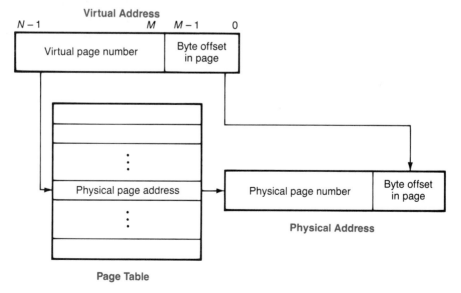

Page Table

segments are constrained to be of equal size, segmentation degenerates into paging.

Of course, the two concepts are not mutually exclusive, and some systems provide both paging and segmentation. In such systems, each segment is divided into a number of pages. The uniformity and consistency of fixed-size pages makes it easier for the operating system to allocate and deallocate space for different users. For example, in a segmentation scheme with paging, the virtual address can be logically broken into three parts, as shown in Figure 12.5. The segment number is used to select one of the entries in the segment table. The segment table entry contains the address of the page table for that segment. Next, the page number field of the virtual address locates one of the page table entries in the selected page table. The physical address is formed by concatenating the physical page address found in the PTE with the byte offset from the virtual address.

This extra level of indirection provided by segmented paging simplifies sharing of code segments between programs. With the one-level page table structure of Figure 12.4, each program would need entries in its own page table to map a shared section of code or data. With the segmented structure, however, the two programs could share a page table. Each program's segment table would have an entry that points to the page table for the shared segment. Therefore, a shared physical page would be mapped by only one PTE. This type of sharing makes it easier for the operating system to account for the page because there is only one descriptor (PTE) telling whether the page is in memory or on disk.

Virtual memory is the term applied to memory systems that allow programs to address more memory than is physically available. The system disk provides the "virtual" memory by storing pieces of the program that are not currently in use. When one of those pieces is referenced, it is brought into physical memory by the operating system, and some piece of a resident program can, in turn, be moved back to the disk. This loading of pages from disk when a nonresident memory location is accessed is called *demand paging*.

In summary, just as the operating system creates a logical temporal environment for each program, it also creates a logical memory environment using the memory-management schemes described here. Memory can be shared by many programs, with each program operating as if it were loaded into contiguous physical memory. The management of physical memory is done by the operating system to increase memory and processor utilization in a manner that is transparent to the program.

Having examined the basic concepts of processor and memory sharing, the rest of this chapter describes those parts of the VAX architecture that support the VAX operating system and its management of resources. Most of these features are invisible to the executing user program. However, an understanding of this level of the architecture will give you a better appreciation for how computers and operating systems

Figure 12.5   Address translation in a typical segmented paging system

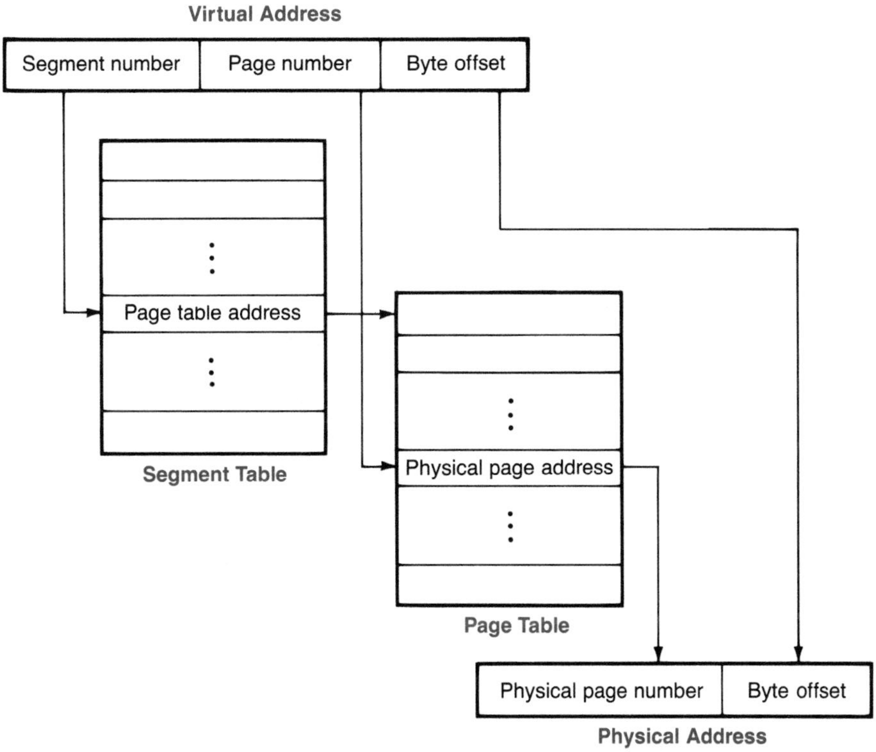

provide the logical environment that is visible to the user. This chapter deals with the hardware mechanisms that are available for the operating system software to use. A later chapter discusses how this support is used to implement policies and to produce a higher-level logical structure for the convenience of the user.

Processes

A user begins a session with a computer by logging into the operating system, that is, by supplying a user identification and a password. After validating this information, the operating system provides the user with an environment in which to edit, run, and debug programs as well as create, update, and maintain a set of permanent files. A *process* is the environment in which these operations are performed. It is the basic logical entity of the hardware and software systems, the environment in which programs execute, and the basic unit scheduled for execution by the operating system.

Each program in the operating system runs in the context of a process. A process is, in effect, a virtual machine that defines the address space and the logical resources for the user. By a virtual or logical

Figure 12.6   User processes in memory

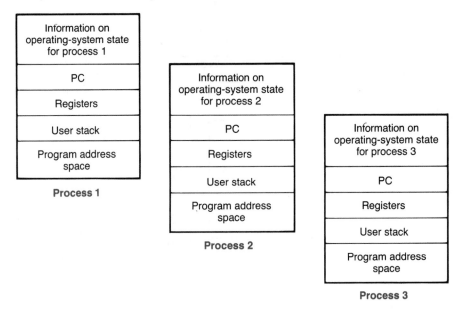

machine, we mean a conceptual environment in which the program sees a machine interface that may or may not exist in physical hardware.

A process is represented by its *state*, or context, which tells (1) the location in physical memory of the instructions and data of the process, (2) the next instruction to execute for the process (that is, its program counter), and (3) the contents of the hardware registers of the process.

Figure 12.6 shows a symbolic representation of the processes in the system. As you will see, the VAX hardware directly supports the concept of a process. But for the time being, we will use the process concept to describe how the VAX architecture allows the operating system to provide sharing and protection among processes.

Processor Access Modes

The four *access modes*, known as *Kernel, Executive, Supervisor,* and *User*, provide the basic protection mechanism of the VAX processor. At any one time, a process executes its instructions in one of these modes. The mode of the process determines its *privilege* for accessing memory and the types of instructions it can execute. For instance, the instruction to halt the processor can be executed only in the most privileged mode, Kernel mode.

Access modes provide *layered protection* for different levels of system software. They are often shown as concentric rings as in Figure 12.7, where the inner rings are more privileged than the outer rings. This

Figure 12.7   Use of access modes by VMS operating system

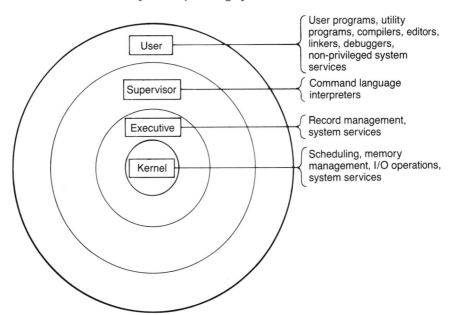

structure permits several distinct functional layers to be constructed, one upon another. Each inner layer provides primitive functions for the next outer layer to use. As each layer of software is added, a new logical interface is constructed, providing higher-level features.

Layering of software simplifies its construction. If careful interfaces are designed between layers to restrict and control the flow of information, layers can be built independently. The VAX access modes allow for the layering of software into four levels. Hardware access modes formalize the structure by providing protection between levels.

In general, routines that execute at a particular mode can protect their code and data from any less privileged mode. Thus, reading or writing certain data structures may require a more privileged access mode. Access modes also allow for restricting certain classes of instructions. Running in Kernel mode, the most privileged mode, the program has complete control of the processor and all its instructions, registers, and memory.

Process Access Mode Stacks

When the concept of the stack was introduced in previous chapters, it appeared that a process needed only one stack to handle subroutine and system calls. In fact, each process has four stacks, one for each processor mode. Each stack can be protected against access by less privileged modes. Having separate stacks allows code running at an inner level, that is, in a more privileged mode, to maintain local information on its stack without worrying about interference from an outer level. For example, a command interpreter that runs in Supervisor mode can use the Supervisor stack for information about its state. Control can be transferred to the user, leaving the Supervisor stack intact until control is returned to the Supervisor level.

The VAX hardware maintains copies of the stack pointer for the four access modes of the current process. The stack pointer (SP) register always contains the stack pointer for the current mode stack. When a mode change occurs, the hardware automatically stores the contents of SP into a temporary location and loads a new value into SP from the copy of the stack pointer of the new mode.

In addition to the four process stacks, there is a fifth system-wide stack called the *Interrupt stack*. While each user process has four stack pointers for each of the four access modes, there is only one Interrupt stack in the system and only one Interrupt stack pointer. The Interrupt stack services events that occur asynchronously to the execution of a process. When the interrupt occurs, the processor automatically switches to the Interrupt stack. (This is examined further in the sections on interrupts and exceptions.)

Changing Modes

Some of the processor-state information is maintained in a hardware register called the *processor status longword* (PSL). The upper 16 bits of the PSL are protected and cannot be modified by a user program. As shown in Figure 12.8, the PSL describes the current and previous modes of the processor. The modes are encoded in two-bit fields, where

00 = Kernel
01 = Executive
10 = Supervisor
11 = User

The one-bit Interrupt stack field indicates that the processor is executing on the Interrupt stack. When this bit is set, the current mode field must be 00, that is, the processor must be in Kernel mode.

Figure 12.8 Processor status longword

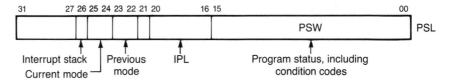

The processor normally runs at the least privileged mode, User mode. To perform a privileged function (for example, an I/O operation), the user calls an operating system service routine for assistance. If the system service routine needs to run at a more privileged mode, the routine executes a Change Mode instruction. For each access mode, there is a Change Mode instruction: CHMK, CHME, CHMS, or CHMU for Change Mode to Kernel, Executive, Supervisor, or User, respectively. The instructions have one operand, a code that specifies what privileged function or procedure to execute.

When a Change Mode instruction is executed, the processor switches to the stack of the specified mode. It does this by saving the contents of the SP in an internal register and loading the SP with the saved stack pointer in the new mode. The PSL and the PC of the process are saved on the new stack. The processor then inserts the caller's mode in the PSL previous mode field and loads the new mode in the current mode field. Now running in the new mode, the processor transfers to a predefined routine within the operating system. This routine, called the change mode dispatcher, examines the code argument and dispatches to the operating system procedure, which performs the requested service. For example,

```
;
; use operating system Kernel mode procedure
; number 10
;

CHMK    #10
```

changes the processor to Kernel mode and invokes the change mode dispatcher to execute a procedure indicated by argument 10. Normally, the user does not specify a Change Mode instruction explicitly, but instead uses a system call to invoke a system function. The called routine executes the Change Mode instruction if needed.

It is important to note that both the dispatching routine and the final service routine execute within the context of the user's process. They behave similarly to local subroutines that a user may call. Therefore, even though the operating system service routine executes in a more privileged mode, it has full access to the user's address space. The Change Mode instructions, then, can be thought of as simple routine calls that cross an access mode boundary. Because the Change Mode dispatcher (which would typically be called a "gatekeeper") intercepts all Change Mode instructions, there is no other way for a program to change to a more privileged mode. Indeed, if a user does execute a Change Mode instruction directly, it will simply call an operating system routine. The routine will check to see if correct arguments are supplied and will return an error code if they are not; otherwise, it will execute the function. There is nothing "privileged" about the Change Mode instruction.

When the service routine completes, it must be able to return to the caller. Moving to a less privileged mode is done with the Return from Exception or Interrupt (REI) instruction. When an REI instruction is executed, the top of the current stack must contain the PSL and the PC for the new mode. The REI instruction causes the CPU to examine the current mode field of the PSL on the stack to ensure that the new mode is the same or less privileged than the current mode. Therefore, the REI instruction cannot be used to increase privilege. The REI instruction restores the PSL and the PC from the stack, changes the processor to the new mode, and restores the new mode's stack pointer from the temporary location where it had been saved. Execution continues in the new mode at the instruction specified by the PC.

The Change Mode and Return from Execution or Interrupt instructions are used to increase and decrease processor access mode, respectively. Increases in access mode are controlled because they are intercepted by the operating system. Using these mechanisms, the operating system itself can be implemented primarily as a collection of routines that the user calls to perform various functions. These routines execute within the context of the user process either at the user's access mode or at a more privileged mode. The routines have the ability to perform functions that require privilege without allowing the user to have direct access to the privileged resources.

Checking for Accessibility

As we discussed, the Change Mode instructions provide a cross-mode service call facility. When such a call is made, the caller often pushes arguments onto the stack for a service routine. Output arguments are specified as the address of a memory location (or locations) in the user's program to receive an output value from the service routine.

Output arguments may cause a problem when the service routine executes in a more privileged mode. The service routine must be able to verify that the caller had access to the memory locations specified. Suppose the service routine executes in Kernel mode and the caller specifies an invalid memory location (for example, an address in the middle of the operating system). If the Kernel mode routine modifies the memory location, it will not be stopped by the hardware, even though the user-mode caller had no authority to reference it.

To protect against such occurrences, two instructions check the accessibility of the previous mode (the caller) to read or write a series of bytes. These instructions are called Probe Read Accessibility (PROBER) and Probe Write Accessibility (PROBEW). A routine executing in a privileged access mode must always check the accessibility of input and output arguments when it is called by a less privileged mode. The section on memory management examines in more detail how memory protection is provided on the VAX.

Process Context Switching

The operating system allocates processor time to each process in the system, scheduling each process to run for a given amount of time. When the time expires or if the process waits for an event, the state of the process is saved so that it can be continued at a later time. A new process is then loaded and run. This operation of changing the processor to a new process is called a *context switch*.

Context switching is a common occurrence in a multiprogrammed environment because processes normally wait for the completion of I/O requests. A multiprogramming system may switch processes several hundred times per second. Consequently, the time necessary to perform this operation has a noticeable effect on system performance.

To switch from one process to another, the operating system must save all the state information of the process, including its registers, stack pointers, program counter, and so on. The context is stored in a software data structure maintained by the operating system. The context for the new process must then be loaded into the hardware registers from its software storage space before the new process can execute. The VAX architecture has simplified context switching by making the loading and storing of these software data structures a hardware operation.

The *process control block* (PCB), shown in Figure 12.9, is the data structure that contains all the hardware state information when the process is inactive. The last four longwords in the PCB contain registers that define the address space of the process. These longwords allow the processor to locate the physical memory for each process. On a context switch, state information is loaded from or stored into the PCB. Loading and storing of the state information are assisted in the VAX hardware by a privileged register, one that only the operating system can access, called the *process control block base register* (PCBB). The PCBB register points to the PCB of the process currently executing.

To perform a context switch, the operating system first executes a Save Process Context (SVPCTX) instruction that causes the hardware to automatically store all the registers of the current process into its PCB, which is pointed to by the PCBB register. Next, the PCBB register is loaded with the address of the PCB of the new process to be run. The operating system executes a Load Process Context (LDPCTX) instruction, which loads all the hardware registers from the new PCB. LDPCTX also pushes the PC and the PSL of the new process on the Interrupt stack (the operating system must run on the Interrupt stack following an SVPCTX, since there is no process and hence no process stack). Next, the operating system executes a Return From Exception or Interrupt (REI) instruction to continue the execution of the new process.

The simplified code sequence in Figure 12.10 shows the instructions executed in a context switch. The Move To Processor Register (MTPR) instruction loads the hardware process control block base register with

Figure 12.9   Hardware process control block

Process Control Block (PCB)

31				00	
KSP					:PCB
ESP					:4
SSP					:8
USP					:12
R0					:16
R1					:20
R2					:24
R3					:28
R4					:32
R5					:36
R6					:40
R7					:44
R8					:48
R9					:52
R10					:56
R11					:60
AP(R12)					:64
FP(R13)					:68
PC					:72
PSL					:76
POBR					:80
MBZ	AST-LVL	MBZ	POLR		:84
PIBR					:88
PME	MBZ		PILR		:92

the physical address of the PCB for the new process. Since every process in the system has private stacks and stack pointers for all access modes, a process can be context switched while executing operating system code in Kernel mode. This is unlike systems in which the operating system executes in a special context from which it cannot be interrupted.

Summary of Process Concepts

We have now covered a number of features that aid the operating system in its management of the processor. First, each program runs in the context of a process. The process is the entity scheduled by the operating

Figure 12.10 Context switch sequence

```
;
; Simplified context switch example.  Assume that this routine
; is entered by an interrupt, as discussed later in this
; chapter.  The PC and PSL of the interrupted process are
; stored on the stack;  these are automatically popped off
; and saved in the PCB by the SVPCTX instruction.
;

SCHEDULE:
        SVPCTX                    ; save current process state
                                  ; ...in current PCB

        <place current PCB in queue of processes
           waiting for the processor>

        <select next process to be run, load the
           physical address of its PCB into R1>

        MTPR    R1,#PCBB          ; load PCB base register with
                                  ; ...new process PCB address
        LDPCTX                    ; load hardware registers from
                                  ; ...the new PCB (also pushes
                                  ; ...PC and PSL onto the stack)
        REI                       ; continue execution of the
                                  ; ...process
```

system scheduler. A process is described by its state information, including its registers, physical memory, program counter, and so on.

A process executes instructions in one of four processor access modes. Normal applications programs execute in User mode. However, the user can call operating system service routines that execute at a more privileged mode. The operating system guards the raising of access modes. Although a process can request a service that will be performed in a more privileged mode, it cannot execute its own code in that mode.

Finally, the processor maintains the hardware-state information for a process in a data structure called a process control block. The operating system scheduler interrupts the execution of one process and begins the execution of another one through the use of special load and store process context instructions.

Having seen how the operating system allows several programs to share the processor, we next examine how the VAX creates a logical memory environment for each process.

VAX Memory Management

Part of the context of each process in the system is its address space. Providing this address space is the job of the operating system memory-management routines and the underlying hardware.

There are two separable functions required of the memory-management subsystem of the operating system. The first gives each user program the impression that it is running in contiguous physical memory, starting at address zero. This is how we have viewed memory since Chapter 2. The second function divides the available physical memory equitably among the users of the system. To obtain efficient memory utilization, the system must allow several processes to exist in memory concurrently.

VAX Memory Structure

One of the most critical decisions in the design of a computer system is the number of bits to be used for an address, since this determines the amount of memory that can be directly accessed (that is, the size of the address space). The address space is the set of unique memory addresses that a program can generate. On the VAX, since addresses are 32-bit unsigned integers, a program can address 2^{32}, or 4,294,967,296, bytes.

To the programmer, then, memory is a contiguous array of 2^{32} individually addressable bytes. Of course, programs and data structures are rarely large enough to require even a fraction of that space. Consequently, the VAX address space is divided into several functional regions, simplifying the user-operating system interface with little loss in addressability.

Besides the functional regions, the VAX address space is divided into 512-byte pages. A program is composed of a linear array of pages numbered from 0 to some large upper limit (actually 2^{23}, or 8,388,608). For example, the first four pages of the address space of a program are numbered as shown in Figure 12.11.

Because pages are 512 (or 2^9) bytes, the low-order 9 bits of the 32-bit virtual address specify the location of the byte within the page being referenced. The high-order bits, called the *virtual page number* (VPN), specify the number of the page within the address space as shown:

31	09 08	00
Virtual page number	Byte offset	

For example, in Figure 12.11, virtual address 514 decimal locates the third byte (byte number 2) in the second page (page 1) of the program's virtual memory space. This is shown more readily in the binary representation of address 514:

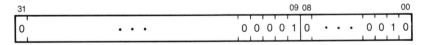

From this we see that address 514 specifies virtual page 1, byte offset 2.

Figure 12.12 shows a sample allocation of process virtual pages to *physical memory*. Like logical memory, physical memory on the VAX is also

Figure 12.11   Division of address space into pages

Virtual Page Number	Decimal Address	Hex Address
0	0 – 511	0 – 1FF
1	512 – 1023	200 – 3FF
2	1024 – 1535	400 – 5FF
3	1535 – 2047	600 – 7FF

Page 0	0
Page 1	512
Page 2	1024
Page 3	1536

⋮

Figure 12.12   Virtual and physical memory

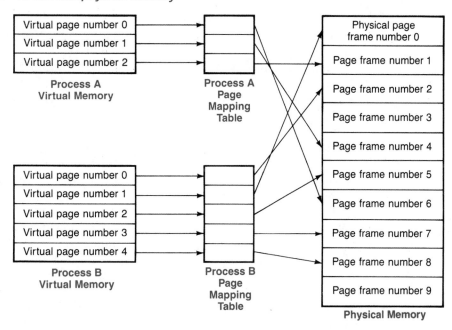

divided into 512-byte pages. Physical memory is addressed via a *physical address*. The physical address can also be viewed as having two components: the upper 21 bits specifying the *physical page number* and the low-order 9 bits specifying the byte within the physical page:

29	09 08	00
Page frame number	Byte offset	

Notice that the VAX physical addresses are 30 bits, although the maximum amount of physical memory allowed on the processor is implementation specific. Because physical memory can be viewed as a list of physical frames or page-sized slots that hold program virtual pages, the physical page number is often called the *page frame number* (PFN).

VAX Page Tables

On a paged virtual memory system, a program is allowed to execute with only some of its pages in physical memory. Because each page is addressed independently of the next, the resident pages can be scattered throughout physical memory. However, when a program references an address in virtual memory, the hardware must calculate the corresponding physical address. The mechanism for this calculation, called *virtual address translation*, uses a data structure called a *page table*.

A page table is an array of longword descriptors, one for each page in the virtual memory of the program. Each descriptor, called a page table entry (PTE), indicates

- what processor access modes can read or write the page

- whether the page is in physical memory

- the page frame number of the corresponding physical page if it is in memory

If the page is not in physical memory, the PTE can specify where to find a copy of the page on disk. We sometimes refer to a structure like this as a map because it gives the directions to (location of) the data in memory.

The VAX page table entry format is shown in Figure 12.13. Bit 31 of the PTE is the Valid bit. When set, the Valid bit indicates that the virtual page is in memory and that bits <20:0> contain the physical page frame number for that page. If the Valid bit is zero, the PTE does not contain a valid page frame number, and the software can use bits <26:0> to keep information about the page location on the system disk. If a program references a virtual address for which the Valid bit is zero, the hardware generates a "translation not valid" fault, or *page fault*. This fault causes the hardware to transfer control to an operating system routine to bring the page into physical memory. Faults are described in more detail later in this chapter.

Bit 26, the Modify bit, is set by the hardware on the first write to the page. When the operating system wants to write a page back to the disk, it first checks the Modify bit to see if the page has been modified. If not, the write can be avoided because the disk already contains an up-to-date copy.

Figure 12.13　VAX page table entry format

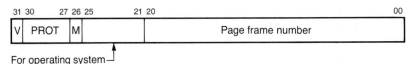

Bits <30:27> of the page table entry contain a protection mask that indicates which processor access modes, if any, are allowed read or write access to the page. If a process references an address it does not have the privilege to access, the hardware generates an *access violation fault*. Even when the Valid bit is zero, the privilege field is checked so that a program cannot cause a page to be faulted for which it has no access rights. Table 12.1 gives the encoding of these bits within the PTE.

The hardware uses the page table for every program memory access, as shown in Figure 12.14. The virtual page number of the virtual address is used to locate the appropriate PTE within the page table. If the Valid bit is set and the protection check succeeds, then the page frame number in the low 21 bits of the PTE is appended to the low 9 bits of the virtual address, forming the 30-bit physical address.

VAX Address-Space Regions

On the VAX, the virtual address space is actually broken into several functional regions or segments. Figure 12.15 shows the division of the virtual address space into two halves, called *system space* and *process space*. Process space is again broken into the program (P0) and control (P1) regions. The high-address half of system space is reserved for future use. The arrows in Figure 12.15 show the direction of dynamic growth in each region.

Table 12.1   PTE Protection Encoding

Code						
Decimal	Binary	K	E	S	U	Comment
0	0000	—	—	—	—	No access
1	0001	Unpredictable	—	—	—	Reserved
2	0010	RW	—	—	—	
3	0011	R	—	—	—	
4	0100	RW	RW	RW	RW	All access
5	0101	RW	RW	—	—	
6	0110	RW	R	—	—	
7	0111	R	R	—	—	
8	1000	RW	RW	RW	—	
9	1001	RW	RW	R	—	
10	1010	RW	R	R	—	
11	1011	R	R	R	—	
12	1100	RW	RW	RW	R	
13	1101	RW	RW	R	R	
14	1110	RW	R	R	R	
15	1111	R	R	R	R	

—	=	No access	K	=	Kernel
R	=	Read only	E	=	Executive
RW	=	Read write	S	=	Supervisor
			U	=	User

Figure 12.14   Virtual address translation

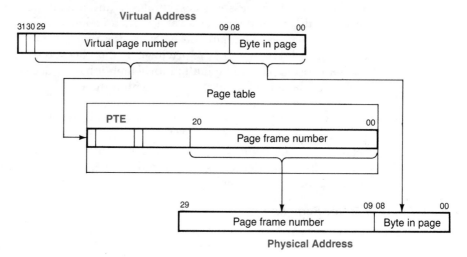

Figure 12.15   VAX process virtual address space

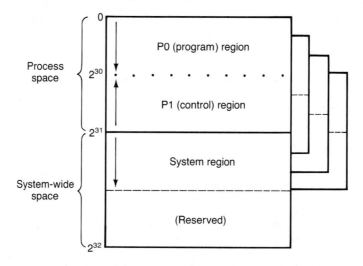

Each region has its own page table. Each page table is described to the hardware by two registers: a base register that contains the page table starting address and a length register that contains the number of page table entries in the table (that is, the number of pages mapped within the region).

The two high-order bits of a virtual address, as shown in Figure 12.16, specify the region that contains the address. When a memory reference is made, the hardware examines bits 31 and 30 of the virtual address to determine which page table to use. The selected base and length registers are then used, along with the virtual page number, to locate the PTE.

Figure 12.16   VAX virtual address

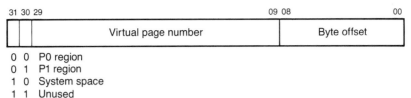

31 30 29   09 08   00

| | | Virtual page number | Byte offset |

0 0   P0 region
0 1   P1 region
1 0   System space
1 1   Unused

System Space

The high-address half of the address space is called system space because it is shared by all processes in the system and because the operating system runs in this region. There is only one page table for system space, called the *system page table* (SPT), that translates all system space references. All processes referencing a virtual address in system space access the same physical location. The operating system is located in system space and is shared by all processes. Thus, the operating system is in the same section of the address space of each process. In fact, the operating system is simply a collection of routines located in the system address space that user programs can call on to perform services.

The system page table is described by its two hardware registers, the *system base register* (SBR) and the *system length register* (SLR). The operating system loads these registers when it is booted. The system base register contains the starting physical address of the system page table, which must be contiguous in physical memory. Notice that the hardware must reference the system page table directly by physical address, since there can be no virtual-to-physical conversion without the page table itself.

The hardware uses the translation process shown in Figure 12.17 to calculate a physical memory address from a system virtual address. The physical address of the page table entry is computed using the contents of the System Base Register and the virtual page number in the specified system virtual address. Figure 12.18 shows an example of the formation of a physical address from a system space virtual address.

Process Space

The low-address half of the VAX address space, shown in Figure 12.19, is called process space. Process space itself is divided in half by bit 30 of the virtual address. The lower half of process space (bit 30 = 0) is known as the *program region*, the upper half (bit 30 = 1) as the *control region*.

Unlike system space, which is shared by all processes, process space is unique to each process in the system. In other words, each process has its own page tables for its private program and control regions. Different processes referencing the same process space virtual address access different physical memory locations.

The reason for having two process regions is to allow for two directions of growth. The program region, P0, holds the user's program.

Figure 12.17 System space address translation flowchart

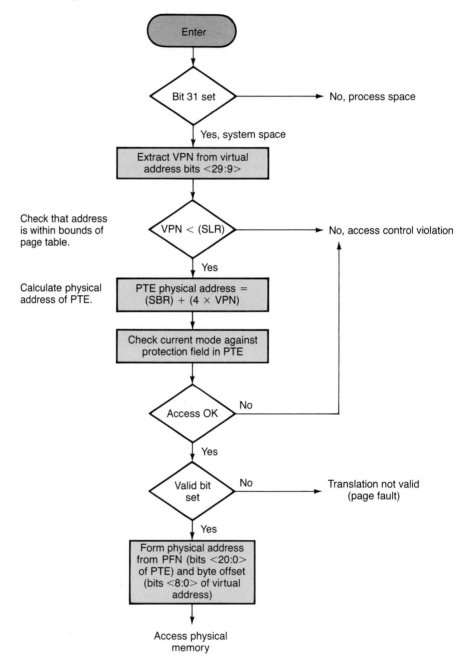

Figure 12.18 System space virtual address translation

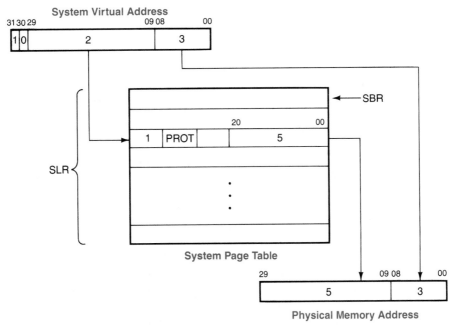

Figure 12.19 Process space

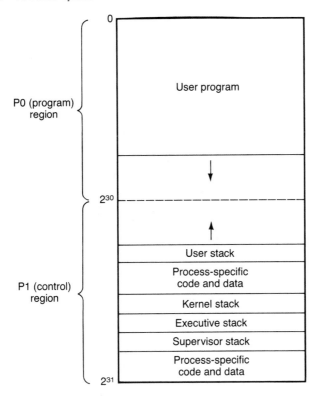

This segment provides the zero-based virtual address space into which most programs expect to be loaded. The program can expand dynamically toward higher addresses. The control region, on the other hand, conveniently accommodates the User mode stack of the process, since stacks grow toward lower addresses. Operating systems can also use the control region, P1, to contain protected process-specific data and code, as well as the stacks for the more privileged access modes.

The P0 and P1 page tables are described by the hardware base and length registers P0BR, P0LR, P1BR, and P1LR. These registers are always loaded with the address and the length of the page tables for the process in execution. Unlike the system page table, which is stored in contiguous physical memory and cannot be paged, the process page tables are stored in contiguous virtual memory in system space and can be paged. The base registers thus contain system space virtual addresses.

Because the process page tables exist in virtual memory, a process space translation demands extra work. The hardware must first use the system page table to compute the physical address of the process page table. Once the physical address of the process table (P0 or P1) is located, the translation process proceeds as it does for system space. Figure 12.20 shows the extra steps in process address translation.

As shown in Figure 12.9, the P0 and P1 base and length registers are part of the PCB. Thus, the process address space is automatically switched by the execution of the VAX context-switch instructions.

Privileged Processor Registers

This chapter has referred to a number of special registers that support the operating system data structures, for example, the process control block base register (PCBB), P0 page table base register (P0BR), and P0 page table length register (P0LR). These registers are known as *privileged processor registers*, or privileged registers, on the VAX. A privileged register is one intended for use only by the operating system. Privileged registers cannot be accessed or modified by user programs.

Each privileged processor register on the VAX has a privileged register number, as shown in Table 12.2. The column labelled "Scope" tells whether the register contains information about the state of the CPU or the state of the current process.

The Move From Processor Register (MFPR) and Move To Processor Register (MTPR) instructions can be used to read and write privileged registers. The source (for MFPR) or destination (for MTPR) is specified by the register number. For example, to store the current value of P0LR in R1 and load a new value from R2, the following instructions would be used:

```
MFPR    #9,R1           ; load P0LR into R1
MTPR    R2,#9           ; load new P0LR from R2
```

The MTPR and MFPR instructions are protected, and execution from any mode other than Kernel causes a fault.

Figure 12.20 Process space versus system space address translation

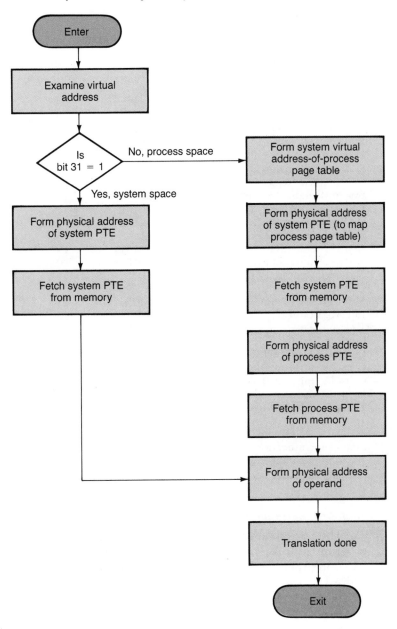

Table 12.2   VAX Privileged Processor Registers

Register Name	Mnemonic	Number	Scope
Kernel Stack Pointer	KSP	0	Process
Executive Stack Pointer	ESP	1	Process
Supervisor Stack Pointer	SSP	2	Process
User Stack Pointer	USP	3	Process
Interrupt Stack Pointer	ISP	4	CPU
P0 Base Register	P0BR	8	Process
P0 Length Register	P0LR	9	Process
P1 Base Register	P1BR	10	Process
P1 Length Register	P1LR	11	Process
System Base Register	SBR	12	CPU
System Length Register	SLR	13	CPU
Process Control Block Base	PCBB	16	Process
System Control Block Base	SCBB	17	CPU
Interrupt Priority Level	IPL	18	CPU
Asynchronous System Trap Level	ASTLVL	19	Process
Software Interrupt Request	SIRR	20	CPU
Software Interrupt Summary	SISR	21	CPU
Interval Clock Control	ICCS	24	CPU
Next Interval Count	NICR	25	CPU
Interval Count	ICR	26	CPU
Time of Year	TODR	27	CPU
Console Receive CSR	RXCS	32	CPU
Console Receive DBR	RXDB	33	CPU
Console Transmit CSR	TXCS	34	CPU
Console Transmit DBR	TXDB	35	CPU
Memory Management Enable	MAPEN	56	CPU
Translation Buffer Invalidate All	TBIA	57	CPU
Translation Buffer Invalidate Single	TBIS	58	CPU
Performance Monitor Enable	PMR	61	Process
System Identification	SID	62	CPU
Translation Buffer Valid Check	TBCHK	63	CPU

Summary of Memory Management Concepts

This section described how the VAX hardware provides for the logical program address space and the sharing of memory by several programs. VAX programs reference a linear virtual address space. The virtual address space, as well as the physical memory address space, is divided into 512-byte pages. As part of its private state information, each process has data structures, called page tables, that describe the physical memory location of each virtual page. While a process is running, the CPU uses the process's page table to translate program-generated addresses into physical memory addresses.

The VAX process address space is divided into several regions. The low-address half is unique to each process. The high-address half is a system-wide address space, used for the operating system, that is shared by all processes. Because system space is part of the address space of every process, a program can directly call operating system routines for service. In addition, since the operating system routine runs in the context of the calling process, it has access to that process's virtual memory (and only that process's memory). The fact that the operating system exists in the process address space and runs in the context of every process greatly simplifies operating system construction.

Now we can understand the need for the processor access modes described earlier. The operating system code and data must be protected because they can be directly addressed by users. The access modes permit the operating system to protect its code and data from user observation and tampering, while still allowing users to call operating system routines for service. The Change Mode instructions provide a protected crossing between user programs and operating system services that operate on protected data structures.

Interrupt and Exception Handling

So far, we have described the VAX architecture features that support the management of the processor and memory. The management of I/O devices is handled at a different level than the management of the processor and memory. For nonshared devices, the program allocates the device while it is in use. The operating system ensures that no other program can use the device while it is allocated. For shared devices, such as disks, the operating system maintains a logical file structure. A request for a file I/O operation is checked against the user's privileges. In either case, the operating system does not worry about guaranteeing fair service. I/O requests are usually processed in order or sequenced according to the priority of the program.

The problems associated with I/O functions are related to the real-time nature of devices. This section looks at how interrupts are used to service devices with real-time requirements; it also examines the use of exceptions in program execution.

Interrupts and Exceptions

Chapter 11 explained that an interrupt is a signal from an I/O device to the CPU. The interrupt causes the CPU to suspend the current process and execute a special operating system service routine to handle the external condition. Interrupts save the processor from having to examine (poll) each device periodically to see if there has been a change in its state. Other conditions that occur within the running program, called exceptions, also require special handling by the operating system. We have already seen examples of exception conditions: the page fault and the Change Mode instructions.

Interrupts

An *interrupt* is an external event asynchronous to the current process execution that causes the processor to change the flow of control. In a sense, it is like an externally triggered subroutine call. Because the interrupt is not related to the running process, the routine initiated by the interrupt executes on the system-wide Interrupt stack. The PC and the PSL of the running process are saved on the Interrupt stack so that the process can be resumed later with a Return from Exception or Interrupt (REI) instruction.

Because interrupts occur asynchronously and because there are many devices that may require service, the processor must be able to arbitrate interrupt requests. Associated with each interrupt request is an *interrupt priority level* (IPL). Because some events have more time-critical requirements than others, the processor grants an interrupt to the request with the highest priority. When that request is serviced, requests with lower priority are granted.

The VAX architecture recognizes thirty-two interrupt priority levels. The lowest priority, IPL 0, is used for all user mode and most operating system code. The next fifteen levels are reserved exclusively for the operating system. The highest sixteen levels are used for hardware interrupts. Peripheral devices interrupt at levels 16 through 23, the system clock interrupts at level 22, and levels 25 through 31 are used for urgent processor error conditions, such as power failure.

The IPL of the processor is contained in bits 16 through 20 of the PSL. Thus, when the processor is interrupted by a higher-priority interrupt request, the current interrupt priority level is saved within the PSL on the stack. When a higher-level routine executes an REI instruction, the PSL of the lower-priority routine is restored, and the processor returns to the lower priority level.

Exceptions

An *exception* is an unusual condition that results from the execution of an instruction that causes the processor to change the flow of control. Because exception conditions are caused by the running process, they are usually serviced within the context of that process on one of the process stacks. The VAX recognizes three types of exceptions: traps, faults, and aborts. When an exception occurs, the processor pushes three longwords onto the stack: the current PSL, the PC, and a type code indicating the cause of the exception.

A *trap* is an exception condition that occurs at the end of an instruction. In this case, the PC pushed on the stack is the PC of the instruction following the one that caused the trap. Some instructions explicitly request an exception. For example, Change Mode instructions always trap to an operating system routine for handling, as explained previously. However, there are really two kinds of traps that concern the

Figure 12.21   *Program status word*

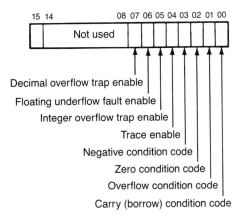

user process. First is the *trace trap*, used to debug programs. The trace trap allows the debugger to gain control following the execution of every instruction. Second is the *arithmetic trap*, which can occur after the completion of an arithmetic operation. Examples include the integer overflow trap, in which the result is too large to be stored in the given format, and integer divide-by-zero trap, in which the supplied divisor was zero. Because some routines may not want to take exceptions for all of these arithmetic conditions, a programmer can disable some exception conditions by clearing bits in the PSW, shown in Figure 12.21.

There is no way to disable exceptions for division by zero and floating-point overflow. Also, because each routine has its own expectations about arithmetic conditions, the VAX calling mechanism allows the called routine to specify the condition of the integer overflow and decimal overflow bits. We explained in Chapter 6 that the word call mask at the call entry site contains bits specifying which registers should be saved on entry. The full format of the call mask is shown in Figure 12.22. Only registers 0 through 11 may be specified (the others are automatically saved in the call frame). The high two bits of the entry mask specify the condition of the integer and decimal overflow bits. Since the PSW is saved in the call frame, a Return instruction automatically restores the previous state of the overflow bits.

An exception condition that arises in the middle of an instruction is a *fault*. A page fault, for example, may occur during instruction operand

Figure 12.22   *VAX call entry mask*

15	14	13	12	11	00
DV	IV	Zero		Registers	

fetching. Floating-point overflow, divide-by-zero, and underflow (in which the resulting exponent is too small to be represented in the data type) are also defined as faults. The registers and memory must be preserved so that the instruction can be restarted and still produce the correct results. Therefore, the PC pushed on the stack points to the instruction that caused the fault. If the operating system routine is able to clear the condition, the instruction is restarted from the beginning.

Finally, an exception condition that arises in the middle of an instruction that cannot be restarted because of the condition of the registers or memory is called an *abort*. Aborts are terminating conditions. For example, if, while pushing information onto the Kernel stack, the processor determines that the Kernel stack pointer contains an illegal address, an abort condition is signaled. This usually indicates an operating system error. Because the Kernel stack pointer is invalid, the abort condition is handled on the Interrupt stack, and the instruction cannot be restarted.

Traps, faults, and aborts are the three types of exceptions recognized by the VAX hardware. Both the exception and the interrupt mechanisms handle special conditions and have the same effect, namely, switching the processor to a special routine to handle the condition. The differences between interrupts and exceptions are summarized in the following list.

Interrupts	*Exception*
Asynchronous to the execution of a process.	Caused by process instruction execution.
Serviced on the system-wide interrupt stack in system-wide context.	Serviced on the process local stack in process context.
Changes the IPL to that of the interrupting device.	Generally does not alter the IPL.
Cannot be disabled, although lower priority interrupts are queued behind higher priority interrupts.	Some arithmetic exceptions can be disabled.

Interrupt and Exception Vectors

When an interrupt or an exception occurs, the hardware transfers to a predefined routine to service the condition. The hardware discovers the address of the service routine by examining a *vector* specific to the condition that occurred. A vector is a longword that dictates the action to be taken when a specific condition occurs. The vector specifies both the address of the service routine and the context in which the condition is to be handled.

The system control block (SCB) is a data structure that contains vectors for each of the various traps and exceptions and for each software and hardware interrupt level. The system control block base (SCBB) register is a privileged register containing the physical address of the system control block. Figure 12.23 shows the layout of the implementation-independent vectors in the SCB (the actual size of the SCB may differ on different processors and configurations).

The vectors are divided into two fields. Bits $<1:0>$ contain a code specifying how the interrupt should be serviced. The binary encoding is as follows:

- 00—If the processor is already running on the Interrupt stack, it continues on the Interrupt stack; otherwise, it services this event on the Kernel stack. Bits $<31:2>$ of the vector contain the virtual address of the service routine. For this and the next encoding, the service routines must begin on a longword boundary, because the virtual address is formed by appending two 0 bits to the address contained in bits $<31:2>$ of the vector.

- 01—This event is serviced on the Interrupt stack, and the IPL is raised to 1F hex if this is an exception. Bits$<31:2>$ of the vector contain the virtual address of the service routine.

- 10—This code is for events handled by *writable control store* (WCS) microcode. Bits $<15:2>$ are passed to the microcode. If WCS does not exist, this operation is undefined.

- 11—This code is reserved.

Software Interrupts

As stated earlier, the VAX processor provides 15 interrupt priority levels (IPLs) for use by the operating system software. Since the hardware contains a separate vector for each IPL, the operating system can use software interrupts as routine calls, where the service routine for each level performs a specific function. A Kernel mode routine can invoke the service by requesting an interrupt at the appropriate level. The IPL at which a specific task is performed indicates its relative importance, and VMS uses IPLs to ensure that more important tasks are performed before less important tasks.

The management of software interrupts uses three of the privileged processor registers. The first register is the *software interrupt summary register* (SISR) as shown in Figure 12.24. SISR contains a bit for each of the 15 software interrupt levels (1–15). When the processor priority level drops below the highest level for which a bit is set in SISR, an interrupt occurs at that level.

Figure 12.23 System control block

Offset	Description	
4	Machine check	
8	Kernel stack not valid	
C	Power fail	
10	Reserved or privileged instruction	
14	Customer reserved instruction	
18	Reserved or illegal operand	
1C	Reserved or illegal addressing mode	
20	Access violation	
24	Translation not valid (page fault)	
28	Trace fault	Exception vectors
2C	Breakpoint fault	
30	Compatibility mode exception	
34	Arithmetic exception	
⋮	⋮	
40	Change mode to Kernel	
44	Change mode to Executive	
48	Change mode to Supervisor	
4C	Change mode to User	
⋮	⋮	
84	Software level 1	
88	Software level 2	
⋮	⋮	
BF	Software level F	
C0	Interval timer	
⋮	⋮	
100	Device level 14, device 0	
101	Device level 14, device 1	
⋮	⋮	
13F	Device level 14, device 15	Interrupt vectors
140	Device level 15, device 0	
⋮	⋮	
17F	Device level 15, device 15	
180	Device level 16, device 0	
⋮	⋮	
1BF	Device level 16, device 15	
1C0	Device level 17, device 0	
⋮	⋮	
1FF	Device level 17, device 15	

Offset from System Control Block Base Register (HEX)

Figure 12.24   Software interrupt summary register

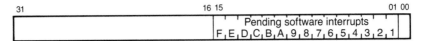

The *software interrupt request register* (SIRR) is used to request an interrupt at a given level. The software requests an interrupt by writing the desired level into the SIRR using the Move To Processor Register (MTPR) instruction. If the requested level is less than the the current processor priority level, the appropriate bit is set in the SISR described previously. If the requested level is higher than the current processor level, an interrupt is immediately generated at the requested level.

Finally, the *interrupt priority level register* is used to read or set the processor priority field of the processor status longword (PSL). Kernel mode software can raise or lower its processor level by writing this register. If the instruction specifies a higher level than the current IPL, the processor is raised to the specified level. If a lower level is specified, the processor priority level is lowered. However, lowering the processor level may cause an interrupt for any pending levels set in the SISR.

Summary of Condition and Exception Handling

This section examined the VAX mechanisms for dealing with special conditions: interrupts and exceptions. An interrupt is an external device-generated signal that tells the operating system to service a device. The exception is the result of an unusual condition in the execution of a program instruction. The existence of exceptions and interrupts reduces the work required of the processor. The software does not have to constantly check for special conditions, completion of device operations, or erroneous arithmetic results. Instead, the hardware automatically reports the occurrence and prioritizes its servicing. Through the use of vectors, the operating system tells the hardware what action to take when a special condition occurs.

Summary

This chapter described how the VAX architecture helps the operating system in the physical management of its three major resources—the processor, the memory, and the I/O devices. The VAX hardware provides process support through the context-switching instructions and layered protection through the processor access modes. It supports a virtual memory environment that protects process-local data while allowing efficient sharing of the operating system. And, it contains an efficient mechanism for servicing external events and conditions. All of these features greatly simplify the job of the operating system. The following chapter examines how the operating system uses these mechanisms to build a logical user environment.

Exercises

1. List some of the functions provided by an operating system.

2. What is a process? Why are processes useful? What is the context of a process? What operating system data structures describe the context of a process?

3. What are VAX processor access modes? What are they used for? How are they controlled?

4. What is process context switching? List the steps involved in a VAX context switch.

5. Explain the difference between virtual and physical memory. Can you have physical page faults? Why must the VAX system page table (SPT) always be resident in contiguous physical memory?

6. Why is the VAX address space divided into several regions? How many memory references are needed to access a location in system space on the VAX? How many for a location in process space?

7. Why do P0BR and P1BR contain virtual addresses?

8. If 90 percent of all references are to process space addresses, what is the average number of memory references required to access a location?

9. Given the process (P0) page table below

E0000028	Virtual page 0 page table entry
70000105	Virtual page 1 page table entry
D0000064	Virtual page 2 page table entry
38000012	Virtual page 3 page table entry

what will happen when a User mode process attempts to first read and then write a 32-bit longword at each of the following virtual addresses? For those operations that succeed, what physical address will be accessed? What effect, if any, does each access have on the page table entry?

a. 0000006E
b. 000001FE
c. 00000214
d. 00000721
e. 00000436

10. Assume that a VAX operating system is initialized to support 64 simultaneous processes, each of which can have a virtual address space of 16 megabytes.

How big is the system page table space required to map the user page tables? What does this imply about the primary memory cost of supporting user virtual memory on the VAX?

11. What is the difference between a fault, a trap, an abort, and an interrupt?

12. Why can't all arithmetic traps be disabled?

13. What is the system control block? Does the SCB reside in physical or virtual memory? Why?

14. The privileged register MAPEN is used to enable VAX virtual memory. When the VAX is first powered on, an initial bootstrapping routine is read into memory. Memory management is turned off, and the routine executes in physical memory. That is, all generated addresses specify physical memory locations directly. What must this routine do before it enables the use of virtual memory?

15. What happens if a VAX/VMS Kernel mode routine running at IPL 0 executes the following code sequence?

```
PR_IPL = 18                 ; define IPL privileged reg.
PR$_SIRR = 20               ; define interrupt request reg.
    .
    .
    .
MTPR    #8,#PR$_IPL
MTPR    #5,#PR$_SIRR
MTPR    #3,#PR$_SIRR
    .
    .
    .
MTPR    #0,#PR$_IPL
```

13

The Structure of a VAX Operating System

The previous chapter began to consider an operating system and its management of physical resources. It then took an in-depth view of the VAX architectural features that support an operating system and its creation of a logical programming environment.

This chapter describes the use of those architectural features by the VAX/VMS (Virtual Memory System) operating system. In particular, this chapter discusses the strategies used by the VMS operating system kernel in its resource-management activities. The material provides a close view of the implementation of the VMS operating system. VMS presents an interesting example because it was designed in parallel with the VAX architecture and takes advantage of the features described in the previous chapter.

Process Scheduling

We have already seen the details of process management in the VAX hardware and briefly described the operating system scheduler, which allocates processor time to executable processes. In a multiprogrammed system, when the scheduler gives the CPU to a process, the process is usually allowed to compute for an interval of time called a *quantum*. If the quantum expires or if the process suspends itself by waiting for an event such as an I/O completion, the scheduler saves the state of the current process and selects another process to execute.

The job of scheduling is one of selecting a process to be run in a way that gives users equitable service. There are many process characteristics that can help select a process to be run, including priority, memory residency, size, and readiness to run. The schedulers for different systems may favor different user processes, depending on the environment. For example, some systems favor computational users, some favor interactive users, and still others favor the service of time-critical events.

In the simplest scheme, a single queue of executable processes is maintained, and processes are scheduled *round-robin*. That is, when the processor becomes available, the scheduler chooses the process at the head of the execute queue. When that process's quantum expires, the scheduler places that process on the tail of the queue and chooses the next process from the head. Thus, the scheduler cycles through all executable processes, giving each process a turn at the chance to execute.

If the operating system wants to favor different types of processes, it usually adopts a priority ordering scheme. Processes with higher priorities are favored over lower-priority processes. Each user might have an initial fixed priority based on a job class assigned by a system manager (for example, depending on the amount of money the user pays), and the priority might be modified as a result of the activity of the process. Or processes could be given priorities depending on the expected remaining service time. Thus, the scheduler may choose to run jobs that are expected to complete quickly. This gives users response time commensurate with the resource requirements of the job. Regardless of the policy implemented, when the quantum expires, the scheduler must again select the next process to run.

VMS Process Scheduling

In the VMS operating system, the scheduler maintains a data structure called the *software* process control block (PCB). Just as the *hardware* process control block contains all of the hardware context information for each process, the software PCB is part of the context for every process and describes the condition of a process at any point in time. For example, the software PCB contains the user's privileges, accumulated resource usage information, user name, and so on. The scheduler keeps track of the condition of each process by maintaining queues of software PCBs organized by process state and priority. Each process's software PCB is linked onto one of the scheduler's queues.

Picking a new process to run in VMS is simple. Each process in the system has an associated priority between 0 and 31. (Process priorities are defined by the operating system and are not related to the processor interrupt priority levels discussed in the last chapter.) When a memory-resident process is ready to compute, it is placed on one of the 32 corresponding runnable priority queues maintained by the scheduler for executable processes, as shown in Figure 13.1. When selecting a new process to run, the scheduler always chooses the process from the head of the highest-priority queue that is nonempty. The software PCB of each process contains a pointer to its hardware PCB, which is used in performing the context switch to restart the program.

This means of selecting a process to run implies that the highest-priority processes could execute forever without allowing lower-priority processes access to the CPU. The problem does not normally occur, however, because the VMS scheduler changes process priorities dynamically. When a process is created during login, it is given the base priority assigned to the user by the system manager. As the process runs, its

Figure 13.1 *VMS executable process queue headers*

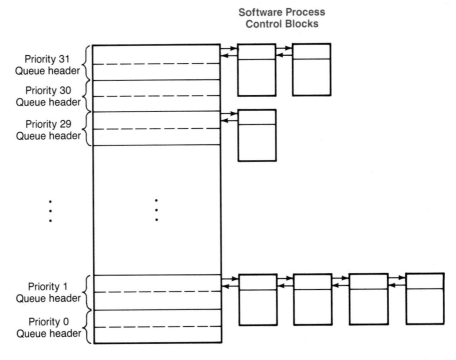

priority can be raised or lowered, depending on its activity. For example, if a process computes until its quantum expires, its priority is reduced, and it is placed on the tail of a lower-priority queue. (A process is never lowered below its initial priority, however.) Alternatively, if an I/O request completes for a waiting process, the process's priority is raised to a higher level so that it has a greater chance of computing.

The events that cause priority reevaluation include

1. execution (priority is decreased when a process is placed into execution)

2. quantum expiration (priority is decreased)

3. terminal-input or terminal-output completion (priority is increased)

4. other input or output completion (priority is increased)

5. resource availability, wake, resume, or deletion (priority is increased)

6. acquisition of a lock (priority is increased)

As a process runs, then, its priority is modified as events occur. Figure 13.2 shows a possible graph of process priority fluctuation over time. The VMS system favors interactive users by raising a process's priority following an interaction (terminal I/O completion) and reducing its priority as the process becomes computational (quantum expiration). The largest priority boost occurs after the completion of a terminal-input operation.

The scheduler manipulates only the priorities of processes whose base priorities are between 0 and 15. The priorities of these processes (known as timesharing processes) are never reduced below their base priority or raised above 15. Processes whose base priorities are between 16 and 31 are real-time processes. Real-time processes deal with time-critical events and can be run only by suitably privileged users. They execute until they reach completion, suspend themselves to wait for an I/O operation or until a higher-priority real-time process becomes runnable, and they are not interrupted by quantum expiration.

Besides selecting the next process to execute, the VMS scheduler is responsible for managing all process-state transitions. In VMS, the *state* of a process is part of its context that describes its condition. The first process state we discussed was the *executable and in-memory* state, for which the scheduler maintains 32 priority queues. There are also 32 queues for processes that are in the executable state but are currently out of memory. An operating system process called the *swapper* (which will be discussed later) is responsible for moving processes between memory and the disk under command of the scheduler.

The remaining states include nonexecutable processes that are waiting for event occurrences, such as the completion of an I/O operation or page-fault or the availability of a hardware or software resource. These processes are linked onto one of the eleven scheduler wait queues described in Table 13.1. As events occur for a process, the software PCB is moved between queues to reflect the state of the process. The differentiation of processes into queues reduces the work needed to locate a waiting process when an event occurs that affects it. For example, when a page

Figure 13.2   Changes in process priority with time

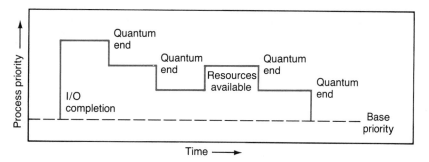

Table 13.1   VMS Process Wait Queues

Process State	Process Condition
Collided Page Wait	Processes faulting a shared page in transition (usually a page in the process of being read or written)
Common Event Wait	Processes waiting for shared event flags (event flags are single-bit interprocess signalling mechanisms)
Free Page Wait	Processes waiting for a free page of physical memory
Hibernate Wait	Processes that have requested hibernation and are resident in memory
Hibernate Wait, swapped out of memory	Processes that have requested hibernation and are swapped out of memory
Local Event Wait	Processes waiting for local event flags (most likely for I/O completion) that are resident in memory
Local Event Wait, swapped out of memory	Processes waiting for local event flags that are swapped out of memory
Suspended Wait	Processes that are suspended and resident in memory
Suspended Wait, swapped out of memory	Processes that are suspended and nonresident
Resource Wait	Processes waiting for miscellaneous system resources
Page Fault Wait	Processes waiting for a faulted page to be read in

fault completes, the scheduler knows that the waiting process can be found on the Page Fault Wait queue. Its software PCB would then be linked onto the appropriate executable queue, based on its priority and whether or not it is in memory. Figure 13.3 shows the possible states and transitions for a process in the VMS system. The arrows in Figure 13.3 show the events that cause a process to move from one state to another.

VMS, then, attempts to provide equitable service by preempting long-running jobs and by modifying process priorities to allow other processes to execute. It does this in a way that favors highly interactive users. When a program is preempted, its state information is saved in system data structures (the hardware and software process control blocks) so that the process can be resumed later. All this is done in a way that is invisible to the process and the user.

Figure 13.3   VMS process state transitions

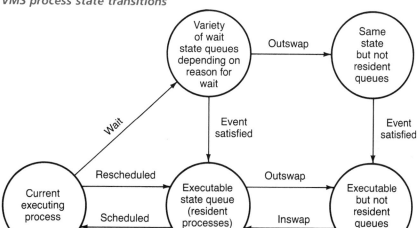

VMS Scheduler Context-Switch Example

It is interesting to look briefly at how the VMS context-switch routine (called the rescheduler) is implemented. Chapter 12 mentioned the use of software interrupts in the operating system as function calls. In VMS, the rescheduler is actually a service routine that executes in response to an interrupt at software IPL 3.

Routines that detect a change in process state or a quantum expiration execute at software IPLs above 3. If the quantum expires or if a detected event causes a process of higher priority than the current process to become executable, a context switch is initiated. To cause the context switch, the event reporting routine simply requests an IPL 3 interrupt using the software interrupt request register, described in Chapter 12. When the event reporting routine returns to a priority level below 3, an interrupt occurs, causing the rescheduling routine to perform a context switch.

Figure 13.4 is a listing of the VMS rescheduling code. (This is the rescheduling code as it existed before symmetric multiprocessing support was added to VMS. Multiprocessing makes this routine somewhat more complicated; we have retained this earlier version for ease of understanding.) This routine is really quite simple, although it may look complex because of the long symbol names. The frequently used notation W^ tells the assembler to generate word-relative addressing. (By default, the assembler uses longword-relative addressing for variables not defined in the same module. Forcing word-relative addressing saves space if the variable is within reach.) To understand what the routine does, we must first define the following symbols that it uses:

Figure 13.4 VMS rescheduling interrupt handler

```
                              .SBTTL  SCH$RESCHED  RESCHEDULING INTERRUPT HANDLER
;++
; SCH$RESCHED - RESCHEDULING INTERRUPT HANDLER
;
; THIS ROUTINE IS ENTERED VIA THE IPL 3 RESCHEDULING INTERRUPT.
; THE VECTOR FOR THIS INTERRUPT IS CODED TO CAUSE EXECUTION
; ON THE KERNEL STACK.
;
; ENVIRONMENT:
;   IPL=3 MODE=KERNEL IS=0
; INPUT:
;   00(SP)=PC AT RESCHEDULE INTERRUPT
;   04(SP)=PSL AT INTERRUPT.
;--
SCH$RESCHED::                              ;RESCHEDULE INTERRUPT HANDLER
        SETIPL  #IPL$_SYNCH                ;SYNCHRONIZE SCHEDULER WITH EVENT REPORTING
    1   SVPCTX                             ;SAVE CONTEXT OF PROCESS
        MOVL    W^SCH$GL_CURPCB,R1         ;GET ADDRESS OF CURRENT PCB
        MOVZBL  PCB$B_PRI(R1),R2           ;CURRENT PRIORITY
        BBSS    R2,W^SCH$GL_COMQS,10$      ;MARK QUEUE NON-EMPTY
10$:    MOVW    #SCH$C_COM,PCB$W_STATE (R1) ;SET STATE TO RES COMPUTE
    2   MOVAQ   W^SCH$AQ_COMT [R2],R3      ;COMPUTE ADDRESS OF QUEUE
        INSQUE  (R1),@(R3)+                ;INSERT AT TAIL OF QUEUE
;+
; SCH$SCHED - SCHEDULE NEW PROCESS FOR EXECUTION
;
; THIS ROUTINE SELECTS THE HIGHEST PRIORITY EXECUTABLE PROCESS
; AND PLACES IT IN EXECUTION.
;-
SCH$SCHED::                                ;SCHEDULE FOR EXECUTION
        SETIPL  #IPL$_SYNCH                ;SYNCHRONIZE SCHEDULER WITH EVENT REPORTING
        FFS     #0,#32,W^SCH$GL_COMQS,R2   ;FIND FIRST FULL STATE
        BEQL    SCH$IDLE                   ;NO EXECUTABLE PROCESS??
        MOVAQ   W^SCH$AQ_COMH[R2],R3       ;COMPUTE QUEUE HEAD ADDRESS
    3   REMQUE  @(R3)+,R4                  ;GET HEAD OF QUEUE
        BVS     QEMPTY                     ;BR IF QUEUE WAS EMPTY (BUG CHECK)
        BNEQ    20$                        ;QUEUE NOT EMPTY
        BBCC    R2,W^SCH$GL_COMQS,20$      ;SET QUEUE EMPTY
20$:    CMPB    #DYN$C_PCB,PCB$B_TYPE(R4)  ;MUST BE A PROCESS CONTROL BLOCK
        BNEQ    QEMPTY                     ;OTHERWISE FATAL ERROR
        MOVW    #SCH$C_CUR,PCB$W_STATE(R4) ;SET STATE TO CURRENT
        MOVL    R4,W^SCH$GL_CURPCB         ;NOTE CURRENT PCB LOC
        CMPB    PCB$B_PRIB(R4),PCB$B_PRI(R4) ;CHECK FOR BASE
        BEQL    30$                        ;PRIORITY=CURRENT
    4   BBC     #4,PCB$B_PRI(R4),30$       ;YES, DONT FLOAT PRIORITY
                                           ;DONT FLOAT REAL TIME PRIORITY
30$:    INCB    PCB$B_PRI(R4)              ;MOVE TOWARD BASE PRIO
        MOVB    PCB$B_PRI(R4),W^SCH$GB_PRI ;SET GLOBAL PRIORITY
    5   MTPR    PCB$L_PHYPCB(R4),#PR$_PCBB ;SET PCB BASE PHYS ADDR
        LDPCTX                             ;RESTORE CONTEXT
        REI                                ;NORMAL RETURN
```

- SCH$GL_COMQS is the address of the 32-bit Compute Queue Status (COMQS) longword. Each bit in COMQS represents one of the 32 executable process queues shown in Figure 13.1. In the actual implementation, both the queues and the bits are ordered from highest to lowest priority. Thus, bit 0 and queue header 0 represent the highest-priority queue, priority 31. Using the Find First Set (FFS) instruction to scan the longword and locate the highest-priority nonempty queue is quite effective. (In fact, the FFS instruction, which scans a field of 32 bits, was included for just this purpose.)

- SCH$AQ_COMH is the address of the first header in the array of 32 computable queue headers shown in Figure 13.1. The bit number from a bit found in SCH$GL_COMQS can be used as an index into the quadword array to address the queue header of a priority queue.

- SCH$AQ_COMT is the address of the tail pointer in the first (highest priority) of the 32 queue headers.

- SCH$GL_CURPCB is the address of a pointer to the software PCB of the process currently executing. (In newer versions of VMS that support multiprocessing, this global variable has been replaced by a field in a processor-specific data structure, since there is a current process executing on each processor.)

The following notes refer to the numbers in the listing. It is not important to understand every instruction. Rather, this routine is a good demonstration of the use of the VAX architecture by the operating system.

1. The routine is entered as a result of an IPL 3 interrupt. It immediately raises its IPL to the VMS synchronizing level (IPL 8, shown symbolically as IPL$_SYNCH) to synchronize with event-reporting routines. This ensures that no process-state changes or database changes will occur while rescheduling is underway.

2. The routine stores the address of the software PCB of the current process into R1 and stores the priority of the process in R2. The PCB is placed on the end of the executable queue for its priority. The corresponding bit in the Compute Queue Status longword is set to note that a process will be placed in the queue. The address of the queue header for this priority is computed, and the PCB is added to the tail.

3. The Find First Set (FFS) instruction locates the first bit set in the Compute Queue Status longword. This indicates the highest-priority nonempty queue. The address of the header for that queue is comput-

ed and the first software PCB is removed. This is the new process to be run. If this PCB was the last entry in the queue, the corresponding bit in the Compute Queue Status longword is cleared.

4. The priority of the process is reduced so that it will automatically be placed on a lower-priority queue if its quantum expires. (This is done with an increment because the queues, bits, and internal priority representations are inverted, that is, 0 is the highest priority.)

5. The address of the hardware PCB of the process is loaded in the process control block base register (PCBB). A Load Process Context instruction then causes the hardware registers to be loaded for the new process. Finally, the Return from Interrupt instruction returns from the original IPL 3 interrupt. If there are no lower-priority interrupts pending, the processor returns to IPL 0 and continues executing instructions for the new process.

The Load Process Context (LDPCTX) instruction at the end of the reschedule routine is the only use of this instruction in the VAX/VMS operating system. The Save Process Context (SVPCTX) instruction does not enjoy quite such a restricted usage. The event-reporting routines will execute a Save Process Context if the current process must be placed in a wait queue. They will then enter the rescheduling code in Figure 13.4 at SCH$SCHED to start the next process.

Process Paging

Chapter 12 examined the VAX hardware support for memory management. The VAX architecture provides for a number of features, including

- a linear logical program address space

- protection of memory

- sharing of operating system code and data

- trapping of references to nonresident pages

Although these architecture features provide the basis for the memory-management system, there are a large number of issues and problem areas in the control of memory. For example, the architecture does not help in deciding how program pages should be loaded or removed from memory. This support must be handled by software, and there are many different strategies that can be chosen for handling memory management, depending on the requirements of the system.

In general, virtual memory is not a performance feature, that is, there is a performance cost in providing the virtual-memory service. First, there is the cost of the extra memory references introduced by page tables, although this can be significantly reduced by additional hardware, as will be discussed in Chapter 14. Second, and more important, is the cost of a reference to a nonresident page. A page fault can require both a disk read and a disk write operation. This is time-consuming to the program and requires some amount of processing by the operating system. Thus, the difficult job of the virtual memory-management system is to optimize performance by trading off the amount of physical memory for each process, which reduces its paging activity, with the number of processes allowed to share memory, which reduces the swapping activity.

The number of page faults generated by a program depends on the memory reference pattern of the program and on the physical memory allocation and page replacement policies of the operating system. Normally, the operating system places some limits on the physical memory available to a program. Figure 13.5 is a graphic representation of program page-fault rate plotted against the ratio of virtual-to-physical memory. Of course, when the virtual-to-physical ratio is 1, there are no page faults once the program is resident in memory (the total number of faults is equal to the program size). As the ratio increases, the fault rate increases. Figure 13.6 is a similar graph of total program page faults versus the program physical memory limit. We see here that there is a point beyond which additional physical memory allocation does not provide any significant decrease in the number of page faults. This point often occurs much before the program becomes fully resident. Therefore, the operating system needs to avoid overcommitting memory to a program. Overcommitting memory reduces the memory available to others, while not benefitting the receiving process.

Figure 13.5 Program page-fault rate versus ratio of virtual-to-physical memory size

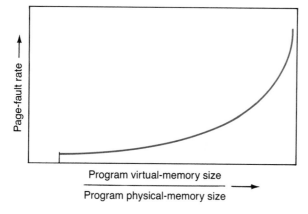

Figure 13.6   *Program page faults versus physical-size limit*

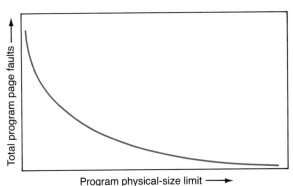

As a program executes, pages are faulted into physical memory until the program reaches the physical memory limit imposed on it by the operating system. At this point, when the program references the next nonresident page, the operating system must choose a page to remove from memory to bring in the newly referenced page. The strategies for selecting a page to remove are known as *page replacement algorithms.*

There are two basic classes of page replacement algorithms. *Fixed-space* replacement algorithms typically place a quota on the number of pages a process may have in memory. The process faults pages into memory until that quota is reached, at which point pages are removed as specified by the replacement algorithm at each new fault. *Variable-space* replacement algorithms attempt to dynamically adjust the number of pages a process has in memory to optimize both fault rate and memory utilization.

The optimal fixed-space replacement strategy, described by Belady, requires full knowledge of the program's future behavior. This method removes the page that will not be referenced for the longest time in the future. Of course, this knowledge is generally not available. Most methods, then, use past program behavior as a predictor of future behavior. For example, in the *least recently used* (LRU) scheme, the page removed is the one that has not been accessed for the longest time. It is assumed that this page will not be needed in the near future. To implement LRU requires that the hardware maintain some amount of usage information on each page. Usually, each page table entry contains a bit, called the *reference bit,* that is set whenever a reference is made to the page. If the software periodically turns off the reference bit, it can keep track of the number of periods since a page has been accessed.

Denning's working set model for program behavior (Denning 1968) provides better intuition concerning the pages required by a program to execute efficiently. Denning defines the *working set* of a program, $W(T,\tau)$, to be the set of pages referenced in the interval $(T-\tau,T)$. The parameter τ is called the *window size*. For different sizes of the window, τ, the working set is the *set* of pages referenced in the last τ references, and the working set size $w(T,\tau)$, is the *number* of pages referenced in that interval. Both the membership of the working set and the size of the working set can be expected to change during the execution of the program, that is, as T increases. In fact, the working set can change at each *reference*. If the window size τ has been appropriately selected (by considering CPU speed and paging-device capacity), then the objective of the memory-management mechanism should be to keep the pages belonging to the program's working set resident in memory at all times.

This model describes a basis for selection of program pages to remain in memory. For a given window size τ, pages that have not been accessed in the last τ references are removed from memory in an attempt to keep exactly the working set in memory at all times. Notice that with this definition, a page can be removed without the occurrence of a page fault. Working set page replacement is a variable-space algorithm because it dynamically adjusts the process's working set either up or down.

There is a tradeoff between the cost of page faults and the complexity of the algorithms required to reduce them. If the replacement algorithm is successful in reducing faults, but requires excessive processor time, it may not be worth the effort. Some simpler but less successful schemes for replacement are *random* replacement, in which the page to be removed is chosen at random, and *first in first out* (FIFO) replacement, in which the page removed is the page that has been in memory for the longest time. In FIFO, the system just keeps a queue of pages. A new page is added to the bottom of the queue, and the oldest page is removed from the top of the queue. FIFO page replacement can suffer from unintuitive anomalies; under some circumstances, a program's fault rate can increase when the program is given more memory in which to execute.

No matter how intelligent the replacement strategy, there is no substitute for primary memory. Regardless of the strategy, the page-fault rate is likely to be high if a process has too little physical memory, as we see in Figure 13.5. Therefore, the main advantage of virtual memory is that it allows processes to operate on a larger address space than would be otherwise possible, but at the cost of performance. The cost, of course, rises with the size of the "virtual" memory needed by the process.

VMS Memory Management

Memory management in VMS actually consists of two parts. The first part of the memory-management system is the *pager*, which handles the reading in of faulted pages and the removing of resident pages from the memory of the process. The pager, which executes within the context of the process, is basically an exception service routine shared by all processes in the system and is invoked by hardware when a nonresident page is addressed. The second part of the VMS memory-management subsystem is the *swapper*, a process whose function is the removal or loading of entire processes from or into memory. The swapper is closely related to the scheduler, since both must cooperate to determine which processes will be moved, or "swapped," between memory and disk.

Paging under VMS

In VMS, each process in the system has a quota or limit for the number of pages of physical memory that it may occupy. This number is called the *resident set limit*. The VMS *resident set* is the set of pages a process has in memory. (The resident set is called the working set in VAX/VMS documentation.) The memory-management system maintains a list for each process, called the *resident set list*, that points to these pages.

When a new process is initially run, the process load file is examined, and page tables are built from information contained there. At first, all page table entry Valid bits are zero, since none of the process pages have been loaded. The resident set of the process is empty, and the resident set list has no entries. When the operating system transfers control to the starting address of the process, a page fault occurs. The page fault causes a transfer of control to the pager so that the first page of the process can be loaded into memory.

When the pager gains control following a page fault, the hardware has pushed the program counter that points to the faulting instruction and the virtual address that caused the fault onto the stack. From the virtual address, the pager is able to locate the process page table entry for the faulted page. This PTE contains information leading to the disk address of the page. The pager obtains an empty page of physical memory and initiates a read of the page from disk. The corresponding PTE is changed so that the Valid bit is set and the page frame number field points to the physical page into which the read will occur. If this is the first faulted page, it will be the first page in the resident set of the process and the first entry in the resident set list. When the read completes, the pager returns to user level to restart the instruction that faulted.

As the program continues to execute, more and more pages are faulted into its resident set. Each time a fault occurs, the pager reads the page from disk and creates a valid PTE to map it. If the program has a large virtual size, the resident set size will eventually reach the resident set limit for the process. At that point, the process cannot use any more physical memory, and reading a new page forces it to return a page from its resident set to the system.

VMS does not use a least recently used page-replacement strategy, because VAX page tables do not have a reference bit (although the VMS operating system avoids removing an active page by checking to see if its PTE is in the translation buffer). Instead of selecting pages to be removed from the system as a whole, VMS pages the process against itself. That is, the page that is removed must come from the process that caused the page fault if it has reached its resident set limit. The page removed from the resident set is selected in round-robin style (first in, first out) from the resident set list. A pointer circles through the resident set list to determine the next page to be removed. Although this method is not optimal, the cost of making an error (that is, throwing out a page to be referenced) is reduced by mechanisms described next.

The VMS memory-management system maintains two lists of physical pages called the *free page list* and the *modified page list*. The free page list is the source of physical pages for the system. When a process needs a physical page to receive a faulted page, it takes the entry from the head of the free page list. The system tries to keep at least a minimal number of pages free at all times.

The free page list also acts as a cache (a fast backup store) of recently used pages. When a page is removed from a resident set, it is placed on the tail of the free page list or the modified page list, depending on the condition of the Modify bit in the page's PTE. If the Modify bit is 0, then there is already an exact copy of the page on disk and the page need not be written back. Such a page is placed on the tail of the free page list. If the Modify bit is set, then the page must be written back to disk and is placed on the tail of the modified page list. The pages of the modified page list are not written back to the disk until the list reaches a predefined threshold. After the modified page list is written to disk, its page frames are placed on the free list.

A page removed from a resident set remains on the appropriate list for some period of time before it is reused. If a process faults a page that is on one of the lists, the page is simply returned to the resident set at little cost. Depending on the list sizes and the activity of the system, these caches have a significant effect on system and process performance by reducing fault time and paging I/O. However, they also have an inherent unfairness because a heavily faulting process can cause a rapid turnover of the lists.

Besides being a cache for pages, the modified page list serves another important purpose. By delaying the writing of modified pages, the system can write pages to the paging file in clusters or groups instead of individually, thus significantly reducing the number of I/O operations and thereby minimizing the time the disk is busy. Moreover, by waiting some period of time, many pages never have to be written at all because they are referenced again or because the program is terminated.

In addition, because many pages are written at one time, the system can attempt to write virtually contiguous process pages on contiguous disk blocks. This way, the system can also cluster reads from the paging file. When the process accesses a page, the system may choose to bring in several pages (a cluster) if they are located together on the disk.

The biggest gain from the clustering of pages on reads occurs when a new program is started. Typically, programs fault heavily when they start until a reasonable working set has been established. When a program faults the first page, VMS actually reads many pages into memory, reducing the high program startup faulting.

A common technique for both reducing paging and optimizing the sharing of programs is to dynamically adjust the resident set size of a program. Some schemes attempt to equalize the fault rate across all processes. VMS checks a process's fault rate over a system-specified interval of time. Based on that rate, the process's resident set limit may be increased or reduced. Processes that are faulting heavily will receive an increment in their physical memory limit, while processes not faulting can have their resident set limit reduced. This takes memory away from processes that don't need it and gives physical memory to processes that make heavy use of virtual memory.

A VMS process also is allowed to grow its resident set past its resident set limit if substantial memory is available. Should the system determine that memory is overcommitted, it begins to trim back the size of process resident sets.

Swapping under VMS

In addition to paging, VMS also swaps entire processes between memory and disk. Swapping is performed by the swapper, a separate process that runs at a high priority and, of course, is never swapped itself.

When the resident set of a process is in memory, it is a member of the *balance set*. While the resident set is the collection of pages for a particular process, the balance set is the set of all resident processes. VMS swaps entire resident sets between the balance set and disk to make room for swapping in resident sets of other processes. Some virtual memory systems force a nonresident process to page itself back into memory. However, before it allows a process to execute, VMS loads the entire resident set as it existed when the process was interrupted. This reduces the number of page faults and the number of disk I/O operations, since all of the resident set pages can be written in or out with a minimal number of disk transfers.

When a process is brought into memory, it will typically execute at least one quantum before it becomes eligible to be swapped out. The algorithm for determining which process to swap in is quite simple. The swapper checks the nonresident executable queues to find the highest-priority process to be brought in. Having selected a process, the swapper must then find enough free pages to hold the resident set of the selected process. Free pages can be located by

- taking them from the free page list

- writing the modified page list back to disk, thereby freeing those pages

- shrinking the resident sets of one or more resident processes

- swapping out a process of lower or equal priority

Input and Output Processing

The input and output processing routines are often the most complex in the operating system. This is due in part to the asynchronous nature of I/O devices and the synchronization problems caused by the parallelism inherent in their operation. In addition, many I/O devices have real-time service requirements, and the I/O system must be carefully tuned to meet those constraints.

The control of I/O devices differs significantly in its purpose from the processor and memory handling described previously. Generally, processor and memory management operations are provided invisibly to the user. They exist to increase resource utilization. On the other hand, I/O operations are initiated at the request of the user program.

A user requests an I/O operation by calling an operating system routine. For high-level languages, the user codes an OUTPUT or WRITE statement (for output), and the language run-time system generates the low-level operating system call (or calls). The operating system call generally specifies the type of operation to be performed (for example, read or write) and the address and length of a user memory buffer for containing the data to be read or written. The I/O service routine then passes the arguments to a separate process, called a *device driver*, that is responsible for invoking the physical I/O operation. In most systems, the calling process is then suspended and placed in a process wait queue until the I/O request completes. In other systems, the process is allowed to continue processing while the I/O operation is in progress.

It is possible for several driver processes to be in various stages of I/O processing at any time. Before a device driver can initiate a device activity, it may need to allocate hardware or software resources. For example, if there are several devices on a single-transfer bus, the driver processes need a mechanism to determine which driver can cause a transfer. Thus, there must be a mechanism that allows a driver to coordinate with other driver processes. There must also be a mechanism for informing devices when a resource becomes available.

Next, we examine the basic structure of the VMS I/O system. Because the VMS I/O system is quite complicated, we do not cover all of its functions or components. In particular, we do not cover the data structures for handling clustered devices (remote MSCP disks, virtual terminals, and so on). For a complete description of VMS operation and data structures, you can refer to Kenah, Goldenberg, and Bate, *VAX/VMS Internals and Data Structures*. Our goal is simply to show how VMS uses the

Figure 13.7 VMS file system layers

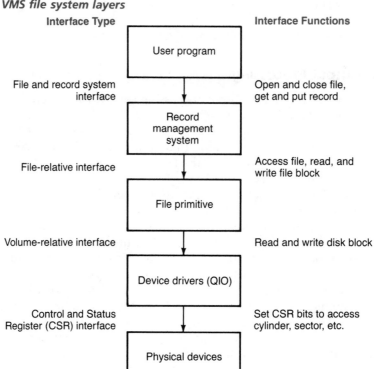

hardware architecture. To this end, we concentrate on the flow of an I/O request between the user process and the system and the use of VAX IPLs to schedule I/O processing.

The VMS I/O System

The VMS I/O system is composed of several layers. Each layer provides a higher-level interface to the level above it, as shown in Figure 13.7. At the highest (most general) level are the record management and database systems that manage named objects such as files, records, fields, and so on. At the lower levels are the kernel routines that interface directly to physical devices. This is the level discussed here.

In general, VMS I/O is asynchronous. In other words, a program can issue an I/O request and continue processing while the request is in progress. Sometime later, the program can check to see if the I/O operation has completed, or it can be notified when the completion occurs. If the program wants to wait until the I/O completes, it calls another operating system routine to request suspension until the I/O operation is done. However, the suspension is not part of the I/O requesting procedure.

VMS I/O Database

Before we examine the functioning of the I/O system components, we introduce a simplified model of the I/O database. The I/O data structures tell as much about the system as the code does.

We have already discussed the PCB, which describes the state of each VMS process. In the I/O system, there are control blocks that describe every bus adapter (for example, UNIBUS, QBUS, or BI), every controller (for example, terminal multiplexer), every device unit (for example, terminal), and every outstanding I/O request (for example, a terminal read operation). These control blocks are linked into a structure that represents the topology of the hardware I/O system.

For example, Figure 13.9 shows a simplified VMS I/O database for the hardware configuration shown in Figure 13.8. The arrows indicate pointers from one control block to another. The six control blocks shown are as follows:

1. The device data block (DDB) contains information common to all devices of a given type connected to a single controller, such as the device name string (for example, TTA for terminals attached to terminal controller A).

2. The unit control block (UCB) describes the characteristics and state for a single device. It also contains the context for the device driver process that controls the device.

3. The I/O request packet (IRP) describes a single user I/O request. For example, the packet contains an identifier for the requesting process, the type of operation requested, and the address and length of the user's memory buffer.

Figure 13.8   Sample VMS system hardware structure

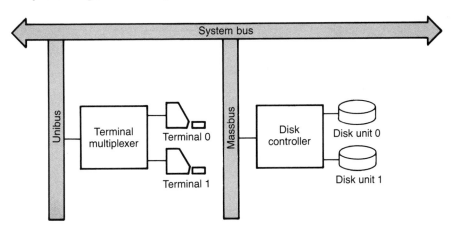

Figure 13.9   VMS I/O and database

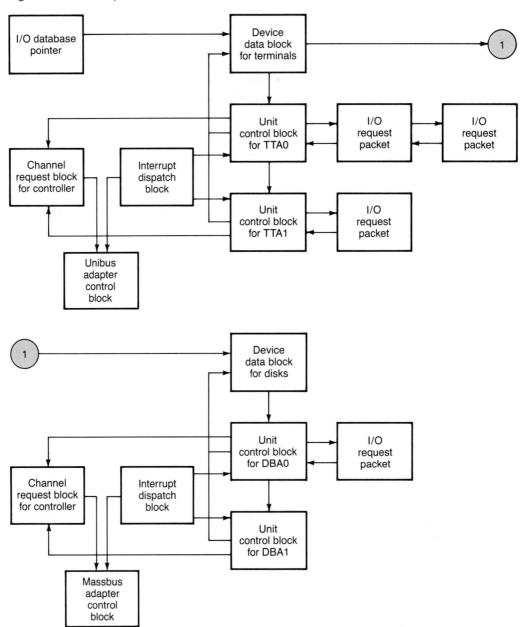

4. The channel request block (CRB) defines the state of a controller. The CRB arbitrates requests for a shared controller. The CRB indicates which device unit is currently transferring and which units are waiting to transfer when the current transfer is complete.

5. The interrupt data block (IDB) describes the current activity on a controller and locates the responsible device when an interrupt occurs. It is a logical extension to the CRB.

6. The adapter control block (ADP) defines the characteristics and state of a bus adapter.

The arrows in Figure 13.9 show the static relationship of the database. However, some control blocks may contain other pointers or be members of other queues, depending on the state of the devices. For example, when a unit is waiting for a free controller on which to transfer, its unit control block is queued to the channel request block for the controller. Thus, the contents of these control blocks precisely define the state of the I/O system at any point in time.

VMS I/O System Components

The VMS I/O system can be logically separated into three components. First is the Queue I/O (QIO) system service, which is called to request all I/O operations on VMS. QIO is a procedure called by the user program. Although it executes in Kernel mode, QIO runs within the context of the user's process and has access to the process address space of the caller. The basic functions of QIO are to validate the user-supplied arguments and to build a data structure in system dynamic memory called an I/O request packet (IRP). The I/O request packet contains all of the information needed by the device driver to perform the physical I/O function. QIO also checks that the calling process is allowed to perform the requested function on the specified device.

Within the unit control block of each device is a header for a queue of outstanding I/O requests, as shown in Figure 13.9. Once QIO has validated the request and built the I/O request packet, it inserts the packet onto the queue for the proper unit and returns control to the caller. (QIO earns its name because it queues the I/O request to the driver.) The calling process can then continue processing or request suspension until the I/O completes. A success indication from QIO means only that the parameters were supplied properly and that the I/O request has been queued to the driver. To see if the I/O has completed successfully, the user program must specify a memory location in which the final status will be placed when the operation completes.

The second component of the I/O system is the device driver. A device driver is a set of routines and data structures that control the operation of a single type of device. VMS uses the routines and data structures in the execution of an I/O request.

When an I/O request is issued for an idle device, VMS creates a driver process to handle the request. A driver process is a limited-context process. By limited context, we mean that the driver is restricted to system-space addressing; it does not execute within the context of a user process. Its state is completely described by its program counter, several registers, and the device database.

The device driver executes at a high processor-priority level. Since it cannot be interrupted by the scheduler, a driver executes until it terminates, performs an explicit wait request, or is interrupted by a driver at a higher IPL. User processes do not run until all driver work is completed.

The context for each driver, its registers and its program counter, are kept within the unit control block for the device. Thus, the UCB is to the device driver what the PCB is to the process. For each active device, the unit's UCB contains the state information of the executing driver process, as well as the status of the unit.

The third component of the VMS I/O system is the I/O postprocessing routine that completes the I/O operation within the caller's address space. Postprocessing, like QIO, is a common routine used for final processing of all device requests. Postprocessing routines are used to return the final status and data to user process memory.

I/O Control Flow

The I/O request begins as a call to QIO. QIO creates an I/O request packet, queues it onto the device UCB, and returns to the user. The IRP is the embodiment of the request and is passed between various components of the I/O system. It contains all the information needed to perform the operation independently of the requesting process and to later complete the operation within the context of the requesting process.

The operations performed by the VMS I/O system to process a request are shown in the flow diagram in Figure 13.10. The user calls the QIO system service routine, which executes in Kernel mode within the context of the user's process. QIO locates the UCB and associated database for the device. It checks device-independent parameters and calls driver subroutines to validate device-specific parameters. QIO then builds an I/O request packet and queues it for the driver by placing it on the unit control block request queue.

The driver process dequeues the request and starts the device. The driver suspends itself so that other processing can continue while the I/O operation proceeds. When the device interrupt occurs, the operating system resumes the driver process. The driver collects any status information from the device and controller registers and copies them into the I/O request packet for the request. The IRP is then placed on a queue for the I/O postprocessing routines.

Figure 13.10 VMS I/O request processing flow

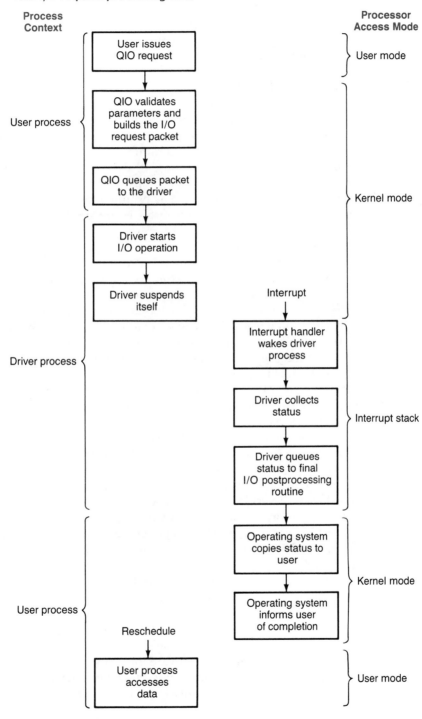

I/O postprocessing examines the IRP to determine how the I/O should be completed. Because the postprocessing routine returns status information into user memory buffers, it must execute with the address space (the context) of the requesting process. Finally, the postprocessing routine notifies the process that the I/O operation has completed.

The Use of Interrupt Priority Levels

The scenario in the previous section showed the sequence of events with respect to a single I/O request. Of course, at any one time there are many processes executing, and many I/O requests in various states of completion. The I/O system has a number of tasks to perform to manage all of the simultaneous operations. It also tries to optimize throughput while retaining real-time device responsiveness. It does this by keeping as many devices busy as possible. For example, as soon as an I/O transfer completes on a device, a new transfer is started if one is queued for the device.

VMS uses the software interrupt priority levels (IPLs) to keep the devices busy while also maintaining responsiveness. This is done by performing different I/O processing functions at different priority levels. Therefore, the I/O system will not process an I/O request sequentially, but will perform all the critical work for each outstanding request at a given level. Then the lower-priority work can be done for each request, and so on. This requires a mechanism for suspending a driver process at one level and continuing its work sometime later at another level.

Figure 13.11 shows the work done at four levels of processing. The VMS I/O system is structured so that all work is completed at the highest level before the next level executes. The highest-priority activity in VMS is the response to a device interrupt. Figure 13.11a shows the flow when an interrupt occurs. The interrupt dispatcher locates the responsible driver and initiates a routine within the driver to service the interrupt. It is a goal of VMS driver interrupt service routines to spend as little time as possible at the device IPL to avoid blocking other hardware interrupts. Therefore, VMS device drivers execute at device IPL only long enough to copy any CSR status information into the UCB. Staying at this IPL ensures that the registers do not change while being copied. As soon as the registers are copied, the driver asks the operating system to continue its execution at a lower level.

The lowering of a driver IPL is known as a *fork* in VMS. It is a continuation of the execution of a process at a different level and time. To initiate a fork, the operating system saves all of the driver context (its PC and registers) in the unit control block for the device. The UCB is placed on a queue for the lower IPL, called the device fork-level queue. The operating system requests a software interrupt at the fork IPL and returns from the hardware device interrupt, allowing other devices to interrupt.

When the processor priority level drops below the IPL requested for

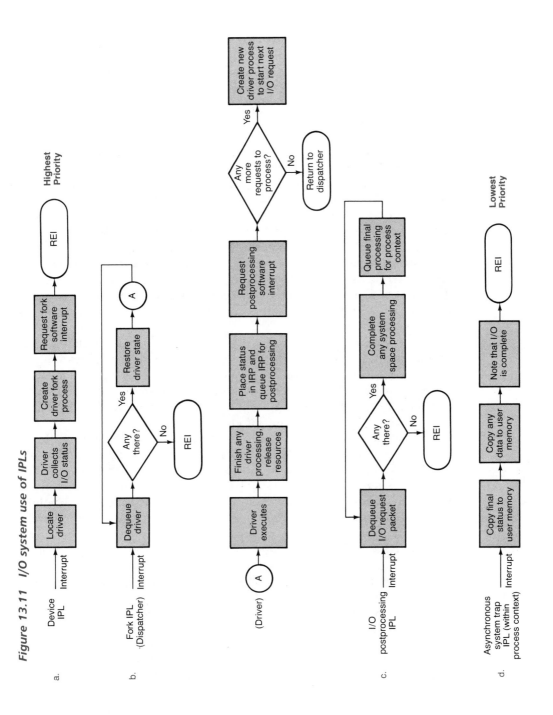

Figure 13.11 I/O system use of IPLs

325

the driver, an interrupt occurs. Figure 13.11b shows the actions at this level. An interrupt dispatcher dequeues the first UCB from its queue and restores the state of the driver process. The driver process continues execution and releases any resources which it has acquired, to increase the level of concurrency possible.

Although processing may still be needed to complete the I/O request, VMS again defers much of it to a lower level. The driver process places any final status in the I/O request packet. This time, the IRP is used to propagate the execution of the I/O request. The packet is placed on a queue of the I/O postprocessing routine, which executes at the lowest priority level once all more crucial work is complete.

After queuing the I/O packet and requesting a software interrupt at the postprocessing IPL, the driver checks its unit control block request queue to see if any more requests are waiting. If so, the driver begins processing the next request. That way, a new request can be started on the device as soon as possible. After the driver initiates the next I/O operation, if there is one, it returns to the fork interrupt dispatcher. The dispatcher checks to determine if any other driver fork processes are waiting to execute at that level.

Once VMS has seen that all possible I/O requests have been initiated, postprocessing can occur. Postprocessing is initiated by a software interrupt. The postprocessing routine dequeues an I/O request packet to finish any processing that can be done in the operating system context, as shown in Figure 13.11c. Then it must switch to process context to perform any final copying of data and status into user memory.

The switch to process context (address space) is done with an *asynchronous system trap* (AST). An AST is a call of a routine within the context of a process, asynchronous to the execution of that process. For example, when a process issues an I/O request, it can specify a routine to be called when the I/O is completed. This routine is called an asynchronous system trap routine, because it is called when an asynchronous event occurs. If the process is executing when the event occurs, it will be interrupted and the AST routine will be called. When the AST routine returns, program execution continues from the interrupt point.

The operating system maintains a queue of AST control blocks in the software PCB of each process. Each entry in the queue describes one requested AST and contains the address of a routine to be called when a specific event occurs. The I/O postprocessing routine queues the address of one of its subroutines, to be executed in Kernel mode when the appropriate process next executes. It also notes in the hardware PCB that a Kernel mode AST is pending for the process. When the process next executes, the VAX hardware automatically causes an interrupt at the AST-level IPL so that the operating system can execute the AST routine.

This final AST routine executes in Kernel mode in the user's address space to copy any information into the user's memory. It may also inform the process that the I/O operation has completed. For example, if the process asked to have its own AST routine executed following the I/O completion, the Kernel mode routine will queue an AST for the user.

We have seen that there are two ways to consider I/O processing. First is the sequential flow of a single I/O request through the system, as shown in Figure 13.10. Second is the actual servicing sequence used by VMS to increase response time, as shown in Figure 13.11. Figure 13.11 shows how a number of fork queues allow for the propagation of a request through several prioritized levels. VMS uses the software interrupt priority levels and the software interrupts to schedule work at each level. It is the hardware, however, that automatically generates an interrupt at the highest level with work to do.

Synchronizing I/O Database Access

The VMS I/O system uses one or two mechanisms for synchronizing its database, depending on whether it is running on a uniprocessor or a multiprocessor. On a uniprocessor, the processor IPL is used to synchronize driver databases. Any driver that wants to access a shared database component for a device or controller must operate at the fork IPL of the device or controller. By forcing all drivers to queue for access to a given level, VMS ensures that only one driver process can access the database at a time. Following an interrupt, the operating system queues drivers at the lower fork IPL. Thus, the forking mechanism is a forced serialization of activity. A driver does not have to worry about synchronizing with other driver processes. It knows implicitly that it is the only process active at that level.

On a symmetric, shared-memory multiprocessor, there is a copy of the VMS operating system running on each node, each capable of addressing the same data structures. Using the processor IPL alone is insufficient to synchronize databases. When a driver rasies IPL, it prevents other processes on the same processor from accessing a controlled data structure; it does not, however, prevent processes on *other* processors from changing their IPLs to the same level or higher.

To prevent multiple processors from simultaneously accessing shared system database, VMS contains a number of semaphores (called *spin locks* because a processor typically busy waits to acquire them) for synchronizing shared multiprocessor data structures. For example, there are spin locks for each of the fork interrupt priority levels. A driver must both acquire the spin lock and change IPL to guarantee mutual exclusion at that priority level on the multiprocessor. Once a driver obtains a spin lock, no other driver (on any processor) can obtain that lock until it is released. Spin locks also exist for various I/O data structures, and these may need to be acquired in order to examine or modify a specific data structure.

System Service Implementation

While examining Change Mode instructions in the previous chapter, we discussed the use of an operating system service routine. In this chapter we have described the most frequently called system service in VMS, the Queue I/O service. This final section discusses how control is actually transferred to a VMS service.

We have already stated that VMS system services are called via the Call instruction. In VMS, macros are available at the assembly language level to access system services. For example, the $QIO macro generates a call to the QIO routine. The name of the QIO entry point in the operating system is SYS$QIO. A high-level language program calls this routine as it calls any other procedure, for example, CALL SYS$QIO (parameters).

Once a program containing a system service call is translated and linked, it contains the virtual address of the service routine entry point. One might ask whether this means that each service routine always remains at the same virtual address or whether the user has to reassemble or relink the program each time a new version of the operating system arrives. The answer to each question is no. VMS was designed so that user programs would run without relinking or reassembling across VMS versions, even though the service routines might be relocated in the system address space. The reason this is possible is that system service calls are made to special system service *vectors*, which are pointers to the system service routines. These vectors are similar to the interrupt vectors in that they give directions to where a routine or system service actually resides in system space.

It is sometimes useful for nonprivileged code to be able to intercept a program's system service calls transparently to that program. For this reason, system service vectors actually appear at two places within a process's virtual address space. While vectors appear in the first several pages of system space, they also appear in the program's P1 region. The VMS linker typically links system service calls to the P1 vector addresses. If a facility wanted to intercept system service calls, it could map the P1 space vector pages to its own handler without disturbing other processes's system service calls. However, under normal circumstances, the P1 space and system space vectors are mapped to the same physical pages.

For each system service, there are several instructions in the vector region to transfer control to the actual service routine. The instructions in the vector region for each service are at fixed virtual addresses for the life of VMS. Consequently, if a new version of VMS is issued in which the service procedures have moved, user programs can still run unchanged because the vectors remain at the same addresses although they transfer control to different locations.

A vector contains instructions to transfer control to a system service routine in system space. If the service routine runs with the access mode of the caller, the vector contains only the 16-bit register save mask (remember that the vector was called as if it were a procedure) and a Jump instruction. The following example of a system service routine called NAME executes in the same mode:

```
SYS$NAME:
        .WORD   ^M<R2,R3,R4,R5>     ; register save mask
        JMP     @#EXE$NAME+2        ; transfer to service
```

The Jump instruction transfers control to the first instruction of the service routine in system space, which is at address EXE$NAME+2. This calling method forces the first instruction of the service to be 2 bytes past its entry point, since the actual service routine has a copy of the register save mask at its beginning. When the service routine executes a Return instruction, it returns directly to the user.

If the system service routine executes in a different mode than the user program, then the vector contains the call mask followed by a Change Mode instruction and a Return instruction:

```
SYS$NAME:
        .WORD   ^M<R2,R3,R4,R5>     ; save registers
        CHMK    #code               ; dispatch to service
        RET                         ; return to caller
```

The Change Mode instruction causes an exception, changing the mode of the processor and transferring control to a special dispatching routine within VMS. This routine examines the code number, which tells which system service should be called. It also builds a new call frame on the stack of the new access mode, first checking that the caller's arguments are valid. When the system service routine executes a Return instruction, it returns to this dispatcher. The dispatcher executes a Return from Exception or Interrupt (REI) instruction, which lowers the access mode and returns to the instruction following the Change Mode. Now running in the caller's access mode, the Return instruction in the service vector executes, returning control to the user.

Summary

This chapter looked closely at the implementation of the VMS operating system. In particular, it examined the operating system's use of the architectural support for managing the processor, memory, and I/O.

VMS uses the hardware process as the basis for program execution. Processes are scheduled to run by VMS using a preemptive priority scheme, where the highest priority process is always run. VMS modifies process priorities, however, as a process executes. The VMS scheduler maintains a number of data structures to manage the scheduling procedure, including the process control block (PCB) introduced in the previous chapter.

The memory-management support implements separate process address spaces and allows sharing of the operating system. VMS uses paging, to allow processes to access large address spaces, and swapping, to allow sharing of memory by many processes. A number of optimizations attempt to decrease the number of I/O operations, including the use of memory lists of recently used pages, reading and writing of pages in clusters, and swapping.

Finally, in the VMS I/O system, the use of software interrupt priority levels (IPLs) helps to schedule the execution of operating system activities to reduce the response time to hardware interrupts.

Exercises

1. How does an operating system scheduler ensure that a single process does not consume the entire CPU, once it has begun executing?

2. What is meant by a real-time process in VMS? How are real-time processes treated differently from timesharing processes?

3. Contrast the scheduling policies you might use when trying to optimize response time with those you would use to optimize throughput.

4. What are the primary states that a process can be in as it makes progress from initiation to completion?

5. Name three page replacement algorithms. Describe the differences.

6. What is the resident set? What algorithms are used to change or replace pages in the resident set? What is the balance set?

7. What is the difference between the working set and the VMS resident set?

8. What is the difference between paging and swapping? Why does VMS use both paging and swapping? Are both paging and swapping needed to implement a VAX virtual memory system?

9. What is the difference between a modified bit and a referenced bit in a page table entry? What is the use of each?

10. What are the functions performed by the VMS I/O device driver?

11. Why does the VMS I/O system use the interrupt priority for processing I/O requests?

12. What is an asynchronous system trap?

13. Why do users call VMS system service routines through vector instructions, instead of calling the routines directly?

14 Caches and Translation Buffers

For any computer architecture, there may be many implementations spanning a wide range of price and performance. For example, in Digital's VAX family, a four-processor VAX 8800 has over 60 times the computational power of the VAX-11/730, the slowest VAX ever produced. The cost ratio between a fully configured four-processor VAX 8800 and the least-expensive VAX, a desktop VAXstation 2000, is over 200.

The implementation of each version of an architecture requires that the designer choose a computer structure that meets cost constraints while providing the best possible performance and reliability. This structure must be built with readily available component technologies and, typically, must be modifiable to accept newer technologies as they become proven.

This chapter considers some of the choices the hardware implementor has in the design of a member of a computer family. It focuses in particular on differences in memory structure that are available to the implementor. It also describes some of the mechanisms that VAX designers have used to enhance performance and some of the differences among VAX implementations. Although invisible to the executing program, these features have a significant effect on system performance and cost.

Choice of Memory Technology and Structure

Throughout the rapid evolution of the computer, the cost of memory has been a major factor in overall system price. Although memories have become relatively inexpensive, there are and always will be memories with varying storage capacities and performance characteristics available at different costs. Since memory speed substantially influences the execution speed of the CPU, selecting a particular memory technology and memory structure is a crucial aspect in designing a computer-family member.

If cost was no object, the entire memory system would be constructed from the fastest available memory, as is done for the CRAY computers. For low-cost computers, this is obviously impossible. However, one option for less expensive systems is organizing the memory system into a layered hierarchy composed of different memory technologies. If this is done with a knowledge of the statistical characteristics and patterns of typical programs in execution, a significant increase in memory performance can be obtained at little added cost.

The Fastest Technology Approach

One way to structure the total memory system is to implement one segment of the memory with the fastest technology available. Exemplifying this strategy, the PDP–11/55 provides for up to 64K bytes of bipolar memory, which the user can fill with data or executable code. The remainder of primary memory is implemented out of slower MOS components. For many real-time applications, this is a perfect solution. The user locks the most time-critical code and data in high-speed memory at program load time, allowing for exact performance prediction. The problem with this approach is that memory is non-uniform from the programmer's point of view, and the programmer must be familiar with the physical-memory structure. This method is unlikely to benefit a multiprogrammed system, in which physical memory is allocated and reallocated among users and time slices.

Cache Memory Approach

Programs, of course, do not execute randomly, but exhibit some locality in their generation of addresses and use of memory. Memory generally is accessed in a logical order, often sequentially, as in processing an array or sequencing through the instructions of the program. Alternatively, a program may repeatedly flow through a loop of instructions, then move to another localized area.

It is possible to take advantage of this locality of reference in programs to build a hierarchical memory system with much better performance than one might expect. This basic structure, shown in Figure 14.1, is called a *cache memory* (from the French *cacher*, "to hide") and was first used in the late 1960s in the IBM 360/85. The idea is to place a small amount of high-speed storage close to the CPU to hold the most recently accessed instructions and data items. When a program makes a memory request, the CPU first checks to see if the data is in the cache. If the data is in the cache, it is returned quickly without using main memory or the bus; this is a cache *hit*. If the data is not in the cache, it is fetched from main memory and loaded into the cache on its way to the CPU; this is a cache *miss*. When new data is loaded into the cache, it typically displaces data that was previously stored there.

The performance of a cache memory is stated in terms of its *hit ratio* or *miss ratio*, where

$$hit\ ratio = \frac{number\ of\ memory\ accesses\ found\ in\ the\ cache}{total\ \#\ of\ memory\ accesses} \times 100$$

and

miss ratio = 1 − hit ratio

Surprisingly, even relatively small caches can achieve hit ratios of 80 to 90 percent. We can easily see the potential impact this has on system performance. The access time of the entire memory system as seen by the CPU is a function of cache hit ratio (H), cache access time (T_C), and primary memory access time (T_M), as expressed by the formula

$$average\ access\ time = H \times T_C + (1 - H) \times T_M$$

This formula becomes more complicated as we consider different cache organizations, but we can see that with cache hit ratios of 90 percent, the average memory access time comes very close to the cache access time, even if memory is significantly slower than the cache. For example, given a system with $H=0.9$, $T_C=200ns$, and $T_M=1400ns$, the average access time is only 320 nanoseconds, which is low considering the high cost of a primary memory access.

The following sections look at some of the organizational choices in cache design.

Associative Memories and Cache Organization

A typical computer memory system is composed of a number of consecutive storage elements, usually bytes, each with a unique physical address. To read the data from a given storage location, the CPU places this unique address in an internal register on the memory bus (often referred to as the memory address register) and receives the return data in another

Figure 14.1   Structure of CPU with cache memory

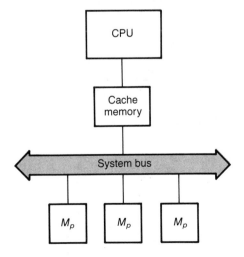

register (the memory data register), as shown in Figure 14.2. The address specified is used as an index into the memory; each address uniquely specifies one memory location to be selected, and no searching is required.

Human memories function by associating or chaining related information together, not by using addresses. We often recall an item committed to memory by remembering something else associated with the item. Thus, to recall the name of an acquaintance called Donald, we conjure up the image of a duck. Such an *associative memory* is represented by the phone book in Figure 14.3. Here we have a list of names and associated information. Although the information could be listed randomly, it is usually presented in alphabetical order. For each name, or *tag*, there is some associated information. Each entry is "addressed" not by its number or position within the list, but by its name or tag field.

If the tags do not uniquely identify the object, then duplications can occur. For instance, the Chicago phone book contains many entries for the name Peter Smith because the name by itself does not uniquely identify one person. Thus, an associative search can yield several alternatives from which one must be selected based on additional information (for example, street name).

A computer memory structure could be constructed as shown in Figure 14.4. Each entry consists of two parts, a tag and an associated data item. The computer presents a tag to memory by writing it into the tag register. If a match (called a hit) is found anywhere in the A half, the associated data item from the B half is returned to the output data register. If no match is found, the memory reports a miss. A complete memory search would be slow if the comparisons were made sequentially from the beginning to the end of the list. Consequently, it is common for the memory system to be constructed to perform all of the comparisons in parallel, at a substantial increase in complexity.

Figure 14.2 *Random access memory*

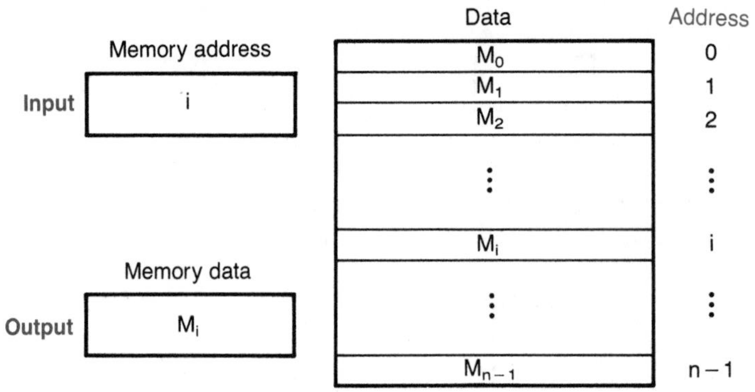

Figure 14.3 Associative list

Name or Tag	Data Item(s)
Cal Cauliflower	281-5610
Bob Blackberry	356-8123
Dora Dandelion	413-1213
Arnold Apple	856-2031

Figure 14.4 Associative memory

Input — Tag A_i

Output — Data B_i

Tag	Data
A_0	B_0
A_1	B_1
A_2	B_2
⋮	⋮
A_{n-1}	B_{n-1}
A half	B half

A cache built in this way with all comparisons done in parallel is called a *fully associative cache*. For the cache, each tag in the A half contains a primary memory address, and the associated B half data entry contains the data stored at that address. For example, if we were designing a simple VAX cache, each tag would be a 32-bit address and the associated data would be a longword. Because of the cost and complexity of the parallel searching structure, very few fully associative caches have been used.

To reduce cost and complexity, it is also possible to use some bits from the tag as an index into the memory, forming a *direct-mapped cache* as illustrated by Figure 14.5. The figure shows a 32-element direct-mapped cache. Given an input tag, the five low-order bits of that tag are used to select one of the 32 cache entries. For example, if the value of the 5-bit field is the integer i, then the ith cache entry will be selected. Many tags may have the same low-order five bits, and therefore collisions may occur; these will potentially decrease the effectiveness of the cache. For instance, if all 5-bit index values are even, only half of the cache will be used.

Thus, the data for each address (tag) can appear in only one location in the cache, as determined by its low-order bits. Once the appropriate cache entry is selected, the twenty-seven high-order bits of the tag are compared with the contents of the A half of entry i (A_i). If a match occurs, data B_i is returned; if not, we have a miss.

Figure 14.5 Direct-mapped cache

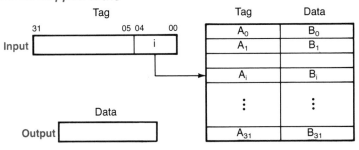

Issues in Cache Design

One problem with the direct-mapped cache is that each datum can be stored at only one location and many data items can map to that same cache location. For example, if two data items that map to the same cache entry are needed alternately within a tight loop, each access to one of them will find the other in the cache, causing a miss and bumping the other item out of the cache.

A solution to this problem is to provide *n* different places where a particular datum can be stored; such a structure is called an *n-way set-associative cache*. Figure 14.6 shows the basic organization of a set-associative cache—the organization used by most contemporary caches. Each box in this figure operates exactly like a direct-mapped cache with *M* entries, except that all of the boxes operate in parallel. When an input tag is presented to the cache, $log_2 M$ bits of the tag are used to form a cache index, *i*, as before. In this case, however, entry *i* of *each* of the *N* boxes is checked for a match simultaneously. Each row of entries in Figure 14.6 is called a *set* and the number of entries in a set (that is, the number of parallel comparisons that must be made) is the *set size* or *set associativity*, which is always a power of 2. A direct-mapped cache is simply a set associative cache with a set size of 1. Caches have been built with set sizes of 2, 4, 8, 16, and 32. As you might imagine, there are diminishing returns; a set size of 2 performs much better than direct mapped, while a set size of 4 performs only a little better than a set size of 2, and so on.

For example, Figure 14.7 shows a typical graph of hit ratio versus cache size for a hypothetical cache memory. As the cache size grows, hit ratios increase to nearly 99 percent. Furthermore, as the cache gets larger, each doubling of cache size gives a smaller gain. This figure also shows the effect of adding associativity. The bottom curve is for a direct-mapped cache. Changing the cache to two-way set-associative, that is, two elements per set, produces a substantial increase in performance, particularly at smaller cache sizes where conflicts are more likely. As we add more associativity, we get better performance but the performance gain becomes smaller and may not be worth the additional complexity.

Figure 14.6   Set-associative cache organization

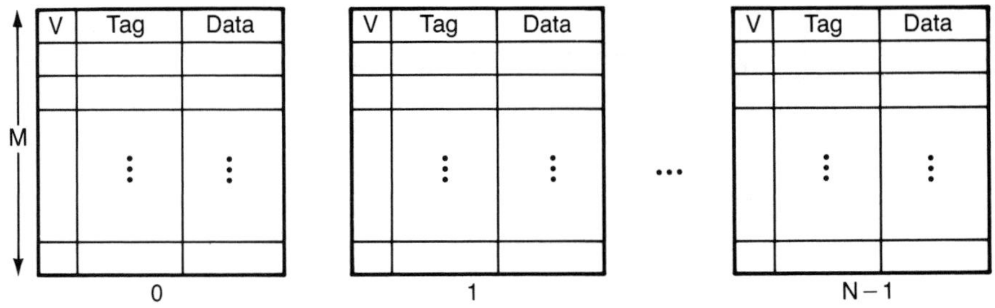

Figure 14.7 Typical cache performance

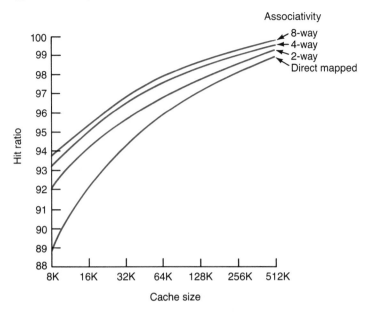

Within this basic structure of a set-associative cache are a number of design decisions that affect both the complexity and the performance of the cache. We consider some of these decisions in the following paragraphs.

Each data slot in a cache is called a *line* or a *block*. One important issue is the cache line size or block size, that is, how much data is stored with each address, and how much data is loaded on each miss. If data were moved from memory and stored in the cache in one-byte units, time would be saved only on a hit to a previously referenced byte. Furthermore, this would waste bus bandwidth. A larger line size can make better use of bus bandwidth and locality, since it *prefetches* a small amount of data with each miss. On the VAX 6200 family, for example, 32 bytes of contiguous data are fetched on each miss. As the line size gets larger, however, the potential increases for the newly loaded data to displace possibly useful data already in the cache.

The time to handle a cache miss depends in part on when the memory fetch is initiated. In the simplest case, the cache is checked for an item and if a miss occurs, the memory fetch is then begun. In this case, the cost of the miss is the sum of the cache lookup time and the memory fetch time. On the other hand, the memory fetch could be started in parallel with the cache lookup; if there is a hit, the memory fetch is simply cancelled. The cost of a miss in this case is only the memory fetch time; however, bus bandwidth may be wasted performing unnecessary fetches.

We have discussed the operation of a cache on reads, but what about writes to memory? The simplest write implementation for handling memory writes in the cache is called *write-through*. When a write request is made, the new data is written "through" the cache to main memory. In this way, both the cache and memory always have valid copies of all data. Although some performance loss may occur because of the time to perform the write, the processor can continue operation while the write into memory proceeds.

There are actually two cases to consider on write requests: those that hit in the cache and those that miss. On a write miss, a write is being performed to data that is not currently in the cache. In most designs, that data will be written to main memory and the cache will not be modified unless that data is subsequently read by the program. On the other hand, some caches employ a strategy called *write allocate*, in which the data is written to memory and loaded into the cache at the same time. On a write hit, the data being written is already cached; in this case, both the cache and main memory are updated.

Another method used to handle writes in cached systems is called *write-back*. With write-back, the new data is written only to the cache and not to main memory. A separate "dirty" bit that is part of the cache tag is set, thereby remembering the cache modification. This method reduces the number of writes to main memory. If a datum is heavily read and written within a tight loop, the loop can proceed without any access to primary memory, saving time, bus bandwidth, and memory cycles. The hardware, however, is more complex because the cache must know when a write to main memory must occur. For example, if a cache miss occurs, the cache must check to see if the data to be displaced is dirty; if so, that data must be written to memory before the new data can be loaded.

If a user with cached data performs a disk write, the memory being written may not be up-to-date. Therefore, either the cache must watch the I/O traffic or else the operating system must cause dirty data to be updated in primary memory before it is output. Similarly, if a user with cached data performs a disk read, some cached elements may need to be invalidated because they no longer reflect the values stored in memory. For this reason, each cache line must have a *valid bit* to indicate whether the data there is valid or not.

Write-back caches are more complex but offer the potential for higher performance. In a multiprocessor with large numbers of processors, a write-back cache is almost a necessity to reduce contention for the system bus and memory. In this case the caches have an additional problem; if one processor writes a datum in its cache, other caches may need to know about it. Such caches are often called "snoopy caches" because they continually keep track of each other's transactions.

One final issue to consider is the separation of the common cache for instructions and data into two separate caches: an instruction cache (I-cache) and a data cache (D-cache). There are two basic reasons for splitting the cache in this way. First, an optimal cache structure for instruction fetches may be different from an optimal structure for data fetches. Instructions show more locality than data, and the fact that instructions are read-only may greatly simplify the I-cache design. Second, on reduced instruction set machines, where most instructions can execute in only one cycle, the cache will be totally saturated by instruction requests. Since the CPU needs to fetch data as well as instructions, a separate I-cache and D-cache may be required to provide the needed parallelism and to prevent a wasted cycle for instructions that read or write memory. On the VAX, this is not an important issue because the average VAX instruction takes about eight to ten cycles, during which there are plenty of free cache cycles to fetch instructions and data.

Cache Coherency in Multiprocessors

As previously stated, a new problem is created by shared-memory multiprocessors. On the one hand, as more processors are added, caches are required to reduce bus traffic and memory contention. On the other hand, the problem of *cache coherency* becomes significant. In a shared-memory multiprocessor, it is possible for a single data item to be cached in several processors' caches. If the data is read-only, there is no problem. However, if one of the processors writes that data, other processors' cached copies will be out of date, that is, incoherent.

There are a number of possible solutions to this problem. One simple solution is for each processor to have a write-through cache. Using a write-through scheme accomplishes two purposes: all writes are broadcast on the bus, and memory always contains the most recent copy of all data. All of the caches watch the bus for memory-write transactions. For example, when processor A modifies variable m, its cache will send a write request to primary memory because the cache is write-through. All other caches will see the transaction and will check to see if they have variable m cached. If processor B's cache finds that it has a copy of m, it will invalidate the cache line containing m. Should processor B subsequently try to read m, it will get a cache miss and the correct data will be loaded from primary memory.

The problem with this strategy is that it requires a write-through cache, which causes more bus traffic and memory contention than the alternative write-back scheme. This is particularly significant in a shared-memory multiprocessor where the bus can be a bottleneck. With a write-back cache, there is additional complexity because writes are not automatically sent to memory; hence, other caches would not normally see write activity. To achieve better performance, multiprocessors with write-back caches typically maintain several additional state bits with each cache entry. These bits describe the state of the cached data and can permit cache writes without updating memory. For example, such a scheme is used in the Firefly, a prototype 7-VAX multiprocessor workstation developed by the DEC System Research Center (and described in the 1987 paper by Thacker and Stewart). Each Firefly processor has a cache; each cache line, which holds one 32-bit word, has two special state bits, called *shared* and *dirty*. These bits are used to reduce write traffic. When a cache knows that its entry is exclusively owned (not shared), that cache can act as a write-back cache, making updates only locally. However, each cache snoops on all bus transactions; when a cache discovers another cache trying to read memory that it currently has exclusively, the owning cache supplies the data and both caches then consider the data to be shared. At that point, all writes to that data item in either cache will be broadcast to all caches and to memory. This mechanism reduces the number of bus writes required to memory locations that are not actively being shared, while maintaining consistency for shared data.

There are many different cache coherence protocols, and the choice of a protocol involves tradeoffs between cache and bus complexity, bus traffic, and performance. For an excellent discussion of these protocols, see the paper by Archibald and Baer (1986).

Multilevel Caches

Several computer systems now employ multilevel caches, that is, two separate caches between the processor and main memory. The basic idea of a two-level cache is to provide a small but fast cache close to the processor; behind that cache is a large, but somewhat slower, second-level cache. The second-level cache is connected to the memory bus. Only misses at the second level are sent to primary memory.

Recently, a two-level structure has become viable for a number of reasons. First, processor speeds are increasing faster than memory speeds. This implies an increasing disparity between processor cycle time and memory access time. The larger this disparity, the more room there is for a multilevel memory hierarchy. Second, primary memories are rapidly increasing in size, and memories of hundreds of megabytes are becoming common. Large memories typically have larger access times because of packaging and physical design constraints. Cache sizes have increased along with memory sizes, but while a large cache reduces misses, it also becomes slow; therefore, a small, fast cache can be used in conjunction with a large, slower cache. Third, because of increasing on-chip densities, it is possible to include small on-chip caches. These caches reduce the number of off-chip memory accesses, but they need to be backed up by larger caches because of their relatively low hit rates. Fourth, shared memory multiprocessors require local caches to reduce bus contention. A large second-level cache can help both to reduce access time on misses in the first-level cache and to reduce bus traffic.

The following section examines a specific two-level cache in more detail.

An Example Cache Organization: The VAX 6200

The beauty of the cache mechanism is that (1) it greatly increases system performance and (2) it is completely invisible to the programmer. Each CPU designer is free to use a cache (or no cache, for that matter) that suits the needs of the CPU. For example, the MicroVAX II computer has no cache, but this system has a relatively balanced CPU speed and memory-access time. Other VAXes require a cache because of a high ratio of memory-access time to CPU cycle time.

This section examines the cache design of a specific computer: the VAX 6200. Two aspects of the VAX 6200 make it interesting to examine. First, it is a multiprocessor system and must deal with cache coherency. Second, the VAX 6200 uses a multilevel cache.

Figure 14.8 shows the general structure of a VAX 6200 system. All CPUs, the primary memory, and the backplane interconnect (BI) buses, which are used to attach I/O and network controllers, are connected through a shared high-speed bus. Each CPU in the VAX 6200 is a single-chip CVAX microprocessor. The CVAX has a small on-chip cache that can hold instructions only or hold both instructions and data. In the VAX 6200, this cache is used to hold only instructions. Between each CPU and the shared bus is a large cache that holds both instructions and data.

The small on-chip instruction cache in the VAX 6200 holds 1K bytes of instruction-stream data. The cache is organized as a two-way set-

Figure 14.8   Organization of the VAX 6200 multiprocessor

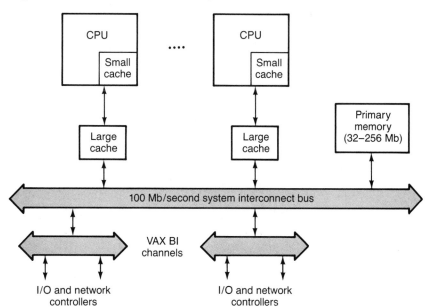

associative cache, as shown in Figure 14.9. Each cache block holds 8 bytes of data. Given a physical memory address, the cache uses the 6-bit index field to select a block in each half of the set-associative cache. The upper 20 bits of the physical address are then compared to the 20-bit tag field in each of the cache blocks selected by the index. If a match occurs, the data is found in the cache block whose tag has matched. The low-order 3 bits of the physical address specify which of the 8 bytes in the cache block is the byte being requested. A lookup in this first-level cache takes 80 nanoseconds, which is the cycle time of the CVAX processors in the VAX 6200.

The second-level cache in the VAX 6200 takes 160 nanoseconds for a lookup, half the speed of the first level, but it is substantially larger, holding 256K bytes of instructions and data. The second-level cache is direct mapped. As previously stated, a direct-mapped cache is simpler to build than a set-associative cache and the associativity becomes less important as the cache size increases. Figure 14.10 shows the structure of the second-level cache in the VAX 6200.

The second-level cache in the VAX 6200 contains 4,096 cache blocks. Each block holds 64 bytes of data; however, a block is divided into two parts that hold 32 bytes each. When a cache miss occurs, 32 bytes of data are loaded into the appropriate half of the selected cache block. Because of this structure, the cache must contain two valid bits (shown as V0 and V1 in Figure 14.10), one for each half of the block. This structure allows the cache to fill in 32-byte units, while reducing by half the tag storage that would be needed if the block size were only 32 bytes.

When a request is made to the second-level cache, the cache extracts a 12-bit index field from the physical address to select one of the 4,096 cache blocks. The cache then compares the high-order 12 bits of the physical address with the 12-bit tag stored in the selected block. The 6-bit offset must also be examined to determine which valid bit is appropriate for the

Figure 14.9   First-level cache in the VAX 6200

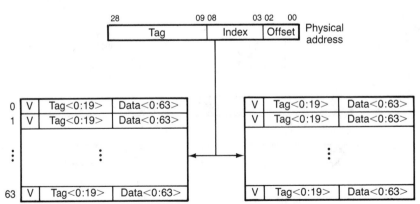

Figure 14.10 Second-level cache in the VAX 6200

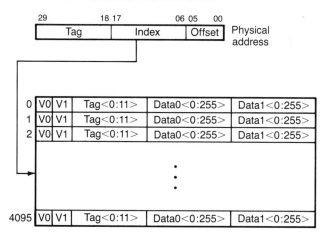

requested data. If the tags match and the appropriate valid bit is set, the offset field specifies the start of the data element requested.

The VAX 6200 is a multiprocessor and must implement cache coherency. The scheme used is fairly simple. All caches are write-through, so memory contains a consistent copy of all data. All caches snoop on the bus and invalidate local copies of any data that is written. Each memory write seen on the bus thus requires a cache lookup. In order to reduce the cache interference that would be caused by those cache lookups, each of the second-level caches has a replicated tag storage. That is, there are two copies of the tag for each block, one copy used for cache lookups from the processor, and one copy used by the logic snooping on the bus. No coherency control is required in the first-level cache because it caches only instructions, which are read-only.[1]

The use of write-through, as previously noted, does cause a substantial increase in write traffic compared to write-back. To reduce this write traffic, the VAX 6200 has a 16-byte write buffer between the second-level cache and memory. This buffer can be thought of as a tiny write-back cache. The buffer is only written to memory when necessary, for example, when a write is made outside of the current 16-byte range of the buffer. Due to the high degree of locality for write references (for example, as a result of consecutive stack writes on procedure calls), this type of write buffer reduces the write traffic to main memory by an average of approximately 50% compared with a standard write-through cache.

---

[1] In fact, although it is strongly discouraged, the VAX does permit writing to the instruction stream; however, the architecture requires software to execute an REI instruction prior to executing modified instruction-stream code. The CVAX automatically flushes its cache on execution of an REI instruction.

The Translation Buffer

On a virtual-memory system such as the VAX, a reference to a single virtual address can cause several memory references to occur before the desired information is finally accessed. For example, a reference to a system space address requires one reference to the system page table, which then yields the final physical address. This extra reference is part of the overhead associated with a virtual memory system. Similarly, a process space access requires references to the system and process page tables to compute the actual physical address.

To reduce the apparent overhead of these levels of indirection, VAX processors contain a high-speed associative memory called the *translation buffer* (TB), which caches the most recently used virtual-to-physical address translations. While not all VAXes have caches, all VAXes must have a translation buffer, if even a small one; otherwise the virtual-memory translation overhead would be intolerable.

Figure 14.11 shows the general system organization of a CPU with a translation buffer. User programs running on the CPU generate virtual addresses of instructions or data to be accessed. These virtual addresses are passed to the translation buffer. The TB is just a cache whose tags are virtual page numbers and whose associated data elements are the page table entries corresponding to those virtual pages. If the translation for the virtual address is found in the TB, the TB performs the translation and sends the correct physical address to the cache. If the TB lookup fails, a TB miss occurs and processor microcode attempts to load the appropriate translation information from the primary memory page tables into the TB.

For example, the VAX-11/780 contains a 128-entry TB whose block structure is shown in Figure 14.12. Like the 780's memory cache, the TB is

Figure 14.11   CPU with cache and translation buffer

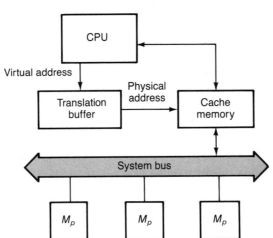

Figure 14.12   VAX-11/780 translation buffer block structure

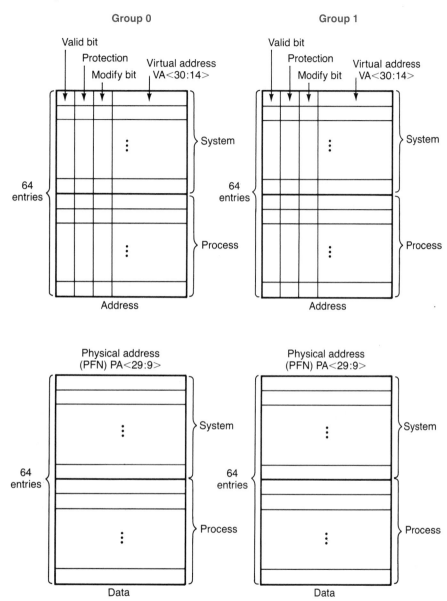

two-way set associative; as a result, there are two possible slots in which a particular page table entry can reside. Moreover, the translation buffer is separated into two parts. In Figure 14.12, the upper thirty-two entries are used for system space translations (system PTEs), the lower thirty-two for process space translations (process PTEs). This structure was chosen because, while system space is shared among all processes, process space translations are local and must be invalidated when a context switch occurs. If these entries are not invalidated, the next process could access the wrong physical-memory location by generating a process virtual address when a previous process translation is in the buffer. Dividing the translation buffer provides a simple structure for invalidating all process translations while leaving system translations unaffected.

The translation of a virtual address is shown in Figure 14.13. Bit 31 of the virtual address selects the top or bottom half of the translation buffer for system or process space. Because there are 32 entries in each half of the buffer, bits <13:9> are used to select one of these entries in both the Group 0 and Group 1 buffers. A validity check is made, and address bits <30:14> are checked against the tag field stored in the buffer. If a match is found, the physical page-frame-number bits stored in the associated data field for the matching entry are appended in the byte-within-page bits <8:0> of the original virtual address, forming the physical address. At the same time, the protection field is compared with the current mode to see if the process has the appropriate privilege to access that page. If not, an access violation fault is generated.

If the operation to be performed is a write, a check must be made to see whether the Modify bit has been set. If it has not, this is the first write to the page, and the Modify bit must be set on both the translation buffer and main memory versions of the PTE.

The operation of all VAX translation buffers is fairly similar, although some are direct mapped and some are two-way set associative. Table 14.1 shows a number of the VAX implementations and the characteristics of their caches and TBs. The table is listed in order of machine performance. The lowest-performance VAX, the VAX-11/730, has no cache. While the MicroVAX II has no cache and only a small on-chip TB, it is a small system with memory packaged close to the CPU (one megabyte is actually on the CPU board). The VAX 6200 multiprocessor, which uses the CMOS MicroVAX chip, has a two-level cache; there is an on-chip cache for instructions and a second-level cache on the CPU board. Each second-level cache on the VAX 6200 is 256K bytes. All VAX systems use the simpler write-through cache structure, except for the VAX 8600/8650, which uses write-back.

Figure 14.13 Translation of a virtual address on the VAX-11/780

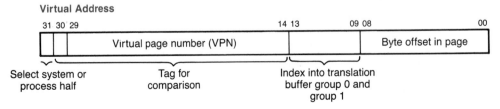

Table 14.1 VAX Cache and TB Characteristics

Machine	Performance	Cycle Time	Cache	TLB
VAX-11/730	.4	270 ns	none	128 entries
VAX-11/750	.6	320 ns	4KB direct mapped	512 entries
MicroVAX II	.9	200 ns	none	8 entries on chip
VAX-11/780	1.0	200 ns	8KB two-way	128 entries
VAX-11/785	1.5	133 ns	32KB two-way	128 entries
VAX 8200	1.0	200 ns	8KB	512 entries
VAX 3500	3.0	90 ns	1K on-chip 64KB 2nd level	28 entries
VAX 6200	3.0	80 ns	1K on-chip 256KB 2nd level	28 entries
VAX 8650	6.0	55 ns	16KB two-way write-back	512 entries
VAX 8800	6.0	45 ns	64KB direct mapped	1024 entries direct mapped

The Instruction Buffer

One area in which the processor particularly benefits from buffering and overlapping operations is the fetching and decoding of the instruction stream. Instructions are almost always executed in a linear or sequential order. If the processor can fetch the next instruction from memory while the current instruction is executing, it rarely has to wait for the memory system between execution of sequential instructions.

On some VAXes, this prefetching of instruction bytes is handled by an *instruction buffer* in the CPU. On the VAX 8800, for example, the instruction buffer is 16 bytes long and is managed as a circular buffer with a read pointer and a write pointer. The read pointer specifies the next byte to be read by the CPU, while the write pointer specifies the first free byte available to be filled by the cache. As a low-priority background activity, the cache continuously attempts to fill the instruction buffer. Such instruction buffer fills may cause cache misses, which will cause instructions to be loaded into the cache before they are accessed. Of course, there is a chance that some instructions will be loaded superfluously because the program may branch before a prefetched instruction is accessed.

Since the average VAX instruction is about 4 bytes long, the VAX 8800 instruction buffer typically holds several instructions at a time. However, whenever a control transfer takes place (as the result of a branch or procedure call), the instruction buffer is flushed and the cache begins refilling the buffer starting with the target address.

To aid the cache in filling the instruction buffer, most VAXes have another optimization structure called the instruction physical address (IPA) register that contains the physical address of the next instruction to be executed. This register makes many address translations unnecessary. Because most instructions are executed sequentially, the IPA register allows the hardware to translate only the first instruction executed within a page. Whenever a branch is taken or IPA is incremented across a page boundary, a translation must be performed to calculate the physical address and to verify protection. Following the translation and loading of IPA, subsequent sequential instructions fetched within the same page do not require virtual-address translation.

Summary

This chapter examined cache memory techniques that are used to increase performance of computer systems. One advantage of the cache and its cousins, the translation buffer and instruction buffer, is that they are invisible to the user program, which thus sees a consistent architecture across all machine implementations. Hardware designers can choose different components and internal structures to obtain machines with different price/performance characteristics.

For more information on caches, read the survey article by Smith (1982). The papers by Clark (1983) and Clark and Emer (1985) provide measurements of cache and translation buffer performance in the VAX-11/780.

Exercises

1. Assuming that a reference to main memory (a cache miss) takes 1200 nanoseconds and a cache hit takes 400 nanoseconds, graph the average access time versus cache hit rate for hit rates of 55, 65, 75, 85, and 95 percent.

2. Previously, we presented the formula

   $$average\ access\ time = H \times T_C + (1 - H) \times T_M$$

   This formula assumes that a cache lookup and memory fetch start simultaneously, and the memory fetch is cancelled if the cache lookup succeeds. Modify the formula for a cache in which the primary memory fetch is not initiated until after the cache lookup fails. Recompute your graph for the previous problem and compare the results.

3. Discuss the three alternative cache organizations. What are the advantages of each?

4. What are advantages and disadvantages of using a write-back cache strategy? Be sure to discuss both the performance and failure implications.

5. Caches are often used to improve the access time to main memory by the CPU. What about using caches for disk I/O to and from main memory? What are the alternatives for placing such a cache? What are the advantages and disadvantages of each option?

6. Describe the similarities and differences between a main memory cache and a translation buffer. How can a translation buffer's performance be improved? Why might a 64-entry translation buffer be sufficient for the VAX?

7. Why is it that enlarging the TB may not pay off in a higher TB hit ratio?

8. Why is organizing a cache as a multiway set-associative cache, as opposed to a direct-mapped cache, more important for small caches than for large caches?

9. The VAX 6200 uses a two-level cache scheme in which the first-level cache is used for instructions only. Why was this decision made (using the first level for instructions only)? What would be required to make the first-level cache a data and instruction cache? What effect would this have on performance of the first-level cache?

10. What must be done to the TB following a process context switch operation? Why? How could you design a TB that would avoid this problem?

11. Is it possible to build a VAX without a cache, TB, or instruction buffer? If you could have one but not all three features, which one would you choose? Why?

15 Microprogramming

Chapter 2 examined the basic structure common to all digital computers. Figure 2.1 showed that the central processing unit contains a control unit, various registers, and an arithmetic and logic unit (ALU) that performs calculations on the data stored in registers under the command of the control unit. This chapter takes a more detailed look at a common technique used for designing the CPU and organizing the data and control portions of the CPU. This technique, called *microprogramming*, is common to many computer systems, particularly to architectural families with sophisticated instruction sets like the VAX, the IBM 370, and the Motorola 68000 series.

Introduction to Microprogramming

The purpose of the CPU is to interpret and execute the instructions that reside in the memory of the computer. The control unit is responsible for fetching instructions and performing the operations that they specify by sending electrical signals to (1) the arithmetic unit to transform data, (2) the memory unit to fetch (or store) data and instructions, (3) the general or special-purpose registers to select registers to be read or written, and (4) the I/O units to access or store aggregate data items. These signals are the "command" inputs to logic gates that determine the flow and control of information throughout the machine.

Typically, two types of control units have been built: *hardwired* and *microprogrammed*. In hardwired machines, the control unit is made up of an interconnection of combinatorial and sequential electrical logic circuits that explicitly execute macro-level[1] instructions for the target architecture. This is often referred to as "random logic" because it is the result of an empirical process that CPU designers go through to design machines. Figure 15.1 shows the organization of a hardwired machine.

Microprogrammed machines have a hardware structure that executes a *different*, and typically simpler, instruction set than that of the macro-

---

[1]As is common when describing microprogramming, we use the term "macro" to mean the machine code of the target computer. This implies a higher level, as opposed to the microprogramming level.

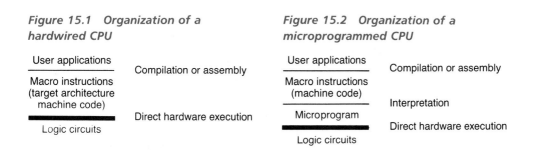

Figure 15.1 Organization of a hardwired CPU

Figure 15.2 Organization of a microprogrammed CPU

level target machine. A program written for that simplified machine *interprets* target-machine instructions. This program, called a *microprogram*, fetches and interprets macro-level instructions, just as the hardware in the hardwired machine interprets macro-level instructions. For example, the microprogram would fetch an instruction from memory, examine its opcode, and do whatever work the instruction is intended to perform. A principal difference between the microprogram and the macro programs that it interprets is that the microprogram is completely stored inside the CPU, while the user and operating system programs reside in main memory. Figure 15.2 shows the structure of a microprogrammed machine.

Most early computers were hardwired. Designing these machines was simple at first because the basic instruction architectures were fairly simple. However, designers quickly sought to build computers with much more complex instruction sets. Complex instructions were needed because memories were slow compared to the speed of the CPU; more powerful instructions could increase performance by keeping the CPU busy while the next instruction was being fetched. Early designers viewed complex instructions as subroutines that were implemented in hardware to reduce the number of instruction fetches needed to perform a complex operation, such as a floating-point multiply.

Building random-logic designs of complex instruction sets has several problems. First, because complexity of the hardware design increases with the complexity of the architecture, it is difficult to design and debug the hardware. Second, once the design is complete, it is difficult to make changes to the architecture. Adding a new instruction could require a major change of the entire hardware design.

Sensing that this process was not well structured, Maurice Wilkes in 1954 suggested a more regular approach to designing the CPU. In his now classic paper on microprogramming, Wilkes separates the design of the CPU into two components: the *data path* and the *microcontrol unit*. The data path consists of all the storage elements, the arithmetic units, and their interconnections. The major innovation is in Wilkes's microcontrol unit, as it is called. The microcontrol unit contains an array of microwords. Each microword is an instruction to control the elements of the data path, signalling data to move from registers onto buses, commanding the ALU, and so on. High-level functions (for example, macro instructions) are implemented as a sequence of microwords that cause the data path to perform the high-level functions.

This structure greatly simplifies the design of the computer control unit. Given a description of the instruction-set architecture and the machine's data path, a microprogram is written to execute that instruction set. That is, for each instruction in the instruction set, the designer writes one or more microinstructions to perform that function. Other microinstructions are written to fetch the next high-level instruction, to examine the opcode, and to branch to the microinstruction sequence responsible for that opcode. Thus, the computer hardware executes *microinstructions*. A program is then written in these microinstructions to interpret the high-level machine instructions.

In this way, a great deal of flexibility is maintained. New instructions can be added simply by writing new microcode. Bugs can be fixed by modifying microcode. The basic hardware design is simplified because the hardware executes the well-structured microinstructions. Also, the hardware and the architecture can be designed somewhat in parallel—it is not necessary to know all the details of the high-level instruction set to design the data path and the microcontrol unit. In fact, different microprograms can be run on the same hardware to emulate different high-level instruction sets. Perhaps different microprograms can be loaded to support execution of different high-level languages. Most important, different hardware implementations can be built to meet different price/performance goals, and each implementation can be microprogrammed to execute the same high-level instruction set. Thus, microprogramming leads to the concept of computer families.

The principal disadvantage of microprogramming is performance. Direct hardware instruction execution is generally faster than microcode emulation. Therefore, direct execution is often used when high performance is a necessity, or on machines with simple instruction-set architectures. Microprogramming is typically used to simplify the design of complex instruction-set architectures, at the cost of performance.

Organization of a Simple Micromachine

The following sections look at the central parts of the microarchitecture—the data path and the control unit—in a little more detail. To describe how these components work, we will construct a prototype microprogrammed data path and control unit for an extremely simple machine. Following the discussion of our simple machine, we will examine the organization of a real microprogrammed computer, the MicroVAX I.

When we examine the microarchitecture of a microprogrammed computer, it is easy to lose track of our place in the hierarchy shown in Figure 15.2. This chapter is concerned with the organization *below* the user-visible architecture, that is, below the double line in Figure 15.2. The purpose of the lowest-level logic circuits is to execute a *single* microprogram, which is typically only a few hundred or a few thousand microinstructions. The purpose of that single microprogram is to fetch and execute machine code as defined by the user-visible architecture of the machine.

The Data Path in a Simple Machine

When studying the hardware organization of either a hardwired or a microprogrammed machine, we normally begin by examining the data path. It is the data path that tells us the basic capabilities of the hardware: how much storage there is, how wide the buses connecting various units are, how many arithmetic units there are, and how much potential there is for parallelism within the computer.

To understand the structure of data paths, we will construct an extremely simple data path for a 32-bit microprogrammed computer system. To begin, let's examine some of the components that will make up our data path. First, the data path contains *buses*, parallel collections of wires that transmit data and addresses between functional units. For our 32-bit computer, it is natural to use buses that are 32 bits wide.

Second, our data path contains storage, which is supplied in the form of registers. We will choose an array of sixteen 32-bit registers, which is depicted as follows:

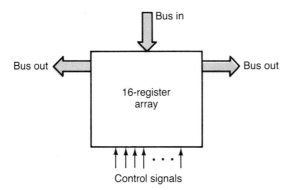

For our particular example, we have chosen a register array that has a single bus leading in. During a particular cycle, one 32-bit value can be written to one of the registers. The register array has two buses leading out. During a particular cycle, two registers (or possibly the same register) can be loaded onto the two output buses. The register array also has a number of control signals leading into it. These signals tell the array when to load the output buses and which registers to load, when to write from the input bus and which register to write, and so on.

Third, the data path has two functional units, a shifter and an ALU. The shifter has an input bus and an output bus. Control signals tell the shifter what operation to perform, as well as when to perform it. This shifter can shift left by one bit, shift right by one bit, or not shift at all, in which case it acts like an intermediate register.

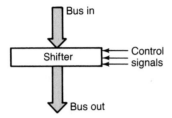

The ALU has two 32-bit buses leading into it, and it produces one 32-bit result that is a function of its inputs. It also outputs several condition code bits depending on the result. Control signals leading into the ALU tell it when to load its inputs and what function to perform. If we call the two inputs A and B respectively, the ALU performs the following operations: NOP (no operation), A AND B, A OR B, A XOR B, A+B, A+B+1, A−B, and A−B−1. The ALU is depicted as follows:

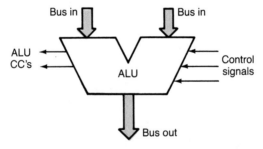

Finally, we may also need one or more multiplexers. A multiplexer takes a number of inputs, usually a power of 2, and selects one of them to be passed to its output. N control signals specify one of the 2^N inputs, as follows:

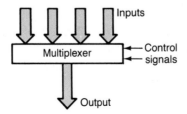

Figure 15.3 **Simple data path organization**

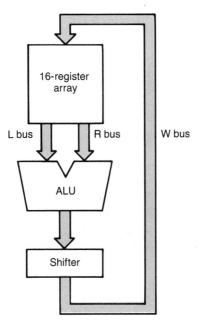

Figure 15.3 shows a simple data path constructed from these parts. The data path as shown is self-contained and has no access to outside memory, but ignore that for the moment and consider what work this data path can do. Imagine that each machine cycle is divided into four subcycles. During the first subcycle the next microinstruction is fetched, and registers are read from the register array, as instructed by control signals to the registers. During the second subcycle, the ALU performs an operation on its inputs, as instructed by its control signals, producing an output. During the third subcycle, the shifter acts on its input to produce a shifted (or nonshifted) output, again as instructed by its control signals. Finally, during the fourth subcycle, the shifter result is stored back into the register array, as instructed by additional control signals to the registers that indicate which register is to be written.

The reason for dividing the complete cycle into subcycles is that each element in the data path has some delay associated with it. For example, it takes time, once valid inputs are available to the shifter or the ALU, for the outputs to be produced. Dividing the cycle into discrete subcycles ensures that each stage of the data path has time to produce correct results. Often the stages are separated by registers to "latch" the results between stages, before the values are fed to the next stage.

In one complete cycle, then, this data path is capable of reading out the values of two registers, performing a logic or arithmetic operation on their values, shifting the result, and storing the final value back in the register array. The arithmetic and shifting functions are simple. However, by performing sequences of data-path operations over multiple cycles, we could perform complex calculations on data in the registers, for example, multiplication or division.

Looking at this data path, we see the basic power of our hardware, its storage, and the primitive functions it can perform. At this point, we might want to ask some questions about how this data path is controlled, for example, where do the control signals come from? How is it possible to execute conditional operations? To answer these questions, we must design a control unit for our simple data path.

The Control Unit in a Simple Machine

The control unit is responsible for issuing commands to the various parts of the data path and for timing those commands so that the operations are performed correctly. For our simple data path, the control signals consist of register selection, ALU function, and shift specifications to the data path. Based on what we've seen, we can make a list of the fields that supply the control signals needed during each cycle, namely,

- a 4-bit control field to tell the register array which of the sixteen registers to load onto its left output bus

- a 4-bit control field to tell the register array which register to load onto its right output bus

- a 4-bit control field to tell the register array which register to write from its input bus

- a 3-bit control field to tell the ALU which of its eight functions to perform

- a 2-bit control field to tell the shifter which of its three functions to perform

These control fields provide the basic commands to the functional units within the data path. In a microprogrammed control unit, as we indicated previously, each microinstruction controls all of the units of the data path; therefore, a microinstruction must have fields to specify all of these bits. In our microprogrammed machine, each microinstruction will specify the actions to be taken in one cycle through our data path.

Figure 15.4 shows a possible microinstruction format for a microcontrol unit for our example data path. Notice that we have added two fields to those specified in the preceding list. The branch control field will be used to specify under what conditions a microcode branch will occur, and the branch address field will specify a destination microinstruction if that a

Figure 15.4   *Example of a microinstruction*

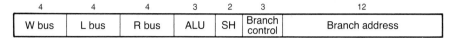

4	4	4	3	2	3	12
W bus	L bus	R bus	ALU	SH	Branch control	Branch address

branch is taken. Since the branch address field is 12 bits, the largest
microprogram that we will be able to write will have 2^{12} (4K) microinstructions.

Now we know what the data path looks like and what a microinstruction looks like. All that's needed to complete our machine is the mechanism for selecting and fetching microinstructions to execute, so we can
write sequences of microinstructions. Such a mechanism, called a *sequencer*, issues the control signals for the micromachine. Figure 15.5
shows a simple sequencer for our micromachine. The sequencer consists
of

- the *microcode control store*, which contains up to 4K microinstructions

- a *microinstruction register*, which holds the current microinstruction
after it is fetched from the control store

- a *microprogram counter* (μPC), which contains the 12-bit address of
the next microinstruction to fetch

- a "+1" unit to increment the microprogram counter

Figure 15.5   *Organization of a simple sequencer*

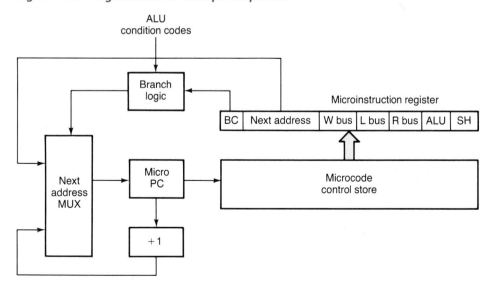

- some branch logic and a next address multiplexer, which selects the next microinstruction to execute

The execution of this hardware should be fairly obvious. At the beginning of each cycle, the microword whose address is held in the microprogram counter is fetched into the microinstruction register. Next, during the subcycles that make up a cycle, the control bits—ALU, SH, W bus, L bus, and R bus—are fed to the data path to direct its operation. Finally, the branch-control field of the microword (BC), which indicates whether a conditional branch should take place, is fed to the branch logic box along with the condition code bits that were produced by the ALU. The branch logic then instructs the next address mutiplexer to load the microprogram counter with either the next sequential microinstruction address (μPC+1) or with the branch target address specified in the microinstruction. Figure 15.6 shows the complete simple machine with its sequencer and data path connected.

This example should give you a basic idea of how a microprogrammed control unit can be used to control the data path of a computer system. Of course, in real systems, the data path is much more complex, permitting high degrees of possible parallelism, multiple functional units, special purpose logic, and so on. An important point is that the simple microprogrammed control unit we have designed has all the components of any computer system, as described in Chapter 2. One major difference is that the program for this machine is stored in a special control store. If we could write microprograms and place them into this control store, we could easily execute user application programs from the microstore. However, this structure is typically used for only one purpose; that is, to execute a *single* microprogram whose task is to interpret macro language programs stored in primary memory.

Armed with this basic understanding of the structure of the data path and the sequencer for a simple microprogrammed computer, we now present a more detailed example: a description of the organization of a real microprogrammed computer, the MicroVAX I. Our intention is to give you a better understanding of how a microprogrammed organization can be used to interpret and execute a complex instruction set, such as the VAX. We have chosen the MicroVAX I because it has a straightforward implementation. Our presentation of the MicroVAX I is somewhat simplified; our objective is to show the work that must be done by the control unit and the data path to execute VAX instructions.

The MicroVAX I Microarchitecture

The MicroVAX I is a 32-bit microprogrammed computer system that executes the VAX instruction set. It is interesting for several reasons. First, it was the first use of custom VLSI to build a small VAX processor. Second,

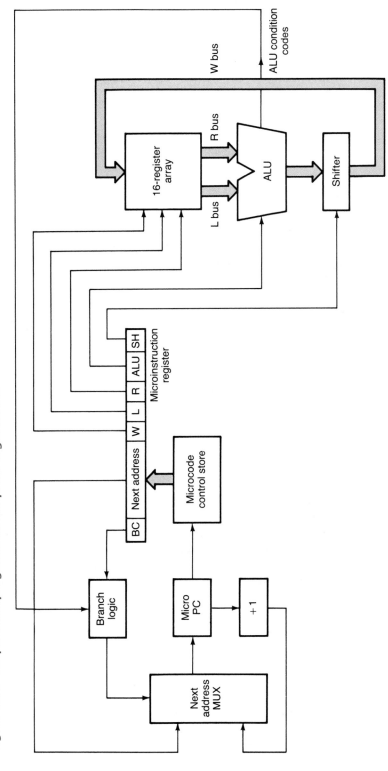

Figure 15.6 Simple microprogrammed computer organization

and more important to this discussion, custom VLSI in the MicroVAX I was used solely for the construction of the data path, which is a single-chip part. One of the crucial goals for the MicroVAX I was short design and development time; in fact, the machine was designed and delivered in about 18 months, an extremely short period for a commercial product. One reason that this goal was met was that the design of the data path was separate from the design of the control section for the microprogrammed control unit.

The MicroVAX I Data Path

Figure 15.7 is an overview of the complete MicroVAX I CPU. The MicroVAX I consists of two boards: the data-path board, shown in the lower part of the figure, and the memory controller board, shown in the upper part. The memory controller board contains the cache, the translation buffer, and the instruction prefetch logic, which supplies VAX instruction bytes to the data-path board. We will not examine the memory controller in any more detail.

The data-path board has a structure somewhat similar to our simple machine. On the right is the data-path chip, which we will discuss in detail shortly. On the left are the control structures, including some familiar components: the microsequencer; the control store; the control store address (CSA) register, also called the MicroPC register; and the condition-code logic. There is also a microstack for microprocedure calls. On the left are logic components that help to interpret VAX opcodes: the IBYTE (instruction byte) register and buffer hold the next bytes of the VAX instruction stream being interpreted, and the decode ROMS (read-only memories) select the proper microcode routine to interpret a particular VAX opcode or operand specifier.

Figure 15.8 shows the structure of the MicroVAX I data-path chip. This structure is not that different from the simple data path presented previously, but let's look at it in some detail. First, there are two 32-bit buses, the A bus and the B bus, that connect all the components in the data path. Starting from the top is an I/O port. This port provides the data interface from the chip to the outside world; data is read from memory into the registers and written from the registers to memory through this interface. A register-save stack provides temporary storage for registers. This is useful for saving registers that may need to be restored, for example, if a page fault occurs in the middle of an instruction. The ROM contains thirty-two constants that are needed by the microprogram. Remember, in the macro machine (that is, VAX assembly instructions) there can be literals of any size in the instructions, so constants do not have to be stored in memory. In microinstructions, however, typically there is no room to store constants. The MicroVAX I does permit 6-bit constants to be stored in its microinstructions, but larger constants, masks, and so on, are stored in the ROM.

Figure 15.7 Block diagram of the MicroVAX I

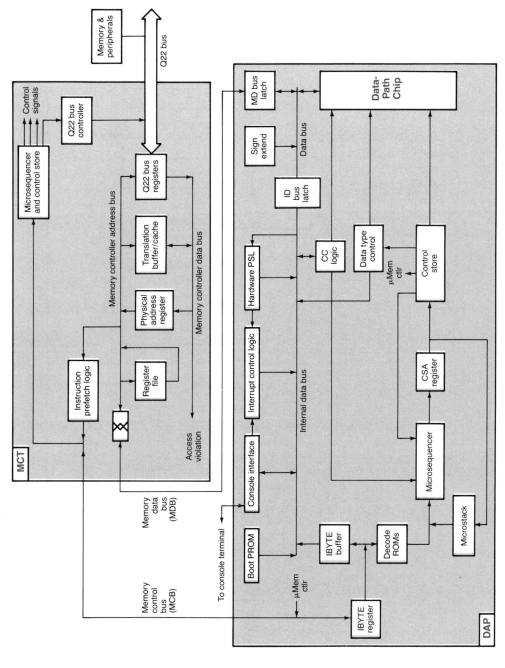

Figure 15.8   MicroVAX I data-path chip

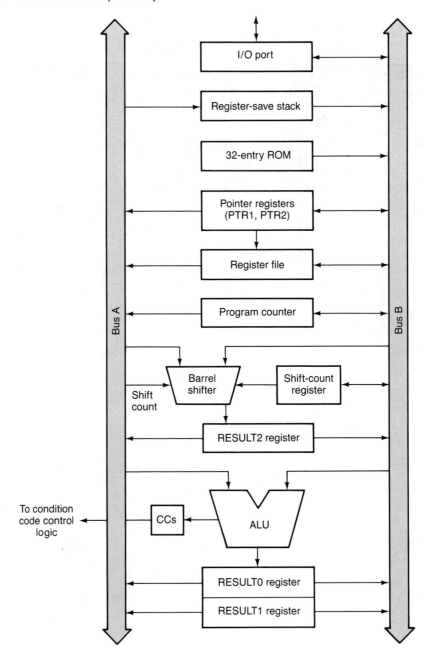

The two pointer registers, POINTER1 and POINTER2, are used to indirectly reference other registers in the data path. These help to modularize the microcode. For example, when the microcode examines the operand specifiers on a two-operand instruction, it can load POINTER1 and POINTER2 with the register numbers of the registers containing the operands. The microcode that performs the operation can then access its operands indirectly without knowing explicitly where they are located.

The register file contains forty-seven 32-bit registers. The registers can be read onto the A and B buses and can be written from the B bus. The first fifteen registers in the register file hold the fifteen VAX general-purpose registers, R0, R1, ... , R11, AP, FP, and SP (PC is handled specially, as we shall see). The remainder of the register file is used for temporaries and special registers needed by the microprogram. In other words, from the point of view of a VAX programmer, the MicroVAX I hardware consists of sixteen registers. From the point of view of the microprogram, the VAX registers are just part of the machine state, which includes forty-eight general-purpose registers; in fact, most of the machine state is invisible to the VAX programmer and even to the VAX operating system.

The next functional unit exists specifically for handling the VAX macro-level program counter (PC). While the microprogram addresses the VAX PC as the sixteenth entry in the register file, the PC is actually stored in this special program counter unit. The PC unit can increment the PC by 1, 2, or 4, which is done automatically as the microcode fetches and decodes the instruction stream.

The simple data path presented in the last section had a shifter that could shift to the left or the right by one bit. The MicroVAX I data path has a *barrel shifter*, which, in one cycle, can shift left or right a variable number of bits. The barrel shifter in the MicroVAX I can read two 32-bit inputs (one each from the A bus and the B bus), concatenate them, and shift the resulting 64-bit quantity by up to 31 bits. The amount of the shift is controlled by either the contents of a shift-count register or a literal in the microinstruction. This variable-sized shift is particularly useful for extracting specific fields or bytes from a word, which is required to execute VAX instructions such as EXTV and INSV. The barrel shifter always produces a 32-bit result, which is placed in the RESULT2 register.

The MicroVAX I ALU reads two inputs from the A bus and the B bus, computes one of sixteen functions of those inputs, as shown in Table 15.1, and stores the result in either the RESULT0 or the RESULT1 register. In addition, the ALU can execute a "multiply-step" operation, which performs a single shift-and-add step used as part of a 32-bit multiply. The multiply-step operation is called thirty-two times to perform a 32-bit multiply.

It is interesting to note that it is possible to implement a VAX, which has a complex instruction set, with such a simple ALU. Of course, this implies that complex arithmetic instructions will require more microcycles to execute; therefore, this VAX implementation may be slower than

Table 15.1   *MicroVAX I ALU and Shifter Operations*

ALU Operations		Shifter Operations
Logical	*Arithmetic*	
A NOP B	A + B	Shift left by count register
A AND B	A + B + a	Shift right by count register
A OR B	A + B + carry bit	Shift right arithmetic by count reg
A XOR B	A − B	Double (64-bit) shift by count reg
NOT A	A − B − 1	Shift left by literal
NOT B	B − A	Shift right by literal
(NOT A) AND B	B − A − 1	Shift right arithmetic by literal
A AND (NOT B)	Compare (set CCs)	

one with more functional units, special-purpose hardware, or a more complex ALU. However, whether a particular implementation is in fact slower or faster than another depends on both the cycle time of the microarchitecture and how much work is accomplished per cycle. In many cases "dumb and fast" beats "smart and slow."

Now that we have described the MicroVAX I data-path chip and the operations it can perform, we will look at the control structure of the machine, that is, the microinstructions that the machine executes.

MicroVAX I Data-Path Control

Figure 15.7 showed the complete MicroVAX I data-path board, which contains the data-path chip as well as the sequencer logic. The purpose of the sequencer is to fetch a microinstruction from the control store, feed signals from that microinstruction to the data path, and select the next microinstruction for execution.

Figure 15.9 shows the format of a MicroVAX I microinstruction. Each next microinstruction is 40 bits long. The microinstruction has a parity bit, a condition code/data type length field (CC/DT) that controls the macro-level condition-code setting and specifies the size of an operand being processed, a 21-bit data-path control field that is sent to the data-path chip, and a next-address field that conditionally selects the next microinstruction to execute.

Of particular interest is the data-path control field, which is shown in detail in Figure 15.9. Notice that this field has an opcode and two operands, much like machine instructions. The 5-bit opcode field can specify one of thirty-two possible opcodes, twenty-three of which were listed in Table 15.1 (we will examine some of the other opcodes in a moment). Microinstructions actually have three operands: two source operands specified by the short- and long-operand fields and a result operand specified by the result-register bit (R1). The R1 bit indicates

Figure 15.9 *Format of a MicroVAX I microinstruction*

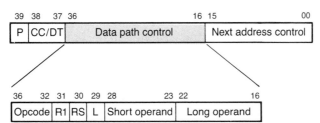

whether an ALU result is stored in RESULT0 or RESULT1. The register-save bit specifies whether the short operand should be pushed onto the register-save stack.

The microinstruction has two operand fields: a 6-bit short-operand field and a 7-bit long-operand field. If the L bit is set in the microword, the short-operand field contains a 6-bit literal. If the L bit is clear, the short-operand field can specify registers 0 to 63. We have already seen that the data-path registers 0 through 47 are stored in the register file, and register addresses 0 through 47 refer to these. Addresses 48 through 63 refer to other data-path registers, such as the result registers and barrel shifter-count register. The 7-bit long-operand field can specify any of these register's addresses, plus additional on-chip and off-chip registers. Addresses 64 through 95 refer to the thirty-two constants stored in the data path ROM, while higher numbers refer to off-chip registers on the data-path module, such as the memory data register and the VAX PSL.

Looking at this microword format gives us a good idea of how the MicroVAX I operates. On each microcycle, a microinstruction is fetched from the control store. That microinstruction has fields for the sequencer (branch control and next address) as well as fields that control the data path. Each microinstruction can specify one data-path operation, which typically reads two registers (or a register and a literal), performs an ALU or a shifter operation, and stores the result in one of the specified result registers.

Our examination of the MicroVAX I data-path operation is almost complete except for three important details that we have ignored up to now: memory accessing, VAX instruction decoding, and branching.

The first detail is how primary memory is accessed. Basically, two of the remaining data-path opcodes that we have not discussed are *Memory Request*, used for reading and writing data from and to primary memory, and *I-stream Request*, used for reading instruction bytes. When a Memory Request microinstruction is specified, the data-path control field is interpreted in a special way. For example, some of the short-operand bits are used to specify the type of memory function: is this a read or a write, is protection checking needed, are we going to specify a virtual address or a physical address, and so on.

On a read request operation, the long operand specifies the register that contains the virtual address, which is transferred to the memory controller module over the memory bus. If the data is available in the cache, the data is returned and written into the data buffer register (one of the off-chip registers). The data is actually returned two microcycles after the read request. Therefore, the microprogrammer must find useful work to do for one microinstruction before the data can be copied into the data-path chip. If the data was not in the cache, the memory controller will fetch it from primary memory (after performing virtual address translation) and will cause the data-path module to wait until the data is ready; this wait is called a *stall*. A memory write operation is similar: the long operand again specifies the virtual address, and the following microinstruction causes the data to be moved from a register on the data-path chip to the memory data buffer register.

If the microprogram wants to read from the instruction stream, it executes an I-stream Request operation, which fetches the next 1, 2, or 4 bytes of instruction into the IBYTE register, and automatically updates the VAX PC.

The second detail is how the microprogram decodes VAX macro-level opcodes. This could be done using the ALU and the shifter, but special hardware support is supplied in the form of the IBYTE register and the decode ROM, which can be seen on the left of Figure 15.7. These are a crucial part of the MicroVAX I data-path module, because decoding VAX opcodes and operand specifiers is the most important task of the microprogram.

The Decode microinstruction, which is used to decode both VAX opcodes and VAX operand specifiers, works in the following way. When the microprogram has fetched the opcode of the next macro instruction into the IBYTE register, it executes a Decode microinstruction. The task of the Decode microinstruction is simply to select the proper microroutine to handle that specific opcode. The Decode microinstruction uses the VAX opcode stored in the IBYTE register as an index into the Decode ROM. The Decode ROM contains the 12-bit control-store addresses of the microroutines that handle every VAX opcode. The Decode microinstruction extracts the appropriate 12-bit control-store address, which is fed to the microsequencer, pushes the current $\mu PC+1$ onto the microstack, and continues at the selected address. (Note the similarity of this decode operation with the jump table example of Figure 6.1.)

At the next microinstruction, the CPU executes the first microinstruction of the microroutine for the particular VAX opcode. For example, if the opcode is an ADDL3 instruction, the microroutine responsible for ADDL3 will execute. The first task of that microroutine will probably be to process the next instruction byte, which is the operand specifier for the first operand. This is also done using a Decode microinstruction that specifies an *operand specifier* decode, as opposed to an *opcode* decode. When an Operand Specifier Decode microinstruction is executed, the operand specifier byte is used as an index into a part of the decode ROM used for operand specifiers. In this case, there are two possibilities. If the operand specifier is a general-purpose register, the register number is placed in a special POINTER register and a signal is generated to cause the next sequential microinstruction to be executed. Since this is the more frequent case, it should be the faster to execute. If the operand is not a register, the next microaddress is constructed from 8 bits found in the decode ROM and 5 bits from the next address field of the Decode microinstruction. Essentially, the microsequencer performs a multiway branch to the microroutine for the specified addressing mode. In any case, the register-number field of the operand specifier is copied to a POINTER register in the data path, so that following microinstructions will know which register is being used for operand addressing. The return address is pushed on the microstack.

When the MicroVAX I data-path processes a Decode of either an opcode or an operand specifier, it automatically increments the VAX PC. In this way, the PC always points to the next instruction byte to be processed.

The last remaining detail to describe is branching, which is examined in the following section.

Microinstruction Branching

The handling of control flow in a microprogram is one of the significant differences between assembly programming and microprogramming. In an assembly program, there are special instructions for testing and branching on conditions. At the microprogram level, it is crucial to minimize the number of microinstructions executed. For this reason, the use of separate microinstructions for branching would be too costly. Instead, a single microinstruction is capable of controlling the data path, testing several conditions in the micromachine, and branching to one of several alternative next addresses based on those conditions.

Figure 15.9 shows that the low-order fifteen bits of a MicroVAX I microinstruction are next-address control bits. These bits control the selection of the next microinstruction for execution. There are eight formats for the next-address control field, each corresponding to a different control flow operation (for example, unconditional jump, conditional branch, and jump to microsubroutine). The operation type is specified by the upper three bits of the next-address control field; these bits are essentially an opcode for the control portion of the microinstruction. Thus, each MicroVAX I microinstruction contains a data-path control field, including an operation code and operands for the data path, and a next-address control field, which includes an operation and operands for the next-address selection logic.

The simplest format of the next-address control field is used for the Jump and Jump to Subroutine microcontrol-flow operations. This format is as follows:

```
 15   13 12                              00
┌────┬────────────────────────────────┐
│Type│    Jump address <12:0>         │
└────┴────────────────────────────────┘
```

Both formats cause an unconditional jump to the specified 13-bit control store address; the only difference is that the Jump to Subroutine saves the microaddress of the current microaddress plus 1 on the microstack.

Most next-address control fields do not contain an entire 13-bit microaddress. Instead, they contain only the low-order eight bits of the address. Logically the microcontrol store is divided into thirty-two pages of 256 microinstructions each. The low-order eight bits of a control-store address specify the instruction within the page, while the high-order bits specify the page number. Therefore, some control fields only permit branching within the current page. For example, the Branch micro-control-flow operation has the format

```
 15   13 12 11   08 07                   00
┌────┬──┬──────┬───────────────────────┐
│Type│  │  JC  │  Jump address <7:0>   │
└────┴──┴──────┴───────────────────────┘
```

where only the low-order eight bits of the transfer address are provided, and the high-order five bits are taken from the high-order five bits of the current microaddress. The four-bit jump control field (JC) specifies the conditions under which the branch should occur. These conditions are listed in Table 15.2. By specifying one of the JC values, the microprogrammer can test whether any one of the possible conditions is true. The conditions that can be tested include the states of the four condition codes, as well as other machine states, such as the occurrence of an interrupt. If the tested state is false, execution continues at the next microinstruction ($\mu PC+1$).

The MicroVAX I microbranch mechanism also allows multiway branches (case microstatements) using a mechanism called the OR

Table 15.2   MicroVAX I Microinstruction Jump Control Field

JC	Condition	JC	Condition
0	Use OR MUX	8	Console Halt
1	OR MUX = 0	9	Interrupt
2	OR MUX ≠ 0	10	Stack register
3	IB OK	11	Register Destination
4	ALU N clear	12	ALU V clear
5	ALU Z clear	13	ALU C clear
6	ALU N set	14	ALU V set
7	ALU Z set	15	ALU C set

multiplexor (OR MUX). This mechanism is particularly useful for the microprogram to quickly check a set of exceptional conditions. The OR MUX is a four-bit value, where the bits are either predefined constants (0 or 1) or micromachine state bits. There are eight possible configurations of the OR MUX, as shown in Table 15.3. Microinstructions that use the OR MUX specify which one of the eight configurations to use. It is not necessary to understand what all of these bits mean, only how the OR MUX is used in multiway branches. For example, the case micro-control-flow operation has the following format:

```
15   13 12   10 09 08 07                      00
  Type | OR | JC | Jump address <7:0>
```

The OR field (OR) specifies which of the OR MUX configurations to use. Suppose that OR is 5; in this case, OR MUX bit 3 is set if there is an overflow or trap, bit 2 is set if there is an interrupt, bit 1 is set if the T bit is on or there is a console halt, and bit 0 is set if the current instruction buffer is invalid. The 2-bit JC field specifies one of the first four conditions from Table 15.2. For example, the JC field can specify that a branch should occur when all of the selected OR MUX bits are 0 (JC = 1) or when the bits are not all zero (JC = 2).

The most interesting feature of the case-style microinstruction is the computation of the branch address. This technique is typical of many microarchitectures. If a case micro-control-flow operation succeeds, the branch target address (which is on the current microstore page) is computed by taking the 8-bit jump address field from the micro-instruction, and ORing the selected 4-bit OR MUX field with the 4 low-order bits of the jump address.

As an example, suppose that the jump address field is 01100000. If the selected OR MUX value is 0010, then we will branch to location 01100010;

Table 15.3   MicroVAX I OR MUX Formats

OR	OR MUX <3>	OR MUX <2>	OR MUX <1>	OR MUX <0>
0	0	0	0	0
1	0	0	0	IB invalid
2	0	0	1	0
3	MEM ERR	Page crossing	TB miss	Modify refuse
4	0	0	BR false	IB invalid
5	Overflow/trap	Interrupt	T bit/Console halt	IB invalid
6	INDEX<3>	INDEX<2>	INDEX<1>	INDEX<0>
7	0	0	SIZE<1>	SIZE<0>

if the OR MUX value is 0110, then we will branch to location 01100110, and so on. Thus, we will branch to one of sixteen possible target micro-instructions, depending on the value of the 4-bit OR MUX. Where the sixteen target microinstructions are located is determined by the high-order four bits of the jump address.

In addition to the case micro-control-flow operation, there is micro-subroutine call that makes a multiway jump within the current microstore page, pushing the μPC+1 on the microstack. A return micro-control-flow operation pops that address from the microstack and returns to the previous flow.

Execution of a VAX Instruction

Now that we have a detailed understanding of how the MicroVAX I hardware operates, we are finally ready to follow the microprogram through the execution of a single VAX instruction. This simplified instruction flow will give you some idea of the work done by the microprogram to interpret a high-level instruction.

Let's assume that the current VAX PC contains address 400 and that at address 400 is the instruction

```
ADDL    (R4),R5
```

so that memory will appear as

| 55 | 64 | C0 | :400 |

where C0 is the opcode (ADDL2), 64 is the first operand specifier (R4 indirect), and 55 is the second operand specifier (R5 register mode). At this point, we make three assumptions:

1. The PC on the data path contains the address of the first byte of our ADDL instruction (400).

2. The microprogram counter (μPC) contains the control-store address of a Decode microinstruction that decodes opcodes.

3. The IBYTE register contains C0, the ADDL opcode.

The following microinstructions are executed by the MicroVAX I to decode and process this single VAX macro instruction. Each microinstruction executes in one MicroVAX I microcycle.

1. *Instruction Decode*. The control store is accessed, and the Instruction Decode microinstruction addressed by the μPC is fetched. The bits from this microinstruction are sent to various parts of the data-path

module and data-path chip. As a result of this Instruction Decode operation, the opcode (C0) stored in the IBYTE register is used to index the Decode ROM. A 12-bit address is read from the ROM; this is the control-store address of the first microinstruction of the ADDL2 microroutine. This microaddress is fed to the sequencer and becomes the new μPC. The PC is incremented by 1 as a result of the Decode and now contains address 401, and the second instruction byte, 64, is fed into the IBYTE register. The old μPC+1 is stored on the microstack as a return address.

2. *Operand Specifier Decode.* The first microinstruction in the ADDL2 microroutine is an Operand Decode microinstruction. The Operand Specifier Decode microinstruction causes the IBYTE register to be used as an index into the operand-specifier decode portion of the ROM, returning some address bits that are used to select the new μPC. The new μPC will be the control-store address of a microroutine to handle register indirect mode. The Operand Specifier Decode micro-instruction causes the register number (in this case, 4) to be fed from the low-order bits of the IBYTE register into a register called POINT-ER1 on the data-path chip. In this way, the microroutine for handling register indirect will have a pointer to the register to use. The PC is incremented by 1 and now contains address 402, and the third instruction byte, 55, is fed into the IBYTE register. The old μPC+1 is stored on the microstack as a return address.

3. *Memory Request.* The first microinstruction in the register indirect microroutine is a Memory Request microinstruction. This microin-struction is fetched and executed. The Memory Request microinstruc-tion sends the virtual-memory address stored in R4 to the memory controller, telling the memory controller to perform a read. The sequencer selects the next microinstruction from the next-address field of the Memory Request microinstruction. The PC is unchanged.

4. *Move.* The next microinstruction simply changes the value of the POINTER1 register that currently points to R4. The POINTER1 register is changed to point to a temporary register in which the data read from memory will be stored; call this register OPERAND1. The next microaddress is taken from the next-address field of the Move microinstruction. The PC is unchanged.

5. *Move Data.* It is two cycles since the Memory Request microinstruc-tion and the data has been returned to the data buffer register by the memory controller. This next microinstruction moves that data from the data buffer register into the OPERAND1 temporary register on the data-path chip. The next-address field specifies that a microreturn

should occur. We have completed processing the first operand, the next address is popped from the microstack, and we return to the microinstruction following step 2. The PC is unchanged.

6. *Operand Specifier Decode.* This microinstruction is an Operand Specifier Decode for the second operand. The second operand specifier, 55, is still in the IBYTE register and PC is still 402. The Operand Specifier Decode microinstruction is fetched and executed. The Operand Specifier Decode moves the register number, 5, into a pointer register, called POINTER2, for the second operand. Because this is register mode, the next microinstruction address is $\mu PC + 1$. PC is incremented as a result of the Decode and now points to the opcode of the next VAX instruction. At this point, both operands have been decoded. Data-path register POINTER1 has the register number of the first operand (which is a temporary register containing the data read from memory). Data-path register POINTER2 has the register number of the second operand (which is R5).

7. *Add.* The next microinstruction, which followed the two Operand Specifier Decode microinstructions, is an Add microinstruction that performs the actual addition of the operands. The add specifies as operands the registers pointed to by POINTER1 and POINTER2. The result is placed in RESULT0. The ALU condition codes are produced and sent to the PSL.

8. *Move.* The next microinstruction copies the result of the add, RESULT0, to the register pointed to by POINTER2. In this case, the result is stored back in its final destination, R5. The next microaddress is taken from the Move microinstruction; it is the address of the Opcode Decode microinstruction so that processing of the next VAX instruction can begin.

While some details have been omitted, the preceding list is approximately the work that the MicroVAX I must do to process a single, two-operand VAX ADDL instruction. The instruction took eight microcycles to execute. One microinstruction completes every 250 nanoseconds on the MicroVAX I, so this instruction would have taken 2 microseconds. This is a best case, assuming a cache hit and so on. A register-to-register instruction would have been faster; a memory-to-memory instruction slower.

The more complex the addressing modes that are used, the slower the instruction because the microprogram will have to use the ALU and/or the shifter to compute the operand address before fetching the operand. For example, if the VAX instruction CLRL (R4)[R5] is processed, the microprogram will shift R5 left by two bits (to multiply by 4), add the shifted value to R4, and use the result to fetch the operand. This address arithmetic will take two additional data-path cycles.

Microarchitecture Alternatives

To conclude our discussion of microprogramming, let's examine some of the options available at the microlevel.

One of the most important tasks performed by the microengine is decoding of the opcode. For this reason, some machines have special data-path support for decoding. There may be special hardware to extract the opcode from an instruction and to use the opcode to look up a microroutine branch address. This hardware assist helps dispatch the microprogram to the appropriate instruction-execution flow without having to explicitly "parse" the opcode bits. Such support exists in the MicroVAX I. Other VAXes have more complex decoding hardware; for example, the VAX/780 can decode a register-to-register arithmetic instruction all at once, so that the instruction can execute in one cycle.

Microinstruction formats vary greatly, depending mainly on the complexity of both the data path and the desired data-path control. In general, there are two options to the structure of microinstructions: horizontal and vertical. A horizontal microinstruction is typically very long. The important characteristic of horizontal instructions is the lack of encoding. A horizontal instruction has many fields, and each field is an unencoded command to control directly a specific part of the data path. Horizontal format is often used to provide lots of concurrency in data paths with multiple functional units that can operate in parallel.

In contrast, a vertical format is a short microinstruction with much encoding. Typically, the microinstruction has an opcode and several operand fields, somewhat like a macro instruction. Because of this, we would say that the MicroVAX I is vertical. Our simple machine presented early in the chapter is more horizontal. That machine has no opcode —each field of the microinstruction controls one of the functional units. With an opcode, as on the MicroVAX I, it might be possible to place a memory-read address on the B bus during the same cycle that a value is loaded onto the A bus and shifted by the shifter. However, there is no way to express this parallelism in the MicroVAX I instruction format, because an opcode specifies only one operation. Furthermore, there must be some decoding logic between the microinstruction register and the data path to turn the opcode into the correct signals to the data path. This decoding logic lengthens the cycle time. On the other hand, vertical microinstructions are easier to program, since there is less parallelism to worry about. In either case, the microprogrammer must be concerned with timing constraints, for example, how long it takes to fetch operands from memory, and how long it takes for the ALU condition codes to be stable.

Because horizontal microinstructions typically do more work than vertical microinstructions, there is sometimes no automatic incrementing of the μPC in such systems. Instead, each microinstruction carries one or more *next-instruction address* fields. In this case, microinstructions can be placed more or less randomly in the microstore. Several next-instruction

Table 15.4   *Horizontal versus Vertical Microinstructions*

	Horizontal	*Vertical*
Microword size	Long instructions	Short instructions
Encoding	Little or none	Highly encoded
Parallelism	Much	Little
Branching	One or more next addresses	Mostly sequential

Table 15.5   *Control Store of VAX Implementations*

CPU	*Microcode Word Size, Bits*	*Control Store Size, Words*
VAX-11/730	24	8K
VAX-11/750	80	6K
VAX-11/780	99	6K
μVAX I	40	8K
μVAX II	39	1.6K
VAX 8200	40	16K
VAX 8600	86	8K
VAX 8700	144	16K
VAX 3500	41	1.6K

address fields permit for multiway branching based on special conditions that may need to be tested.

In reality, most microword formats are somewhere between horizontal and vertical. Table 15.4 reviews some of the differences. Table 15.5 shows some of the sizes of the control stores in various VAX implementations.

Exercises

1. Contrast the microprogrammed approach with the hardwired approach. What are the advantages and disadvantages of microprogramming?

2. What do you think is the relationship between microprogramming and the reduced instruction set approach (described in Chapter 10)? Discuss tradeoffs between microprogrammed complex instruction set machines and directly executed reduced instruction set machines.

3. The simple data path shown in Figure 15.3 has no access to memory. Modify the data path so that memory can be accessed. Show the changes to the data path and the changes to the microword that will be needed. (Suggestion: Connect two registers to the W bus, a memory address register and memory

data register, as the interface to memory. To read from memory, the memory address register must be written with the requested memory address, and memory will then deposit the data in the memory data register. On a write to memory, the data path must put the address in the memory address register and data in the memory data register. You will need control signals to control loading of these registers and to tell memory what kind of operation is being performed.)

4. Describe, in as much detail as you can, what the MicroVAX I microinstruction sequence would look like for executing the VAX instruction MOVAL (R1)+,R2.

5. Describe how multiway branching works in the MicroVAX I microarchitecture. What is the advantage of having a next address field in every microinstruction? How could you imagine using this idea at the macro instruction level?

6. What are the differences between vertical and horizontal microcode? Why would a designer choose one or the other?

16 *Parallelism and Parallel Computer Systems*

No matter how powerful the newest computer is, users will eventually require more memory (physical and virtual), more processing power (to support faster execution and/or more users), and more file space (larger disk capacities and more disk drives). Computer vendors often meet these needs by offering a family of machines with a range of capacities and speeds. As long as your needs can be met by a member of the computer family in the middle of its performance range, you have an upward growth path. Individual components can be added (such as more disk drives or memory), or enhanced (such as the model 35 processor replaced by the model 55). But what happens when you acquire the family member at the top of the line? Where do you go from there?

A quick answer might be to switch to a vendor that makes higher-performance computers. While this might help, in some cases the costs of switching vendors may be high in retraining and reprogramming. In any case, although it is possible to spend more money to buy a more powerful machine, there are diminishing returns. Each additional increment in performance costs more to obtain.

One issue is that a particular design pushes the use of technology as far as it can go when that design is committed to manufacturing. At that point, its speed can't be easily improved because the logic chosen is at the cutting edge and performance has been reached using all the best architectural and implementation techniques (caches, memory interleaving, pipelining, and coprocessor support). With a typical cost-performance curve, as shown in Figure 16.1, it is clearly prohibitive to go beyond the "knee of the curve," where the cost for improved performance rises exponentially. A second issue is the relative costs of microprocessors and higher-speed but less-dense technologies. Today's microprocessors are amazingly fast; a contemporary single-chip microprocessor is 3-10 times faster than a large midrange computer of only five years ago. It is possible to build computers faster than the fastest microprocessors, but again the cost rises exponentially, particularly compared to the cost of just adding one or more additional microprocessors to the system. A third issue is that the processor may be a small part of the total cost of a computer system. Disks, tapes, and other peripherals are often more expensive than the processor. Customers want to be able to increase performance while saving their investment in peripherals, software, and so on.

Figure 16.1   Typical cost-performance curve

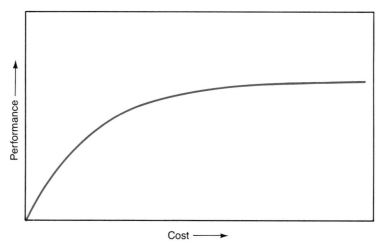

The best possible solution then is to offer a multicomputer system. We use the term "multicomputer system" to describe the wide range of possible computer systems where there is more than one central processor. For example, we have already described networks where ring, star, and LAN configurations offer the ability to share programs and data among different computers or nodes. Depending on the sophistication of the network software, the users may or may not be aware of all the underlying work that goes on to support this added functionality. However, in most cases, the users are aware that they must log in to some node and operate on some computer, most likely one located physically nearby. Programs in a network communicate only on a coarse scale, sending messages between them.

It would be more desirable if we could increase the computational power of a computer in the same way that we increase the memory or disk space, that is, by simply attaching one or more additional processors. In the best case, this addition of more processors in the multicomputer system, called a *multiprocessor,* would be completely transparent to the users. Nothing different would be required of users, and the only noticeable change would be an increase in the responsiveness of the system or the number of users that could be supported. There are more processors in the system, so a user gets more time on any one of them; in a sense there is a larger quantum of time before the user's program is interrupted. The addition of more processors introduces parallelism, which is used to execute additional user processes. On the other hand, adding additional processors typically will not make a single application run faster when that application is running stand-alone on the multiprocessor.

Parallelism can be used in many ways to improve system performance. As another example, we could construct each user program so that different parts of a single program can be executed in parallel. Thus, if the program adds a constant to each element of an array, such that the change to one element doesn't depend on another, then it is easy to imagine performing all the adds in parallel rather than sequentially, as is implied by the way a user typically creates a program. Some computer systems, called *vector, array,* or simply *parallel processing systems,* permit this kind of parallelism. Vector computation is typically associated with supercomputer technology; however, as with everything else, the same techniques can be applied to every type of computer system from microcomputers to mainframes.

This chapter describes various ways of introducing parallelism into computer systems, to increase both the performance of individual programs and the number of users that can be supported. First, let's look at ways of classifying parallelism in multicomputers.

Classifying Multicomputer Systems

Having considered the forms of parallelism, Michael Flynn in 1966 divided all computer systems into four classes. This separation between classes was based on the recognition that parallelism can occur both in the instruction stream, with multiple instructions being issued in parallel, and in the data stream, with multiple data elements being delivered in parallel. Flynn described the possible combinations of instruction and data stream parallelism:

- SISD (single instruction stream, single data stream). The computers considered so far in this book are all SISD machines. A control unit issues a single instruction to the arithmetic processor, which fetches operands to perform that instruction, as shown in Figure 16.2a.

- SIMD (single instruction stream, multiple data stream). An SIMD machine is a parallel processor, typically designed to operate on large arrays and data structures. Such a machine has a single control unit that fetches and broadcasts a single instruction to multiple arithmetic processors. Each arithmetic processor executes that instruction on data from its local memory. For example, an SIMD instruction might cause all arithmetic processors to add their local memory location 100 to their local memory location 200. This structure is shown in Figure 16.2b.

- MISD (multiple instruction stream, single data stream). Shown in Figure 16.2c, the MISD system consists of multiple control units that fetch instructions and issue them to multiple arithmetic units, which perform the operation on a single data item.This is more a conceptual model for completeness than a practical model on which to build a system.

Figure 16.2 **Flynn's classifications of computer systems**

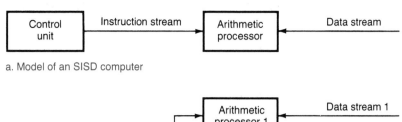

a. Model of an SISD computer

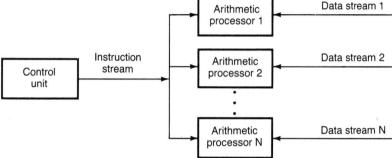

b. Model of an SIMD computer

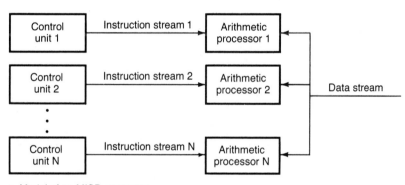

c. Model of an MISD computer

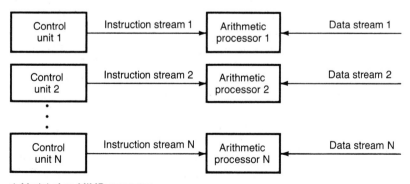

d. Model of an MIMD computer

- MIMD (multiple instruction stream, multiple data stream). An MIMD machine, shown in Figure 16.2d, has multiple independent control units, each of which fetches its own instructions. Each control unit then issues instructions to its own arithmetic processor,which fetches operands, possibly from a large shared memory. Most contemporary microprocessor-based multiprocessors are MIMD machines. The MIMD structure accommodates both the execution of multiple independent processes (for example, for timesharing) and the execution of single, multithreaded applications (that is, parallel programs).

The significance of Flynn's classification scheme is that it makes it easier to describe systems. For example, if a machine is built that includes the ability to operate on a vector, such as performing a simple arithmetic operation like add, subtract, multiply, or divide, to all the elements of the vector at the same time, then this machine can be classified as a SIMD machine. Alternatively, if several computers are interconnected so as to share the same memory and file space, but they operate independently of each other, then that machine can be classified as a MIMD computer.

There are, of course, many other classifications, depending on the underlying architecture of the machine. Gordon Bell described machines based on their degree of parallelism. His four categories, shown in Table 16.1, relate more to the needs of the application than the specific hardware. Bell's model is based on the granularity of parallelism permitted by a particular system. A system with fine-grained parallelism permits an application to spawn multiple parallel threads, each of which executes only a few instructions. In such a system, the overhead of managing the parallel activities must be small, so that the benefits of executing such small parallel tasks are not dominated by that overhead. At the next level, medium-grained parallelism, the system permits parallel activities that are, say, the size of a small procedure, that is, several hundred instructions.

There are many other ways to classify multiple computer systems. For instance, you might base a classification on the cost of communication between entities executing in parallel. If processors share a common memory and can communicate through that memory (typically in nanoseconds or microseconds), then we say they are *tightly coupled*. If the processors communicate via a network, where messages take tens of milliseconds, we say they are *loosely coupled*. Another dimension might have to do with availability and reliability. Clearly, attaching two machines together doesn't necessarily make them more reliable, although for a user who has automatically been switched from one to the other, availability might increase. Suffice it to say that there are many ways to categorize multiple computer systems.

Our examination of parallel computation begins with ways to introduce parallelism into standard SISD computers. Later we look at more complex SIMD and MIMD structures.

Table 16.1 Degrees of Parallelism

Granularity	*Parallelism*	*Synchronization Interval (instructions)*
Fine	Instruction	<20
Medium	Procedure	20-200
Coarse	Process	200-2000
Very coarse	Environment	2000-1M

Pipelined Processors

Parallelism can be used in many ways to increase the performance of computer systems. *Pipelining* is a common technique that can be applied to introduce parallelism both into sequential SISD machines and into machines that have more inherent parallelism, for example, multiple functional or arithmetic units.

Looking at the concept of the von Neumann machine (presented in Chapter 21, we find the genesis of the idea that often constrains us today. The concept is that instructions are fetched, interpreted, and executed sequentially. Obviously, it makes little sense to execute an instruction before it is fetched and interpreted. But carried to its extreme, this concept means that there is no overlap between instructions. This made sense when computers were first designed, but today we know that instruction processing can be broken down into independent steps (such as fetch, interpret, and execute), and that these steps can be decoupled. Furthermore, it is possible to design a machine so that at any time, different instructions are in various stages of processing within the machine.

Figure 16.3a shows the sequential nature of instruction processing in a purely sequential machine. The table in Figure 16.3 is a *reservation table*; it tells what functional components are required for each stage of

Figure 16.3 Pipelined instruction execution

Time →	1	2	3	4	5	6	7
Fetch	I1			I2			I3
Interpret		I1			I2		
Execute			I1			I2	

a. Nonpipelined execution

Time →	1	2	3	4	5	6	7
Fetch	I1	I2	I3	I4	I5	I6	I7
Interpret		I1	I2	I3	I4	I5	I6
Execute			I1	I2	I3	I4	I5

b. Pipelined execution

instruction processing. Here we see that instruction execution is broken into three independent stages: fetch, interpret, and execute. In this figure, we assume that each stage takes exactly one time unit to complete. Each instruction therefore takes three time units to complete, and we finish one instruction every three time units. We also notice that each stage is busy only one third of the time; for example, the instruction fetch stage is idle during time units 2, 3, 5, 6, and so on.

Figure 16.3b shows the pipelined processing of the same instruction stream. In the pipelined execution, instruction executions overlap. Basically, as soon as a pipeline stage is idle, the next instruction is fed into that stage. The concept seems pretty simple when presented this way, and the connotation of a pipeline seems appropriate in that instructions are fed in one end and results come out the other end. The pipeline shown in Figure 16.3 is "perfect"; once the pipe is loaded, there are no idle stages. In reality, however, this is often difficult to accomplish. Most pipelines have idle stages; in fact, depending on how well different instructions overlap in the pipe, performance can sometimes be improved by introducing delays during some instruction processing.

With the pipelined organization, each instruction still takes three time units to complete. However, once the pipeline is full, one instruction is finished every time unit. The shorter the pipeline stages, the more rapidly instructions are completed, on average. In general, if we have a perfect m-stage instruction execution process and want to execute n instructions, a nonpipelined organization will take n × m time units, while a pipelined organization will take (n + m−1), where the m−1 units are the cycles required to load the pipeline.

A number of observations are appropriate here. The *average* time to produce the finished result is faster if each stage is specialized than if one general-purpose stage does it all, even if the total time to produce each result, start to finish, is lengthened. There is an implication that each stage takes the same amount of time, and as a result of this constant time per stage, we get results on a regular basis. In addition, as a result of the fixed time per stage (and many stages), there is no output while the pipe fills up. Obviously it also takes a while to empty the pipeline. Finally, any problems in the pipeline will cause it to halt, and the result coming off at the end when the pipeline halts will not likely be the one that had the problems.

Thus, we can make the following assumptions:

- A pipeline is fine once it gets started up.

- Multiple stages mean more results per unit of time.

- An exception somewhere within the pipe is more difficult to handle because it does not necessarily relate to the current results.

- Stopping the pipeline to start up another sequence of instructions helps to negate some of the speed-up improvements (this occurs when a branch is taken or any change to the PC occurs).

In fact, if a change to the PC occurs late in the pipeline, in the worst case we may need to undo some of the computations that have been carried out by partially completed instructions in previous stages.

There is no reason to believe that instruction execution pipelining can be subdivided into only three stages. Pipelines of five, six, or seven stages are not uncommon. Pipelining can also be applied in several places within a single processor. One common application of pipelining is within a floating-point unit, where, for example, each floating-point addition is broken down into its various stages of subtracting exponents, aligning the mantissas, adding, shifting, normalizing, and so on.

Pipelining can be applied at several levels. For example, in the VAX 8600 processors, VAX instructions are pipelined; at any point, several VAX instructions are being executed. The VAX 8600 pipeline has four stages: instruction fetch and decode, operand-address generation and fetch, execute, and result store. On the VAX 8800, however, a five-stage pipeline is used for executing *microinstructions*, that is, the fetching and execution of microinstructions is overlapped, and multiple microinstructions are in the process of being executed at any given time. The effect is to reduce the *micro*cycle time, thereby reducing the instruction execution time.

Multiple Functional Units and Hazards

In addition to pipelining, it is possible to increase parallelism in the execution of a sequential instruction stream through multiple functional units. For example, a computer can contain several arithmetic and logic units. These units can be specialized, for example, can have several fixed-point adders and multipliers, several boolean logic units, and several floating-point multiply and divide units. These functional units can also be pipelined, so that if many operands are fed to them one after another, the average completion time will be reduced.

If we imagine a machine with multiple functional units as just described, it is clear that the time through these units will be different; a floating-point divide will clearly take more time than a boolean operation. What is the implication of these timing differences on instruction execution, particularly if we want to keep as many units busy as possible? For example, if we have a floating divide instruction followed by a boolean OR, does the OR have to wait for the divide to complete?

The answer to that question is that it depends on the instructions. However, it is not strictly necessary that instructions be executed in the order in which they are fetched by the program counter. A number of high-performance computers perform out-of-order execution of a user's instructions. The constraint that must be maintained, of course, is that the result of the out-of-order computation must be the same as if the instructions were executed in order. To ensure this constraint, the hardware or microcode must check for and prevent the occurrence of *hazards*. A hazard is a potential error condition that would result if events completed in a different time sequence than that originally intended by the programmer. Or, in some cases, the compiler generates code to ensure that hazards do not exist. Let's examine some code sequences to demonstrate the problem.

Suppose we have the following instruction sequence (we use VAX assembly language for expressing instructions):

```
ADDL    R1,R2
DIVL    R3,R4
BICL    R5,R6
ADDL    R7,R8
```

In this case, the order in which these instructions is executed is immaterial because there are no *dependencies* among instructions. That is, the operands of each instruction are independent of the operands of the others. On the other hand, suppose we had written

```
ADDL    R1,R2
DIVL    R2,R3
```

Here, the ordering does matter because one source of the divide instruction (R2) is a destination of the add instruction. The add must complete first to produce the result needed by the divide. This is called a *read after write* (RAW) hazard. Similarly, we can have a *write after read* (WAR) hazard if we had written

```
DIVL    R2,R3
ADDL    R1,R2
```

Should the add complete before the division is started, the divide will mistakenly use the new value of R2 instead of the old value.

In any computer with out-of-order execution, the processor must keep track of the inputs and outputs of instructions as they are fetched. Before an instruction can begin execution, the processor must ensure that no hazards exist in the execution of that instruction. Typically this is done by keeping track of which registers are used for sources or results. When the sources needed by an instruction are available, the instruction can be started, as long as its results will not produce hazards for other instructions. When memory locations are used for sources or results, the check can become more complex, but it's still possible to keep track of several operand addresses and how they're being used.

It is possible for hazards to exist in a pipelined organization, depending on how the pipeline is structured. For example, a hazard can exist if there are many pipeline stages and an instruction in an earlier stage can produce a result before an instruction in a later stage can read one of its sources. Hazards can even exist within a single instruction. For example, the VAX instruction ADDL (R1)+, (R1)+ modifies R1 in the middle of the instruction, and that modification must complete before R1 is read to be used for the second operand.

Vector Machines: The Cray-1

An example of a computer that uses both pipelining and multiple functional units is the Cray-1, certainly the most powerful supercomputer during the late 1970s. In addition to its use of techniques that we have just discussed, the Cray-1 is a vector machine, that is, it is designed to operate on large vectors of data.

The basic structure of the Cray-1 is shown in Figure 16.4. On the left of the figure is the large primary memory, organized as one million 64-bit words. Memory cycle time is 50 nanoseconds. In the center are the machine's internal registers. On the right are the multiple functional units: twelve different units organized into groups for vector operations, floating-point operations, scalar arithmetic, and address arithmetic. These functional units are capable of operating in parallel, producing more than one result per cycle.

The basic machine registers are similar to those of the CDC family, described in Chapter 10 (Seymour Cray designed both the CDC family and the Cray computers). The eight 24-bit A registers are used for addressing and address arithmetic. Sixty-four B registers (numbered 0 through 77 octal) provide buffers between the A registers and primary memory. Eight 64-bit S registers form the scalar register set for scalar arithmetic. Sixty-four T registers provide buffers between the S registers and primary memory. Most interesting are the eight vector registers, V0 through V7, shown at the top of the figure. Each of these is actually an array of sixty-four 64-bit registers.

The Cray-1 is particularly effective at performing vector arithmetic. For example, suppose we want to compute the operation

$$A = k1 * B + k2$$

where A and B are vectors and k1 and k2 are constants. The compiler would generate code to load one of the vector registers with sixty-four elements from array B. The constants would be loaded into two of the

Figure 16.4 Organization of the Cray-1

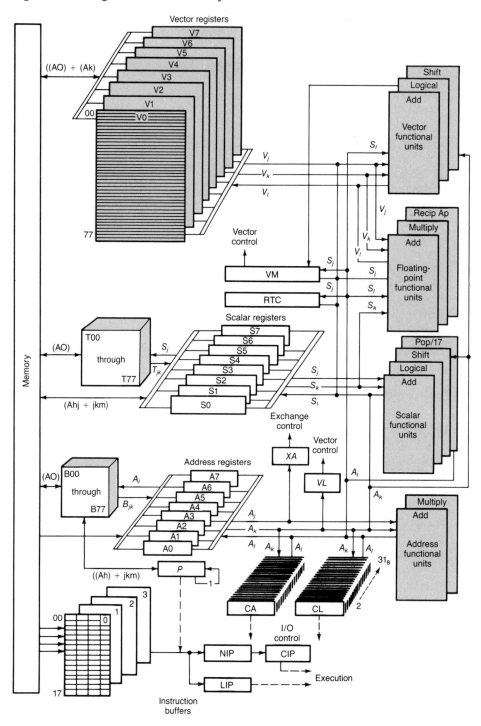

scalar registers. The compiler would then generate a single multiply instruction to multiply the sixty-four elements of the vector register containing part of B by a constant, storing the result in another vector register. (The Cray performs instructions of the form vector ← vector op scalar, as well as vector ← vector op vector.) A second vector instruction would add a constant to each element of that result register. Thus, the Cray requires only two instructions to perform the sixty-four multiplications and sixty-four additions. If the array has more than sixty-four elements, the compiler generates code to load parts of the array, sixty-four elements at a time.

The Cray does not have sixty-four parallel functional units to perform the multiply operations in parallel, but it has a heavily pipelined multiply unit for vectors. Pipelining works well in this case, because we can ensure that there are enough operands to be piped through the unit to keep it busy. Once the pipeline is full, the Cray vector units will produce a result every minor cycle, that is, every 12.5 nanoseconds. The complete time through the pipeline (also the time to fill the pipeline) is only six cycles for the floating-point add unit and seven cycles for the floating-point multiply unit.

In addition to pipelining, the Cray can also perform *chaining* of operands, a mechanism by which results from one functional unit can be fed to another functional unit, even before the first functional unit has completed processing of all its inputs. For example, in our previous computation, if instructions were executed strictly in sequence, all sixty-four multiply operations would have to complete before the additions begin. In this case, however, the machine can recognize that the inputs to the add vector unit for the second instruction are the outputs of the multiply vector unit. By feeding the multiply results directly into the add vector unit as they are produced, the time for the additions is mostly absorbed into the multiply time. Essentially, the chaining of the multiply and add instructions produces one longer pipeline.

Since the introduction of the Cray-1, Cray has introduced several newer supercomputers, including the Cray X-MP, a four-processor super-computer, and the Cray-2, which has an impressive 4.1-nanosecond clock cycle and holds one gigabyte of primary memory. The Cray-2 is completely immersed in fluorocarbon liquid to dissipate heat because at only 45 inches high and 53 inches in diameter, it consumes 195 KW of power.

Multiprocessors

Multiprocessor systems are generally designed to increase system performance economically, offer more flexibility in terms of the system configuration, and provide greater availability or reliability to a particular system. Multiprocessors are particularly desirable when it becomes prohibitively expensive to build faster uniprocessors. They offer a solution to the limited amount of memory, number of channels and devices that can hang on one processor, and the terminals that can be supported. Finally, multiprocessors offer real redundancy, so that if a failure occurs, it is possible to isolate failed units and still keep the system running.

For our purposes, a multiprocessing system is one in which all the processors share a global memory, although each is allowed to have some small amount of local memory. The processors cannot be highly specialized. Thus, an I/O processor, a floating-point processor, or a graphics processor attached to the main CPU does not make a system a multiprocessor. Each of the processors must be capable of performing significant computational work, and each must be capable of accessing or controlling all the I/O devices. The processors must share a single, integrated operating system that allows intimate interaction at all levels (e.g., processes, jobs, data sets, I/O devices, and user-operator interaction).

Given this definition, there are typically two classes of such systems: symmetric and asymmetric. The distinction is really one of style and relates to the operating system that controls the multiprocessor, as well as to the hardware. In a symmetric system, the operating system can run on any of the processors; in fact, several processors may be executing the operating system simultaneously. Processors are scheduled dynamically so as to keep all of them busy with the highest priority jobs. Programs are reentrant and serially queued so that service conflicts are resolved rapidly and operating system code and data is shared but without the possibility of corruption.

Asymmetric systems are those where one of the processors, called the master, is always selected to run the operating system. Since this environment is not unlike the typical multiprogramming environment, the operating system code need not be changed, because only the master processor executes it. Also, since the computational needs of the master processor are different from those of the slave processors (the master spends most of its time executing the operating system code), the slave processors may be more computationally powerful to handle the user application workload. Typically, I/O is handled only by the master.

The advantages and disadvantages of both types of multiprocessor systems are many. Generally it is more difficult to modify an old operating system to run in a symmetric fashion. However, there is greater availability in a symmetric system, since there is true redundancy in the hardware and software, and it is possible to reconfigure the symmetric system should the hardware or software fail. Symmetric systems may be more expensive to build since all components are generally duplicated. However, with many identical processors, programs and jobs have more resources for processing and throughput is better.

Asymmetric systems can offer lower costs to construct if the slaves are simply computational engines that are directed by the master. Thus, only slight changes to the operating system are needed to schedule the slaves to keep them busy. All the overhead associated with I/O and interrupts is handled by the master processor. There is little, if any, redundancy in such systems; if the master processor fails, the entire system is down. Historically, asymmetric systems are often the first to be offered by a computer vendor. For obvious reasons of cost, this allows the vendor to "test the waters" to see what the market will accept. As users come onboard, such systems are often reworked to make them truly symmetric systems. This has happened in the VAX line, as the VMS operating system treated the first VAX multiprocessors in an asymmetric fashion. Newer VAX multiprocessors are supported in a symmetric fashion. In fact, all VAX multiprocessors are capable of symmetric operation. The difference is really a change to the VMS operating system to support symmetric multiprocessing, rather than a fundamental change to hardware. Symmetric multiprocessing required a fundamental change to the structure of VMS so that operating system data structures could be properly synchronized when accessed simultaneously by copies of the operating system running on different processors.

As the number of processors in a multiprocessor increase, the need for symmetric processing increases; otherwise the master will not be able to service all the needs of the slaves. In a large multiprocessor, it is important to distribute the operating system overhead among the processors, which requires a symmetric operating system.

Multiprocessor Organizations

The crucial issue in multiprocessor organization is the interconnection of processors and memories. Some of the alternative structures are

- common bus

- crossbar switch

- multiport memory

- interconnection network

- special-purpose buses for memories and processors

The most common structure is a single shared bus, as shown in Figure 16.5a. All processors, memories, and I/O devices attach to this bus, which they timeshare. Bus bandwidth is critical in terms of the speed at which processors can access memory and devices on the bus. How the bus is controlled and how processors determine when they can transmit or receive (called *arbitration*) are other considerations. Shared buses often slow down when several processors simultaneously try to arbitrate for use of the bus. One solution is to use multiple shared buses (Figure 16.5b) to increase the available bandwidth, but this increases the system complexity and cost because devices need multiple ports to connect to each bus.

Figure 16.5 *Alternative multiprocessor organizations*

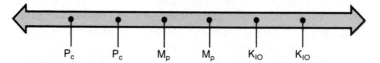

a. Timeshared common bus

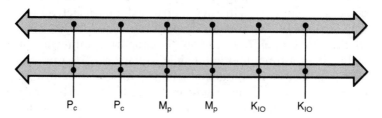

b. Multiple timeshared common buses

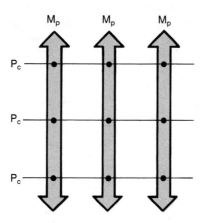

c. Crossbar switch

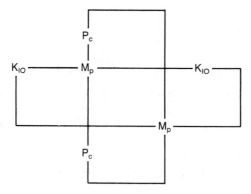

d. Multiport and multibus

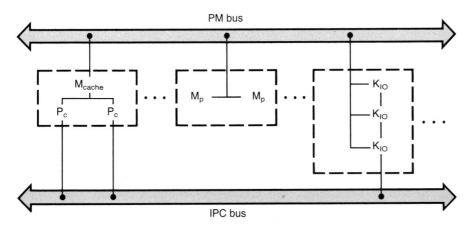

e. Special bus

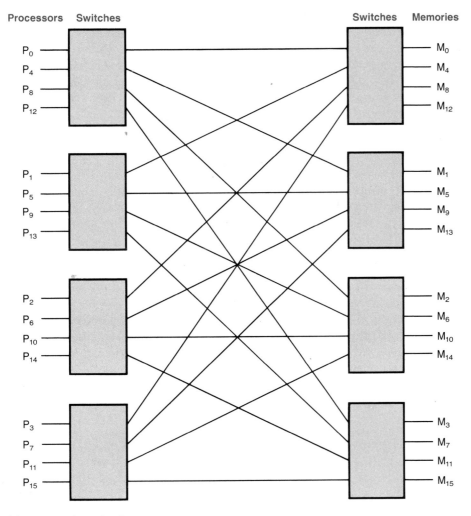

f. Interconnection network

Traffic on a shared bus can be reduced and bus bandwidth increased by using a cache on each of the processors. Caches reduce much of the memory read traffic and possibly some of the memory write traffic, depending on the write strategy used. One problem, discussed in Chapter 14, is keeping the data in the caches consistent, since multiple processors may be attempting to read and write a single word of memory at the same time. With large write-back caches using a good distributed-write cache coherence algorithm, the number of processors that a bus will support can be significantly increased.

Another means of interconnecting processors and memories is a crossbar switch. In the shared bus, a single bus cable connects all processors and memories. In a crossbar, a separate bus leads from each processor and memory, and these are fully interconnected through a switch (Figure 16.5c). Because of this direct connection, there is no timesharing and multiple memory transactions can be done simultaneously, as long as the transactions are to different memories. If two processors attempt to access the same memory at the same time, some arbitration must occur, and one processor will retry or its request will be queued. With a crossbar, the switching must be done quickly or there is a significant penalty in trying to share programs and data. Furthermore, the higher the speed of the switch, the more complex it becomes and the more costly it is to build. In fact, the major problem with a crossbar is that its complexity grows with the square of the number of processor-memory pairs, making it unsatisfactory for large multiprocessors. Finally, because the switch is a single point of failure, its reliability is important. A primary example of the use of a crossbar switch was the C.mmp (multi-minicomputer), developed at Carnegie-Mellon University in the early 1970s. C.mmp consisted of sixteen PDP−11 minicomputers, interconnected to sixteen global memory units through a 16x16 crossbar.

The multiport and multibus configuration, shown in Figure 16.5d, is one where both memory and devices are accessible through different paths. Essentially, a fast multiplexor is placed in front of each memory module and each I/O device so that access can be granted quickly from one port to another. Multiplexors are relatively cheap and reliable, so this has been a popular way to build multiprocessing systems. Also, with duplication of both memory and I/O devices, it is generally possible to reconfigure the system within minutes so that it can remain operational after a failure occurs. The difficulty is that the multiplexors cannot be added to the memories and devices after the complete computer system is installed at the customer's site. Thus, purchasers must buy more hardware than required if they expect to eventually upgrade to a multiprocessor system.

Another way to reduce bus traffic and to increase system availability is to add a special bus for interprocessor communication. Unlike the traditional bus to which the I/O devices are connected, the special bus is used to serialize requests for nonsharable system resources (such as operating system queues, I/O devices like printers or locked files, and critical sections of operating-system code), as well as to pass high-speed messages between processors to maintain system integrity and to pass "I'm all right," or "alive," messages as operational checks. The computer systems from Tandem and Sequent use this technique.

Finally, there is the generalized form of interconnection, much like a typical communications network. Every processing node, consisting of a processor and possibly some local memory, connects to a communications network of switching nodes. To access nonlocal memory, or to communicate with another processor, a connection path has to be built from machine to machine or from machine to memory. In a sense, then, you can consider such a system as containing a large shared memory with an access cost that depends on the distance to the memory. The advantage of such a structure is its ability to scale in order to handle large numbers of processors. The Butterfly multiprocessor from Bolt Beranek and Newman Inc. (BB&N) and the Intel iPSC hypercube, both which are described later, use this technique.

What Is Required for Multiprocessing?

Regardless of the actual bus configuration and type of multiprocessing system, the following basic ingredients are found in many multiprocessors:

1. a locking mechanism

2. interprocessor communications

3. processor identification

4. separate processor address spaces

5. reconfiguration

6. failure isolation

A lock is a mechanism that serializes access to a single resource from multiple parallel instruction streams. Locks can be implemented in hardware, software, or both. In fact, a lock is usually a combination of hardware and software, because that is the easiest way to implement one.

Typically, a lock is implemented as a single bit in memory. Several processes, who are sharing a resource, use the lock to gain exclusive access to the resource. Imagine that the bit has a value of 1 to indicate that the resource is free, and 0 to indicate that it is in use. To access the shared resource, a process must gain exclusive access by first setting the bit to 0.

The first process to set the bit to 0 can access the resource; other processes trying to access the resource will then be forced to wait until the lock bit becomes 1 again. When the process using the resource has finished, it sets the bit back to 1, making it available again. This is a simple binary semaphore.

The problem on a multiprocessor is guaranteeing that only one process can set the bit to zero. For example, suppose that the lock bit is implemented as bit 0 of a word and a process attains the lock by decrementing the word. The problem is that a decrement normally takes several cycles: a read of the word into the processor's memory, a decrement of the word within the processor, and then a write of the modified value back to memory. It is possible that, while one processor is decrementing the word, another processor performs a read of the same memory location. Now both processors have read a value of 1, both decrement the lock to 0, and both write a 0 back to memory, thinking that they now have exclusive access.

The solution is to make the sequence of actions *atomic*, that is, noninterruptable by other operations, at least to the same data element. This is called a *read-modify-write* sequence. A typical solution is to permit a processor performing a read-modify-write to hold the bus for the entire transaction, thus prohibiting other processors from accessing memory. In general, the system should be able to differentiate lock manipulation instructions from other read-modify-write sequences (for example, normal arithmetic) so that more concurrency is allowed on the bus.

For example, the VAX has special interlocked bit instructions (BBSSI, BBCCI) that perform atomic read-modify-write cycles on a bit in memory. Such instructions are often known as test-and-set instructions because they atomically test the condition of a bit and set it to a new value. These instructions use primitive interlocked bus cycles to perform the operations atomically. A more complicated example is the VAX interlocked queue instructions (INSQHI, REMQHI), which must perform multiple reads and writes on the queue data structure in an atomic fashion. The trick, in this case, is that hardware uses a single lock bit to guarantee mutual exclusion to the data structure. Because interlocked queue elements must be aligned on quadword address boundaries, it is guaranteed that the low-order two bits in the queue header are zero (because the address of the forward link is evenly divisible by four). The hardware can therefore use one of the two bits in the queue header as a lock to guarantee that another processor will not access the queue while an interlocked queue manipulation is in progress. Hardware resets the lock bit when the operation has completed. Only the setting of the lock bit requires a primitive interlocked bus transaction.

The second requirement listed was that address spaces be separate. This is not, in fact, an absolute requirement, and it is possible (and sometimes desirable) for all processors to share a single address space. From a reliability and protection point of view, however, there is often data that is only related to a particular processor, such as its stack, its interrupt vectors, and its processor ID, that is not meaningfully shared. For this, a separate address space can ensure that a failure in one processor does not damage data stored by another processor.

The need for interprocessor communications has already been described. It is useful for any processor to be able to interrupt another processor, for example, to force it to reschedule because a higher priority job has entered the system. Given an interrupt capability and shared memory, processors can communicate through shared message queues, with interrupts telling a processor when to look at its queue. Processors may have individual queues for processor-specific messages, and may also share queues for common work that can be distributed among the processors. It is of course important that each processor be uniquely identifiable with some unique processor ID.

Reconfiguration and failure isolation are important because, as the complexity of a system increases, the probability of failure increases. Multiprocessors are complex for many reasons, including the number of processors and devices, the amount of memory, and typically, the complex interconnection of those units. Because the components of a multiprocessor are often intimately connected, a failure in one component can easily lead to a system failure. Some multiprocessors are designed for high reliability; such systems implement online error detection and isolation of the faulty component. These systems may even permit diagnosis and replacement of faulty components while the system is operating. More typically, as with uniprocessors, multiprocessors crash when a failure occurs. Unlike a uniprocessor, however, in which the system is either all up or all down, a single faulty processor can be removed from a multiprocessor, and it can reboot and continue operating in a somewhat degraded mode.

Examples of Multiprocessor Systems

The previous sections described some of the alternatives for multiprocessor organization, as well as some of the requirements for multiprocessors. This section briefly describes three multiprocessor systems that have been constructed: the Connection Machine, the Butterfly, and the hypercube. These are examples of a new generation of highly parallel computers with complex interconnection structures. While it is possible to build these and other complex structures, the difficult problem for the future is how to best produce software that fully utilizes the capabilities of these machines.

The Connection Machine: A Highly Parallel SIMD Machine

The Connection Machine, a product of Thinking Machines Corporation, is an example of a new generation of very highly parallel computers. By very highly parallel, we mean that it has tens of thousands, rather than tens or hundreds, of processors. In fact, the CM-1, the first prototype of the Connection Machine, is implemented as four quadrants of 16K processors each, for a total of 64K processors. The CM-1 is actually a coprocessor to a more conventional computer, such as a VAX or Symbolics, which is used to control the Connection Machine.

Figure 16.6 shows the structure of each processor in the CM-1. Processors are extremely simple. Each processor consists of a 1-bit ALU, 4K bits of local memory, and 16 local flag bits. During a single instruction, the ALU takes three 1-bit operands—2 bits from memory and 1 bit from the local flags—and produces a 1-bit result that is written back to memory and possibly to the flags. The result is computed as one of 256 possible logical functions of the three 1-bit source operands. Although each cycle produces only one 1-bit result in a processor, the power of the machine comes from the huge number of processors.

The CM-1 processors are implemented using VLSI technology with sixteen processors per chip. Each chip also has a router through which processors are interconnected, allowing processor-to-processor messages. On the chip, and across chip boundaries, each chip is connected to its four neighbors in a grid. However, using the routing network, any processor can send a message to any other processor.

Each of the 4,096 routers (that interconnect the 64K processors) has a unique 12-bit address. The structure of the interconnection network is that

Figure 16.6   Organization of the CM-1 processor

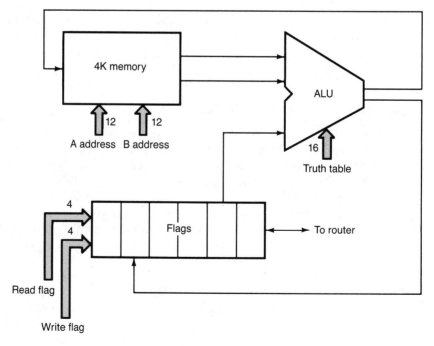

of a boolean n-cube. Each of the routers connects to all of the other routers whose 12-bit addresses differ by only one address bit. In the worst case, therefore, a message from one node to its topologically farthest neighbor will travel through 12 routers, since one address can differ from another by no more than 12 bits.

The CM-1 is an SIMD computer, meaning that a single instruction stream controls the operation of all 64K processing elements. Instructions are issued by a Lisp or C program running on a host computer to the CM-1 microcontroller, which is responsible for managing 16K processors in a quadrant. The microcontroller translates the high-level instruction into one or perhaps hundreds of CM-1 *nanoinstructions* that accomplish the action. The nanoinstructions are broadcast to all processors, which execute them in parallel. For example, one instruction might tell all processors to AND locations i and j in their local memories. While nanoinstructions are really 1-bit instructions, higher-level operations are easily performed on sets of data spread over multiple processors.

For executing conditional operations, each processor has a context bit as one of its flags that tells the processor whether or not to execute the current nanoinstruction. Thus, during a particular instruction, some processors may be active and others may be passive. The machine context, that is, the set of all context bits, can be quickly changed for different situations.

The Butterfly: An Interconnection Network Machine

The Butterfly, a product of Bolt Beranek and Newman, Inc., is probably the best example of a parallel networked multiprocessor. The Butterfly is interesting because it is an MIMD machine built from conventional multiprocessors, but its switching network interconnection structure permits expansion to up to 256 processors. This would be difficult to accomplish with a shared-bus approach.

Each node in the Butterfly consists of a Motorola 68020 microprocessor, a floating-point coprocessor, and up to 4 megabytes of local memory. Processors execute code out of their local memory; however, a processor can address any of the memories in the system, including its own. Thus, each processor has a local memory and all the local memories together form a global memory. The only difference in accessing local or nonlocal memory is performance.

Attached to each processor is a microprogrammed processor node controller (PNC), whose function is the handling of both local and remote memory requests. The PNC performs virtual-to-physical address translation, examines the physical address, and determines whether the reference is local or remote. If the reference is remote, the PNC initiates the remote reference. The PNC also handles local memory requests from remote systems and is used to implement atomic operations.

The most significant feature of the Butterfly is its interconnection structure. Figure 16.5f shows the structure of a sixteen-node Butterfly multiprocessor. While each processor and its local memory are colocated, in Figure 16.5f they are pictorially split apart to show the logical interconnection of processors and memories. The Butterfly interconnection network is composed of switching nodes, which are the rectangles in the figure. Each switching node has four inputs and four outputs. A switch is a custom VLSI part, and eight switches are packaged on a module to implement a sixteen input and sixteen output switch.

The switches perform packet switching of messages from processor to memory. When a processor issues a memory request to a remote memory, its PNC builds a packet with the request and passes it to the switch. The destination memory address in the packet is used to route the packet. At each switch, two bits of the address are used to select one of the four possible switch output paths. In Figure 16.5f, for example, suppose node 2 wants to send a request to node 9. Node 2's PNC builds a packet with node 9's address (1001 in binary). At the first switch, the low-order two bits (01) select the second output path of that switch. At the next switch, the next two bits (10) select the third output path of that switch, which leads to processor 9.

There are several advantages of a such a switching structure, as previously noted, including its scalability and parallelism. Several switches can operate in parallel, so several memory accesses can be in progress at a time. If two messages for the same destination arrive at a single switch at the same time, one of the messages is queued and then retransmitted. Redundancy can be added by having multiple paths between nodes. An increase to sixty-four nodes is accomplished by adding another level of switches, as shown in Figure 16.7.

MIMD Hypercube Machines

The final parallel architecture that we examine is the *hypercube*. A hypercube is an MIMD computer consisting of nodes that are independent processors with local memories. Each processor in a hypercube of size 2^n processors connects directly to n of its neighbor processors through n bidirectional communications channels. This structure is called a binary n-cube. For example, in a 4-cube there are sixteen nodes, and each node is connected to four neighbors; in a 6-cube there are sixty-four nodes, and each node is connected to six of its neighbors.

Figure 16.8 shows the interconnection structure of a 16-node hypercube. Each node has a 4-bit address, as shown in the figure. Also, each node has connections to its four "nearest" neighbors, where a nearest neighbor is one whose address differs in only one bit position. The four neighbors of node 1111 are thus 1110, 1101, 1011, and 0111. Any node can thus communicate with any other node in from one to four hops. An important issue in such machines, therefore, is mapping application

Figure 16.7   *Butterfly 64-element switch*

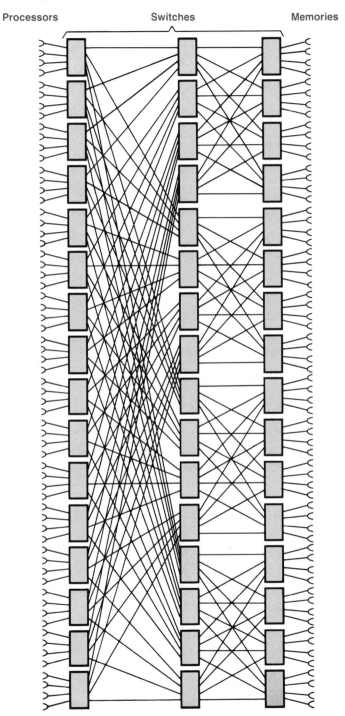

Processors   Switches   Memories

Figure 16.8   16-node hypercube

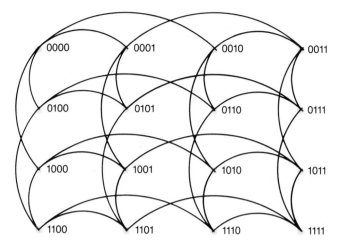

processes onto processors in a way that locates heavily-communicating processes onto topologically close processors.

Two examples of hypercubes are the Cosmic Cube, a prototype 64-node hypercube implementation designed at Caltech, and the Intel iPSC (for Intel Personal SuperComputer), a hypercube product developed and sold by Intel Corporation.

Summary

This chapter has described both methods of introducing parallelism into sequential (SISD) processors and alternatives for organizing multiprocessors. Changes in technology, particularly those leading to the high performance that microprocessors currently enjoy, are making multiprocessors a cost-effective way to produce high-performance computer systems. The important issue for the future will be whether software will be capable of effectively utilizing the multiprocessor systems that technology is providing.

Exercises

1. Give an example of each of Flynn's four computer system classifications. Can you find an example of an MISD machine?

2. Explain how a pipeline works. Suppose a computer has a three-stage pipeline with fetch, decode, and execute stages that take 1, 1, and 2 time units to complete, respectively. Show the reservation table for this pipeline. Once this pipeline is full, how frequently are results generated?

3. What problems do branch instructions cause on pipelined computers? Describe how this situation can be helped by a delayed branch mechanism, such as that used in the Berkeley RISC (discussed in Chapter 10).

4. What is the difference between availability and reliability? Give an example of an available system that is not reliable and a reliable system that is not available.

5. What is a hazard? Give a code sequence that demonstrates a write-after-write hazard and discuss the problem that it presents.

6. Discuss the advantages and disadvantages of symmetric and asymmetric multiprocessor systems.

7. Find a technical description of a commercially available multiprocessor bus and describe the features that specifically support multiprocessing.

8. What is a critical section as found in a typical operating system? What are the differences, if any, between the handling of critical sections in a uniprocessor and in a multiprocessor?

9. If a read-modify-write decrement instruction is used to implement a lock in a two-processor system and each executes it at the same time, what are the consequences? Also, consider how unlocking is done.

10. What happens if a processor sets a lock and then fails? What can be done to correct this and keep a multiprocessor system running after such a failure?

Appendix A
The Ultrix Assembler

This appendix describes the operation of the Ultrix Assembler. It is intended to be an introduction for those who wish to write small assembly language programs on Ultrix or Berkeley VAX/Unix. (We'll use the name Ultrix in this section to refer·to Ultrix, Berkeley VAX/Unix, or any of its derivatives.) There are a number of differences between the Ultrix assembler and the VAX/VMS assembler, which we described in Chapter 3. For most programs, however, it should be easy for anyone who understands the VAX instruction set to use either assembler. For those using this book with Ultrix, we recommend first reading the assembler portion of Chapter 3, and then reading this appendix to understand the differences.

In general, the Ultrix assembler is designed to be a target language for compilers and not for hand-coding of assembler. One can assemble Ultrix assembly programs using the C compiler.

Differences Between Ultrix and VAX/VMS Assemblers

Following are some of the important syntactic similarities and differences between the Ultrix and the VAX/VMS assemblers. These differences need to be kept in mind when switching from one to the other.

- The instruction format is similar to that used in VAX/VMS. Each assembler statement begins with an optional label, followed by a VAX instruction (or assembler pseudo-operation), followed by an optional comment, for example:

```
mylabel:    addl2    r0,r3            # sum two variables
```

- Program text should be entered in lowercase. VAX instruction names are lowercase, and register names (r0 through r15; ap, fp, sp, and pc) are lowercase.

- The VAX 2- and 3-operand instruction names must be explicitly listed by "proper" name, that is, one must write *addl2* or *addl3*; the assembler does not recognize *addl* without the following digit, 2 or 3, to specify the number of operands.

- Comments use the C comment conventions. Multiline block comments are delimited with /* and */. The sharp (#) character, as shown previously, signals that the remainder of the current line is a comment (sharp replaces the semicolon, used in VAX/VMS assembler).

403

- Immediate mode operands (literals) are specified by a preceding dollar sign ($) instead of the sharp used by VAX/VMS. For example, the instruction

```
subl2    $5,myint          # decrease myint by 5
```

subtracts the integer 5 from the longword myint.

- Indirect memory addressing is specified by an asterisk (*) instead of the at sign (@) used by VAX/VMS, for example,

```
subl3    $5,*mypointer,(r2)
```

subtracts the integer 5 from the longword whose address is stored in mypointer; the result is stored in the longword pointed to by r2. Indirect register addressing mode is specified using parentheses.

- The default radix for numbers is decimal. However, a non-zero number that begins with a 0 is assumed to be octal, while a number that begins with 0x is assumed to be hexadecimal. For example,

```
stuff:    .long    124,0124,0x124
```

stores the values 124_{10}, 124_8 (84 decimal), and 124_{16} (292 decimal) in three adjacent longwords starting at symbolic address *stuff*.

Storage Allocation

Storage allocation is similar to the VAX/VMS assembler. The Ultrix storage directives are shown in Table A.1. These directives are similar to the VAX/VMS directives. Two different directives are *.space* and *.fill*. The *.space* directive simply allocates a contiguous number of zero-valued bytes, as specified by the expression parameter. The *.fill* directive has three parameters: a repetition count, a size (of value 1–8), and a fill value. The result of *.fill* is to allocate size*repetition_count bytes; each unit of size bytes is initialized to the fill value.

There are two string directives, *.ascii* and *.asciz*. In both cases, these strings are delimited by double quotes. In Ultrix, the typical method of storing strings is as zero-terminated strings (.asciz). There are no string descriptors.Strings can include normal Ultrix backslash escapes. The escapes are newline (\n), tab (\t), backspace (\b), carriage return (\r), form feed (\f), backslash (\\), double quote (\"), and single quote (\'). Any arbitrary binary pattern can be inserted in a string using the notation \ddd where ddd is one to three octal digits. For example, the string

```
str:    .ascii "Hello there\n\0"
```

contains the characters "Hello there" followed by a newline character, followed by a null character. This could have been defined equivalently by using *.asciz* and omitting the final null.

In addition to these directives, the Ultrix assembler also recognizes the floating point allocation directives *.ffloat*, *.dfloat*, *.gfloat*, and *.hfloat*.

Table A.1   Ultrix Assembler Storage Allocation Directives

Directive	*Meaning*
label: .byte value_list	Store specified values in successive bytes in memory at symbolic address "label."
label: .word value_list	Store specified values in successive words in memory.
label: .long value_list	Store specified values in successive longwords in memory.
label: .quad value_list	Store specified values in successive quadwords in memory.
label: .octa value_list	Store specified values in successive octawords in memory.
label: .ascii "string"	Store ASCII representation of the delimited character string in successive bytes in memory.
label: .asciz "string"	Store the ASCII representation of the string, followed by a zero byte.
label: .space expression	Allocates *expression* bytes of zeros.
label: .fill rep,size,fill	Allocates *rep * size* bytes, where each of the size-byte units is initialized to *fill*. *Size* must be between 1 and 8.

Labels

The Ultrix assembler uses several different naming conventions for labels, primarily for use by compilers. By convention, there are five different types of labels.

1. Labels that begin with capital L are labels that will not be needed at run time. That is, they are not retained in the run-time symbol table, cannot be referred to globally, and cannot be accessed by a debugger.

2. Labels that begin with any lowercase or uppercase alphabetic character (except L) are labels that are used by assembly language programmers. They cannot be referred to by C programs.

3. Labels that begin with underscore (_) are visible from C programs that are linked with the modules in which they are defined. For example, an assembly procedure named _myproc can be referred to as *myproc* within a C program that will be linked with that procedure. The main program of an assembly program is always named _main.

4. Labels that begin with two underscores refer to global procedures used by the C library. Assembly programmers should not begin labels with two underscores.

5. The assembler permits the use of nine local labels "1:" through "9:." The scope of a local label is active until that local label is redefined (by using it again). A consequence of the small number of local labels and their scoping is that branch instructions require a special notation for the branch destination, since a branch may be placed between two definitions of a single local label. When a local label is used in a branch or jump instruction, it is specified as the local label number followed by the letter *b* or *f* for backward or forward, respectively. For example, in the code

```
1:  incl r5
    cmpl r5,r6
    bgtr 1b
1:  movl r5,saveit
```

the label "1:" has been used in two places. The statement *bgtr 1b* branches to the previous "1:" because the *b* specifies a branch backwards.

Input and Output

Terminal input and output are performed using the standard C library routines, *printf* and *scanf*. (These routines are named *_printf* and *_scanf* inside of an assembly program because they refer to procedures in the global C library.) These procedures are defined in most Ultrix, Unix, and C manuals. *Printf* is an output procedure that takes a variable number of arguments. In a high level language call, a call to printf might look like

```
printf (control_string, param1, param2, ... , paramN)
```

The first argument is the address of a zero-terminated control string. If the control string contains no special control codes, it is simply output to the terminal. However, special control codes can be used to cause additional parameters to printf to be converted to ASCII and output as part of the string. The standard conversion characters are shown in Table A.2. In C, if we wished to print the ASCII decimal and hexadecimal equivalent of an integer *xyz*, we would simply write

```
printf ("xyz is %d in decimal and %x in hex", xyz, xyz )
```

Note that the control string contains two special control codes, so we need to pass two parameters, in this case both are the integer *xyz*. In assembly language, we need to perform the call by pushing the parameters on the stack in *reverse* order, and then executing the proper call instruction. We also need to remember that integers are passed by value (using *pushl*) while strings would be passed by reference (using *pushab*).

As an example of the use of *printf*, and to demonstrate how Ultrix assembler programs are written, Figure A.1 is a simple output program that corresponds to Figure 3.4. The program simply outputs two messages.

To run this program, first create a file named *prog1.s*. The *.s* is the file extension required for assembler programs. Now compile the program with the C compiler using the command line:

```
cc -o prog1.x prog1.s
```

Table A.2   Simple printf Control Codes

Code	Meaning
%d	Decimal
%o	Octal
%x	Hexadecimal
%u	Unsigned decimal
%c	Single character
%s	Zero-terminated string

Figure A.1   Simple string output program

```
/*               First Example Program
 *
 * First program to output a simple string to the terminal
 */

        .data 0                 # begin data segment
himsg:  .asciz "hello there\n"  # initial message descriptor
byemsg: .asciz "bye now\n"      # final message descriptor

# The main program entry point is defined as _main.

        .text  0                # begin text segment
        .globl  _main           # define _main as external

_main:  .word  0                # main entry point
                                # saves no registers

# Output the initial message to the terminal.

        pushab  himsg           # push control string address
        calls   $1,_printf      # call output format routine

# Output the final message to the terminal.

        pushab  byemsg          # push control string address
        calls   $1,_printf      # call output format routine
        ret                     # return from _main to system
```

This invokes the C compiler (named *cc*), specifies the production of an executable output file named *prog1.x* (using the −*o* switch), and specifies an input file named *prog1.s*. Seeing that the input is an assembler program (because of its name), the C compiler invokes the assembler on *prog1.s* and links the resulting object file with the C run-time library. The program can then be run simply by typing *prog1.x*.

The program in Figure A.1 illustrates some other important issues in using the Ultrix assembler. First, each program consists of up to four data segments and up to four text segments (numbered 0 through 4). A text segment is read-only and normally contains program instructions. Our first sample program has only one data segment and one text segment, as defined by the *.data* and *.text* statements. Second the entry point for your program is defined by the label *_main*, as previously described. In order to define the symbol *_main* externally, the *.globl* directive is used; this permits the linker or loader to find the address of the symbol *_main*. Third, because *_main* is a procedure entry, it must begin with a word register save mask. The Ultrix assembler has no special notation for specifying a procedure entry point or a register mask, so the mask must be specified using the *.word* directive followed by the correct decimal or hexadecimal value. For example, to save registers r2 and r3, we would specify .word 0x000c, which sets bits 2 and 3 and therefore causes registers 2 and 3 to be saved. Fourth, note that the *.asicz* strings contain the \n control character to ensure that a newline is output at the end of the line.

Figure A.2 shows the Ultrix version of Figure 3.5. This program simply outputs the integers 10 through 0. In this case, *printf* is used both to output strings and to convert and output the integers in ASCII format. Note that in Figure A.2 we use the local label "1:" and the branch backward to that label.

As our final example, we show the use of the procedure *scanf* for reading terminal input. *Scanf* takes a control string and several parameters, all of which are passed by reference. The control string specifies the format in which input is to be processed and converted, and each parameter is the address of the place to store the next input item. For example, in Figure A.3, we use scanf to read an integer and a string from the terminal. The C high-level call would look like

```
scanf ("%d %s", &in_int, &inbuf)
```

where the & implies that the address of these variables is to be passed. As a result of this call, the integer typed on the terminal is converted to binary and placed in the variable in_int, and the string typed on the terminal is stored as a zero-terminated string in inbuf. Notice that when we use *printf* to output the integer and string, the integer is passed by value and the string is passed by reference.

For more detailed information on the use of *printf* and *scanf*, we recommend looking at books on C, such as the one by Kernighan and Ritchie [1978].

Finally, the Ultrix assembler does not produce a listing file. However, to find the load addresses of defined labels and variables, the *nm* utility will dump all labels and addresses (just type *nm prog.x* to display the symbols in the executable program *prog.x* sorted alphabetically, or *nm* −*n* *prog.x* to sort the symbols numerically). Because the program is linked with the C library, there will be many symbols in the list. There are several Ultrix debuggers which we do not describe here. Documentation can be found in the Berkeley VAX/Unix or Ultrix manual set (for example, see the tutorial by Maranzano and Bourne [1985]).

Figure A.2   Simple integer printing program

```
/*        Second Program
 *
 *        Program to print integers from 10 down to 0.
 */

          .data  0
himsg:    .asciz "hello there\n"    # initial message descriptor
byemsg:   .asciz "bye now\n"        # final message descriptor
numstring:                         # printf control string...
          .asciz "%d\n"            # ... to print decimal value
counter:  .long  10                # init integer counter to 10

# Define main entry point.

          .text  0                 # begin text segment
          .globl _main             # define _main as external

_main:    .word  0                 # main entry point
                                   # saves no registers

# Output the initial message to the terminal.

          pushab himsg             # push control string address
          calls  $1,_printf        # call output format routine

# Loop to process integers.  On each pass printf is
# called to print the integer in ASCII format.  This
# call looks like    printf(numstring,counter)   where
# numstring is the control string address and counter is
# the value to be converted as specified in the string.

1:        pushl  counter           # push parameter to printf
          pushab numstring         # push control string address
          calls  $2,_printf        # output next integer
          decl   counter           # decrement counter
          bgeq   1b                # branch back if \ 0

# Output the final message to the terminal.

          pushab byemsg            # control string...
          calls  $1,_printf        # ...for final message
          ret                      # return from _main to system
```

Figure A.3   Simple terminal reading program

```
/*          Program to read input
 *
 *    This program simply prompts the user for an integer
 *    and a string, and then echoes both.  The string cannot contain
 *    blanks.  The program exits if the string entered is a $.
 */



        .data   0               # begin data segment
inbuf:  .space  100             # space for input string
in_int: .long   0               # space for integer
in_msg: .asciz "enter an integer and a string (exit with a \"$\"): "
read_it:.asciz "%d %s"
out_msg:.asciz "you typed the integer %d and the string \"%s\"\n"

# Define main entry point.

        .text   0               # begin text segment
        .globl  _main           # define _main as external

_main:  .word   0               # main entry point
                                # saves no registers

# Output the initial message to the terminal.

loop:   pushab  in_msg          # push control string address
        calls   $1,_printf      # print the prompt message

# Read user's string and integer

        pushab  inbuf           # push address of user string
        pushal  in_int          # push address of integer
        pushab  read_it         # scanf control string
        calls   $3,_scanf       # read input into inbuf

/*
   The user's string has been read into inbuf, and
   the binary integer is in in_int.
   Write out the user's input to the terminal
   and then check if we're finished.
*/
        pushab  inbuf           # push address of string
        pushl   in_int          # push address of integer
        pushab  out_msg         # printf control string
        calls   $3,_printf      # echo what was typed

        cmpb    $0x24,inbuf     # did user type a "$"?
        bneq    loop            # continue if not
        ret                     # else return
```

Appendix B
VAX Instruction Set Description

Operand Specifier Notation Legend

The standard notation for operand specifiers is:

<name>.<access type><data type>

where:

1. Name is a suggestive name for the operand in the context of the instruction. It is the capitalized name of a register or block for implied operands.

2. Access type is a letter denoting the operand specifier access type.

   a Calculate the effective address of the specified operand. Address is returned in a pointer which is the actual instruction operand. Context of address calculation is given by data type given by <data type>.

   b No operand reference. Operand specifier is branch displacement. Size of branch displacement is given by <data type>.

   m Operand is modified (both read and written).

   r Operand is read only.

   v If not "Rn," same as a. If "RN," R[n + 1]R[n].

   w Operand is written only.

3. Data type is a letter denoting the data type of the operand.

   b denotes byte data

   d denotes D_floating data

   f denotes F_floating data

   g denotes G_floating data

   h denotes H_floating data

411

l denotes longword data

o denotes octaword data

q denotes quadword data

w denotes word data

x denotes the first data type specified by instruction

y denotes the second data type specified by instruction

4. Implied operands, that is, locations that are accessed by the instruction, but not specified in an operand, are denoted in enclosing brackets,[ ].

Condition Codes Legend

. = conditionally cleared/set   0 = cleared
– = not affected   1 = set

Table B.1   List of VAX Instructions by Mnemonic

OP	Mnemonic	Description	Arguments	N	Z	V	C
9D	ACBB	Add compare and branch byte	limit.rb, add.rb, index.mb, displ.bw	.	.	.	–
6F	ACBD	Add compare and branch D_floating	limit.rd, add.rd, index.md, displ. bw	.	.	.	–
4F	ACBF	Add compare and branch F_floating	limit.rf, add.rf, index.mf, displ.bw	.	.	.	–
4FFD	ACBG	Add compare and branch G_floating	limit.rg, add.rg, index.rg, displ.bw	.	.	.	–
6FFD	ACBH	Add compare and branch H_floating	limit.rh, add.rh, index.rh, displ.bw	.	.	.	–
F1	ACBL	Add compare and branch long	limit.rl, add.rl, index.ml, displ.bw	.	.	.	–
3D	ACBW	Add compare and branch word	limit.rw, add.rw, index.mw, displ.bw	.	.	.	–
58	ADAWI	Add aligned word interlocked	add.rw, sum.mw	.	.	.	.
80	ADDB2	Add byte 2-operand	add.rb, sum.mb	.	.	.	
81	ADDB3	Add byte 3-operand	add1.rb, add 2.rb, sum.wb	.	.	.	0
60	ADDD2	Add D_floating 2-operand	add.rd, sum.md	.	.	.	0
61	ADDD3	Add D_floating 3-operand	add1.rd, add2.rd, sum.wd	.	.	.	0
40	ADDF2	Add F_floating 2-operand	add.rf, sum.mf	.	.	.	0
41	ADDF3	Add F_floating 3-operand	addl.rf, add2.rf, sum.wf	.	.	.	0
40FD	ADDG2	Add G_floating 2-operand	add.rg, sum.mg	.	.	.	0
41FD	ADDG3	Add G_floating 3-operand	addl.rg, add2.rg, sum.wg	.	.	.	0

OP	Mnemonic	Description	Arguments	N	Z	V	C
					Condition Codes		

OP	Mnemonic	Description	Arguments	N	Z	V	C
60FD	ADDH2	Add H_floating 2-operand	add.rh, sum.mh	.	.	.	0
61FD	ADDH3	Add H_floating 3-operand	add1.rh, add2.rh, sum.wh	.	.	.	0
C0	ADDL2	Add long 2-operand	add.rl, sum.ml	.	.	.	.
C1	ADDL3	Add long 3-operand	addl.rl, add2.rl, sum.wl	.	.	.	0
20	ADDP4	Add packed 4-operand	addlen.rw, addaddr.ab, sumlen.rw, sumaddr.ab, [R0-3.wl]	.	.	.	0
21	ADDP6	Add packed 6-operand	add1len.rw, add1addr.ab, add2len.rw, add2addr.ab, sumlen.rw, sumaddr.ab, [R0-5.wl]	.	.	.	0
A0	ADDW2	Add word 2-operand	add.rw, sum.mw	.	.	.	.
A1	ADDW3	Add word 3-operand	add1.rw, add2.rw, sum.ww	.	.	.	0
D8	ADWC	Add with carry	add.rl, sum.ml	.	.	.	.
F3	AOBLEQ	Add one and branch on less or equal	limit.rl, index.ml, displ.bb	.	.	.	−
F2	AOBLSS	Add one and branch on less	limit.rl, index.ml, displ.bb	.	.	.	−
78	ASHL	Arithmetic shift long	count.rb, src.rl, dst.wl	.	.	.	0
F8	ASHP	Arithmetic shift and round packed	count.rb, srclen,rw, srcaddr.ab, round.rb, dstlen.rw, dstaddr.ab, [R0-3.wl]	.	.	.	0
79	ASHQ	Arithmetic shift quad	count.rb, src.rq, dst.wq	.	.	.	0
E1	BBC	Branch on bit clear	pos.rl, base.vb, displ.bb, [field.rv]	−	−	−	−
E5	BBCC	Branch on bit clear and clear	pos.rl, base.vb, displ.bb, [field.mv]	−	−	−	−
E7	BBCCI	Branch on bit clear and clear interlocked	pos.rl, base.vb, displ.bb, [field.mv]	−	−	−	−
E3	BBCS	Branch on bit clear and set	pos.rl, base.vb, displ.bb, [field.mv]	−	−	−	−
E0	BBS	Branch on bit set	pos.rl, base.vb, displ.bb, [field.rv]	−	−	−	−
E4	BBCS	Branch on bit set and clear	pos.rl, base.vb, displ.bb, [field.mv]	−	−	−	−
E2	BBSS	Branch on bit set and set	pos.rl, base.vb, displ.bb, [field.mv]	−	−	−	−
E6	BBSSI	Branch on bit set and set interlocked	pos.rl, base.vb, displ.bb, [field.mv]	−	−	−	−
1E	BCC	Branch on carry clear	displ.bb	−	−	−	−
1F	BCS	Branch on carry set	displ.bb	−	−	−	−
13	BEQL	Branch on equal	displ.bb	−	−	−	−
13	BEQLU	Branch on equal unsigned	displ.bb	−	−	−	−
18	BGEQ	Branch on greater or equal	displ.bb	−	−	−	−
1E	BGEQU	Branch on greater or equal unsigned	displ.bb	−	−	−	−

OP	Mnemonic	Description	Arguments	N	Z	V	C
				for Condition Codes			

OP	Mnemonic	Description	Arguments	N	Z	V	C
14	BGTR	Branch on greater	displ.bb	–	–	–	–
1A	BGTRU	Branch on greater unsigned	displ.bb	–	–	–	–
8A	BICB2	Bit clear byte 2-operand	mask.rb, dst.mb	.	.	0	–
8B	BICB3	Bit clear byte 3-operand	mask.rb, src.rb, dst.wb	.	.	0	–
CA	BICL2	Bit clear long 2-operand	mask.rl, dst.ml	.	.	0	–
CB	BICL3	Bit clear long 3-operand	mask.rl, src.rl, dst.wl	.	.	0	–
B9	BICPSW	Bit clear processor status word	mask.rw	.	.	.	.
AA	BICW2	Bit clear word 2-operand	mask.rw, dst.mw	.	.	0	–
AB	BICW3	Bit clear word 3-operand	mask.rw, src.rw, dst.ww	.	.	0	–
88	BISB2	Bit set byte 2-operand	mask.rb, dst.mb	.	.	0	–
89	BISB3	Bit set byte 3-operand	mask.rb, src.rb, dst.wb	.	.	0	–
C8	BISL2	Bit set long 2-operand	mask.rl, dst.ml	.	.	0	–
C9	BISL3	Bit set long 3-operand	mask.rl, src.rl, dst.wl	.	.	0	–
B8	BISPSW	Bit set processor status word	mask.rw	.	.	.	.
A8	BISW2	Bit set word 2-operand	mask.rw, dst.mw	.	.	0	–
A9	BISW3	Bit set word 3-operand	mask.rw, src.rw, dst.ww	.	.	0	–
93	BITB	Bit test byte	mask.rb, src.rb	.	.	0	–
D3	BITL	Bit test long	mask.rl, src.rl	.	.	0	–
B3	BITW	Bit test word	mask.rw, src.rw	.	.	0	–
E9	BLBC	Branch on low bit clear	src.rl, displ.bb	–	–	–	–
E8	BLBS	Branch on low bit set	src.rl, displ.bb	–	–	–	–
15	BLEQ	Branch on less or equal	displ.bb	–	–	–	–
1B	BLEQU	Branch on less or equal unsigned	displ.bb	–	–	–	–
19	BLSS	Branch on less	displ.bb	–	–	–	–
1F	BLSSU	Branch on less unsigned	displ.bb	–	–	–	–
12	BNEQ	Branch on not equal	displ.bb	–	–	–	–
12	BNEQU	Branch on not equal unsigned	displ.bb	–	–	–	–
03	BPT	Break point fault	[-(KSP).w*]	0	0	0	0
11	BRB	Branch with byte displacement	displ.bb	–	–	–	–
31	BRW	Branch with word displacement	displ.bw	–	–	–	–
10	BSBB	Branch to subroutine with byte displacement	displ.bb, [-(SP).wl]	–	–	–	–
30	BSBW	Branch to subroutine with word displacement	displ.bw, [-(SP).wl]	–	–	–	–
FDFF	BUGL	Bugcheck longword	message.bx	–	–	–	–
FEFF	BUGW	Bugcheck word	message.bx	–	–	–	–
1C	BVC	Branch on overflow clear	displ.bb	–	–	–	–
1D	BVS	Branch on overflow set	displ.bb	–	–	–	–
FA	CALLG	Call with general argument list	arglist.ab, dst.ab, [-(SP).w*]	0	0	0	0
FB	CALLS	Call with argument list on stack	numarg.rl, dst.ab, [-(SP).w*]	0	0	0	0
8F	CASEB	Case byte	selector.rb, base.rb, limit.rb, displ.bw-list	.	.	0	.
CF	CASEL	Case long	selector.rl, base.rl, limit.rl, displ.bw-list	.	.	0	.

OP	Mnemonic	Description	Arguments	Condition Codes			
				N	Z	V	C
AF	CASEW	Case word	selector.rw, base.rw, limit.rw, displ.bw-list	.	.	0	.
BD	CHME	Change mode to executive	param.rw, [−(ySP).w*] y=MINU(E, PSL*current-mode*)	0	0	0	0
BC	CHMK	Change mode to kernel	param.rw, [−(KSP).w*]	0	0	0	0
BE	CHMS	Change mode to supervisor	param.rw, [−(ySP).w*] y=MINU(S, PSL*current-mode*)	0	0	0	0
BF	CHMU	Change mode to user	param.rw, [−(SP).w*]	0	0	0	0
94	CLRB	Clear byte	dst.wb	0	1	0	−
7C	CLRD	Clear D_floating	dst.wd	0	1	0	−
D4	CLRF	Clear F_floating	dst.wf	0	1	0	−
7C	CLRG	Clear G_floating	dst.wg	0	1	0	−
7CFD	CLRH	Clear H_floating	dst.wh	0	1	0	−
D4	CLRL	Clear long	dst.wl	0	1	0	−
7CFD	CLRO	Clear Octoword	dst.wo	0	1	0	−
7C	CLRQ	Clear quad	dst.wq	0	1	0	−
B4	CLRW	Clear word	dst.ww	0	1	0	−
91	CMPB	Compare byte	srcl.rb, src2.rb	.	.	0	.
29	CMPC3	Compare character 3-operand	len.rw, srcladdr.ab, src2addr.ab, [R0-3.wl]	.	.	0	.
2D	CMPC5	Compare character 5-operand	srcllen.rw, srcladdr.ab, fill.rb, src2len.rw, src2addr.ab, [R0-3.wl]	.	.	0	.
71	CMPD	Compare D_floating	srcl.rd, src2.rd	.	.	0	0
51	CMPF	Compare F_floating	srcl.rf, src2.rf	.	.	0	0
51FD	CMPG	Compare G_floating	srcl.rg, src2.rg	.	.	0	0
71FD	CMPH	Compare H_floating	srcl.rh, src2.rh	.	.	0	0
D1	CMPL	Compare long	srcl.rl, src2.rl	.	.	0	.
35	CMPP3	Compare packed 3-operand	len.rw, srcladdr.ab, src2addr.ab, [R0-3.wl]	.	.	0	0
37	CMPP4	Compare packed 4-operand	srcllen.rw, srcladdr.ab, src2len.rw, src2addr.ab, [R0-3.wl]	.	.	0	0
EC	CMPV	Compare field	pos.rl, size.rb, base.vb, [field.rv], src.rl	.	.	0	.
B1	CMPW	Compare word	srcl.rw, src2.rw	.	.	0	.
ED	CMPZV	Compare zero extended field	-pos.rl, size.rb, base.vb, [field.rv], src.rl	.	.	0	.
0B	CRC	Calculate cyclic redundancy check	tbl.ab, initialcrc.rl, strlen.rw, stream.ab, [R0-3.wl]	.	.	0	0
6C	CVTBD	Convert byte to D_floating	src.rb, dst.wd	.	.	.	0
4C	CVTBF	Convert byte to F_floating	src.rb, dst.wf	.	.	.	0
4CFD	CVTBG	Convert byte to G_floating	src.rb, dst.wg	.	.	.	0
6CFD	CVTBH	Convert byte to H_floating	src.rb, dst.wh	.	.	.	0
98	CVTBL	Convert byte to long	src.rb, dst.wl	.	.	.	0

OP	Mnemonic	Description	Arguments	Condition Codes			
				N	Z	V	C
99	CVTBW	Convert byte to word	src.rb, dst.ww	.	.	.	0
68	CVTDB	Convert D_floating to byte	src.rd, dst.wb	.	.	.	0
76	CVTDF	Convert D_floating to floating	src.rd, dst.wf	.	.	.	0
32FD	CVTDH	Convert D_floating to H_floating	src.rd, dst.wh	.	.	.	0
6A	CVTDL	Convert D_floating to long	src.rd, dst.wl	.	.	.	0
69	CVTDW	Convert D_floating to word	src.rd, dst.ww	.	.	.	0
48	CVTFB	Convert F_floating to byte	src.rf, dst.wb	.	.	.	0
56	CVTFD	Convert F_floating to double	src.rf, dst.wd	.	.	.	0
99FD	CVTFG	Convert F_floating to G_floating	src.rf, dst.wg	.	.	.	0
98FD	CVTFH	Convert F_floating to H_floating	src.rf, dst.wh	.	.	.	0
4A	CVTFL	Convert F_floating to long	src.rf, dst.wl	.	.	.	0
49	CVTFW	Convert F_floating to word	src.rf, dst.ww	.	.	.	0
48FD	CVTGB	Convert G_floating to byte	src.rg, dst.wb	.	.	.	0
33FD	CVTGF	Convert G_floating to F_floating	src.rg, dst.wf	.	.	.	0
56FD	CVTGH	Convert G_floating to H_floating	src.rg, dst.wh	.	.	.	0
4AFD	CVTGL	Convert G_floating to longword	src.rg, dst.wl	.	.	.	0
49FD	CVTGW	Convert G_floating to word	src.rg, dst.ww	.	.	.	0
68FD	CVTHB	Convert H_floating to byte	src.rh, dst.wb	.	.	.	0
F7FD	CVTHD	Convert H_floating to D_floating	src.rh, dst.wd	.	.	.	0
F6FD	CVTHF	Convert H_floating to F_floating	src.rh, dst.wf	.	.	.	0
76FD	CVTHG	Convert H_floating to G_floating	src.rh, dst.wg	.	.	.	0
6AFD	CVTHL	Convert H_floating to longword	src.rh, dst.wl	.	.	.	0
69FD	CVTHW	Convert H_floating to word	src.rh, dst.ww	.	.	.	0
F6	CVTLB	Convert long to byte	src.rl, dst.wb	.	.	.	0
6E	CVTLD	Convert long to D_floating	src.rl, dst.wd	.	.	.	0
4E	CVTLF	Convert long to F_floating	src.rl, dst.wf	.	.	.	0
4EFD	CVTLG	Convert longword to G_floating	src.rl, dst.wg	.	.	.	0
6EFD	CVTLH	Convert longword to H_floating	src.rl, dst.wh	.	.	.	0
F9	CVTLP	Convert long to packed	src.rl, dstlen.rw, dstaddr.ab, [R0-3.wl]	.	Z	V	0
F7	CVTLW	Convert long to word	src.rl, dst.ww	.	.	.	0
36	CVTPL	Convert packed to long	srclen.rw, srcaddr.ab, [R0-3.wl], dst.wl	.	.	.	0
08	CVTPS	Convert packed to leading separate	srclen.rw, srcaddr.ab, dstlen.rw, dstaddr.ab, [R0-3.wl]	.	.	.	0
24	CVTPT	Convert packed to trailing	srclen.rw, srcaddr.ab, tbladdr.ab, dstlen.rw, dstaddr.ab, [R0-3.wl]	.	.	.	0

OP	Mnemonic	Description	Arguments	N	Z	V	C
6B	CVTRDL	Convert rounded D_floating to long	src.rd, dst.wl	.	.	.	0
4B	CVTRFL	Convert rounded F_floating to long	src.rf, dst.wl	.	.	.	0
4BFD	CVTRGL	Convert rounded G_floating to longword	src.rg, dst.wl	.	.	.	0
6BFD	CVTRHL	Convert rounded H_floating to longword	src.rh, dst.wl	.	.	.	0
09	CVTSP	Convert leading separate to packed	srclen.rw, srcaddr.ab, dstlen.rw, dstaddr.ab, [R0-3.wl]	.	.	.	0
26	CVTTP	Convert trailing to packed	srclen.rw, srcaddr.ab, tbladdr.ab, dstlen.rw, dstaddr.ab, [R0-3.wl]	.	.	.	0
33	CVTWB	Convert word to byte	src.rw, dst.wb	.	.	.	0
6D	CVTWD	Convert word to D_floating	src.rw, dst.wd	.	.	.	0
4D	CVTWF	Convert word to F_floating	src.rw, dst.wf	.	.	.	0
4DFD	CVTWG	Convert word to G_floating	src.rw, dst.wg	.	.	.	0
6DFD	CVTWH	Convert word to H_floating	src.rw, dst.wh	.	.	.	0
32	CVTWL	Convert word to long	src.rw, dst.wl	.	.	.	0
97	DECB	Decrement byte	dif.mb	.	.	.	.
D7	DECL	Decrement long	dif.ml	.	.	.	.
B7	DECW	Decrement word	dif.mw	.	.	.	.
86	DIVB2	Divide byte 2-operand	divr.rb, quo.mb	.	.	.	0
87	DIVB3	Divide byte 3-operand	divr.rb, divd.rb, quo.wb	.	.	.	0
66	DIVD2	Divide D_floating 2-operand	divr.rd, quo.md	.	.	.	0
67	DIVD3	Divide D_floating 3-operand	divr.rd, divd.rd, quo.wd	.	.	.	0
46	DIVF2	Divide F_floating 2-operand	divr.rf, quo.mf	.	.	.	0
47	DIVF3	Divide F_floating 3-operand	divr.rf, divd.rf, quo.wf	.	.	.	0
46FD	DIVG2	Divide G_floating 2-operand	divr.rg, quo.mg	.	.	.	0
47FD	DIVG3	Divide G_floating 3-operand	divr.rg, divd.rg, quo.wg	.	.	.	0
66FD	DIVH2	Divide H_floating 2-operand	divr.rh, quo.mh	.	.	.	0
67FD	DIVH3	Divide H_floating 3-operand	divr.rh, divd.rh, quo.wh	.	.	.	0
C6	DIVL2	Divide long 2-operand	divr.rl, quo.ml	.	.	.	0
C7	DIVL3	Divide long 3-operand	divr.rl, divd.rl, quo.wl	.	.	.	0
27	DIVP	Divide packed	divrlen.rw, divraddr.ab, divdlen.rw, divdaddr.ab, quolen.rw, quoaddr.ab, [R0-5.wl,-16(SP): -1(SP).wb]	.	.	.	0
A6	DIVW2	Divide word 2-operand	divr.rw, quo.mw	.	.	.	0
A7	DIVW3	Divide word 3-operand	divr.rw, divd.rw, quo.ww	.	.	.	0
38	EDITPC	Edit packed to character string	srclen.rw, srcaddr.ab, pattern.ab, dstaddr.ab, [R0-5.wl]	.	.	.	.
7B	EDIV	Extended divide	divr.rl, divd.rq, quo.wl, rem.wl	.	.	.	0
74	EMODD	Extended modulus double	mulr.rd, mulrx.rb, muld.rd, int.wl, fract.wd	.	.	.	0
54	EMODF	Extended modulus F_floating	mulr.rf, mulrx.rb, muld.rf, int.wl fract.wf	.	.	.	0

OP	Mnemonic	Description	Arguments	Condition Codes N	Z	V	C
54FD	EMODG	Extended modulus G_floating	mulr.rg, mulrx.rb, muld.rg, int.wl, fract.wg	.	.	.	0
74FD	EMODH	Extended modulus H_floating	mulr.rh, mulrx.rb, muld.rh, int.wl, fract.wg	.	.	.	0
7A	EMUL	Extended multiply	mulr.rl, muld.rl, add.rl, prod.wq	.	.	0	0
EE	EXTV	Extract field	pos.rl, size.rb, base.vb, [field.rv], dst.wl	.	.	0	–
EF	EXTZV	Extract zero extended field	-pos.rl, size.rb, base.vb, [field.rv], dst.wl	.	.	0	–
EB	FFC	Find first clear bit	startpos.rl, size.rb, base.vb, [field.rv], findpos.wl	0	.	0	0
EA	FFS	Find first set bit	startpos.rl, size.rb, base.vb, [field.rv], findpos.wl	0	.	0	0
00	HALT	Halt (Kernel Mode only)	[–(KSP).w*]	.	.	.	.
96	INCB	Increment byte	sum.mb	.	.	.	.
D6	INCL	Increment long	sum.ml	.	.	.	.
B6	INCW	Increment word	sum.mw	.	.	.	.
0A	INDEX	Index calculation	subscript.rl, low.rl, high.rl, size.rl, entry.rl, addr.wl	.	.	0	0
5C	INSQHI	Insert at head of queue, interlocked	entry.ab, header.aq	0	.	0	.
5D	INSQTI	Insert at tail of queue, interlocked	entry.ab, header.aq	0	.	0	.
0E	INSQUE	Insert into queue	entry.ab, addr.wl	.	.	0	.
F0	INSV	Insert field	src.rl, pos.rl, size.rb, base.vb, [field.wv]	–	–	–	–
17	JMP	Jump	dst.ab	–	–	–	–
16	JSB	Jump to subroutine	dst.ab, [–(SP)+.wl]	–	–	–	–
06	LDPCTX	Load process context (only legal on interrupt stack)	[PCB.r*, –(KSP).w*]	–	–	–	–
3A	LOCC	Locate character	char.rb, len.rw, addr.ab, [R0-1.wl]	0	.	0	0
39	MATCHC	Match characters	len 1.rw, addr 1.ab, len2.rw,addr2.ab, [R0-3.wl]	0	.	0	0
92	MCOMB	Move complemented byte	scr.rb, dst.wb	.	.	0	–
D2	MCOML	Move complemented long	scr.rl, dst.wl	.	.	0	–
B2	MCOMW	Move complemented word	src.rw, dst.ww	.	.	0	–
DB	MFPR	Move from processor register (Kernel Mode only)	procreg.rl, dst.wl	.	.	0	–
8E	MNEGB	Move negated byte	src.rb, dst.wb	.	.	.	.
72	MNEGD	Move negated D_floating	src.rd, dst.wd	.	.	0	0
52	MNEGF	Move negated F_floating	src.rf, dst.wf	.	.	0	0

OP	Mnemonic	Description	Arguments	Condition Codes			
				N	Z	V	C
52FD	MNEGG	Move negated G_floating	src.rg, dst.wg	.	.	0	0
72FD	MNEGH	Move negated G_floating	src.rh, dst.wh	.	.	0	0
CE	MNEGL	Move negated long	src.rl, dst.wl	.	.	.	.
AE	MNEGW	Move negated word	src.rw, dst.ww	.	.	.	.
9E	MOVAB	Move address of byte	src.ab, dst.wl	.	.	0	–
7E	MOVAD	Move address of D_floating	src.aq, dst.wl	.	.	0	–
DE	MOVAF	Move address of F_floating	src.al, dst.wl	.	.	0	–
7E	MOVAG	Move address of G_floating	src.ag, dst.wl	.	.	0	–
7EFD	MOVAH	Move address of H_floating	src.ah, dst.wl	.	.	0	–
DE	MOVAL	Move address of long	src.al, dst.wl	.	.	0	–
7EFD	MOVAO	Move address of octa	src.ao, dst.wl	.	.	0	–
7E	MOVAQ	Move address of quad	src.aq, dst.wl	.	.	0	–
3E	MOVAW	Move address of word	src.aw, dst.wl	.	.	0	–
90	MOVB	Move byte	src.rb, dst.wb	.	.	0	–
28	MOVC3	Move character 3-operand	len.rw, srcaddr.ab, dstaddr.ab, [R0-5.wl]	0	1	0	0
2C	MOVC5	Move character 5-operand	srclen.rw, scraddr.ab, fill.rb, dstlen.rw, dstaddr.ab, [R0-5.wl]	.	.	0	.
70	MOVD	Move D_floating	scr.rd, dst.wd	.	.	0	–
50	MOVF	Move F_floating	src.rf, dst.wf	.	.	0	–
50FD	MOVG	Move G_floating	src.rg, dst.wg	.	.	0	–
70FD	MOVH	Move H_floating	src.rh, dst.wh	.	.	0	–
DO	MOVL	Move long	src.rl, dst.wl	.	.	0	–
7DFD	MOVO	Move octa	src.ro, dst.wo	.	.	0	–
34	MOVP	Move packed	len.rw, srcaddr.ab, dstaddr.ab, [R0-3.wl]	.	.	0	–
DC	MOVPSL	Move processor status longword	dst.wl	–	–	–	–
7D	MOVQ	Move quad	src.rq, dst.wq	.	.	0	–
2E	MOVTC	Move translated characters	srclen.rw, srcaddr.ab, fill.rb, tbladdr.ab, dstlen.rw, dstaddr.ab, [R0-5.wl]	.	.	0	.
2F	MOVTUC	Move translated until character	srclen.rw, srcaddr.ab, escape.rb, tbladdr.ab, dstlen.rw, dstaddr.ab, [R0-5.wl]	.	.	.	.
BO	MOVW	Move word	src.rw, dst.ww	.	.	0	–
9A	MOVZBL	Move zero-extended byte to long	src.rb, dst.wl	0	.	0	–
9B	MOVZBW	Move zero-extended byte to word	src.rb, dst.ww	0	.	0	–
3C	MOVZWL	Move zero-extended word to long	src.rw, dst.wl	0	.	0	–
DA	MTPR	Move to processor register (Kernel Mode only)	src.rl, procreg.rl	.	.	0	–
84	MULB2	Multiply byte 2-operand	mulr.rb, prod.mb	.	.	.	0
85	MULB3	Multiply byte 3-operand	mulr.rb, muld.rb, prod.wb	.	.	.	0

OP	Mnemonic	Description	Arguments	N	Z	V	C
						Condition Codes	
64	MULD2	Multiply D_floating 2-operand	mulr.rd, prod.md	.	✓	.	0
65	MULD3	Multiply D_floating 3-operand	mulr.rd, muld.rd, prod.wd	.	.	.	0
44	MULF2	Multiply F_floating 2-operand	mulr.rf, prod.mf	.	.	.	0
45	MULF3	Multiply F_floating 3-operand	mulr.rf, muld.rf, prod.wf	.	.	.	0
44FD	MULG2	Multiply G_floating 2-operand	mulr.rg, prod.mg	.	.	.	0
45FD	MULG3	Multiply G_floating 3-operand	mulr.rg, muld.rg, prod.wg	.	.	.	0
64FD	MULH2	Multiply H_floating 2-operand	mulr.rh, prod.mh	.	.	.	0
65FD	MULH3	Multiply H_floating 3-operand	mulr.rh, muld.rh prod.wh	.	.	.	0
C4	MULL2	Multiply long 2-operand	mulr.rl, prod.ml	.	.	.	0
C5	MULL3	Multiply long 3-operand	mulr.rl, muld.rl, prod.wl	.	.	.	0
25	MULP	Multiply packed	mulrlen.rw, mulradr.ab, muldlen.rw, muldadr.ab, prodlen.rw, prodadr.ab, [R0-5.wl]	.	.	.	0
A4	MULW2	Multiply word 2-operand	mulr.rw, prod.mw	.	.	.	0
A5	MULW3	Multiply word 3-operand	mulr.rw, muld.rw, prod.ww	.	.	.	0
01	NOP	No operation		–		–	–
75	POLYD	Polynomial evaluate D_floating	arg.rd, degree.rw, tbladdr.ab, [R0-5.wl]	.	.	.	0
55	POLYF	Polynomial evaluate F_floating	arg.rf, degree.rw, tbladdr.ab, [R0-3.wl]	.	.	.	0
55FD	POLYG	Polynomial evaluate G_floating	arg.rg, degree.rw, tbladdr.ab, [R0-5.wl]	.	.	.	0
75FD	POLYH	Polynomial evaluate H_floating	arg.rh, degree.rw, tbladdr.ab, [R0-5.wl, –16(SP): –1(SP).wb]	.	.	.	0
BA	POPR	Pop registers	mask.rw, [(SP)+.r*]	–	–	–	–
0C	PROBER	Probe read access	mode.rb, len.rw, base.ab	0	.	0	–
0D	PROBEW	Probe write access	mode.rb, len.rw, base.ab	0	.	0	–
9F	PUSHAB	Push address of byte	src.ab, [–(SP).wl]	.	.	0	–
7F	PUSHAD	Push address of D_floating	src.aq, [–(SP).wl]	.	.	0	–
DF	PUSHAF	Push address of F_floating	src.al, [–(SP).wl]	.	.	0	–
7F	PUSHAG	Push address of G_floating	src.ag, [–(SP).wl]	.	Z	0	–
7FFD	PUSHAH	Push address of H_floating	src.ah, [–(SP).wl]	.	.	0	–
DF	PUSHAL	Push address of long	src.al, [–(SP).wl]	.	.	0	–
7FFD	PUSHAO	Push address of octa	src.ao, [–(SP).wl]	.	.	0	–
7F	PUSHAQ	Push address of quad	src.aq, [–(SP).wl]	.	.	0	–
3F	PUSHAW	Push address of word	src.aw, [–(SP).wl]	.	.	0	–
DD	PUSHL	Push long	src.rl, [–(SP).wl]	.	.	0	–
BB	PUSHR	Push registers	mask.rw, [–(SP).w*]	–	–	–	–
02	REI	Return from exception or interrupt	[(SP)+.r*]	.	.	.	.

OP	Mnemonic	Description	Arguments	N	Z	V	C
				Condition Codes			
5E	REMQHI	Remove from head of queue, interlocked	header.aq, addr.wl	0	.	.	.
5F	REMQTI	Remove from tail of queue, interlocked	header.aq, addr.wl	0	.	.	.
0F	REMQUE	Remove from queue	entry.ab, addr.wl	.	.	.	.
04	RET	Return from procedure	[(SP)+.r*]	.	.	.	.
9C	ROTL	Rotate long	count.rb, src.rl, dst.wl	.	.	0	–
05	RSB	Return from subroutine	[(SP)+.rl]	–	–	–	–
D9	SBWC	Subtract with carry	sub.rl, dif.ml	.	.	.	.
2A	SCANC	Scan for character	len.rw, addr.ab, tbladdr.ab, mask.rb, [R0-3.wl]	0	.	0	0
3B	SKPC	Skip character	char.rb, len.rw, addr.ab, [R0-1.wl]	0	.	0	0
F4	SOBGEQ	Subtract one and branch on greater or equal	index.ml, displ.bb	.	.	.	–
F5	SOBGTR	Subtract one and branch on greater	index.ml, displ.bb	.	.	.	–
2B	SPANC	Span characters	len.rw, addr.ab, tbladdr.ab, mask.rb, [R0-3.wl]	0	.	0	0
82	SUBB2	Subtract byte 2-operand	sub.rb, dif.mb	.	.	.	.
83	SUBB3	Subtract byte 3-operand	sub.rb, min.rb, dif.wb	.	.	.	0
62	SUBD2	Subtract D_floating 2-operand	sub.rd, dif.md	.	.	.	0
63	SUBD3	Subtract D_floating 3-operand	sub.rd, min.rd, dif.wd	.	.	.	0
42	SUBF2	Subtract F_floating 2-operand	sub.rf, dif.mf	.	.	.	0
43	SUBF3	Subtract F_floating 3-operand	sub.rf, min.rf, dif.wf	.	.	.	0
42FD	SUBG2	Subtract G_floating 2-operand	sub.rg, dif.mg	.	.	.	0
43FD	SUBG3	Subtract G_floating 3-operand	sub.rg, min.rg, dif.rg	.	.	.	0
62FD	SUBH2	Subtract H_floating 2-operand	sub.rh, dif.mh	.	.	.	0
63FD	SUBH3	Subtract H_floating 3-operand	sub.rh, min.rh, dif.rh	.	.	.	0
C2	SUBL2	Subtract long 2-operand	sub.rl, dif.ml	.	.	.	.
C3	SUBL3	Subtract long 3-operand	sub.rl, min.rl, dif.wl	.	.	.	0
22	SUBP4	Subtract packed 4-operand	sublen.rw, subaddr.ab, diflen.rw, difaddr.ab, [R0-3.wl]	.	.	.	0
23	SUBP6	Subtract packed 6-operand	sublen.rw, subaddr.ab, minlen.rw, minaddr.ab, diflen.rw, difaddr.ab, [R0-5.wl]	.	.	.	0
A2	SUBW2	Subtract word 2-operand	sub.rw, dif.mw	.	.	.	.
A3	SUBW3	Subtract word 3-operand	sub.rw, min.rw, dif.ww	.	.	.	0
07	SVPCTX	Save process context	[(SP)+.r*, –(KSP).w*]	–	–	–	–

OP	Mnemonic	Description	Arguments	N	Z	V	C
		(Kernel Mode only)					
95	TSTB	Test byte	src.rb	.	.	0	0
73	TSTD	Test D_floating	src.rd	.	.	0	0
53	TSTF	Test F_floating	src.rf	.	.	0	0
53FD	TSTG	Test G_floating	src.rg	.	.	0	0
73FD	TSTH	Test H_floating	src.rh	.	.	0	0
D5	TSTL	Test long	src.rl	.	.	0	0
B5	TSTW	Test word	src.rw	.	.	0	0
FC	XFC	Extended function call	user defined operands	0	0	0	0
8C	XORB2	Exclusive OR byte 2-operand	mask.rb, dst.mb	.	.	0	–
8D	XORB3	Exclusive OR byte 3-operand	mask.rb, src.rb, dst.wb	.	.	0	–
CC	XORL2	Exclusive OR long 2-operand	mask.rl., dst.ml	.	.	0	–
CD	XORL3	Exclusive OR long 3-operand	mask.rl, src.rl, dst.wl	.	.	0	–
AC	XORW2	Exclusive OR word 2-operand	mask.rw, dst.mw	.	.	0	–
AD	XORW3	Exclusive OR word 3-operand	mask.rw, src.rw, dst.ww	.	.	0	–

Table B.2   List of VAX Instructions by Opcode

Opcode	Mnemonic	Opcode	Mnemonic	Opcode	Mnemonic
00	HALT	1B	BLEQU	36	CVTPL
01	NOP	1C	BVC	37	CMPP4
02	REI	1D	BVS	38	EDITPC
03	BPT	1E	BGEQU	39	MATCHC
04	RET	1E	BCC	3A	LOCC
05	RSB	1F	BLSSU	3B	SKPC
06	LDPCTX	1F	BCS	3C	MOVZWL
07	SVPCTX	20	ADDP4	3D	ACBW
08	CVTPS	21	ADDP6	3E	MOVAW
09	CVTSP	22	SUBP4	3F	PUSHAW
0A	INDEX	23	SUBP6	40	ADDF2
0B	CRC	24	CVTPT	41	ADDF3
0C	PROBER	25	MULP	42	SUBF2
0D	PROBEW	26	CVTTP	43	SUBF3
0E	INSQUE	27	DIVP	44	MULF2
0F	REMQUE	28	MOVC3	45	MULF3
10	BSBB	29	CMPC3	46	DIVF2
11	BRB	2A	SCANC	47	DIVF3
12	BNEQ	2B	SPANC	48	CVTFB
12	BNEQU	2C	MOVC5	49	CVTFW
13	BEQL	2D	CMPC5	4A	CVTFL
13	BEQLU	2E	MOVTC	4B	CVTRFL
14	BGTR	2F	MOVTUC	4C	CVTBF
15	BLEQ	30	BSBW	4D	CVTWF
16	JSB	31	BRW	4E	CVTLF
17	JMP	32	CVTWL	4F	ACBF
18	BGEQ	33	CVTWB	50	MOVF
19	BLSS	34	MOVP	51	CMPF
1A	BGTRU	35	CMPP3	52	MNEGF

Opcode	Mnemonic	Opcode	Mnemonic	Opcode	Mnemonic
53	TSTF	81	ADDB3	B5	TSTW
54	EMODF	82	SUBB2	B6	INCW
55	POLYF	83	SUBB3	B7	DECW
56	CVTFD	84	MULB2	B8	BISPSW
57	*Reserved*	85	MULB3	B9	BICPSW
58	ADAWI	86	DIVB2	BA	POPR
59	*Reserved*	87	DIVB3	BB	PUSHR
5A	*Reserved*	88	BISB2	BC	CHMK
5B	*Reserved*	89	BISB3	BD	CHME
5C	INSQHI	8A	BICB2	BE	CHMS
5D	INSQTI	8B	BICB3	BF	CHMU
5E	REMQHI	8C	XORB2	C0	ADDL2
5F	REMQTI	8D	XORB3	C1	ADDL3
60	ADDD2	8E	MNEGB	C2	SUBL2
61	ADDD3	8F	CASEB	C3	SUBL3
62	SUBD2	90	MOVB	C4	MULL2
63	SUBD3	91	CMPB	C5	MULL3
64	MULD2	92	MCOMB	C6	DIVL2
65	MULD3	93	BITB	C7	DIVL3
66	DIVD2	94	CLRB	C8	BISL2
67	DIVD3	95	TSTB	C9	BISL3
68	CVTDB	96	INCB	CA	BICL2
69	CVTDW	97	DECB	CB	BICL3
6A	CVTDL	98	CVTBL	CC	XORL2
6B	CVTRDL	99	CVTBW	CD	XORL3
6C	CVTBD	9A	MOVZBL	CE	MNEGL
6D	CVTWD	9B	MOVZBW	CF	CASEL
6E	CVTLD	9C	ROTL	D0	MOVL
6F	ACBD	9D	ACBB	D1	CMPL
70	MOVD	9E	MOVAB	D2	MCOML
71	CMPD	9F	PUSHAB	D3	BITL
72	MNEGD	A0	ADDW2	D4	CLRL
73	TSTD	A1	ADDW3	D4	CLRF
74	EMODD	A2	SUBW2	D5	TSTL
75	POLYD	A3	SUBW3	D6	INCL
76	CVTDF	A4	MULW2	D7	DECL
77	*Reserved*	A5	MULW3	D8	ADWC
78	ASHL	A6	DIVW2	D9	SBWC
79	ASHQ	A7	DIVW3	DA	MTPR
7A	EMUL	A8	BISW2	DB	MFPR
7B	EDIV	A9	BISW3	DC	MOVPSL
7C	CLRQ	AA	BICW2	DD	PUSHL
7C	CLRD	AB	BICW3	DE	MOVAL
7C	CLRG	AC	XORW2	DE	MOVAF
7D	MOVQ	AD	XORW3	DF	PUSHAL
7E	MOVAQ	AE	MNEGW	DF	PUSHAF
7E	MOVAD	AF	CASEW	E0	BBS
7E	MOVAG	B0	MOVW	E1	BBC
7F	PUSHAQ	B1	CMPW	E2	BBSS
7F	PUSHAD	B2	MCOMW	E3	BBCS
7F	PUSHAG	B3	BITW	E4	BBSC
80	ADDB2	B4	CLRW	E5	BBCC

Opcode	Mnemonic	Opcode	Mnemonic	Opcode	Mnemonic
E6	BBSSI	4AFD	CVTGL	7DFD	MOVO
E7	BBCCI	4BFD	CVTRGL	7EFD	MOVH
E8	BLBS	4CFD	CVTBG	7EFD	MOVAO
E9	BLBC	4DFD	CVTWG	7FFD	PUSHAH
EA	FFS	4EFD	CVTLG	7FFD	PUSHAO
EB	FFC	4FFD	ACBG	80FD	Reserved
EC	CMPV	50FD	MOVG	.	.
ED	CMPZV	51FD	CMPG	.	.
EE	EXTV	52FD	MNEGG	.	.
EF	EXTZV	53FD	TSTG	8FFD	Reserved
F0	INSV	54FD	EMODG	90FD	Reserved
F1	ACBL	55FD	POLYG	.	.
F2	AOBLSS	56FD	CVTGH	.	.
F3	AOBLEQ	57FD	Reserved	.	.
F4	SOBGEQ	.	.	97FD	Reserved
F5	SOBGTR	.	.	98FD	CVTFH
F6	CVTLB	.	.	99FD	CVTFG
F7	CVTLW	5FFD	Reserved	9AFD	Reserved
F8	ASHP	60FD	ADDH2	.	.
F9	CVTLP	61FD	ADDH3	.	.
FA	CALLG	62FD	SUBH2	.	.
FB	CALLS	63FD	SUBH3	9FFD	Reserved
FC	XFC	64FD	MULH2	A0FD	Reserved
FD	Reserved	65FD	MULH3	.	.
FE	Reserved	66FD	DIVH2	.	.
FF	Reserved	67FD	DIVH3	.	.
00FD	Reserved	68FD	CVTHB	EFFD	Reserved
.	.	69FD	CVTHW	F0FD	Reserved
.	.	6AFD	CVTHL	.	.
.	.	6BFD	CVTRHL	.	.
31FD	Reserved	6CFD	CVTBH	.	.
32FD	CVTDH	6DFD	CVTWH	F5FD	Reserved
33FD	CVTGF	6EFD	CVTLH	F6FD	CVTHF
34FD	Reserved	6FFD	ACBH	F7FD	CVTHD
.	.	70FD	MOVH	F8FD	Reserved
.	.	71FD	CMPH	.	.
.	.	72FD	MNEGH	.	.
3FFD	Reserved	73FD	TSTH	.	.
40FD	ADDG2	74FD	EMODH	FFFD	Reserved
41FD	ADDG3	75FD	POLYH	00FF	Reserved
42FD	SUBG2	76FD	CVTHG	.	.
43FD	SUBG3	77FD	Reserved	.	.
44FD	MULG2	.	.	FCFF	Reserved
45FD	MULG3	.	.	FDFF	BUGL
46FD	DIVG2	7BFD	Reserved	FEFF	BUGW
47FD	DIVG3	7CFD	CLRH	FFFF	Reserved
48FD	CVTGB	7CFD	CLRO		
49FD	CVTGW				

Bibliography

David W. Archer, David R. Deverell, Thomas F. Fox, Paul E. Gronowski, Anil K. Jain, Michael Leary, Daniel G. Miner, Andrew Olesin, Shawn D. Persels, Paul I. Rubinfeld, and Robert M. Supnik. A CMOS VAX Microprocessor with On-Chip Cache and Memory Management. *IEEE Journal of Solid-State Circuits*, October 1987.

James Archibald and Jean-Loup Baer. Cache Coherence Protocols: Evaluation Using a Multiprocessor Simulation Model. *ACM Transactions on Computer Systems*, Volume 4, Number 4, November 1986.

Robert G. Babb II, editor. *Programming Parallel Processors*. Addison-Wesley Publishing Company, Reading, Massachusetts, 1988.

Maurice J. Bach. *The Design of the UNIX Operating System*. Prentice-Hall, Inc., Englewood Cliffs, New Jersey, 1986.

Jean-Loup Baer, *Computer Systems Architecture*. Computer Science Press, Rockville, Maryland, 1980.

Mario R. Barbacci and Daniel P. Siewiorek. *The Design and Analysis of Instruction Set Processors*. McGraw-Hill Book Company, New York, 1982.

BB&N. *Butterfly Parallel Processor Overview*. Version 1, December 8, 1985. BBN Laboratories Incorporated, Cambridge, Massachusetts.

C. Gordon Bell, J. Craig Mudge, and John E. McNamara. *Computer Engineering: A DEC View of Hardware Systems Design*. Digital Press, Bedford, Massachusetts, 1978.

Lubomir Bic and Alan C. Shaw. *The Logical Design of Operating Systems* (Second Edition). Prentice-Hall, Inc., Englewood Cliffs, New Jersey, 1988.

Richard P. Case and Andris Padegs. Architecture of the IBM System/370. *Communications of the ACM*, Volume 21, Number 1, January 1978.

Douglas W. Clark. Cache Performance in the VAX-11/780. *ACM Transactions on Computer Systems*, Volume 1, Number 1, February 1983.

Douglas W. Clark. Pipelining and Performance in the VAX 8800. *Proceedings of the Second International Conference on Architectural Support for Programming Languages and Operating Systems*, IEEE Computer Society, October 1987.

Douglas W. Clark and Joel S. Emer. Performance of the VAX-11/780 Translation Buffer: Simulation and Measurement. *ACM Transactions on Computer Systems*, Volume 3, Number 1, February 1985.

Douglas W. Clark and Henry M. Levy. Measurement and Analysis of Instruction Use in the VAX-11/780. *Proceedings of the 9th International Symposium on Computer Architecture*, Austin, Texas, October 1982.

Peter J. Denning. The Working Set Model for Program Behavior. *CACM*, Volume 11, Number 5, 1968.

John DeRosa, Richard Glackemeyer, and Thomas Knight. Design and Implementation of the VAX 8600 Pipeline. *Computer*, Volume 18, Number 5, May 1985.

Digital Equipment Corporation, *MicroVAX I CPU Technical Description*, Second Edition. Order Number EK-KD32A-TD-002. Digital Equipment Corporation, Maynard, Massachusetts, August 1984.

Digital Equipment Corporation, *VAX Architecture Handbook*. Digital Equipment Corporation, Maynard, Massachusetts, 1986.

Richard H. Eckhouse, Jr. and L. Robert Morris. *Minicomputer Systems: Organization, Programming, and Applications (PDP-11)*. Prentice-Hall, Inc., Englewood Cliffs, New Jersey, 1979.

Joel S. Emer and Douglas W. Clark. A Characterization of Processor Performance in the VAX-11/780. *Proceedings of the 11th Annual Symposium on Computer Architecture*, June 1984.

Edward F. Gehringer, Daniel P. Siewiorek, and Zary Segall. *Parallel Processing: The Cm* Experience*. Digital Press, Bedford, Massachusetts, 1987.

V. Carl Hamacher, Zvonko G. Vranesic, and Safwat G. Zaky. *Computer Organization* (Second Edition). McGraw-Hill Book Company, New York, 1984.

John L. Hennessy. VLSI Processor Architecture. *IEEE Transactions on Computers*, Volume C-33, Number 12, December 1984.

W. Daniel Hillis. *The Connection Machine*. The MIT Press, Cambridge, Massachusetts, 1985.

W. Daniel Hillis and Guy L. Steele, Jr. Data Parallel Algorithms. *Communications of the ACM*, Volume 29, Number 12, December 1986.

Kai Hwang and Fayé A. Briggs. *Computer Architecture and Parallel Processing*. McGraw-Hill Book Company, New York, 1984.

Intel Corporation. *Intel 80386 Programmer's Reference Manual*. Intel Corporation, Santa Clara, California, 1986, Order Number 230985-001.

Manolis G. H. Katevenis. *Reduced Instruction Set Computer Architectures for VLSI*. The MIT Press, Cambridge, Massachusetts, 1985.

Lawrence J. Kenah, Ruth E. Goldenberg, and Simon F. Bate. *VAX/VMS Internals and Data Structures* (Version 4.4). Digital Press, Bedford, Massachusetts, 1988.

Brian W. Kernighan and Dennis M. Ritchie. *The C Programming Language.* Prentice-Hall, Inc., Englewood Cliffs, New Jersey, 1978.

Brian W. Kernighan and Rob Pike. *The UNIX Programming Environment.* Prentice-Hall, Inc., Englewood Cliffs, New Jersey, 1984.

Peter M. Kogge. *The Architecture of Pipelined Computers.* McGraw-Hill Book Company, New York, 1981.

Nancy P. Kronenberg, Henry M. Levy, and William D. Strecker. VAXclusters: A Closely-Coupled Distributed System. *ACM Transactions on Computer Systems,* Volume 4, Number 2, May 1986.

Timothy E. Leonard, editor. *VAX Architecture Reference Manual.* Digital Equipment Corporation, 1987.

Henry M. Levy and Richard H. Eckhouse, Jr. *Computer Programming and Architecture: The VAX-11.* Digital Press, Bedford, Massachusetts, 1980.

Henry M. Levy and Peter H. Lipman. Virtual Memory Management in VAX/VMS. *Computer,* Volume 15, Number 3, March 1982.

J. F. Maranzano and S. R. Bourne. A Tutorial Introduction to ADB. In *ULTRIX-32 Supplementary Documents, Volume 2: Programmer.* Digital Equipment Corporation, Merrimack, New Hampshire, Order Number AA-CN31A-TE, 1985.

Glenford J. Myers. *Digital System Design with LSI Bit-Slice Logic.* John Wiley and Sons, New York, 1980.

David A. Patterson. Reduced Instruction Set Computers. *Communications of the ACM,* Volume 28, Number 1, January 1985.

James L. Peterson and Abraham Silberschatz. *Operating System Concepts.* Addison-Wesley Publishing Company, Reading, Massachusetts, 1983.

John F. Reiser and Robert R. Henry. Berkeley VAX/Unix Assembler Reference Manual. In *ULTRIX-32 Supplementary Documents, Volume 2: Programmer.* Digital Equipment Corporation, Merrimack, New Hampshire, Order Number AA-CN31A-TE, 1985.

Randall Rettberg and Robert Thomas. Contention is no obstacle to shared-memory multiprocessing. *Communications of the ACM,* Volume 29, Number 12, December 1986.

Richard M. Russell. The CRAY-1 Computer System. *Communications of the ACM,* Volume 21, Number 1, January 1978.

Charles L. Seitz. The Cosmic Cube. *Communications of the ACM,* Volume 28, Number 1, January 1985.

Robert T. Short and Henry M. Levy. A Simulation Study of Two-Level Caches. *Proceedings of the 15th International Symposium on Computer Architecture,* May 1988.

Daniel P. Siewiorek, C. Gordon Bell, and Allen Newell. *Computer Structures: Principles and Examples.* McGraw-Hill Book Company, New York, 1982.

Alan J. Smith. Cache Memories. *ACM Computing Surveys*, Volume 14, Number 3, September 1982.

Harold S. Stone. *High-Performance Computer Architecture*. Addison-Wesley Publishing Company, Reading, Massachusetts, 1987.

William D. Strecker. VAX-11/780—A Virtual Address Extension to the DEC PDP-11 Family. *Proceedings of the NCC*, AFIPS Press, Montvale, New Jersey, 1978.

William D. Strecker. Cache Memories for the PDP-11 Family Computers. *Proceedings of the 3rd Annual Symposium on Computer Architecture*, January 1976.

George Struble. *Assembler Language Programming: The IBM System/360*. Addison-Wesley Publishing Company, Reading, Massachusetts, 1969.

Robert M. Supnik. MicroVAX 32, A 32 Bit Microprocessor. *IEEE Journal of Solid-State Circuits*, Volume SC-19, Number 5, October 1984.

Andrew S. Tanenbaum. *Structured Computer Organization* (Second Edition). Prentice-Hall, Inc., Englewood Cliffs, New Jersey, 1984.

Andrew S. Tanenbaum. *Operating Systems: Design and Implementation*. Prentice-Hall, Inc., Englewood Cliffs, New Jersey, 1987.

Charles P. Thacker and Lawrence C. Stewart. Firefly: a Multiprocessor Workstation. *Proceedings of the Second International Conference on Architectural Support for Programming Languages and Operating Systems*, October 1987.

Cheryl A. Wiecek. A Case Study of VAX-11 Instruction Set Usage for Compiler Execution. *Proceedings of the Symposium on Architectural Support for Programming Languages and Operating Systems*, March 1982.

Index